Strategic Reading in the Content Areas

Practical Applications for Creating a Thinking Environment

by Rachel Billmeyer

Second Edition
June 2010
Printco Graphics
Omaha, Nebraska

Strategic Reading in the Content Areas
Practical Applications for Creating a Thinking Environment

Compiled and written
by Dr. Rachel Billmeyer

Foreword
by Dr. Arthur L. Costa

Credit
Every effort has been made to contact copyright holders for permission to reproduce borrowed material where necessary. We apologize for any oversights and would be happy to rectify them in future printings.

Published by   Rachel Billmeyer, Rachel & Associates, Inc.
           17445 Riviera Drive, Omaha, NE 68136

Printed by Printco Graphics 14112 Industrial Road, Omaha, NE 68144-3332
Desktop Published by Donna Flood and Chris Warner
Cover by Tom Wise
Edited by Marilyn Kelly

First Printing August, 2004
Printed in the United States of America

ISBN   978-0-9711292-6-9   Softcover
Library of Congress Control Number: 2004094214

Strategic Reading in the Content Areas
Practical Applications for Creating a Thinking Environment

Table of Contents

Dedication

This book is dedicated to my parents,
Bernard and Luella Klein. Their work ethic and love for learning
has provided the platform for my continued efforts as an educator.

"My love and my thanks, Mom and Dad!"

Acknowledgments

Strategic Reading in the Content Areas: Practical Applications for Creating a Thinking Environment is the final piece in the Literacy and Learning Trilogy. Since 1996 when my friend Fran Mayeski invited me to write *Teaching Reading in the Content Areas: If Not Me Then Who?* educators have learned a great deal about influencing the reading efforts of students. I have been fortunate to work with hundreds of teachers, implementing reading practices to develop strategic readers. Their many ideas as well as current research on literacy encouraged me to update and expand my work. My hope is that *Strategic Reading in the Content Areas* will advance the work of teachers in developing strategic readers and ultimately will enrich their reading lives.

This book is the product of many colleagues' experimentation, exploration, and application of reading research and strategies. Through their devotion to learning and dedication to developing strategic readers, they have produced numerous suggestions, examples, and strategies for the benefit of all. I offer special thanks to the talented contributors who provided the information in chapters 6 and 7. I am indebted for their willingness to spend big chunks of time to revamp draft after draft and to share how they have incorporated reading ideas within their content areas. Specific information about each author is shared on pages 266.

Writing a book requires the ongoing support of many people; I am fortunate to be surrounded with superb help. I am particularly grateful to Marilyn Kelly, my reader-responder extraordinaire, who spent countless hours reviewing and discussing each draft of the book. Her loyal support and words of encouragement have made this publication possible. Thank you Marilyn! Donna Flood and Chris Warner worked their magic as desktop publishers; I thank them for their major contribution in compiling and designing the masterpiece. I extend a special thanks to Wendy Grojean for her superb work and countless hours updating the annotated bibliography in chapter 9. I appreciate the contribution of my colleague Sue Presler for designing the learning team activities for each chapter. Special thanks to Stacy Rulla-Parroquin and Ashley Clark from Bellevue Public Schools for providing instructional strategies for the foreign language section.

I am grateful to the talented people who spent hours proofreading the book. Thanks to:
Cheryl Becker Dobbertin, School Designer with Expeditionary Learning, Rochester, NY
Gina Davis, Director Professional Development, Cedar Bridge Academy, Devonshire, Bermuda
Brian Kirkpatrick, Middle School Teacher, Charles F. Bolden, Beaufort, SC
Carolyn Law, Retired Elementary Principal for Westside Schools, Omaha, NE
Linda Nakashima, Consultant for Department of Education, Honolulu, HI
Christine Parker, Teacher/Literacy Coach at Hightower Elementary, Doraville, GA
Sandy Kappmeyer, Coordinator of Instructional Services for Genesee Valley Educational Partnership, Rochester, NY

A special thank you to my family. Ellen, teacher extraordinaire, keeps me focused with "real-life" examples and strategies for creating readers. And finally, thanks to my husband Lance whose patience, support, and words of encouragement made the rewrite of this book a reality.

Foreword

When I was invited to write this Foreword to Rachel Billmeyer's book, *Strategic Reading in the Content Areas*, I asked myself, "What do I know about reading?" "Precious little," I answered. I vaguely remember how I learned to read—decoding the cereal boxes on the breakfast table, having my parents read to me, seeing them read, realizing my father's love of books, and my fascination with the boyhood adventures of Richard Haliburton. But learning to read in school, I reminisced, consisted of the obligatory "cat, bat, hat, rat, mat" tedium, with a sprinkling of "seeing Dick, Jane and Spot run."

Then I thought, "What do I know about *teaching* reading?" Still less, I answered again. Foggy images of my teacher-preparation methods classes emerged. Abstract lectures on reading theory, dim recall about phonetic analysis, word recognition, and experience charts. As a middle school science teacher I had little concern with teaching reading. That was someone else's job. Furthermore, I believed students should be able to read by the time they reached middle grades. If they were having difficulties, their primary grade teachers' inadequacies were to blame. My reading assignments to students basically were to learn the steps of the scientific method, to follow the directions in the lab manual, to read the text with enough recall to answer the end-of-chapter questions, and to draw logical conclusions about the experimental data they generated.

I thought maybe I could learn something from Rachel's book, however. I wanted to know more about her approach to reading and I was curious about what she meant by "Strategic" reading and how this was performed in relation to content areas. So, I accepted the challenge as a means of continuing my own education.

As I started to consume each chapter, I initially thought that Rachel's message was more about thinking than about reading. I resonated with that notion as I too have a career-long affinity for helping students think more skillfully! I soon realized, however, that's not quite right. Rachel's messages are that the complex act of constructing meaning from text involves intellectual processes that can be taught, learned, and perfected over time. That student learning from text is greatly enhanced with the addition of these processes, that students can learn to employ such processes autonomously when they are reading on their own, and that all teachers——regardless of the subjects or grade levels they teach— need to increase their understanding and use of these intellectual processes with all students.

I learned that:
• Strategic readers are **self-managing**. They approach their text as a form of problem solving and the problem is to create meaning from the text. They come to the task equipped with clarity of outcomes, questions in mind, a flexible plan, necessary data drawn from past experiences, anticipation of success indicators, and creative alternatives for constructing meaning.

• Strategic readers are **self-monitoring**. They think about their thinking. They establish metacognitive strategies such as pattern finding, making connections to previous learning, comparing with other text materials, and visualizing scenarios. They monitor their own comprehension, being conscious of not only the meaning they are making but also the adequacy of the processes they are employing to construct that meaning.

• Strategic readers are **self-modifying.** They reflect upon, analyze, and evaluate the reading experience, and they are open to altering their perceptions, biases and conclusions, synthesizing new learnings and applying them to future activities, tasks, and challenges. They view each reading task as a learning experience—an opportunity to continuously evaluate and improve their meaning-making skills.

I also found the book contains many practical strategies for teachers to employ to help students expand their capacities for reading more strategically in all content areas. To adopt and employ these strategies may mean that some teachers will need to undergo a mind shift in their approach to teaching reading. With strategic reading, our perceptions of teaching and learning shift from educational outcomes that are primarily collections of sub-skills that teachers transmit to students, to instead include successful participation in socially organized activities that develop students' identities as conscious, flexible, and efficacious meaning makers. Knowledge is a constructive process; it is not the content that gets stored in memory but rather the activity of constructing it that gets stored. Meaning making is not a spectator sport— humans don't **get** ideas; they **make** ideas.

Furthermore, meaning making is not just an individual operation; students interact with others to construct shared knowledge through interdependent social participation. Strategic reading, therefore, is viewed as a reciprocal process in that the individual influences the group's meaning and the group influences the individual's meaning.

Now, having read the manuscript in its entirety, and as I meander back through my learning, I realize that Rachel has even a larger message. Becoming a strategic learner is a goal of education, and reading provides one more avenue for the learning, practice, and application of such life-long dispositions as flexibility, consciousness, questioning, drawing upon past knowledge, communicating ideas with clarity and precision, and thinking interdependently.

These intellectual dispositions transcend all subject matter commonly taught in school. They are characteristics of peak performers whether they are in homes, schools, athletic fields, organizations, the military, governments, churches or corporations. They are what make marriages successful, learning continuous, workplaces productive, and democracies enduring. One major goal of reading instruction, therefore, should be to support others and ourselves in developing, liberating, and habituating these intellectual dispositions more fully. I have uncovered Rachel Billmeyer's real goal: to make classrooms, schools, and the world more thoughtful places.

Arthur L. Costa, Ed. D.
Search Models Unlimited
Granite Bay, California
June 2004

About This Book

Strategic Reading in the Content Areas: Practical Applications for Creating a Thinking Environment, Second Edition incorporates "guides" to focus thinking. A graphic organizer is used as a point of entry into each chapter, outlining the major elements of the book. The border, Principles of Learning, frames all ideas discussed in *Strategic Reading in the Content Areas*. Strategies to engage the mind of the reader serve as the backdrop and provide avenues for creating strategic readers. Strategic reading in the content areas involves three interactive reading ingredients: Reader, Context, and Text. These reading ingredients work interdependently but are addressed separately to assist educators in making reading accessible to ALL students. Developing strategic readers who "think about their thinking" and strategic reading in the content areas are the central focus, or target, for all ideas presented in this book. The graphic organizer is intended to assist you in understanding how a given chapter or section fits into the "larger picture" or current context of your learning.

Strategic Reading in the Content Areas is Volume 1 of the Literacy and Learning Trilogy. Strategies and examples referenced in this book are extensively presented in Volume 2, *Strategies to Engage the Mind of the Learner* (Billmeyer, 2006b). The traits and attributes of a strategic reader introduced in chapter 3 are extensively detailed in Volume 3, *Capturing All of the Reader Through the Reading Assessment System* (Billmeyer, 2006a). Children's and adolescent literature referenced in the book can be found in chapter 10.

A learning team format has been incorporated to assist your learning. It is my hope that teams of educators will read, discuss, and use the process activities outlined at the beginning of each chapter or section. Specific learning team information is provided in the appendix, pages 263-265. For quick reference, strategies explained in chapters 6 and 7 are indexed on the following page. The icons will help to focus your attention on specific portions of the text.

☞ At the beginning of chapters and sections, you will discover a page that prepares you for reading. The icon of a pointing finger signifies major upcoming topics of a chapter.

〰 Another frequently used icon is the "notes" icon. It directs you to spaces where notes might be written.

☯ At various junctures in your learning you will be challenged to reflect on your reading, either alone or with a colleague. The yin-yang icon denotes an opportunity for reflection.

⌘ Strategies and Process activities are found throughout the text. The synergy icon depicts an opportunity to process information—usually with one or more colleagues.

◻ As stated earlier in the book, the purchaser of the text has permission to reproduce specific pages for classroom use. These pages are denoted by the blackline master icon.

⚑ And finally, you frequently will note examples of strategies provided throughout the text, highlighted with a flag icon.

I hope this information will complement your style of learning. Happy Reading! RB

Strategies Incorporated in Strategic Reading in the Content Areas

Vocabulary	*Content Areas*	*Pages*
Categories and Labels	Career & Tech. Ed.	128
Concept Definition Mapping	Science, Young Child, ELL	183, 202, 210
Forecast	English, Social Studies	134, 190
Frayer Model	Art, Music, Science	122, 162, 177
Mind Sketching	Science	182
Preview Content Vocabulary	Career & Tech. Ed.	125
Prevoke	Foreign Language	144
SAW Model	Young Child	201
Vocabulary Writing	Math	156
Word Sift and Word Sort	21st Century Learners, Math, ELL, Special Ed.	115, 157, 209, 214
Word Wall	Music, PE & Health	163, 173

Narrative/Informative Text	*Content Areas*	*Pages*
Anticipation Guide	Career & Tech., Science, Social Studies	127, 180, 187
Boolean Operators	Internet	149
Carousel Brainstorming	English	133
Character Map	Foreign Language	145
Click or Clunk	Foreign Language	145
Collaborative Summarizing	Music	167
Concept Circles or Maps	Art, Career & Tech. Ed.	121, 126
Directed Reading/Thinking Activity	Science, Reluctant Reader	181, 222
FQR	Special Ed.	216
Focused Reading, Text Tag, Post-it Notes	Career & Tech., Math, Science, Soc. St., Sp. Ed.	127, 157, 184, 188, 215
Give 1 to Get 1	Young Child	204
Graphic Organizers	Internet, PE & Health, Science, Social St., ELL	147, 172, 179, 189, 207
K-N-L	Math	155
Learning Logs	Reluctant Reader	218
L.E.T.S. Connect	Social Studies, Young Child	192, 202
Literature Circles	Reluctant Reader	220
Pairs Read or Pairs Share	Math, PE & Health	157, 174
Paired Verbal Fluency	Foreign Language	145
Pinwheel Discovery	Foreign Language	146
Preview, Read, Examine, Prompt	Foreign Language	143
Problem Solving/Process Writing	Math	158
Question-Answer Relationship (QAR)	PE & Health, Science, Young Child	173, 181, 202
Questioning the Author	Social Studies	190
Quotation Marks	Internet	150
RGB Notetaking	21st Century Learners	116
Read and Respond	Art	120
Reading from Different Perspectives	English	138
Reading Lenses	Art	120
Reciprocal Teaching	Special Ed.	214
Role, Audience, Format, Topic (RAFT)	Social Studies	190
Save the Last Word for Me	English	130
Scavenger Hunt	Internet	150
Story Maps	Music	165
STARS Strategy	Music	164
Summary Wheel	English, Young Child	139, 203
SQ4R	ELL	207
Synthesis Chart	Internet	152
T+B=I Inference	Special Ed.	215
Think-Aloud	English, Math	135, 156

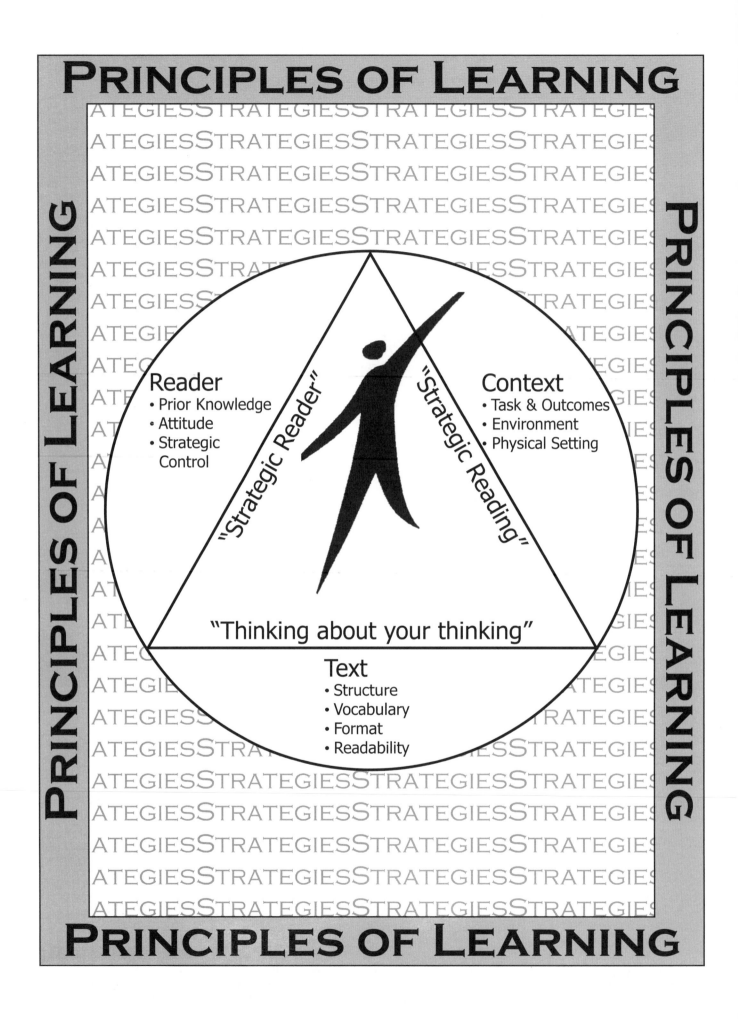

Chapter 1

Strategic Reading in the Content Areas: Practical Applications for Creating a Thinking Environment

"Learning Teams"

As a result of working through this chapter you will:
- Understand the importance of creating a thinking environment through reading
- Understand the organization of this book

Questions to ponder before, during, and after reading

Before reading – Why is it important to develop strategic readers?

During reading – Think about turning points in becoming the strategic reader you are today. How might you use awareness of these turning points to support developing strategic readers in your classroom? Be ready to share turning points and the ways these experiences have impacted your teaching.

After reading – As you think about reading and studying the information in this book, which areas are of most importance to you? How will this awareness focus your thinking as you read through the text?

Process Activity

The process activity used for this chapter is Round-Robin Sharing. Each person will share responses to the before, during, and after questions listed above. Participants answer the questions individually, and then in round-robin fashion, everyone in the group responds to the question. The process is a great strategy for balancing participation because everyone has the opportunity to respond without having to "jump in."

Chapter 1

Strategic Reading in the Content Areas

Adolescents entering the adult world in the 21st century will read and write more than at any other time in human history. They will need advanced levels of literacy to perform their jobs, run their households, and act as citizens.

- Richard Vacca

Introduction

Children must be lured into the wonderful world of books; the joy of reading begins at birth through modeling, reading aloud, and exposure to quantities of reading material. Reading shapes our lives, positively or negatively. Think of turning points in your path to becoming a reader. What attracted you to reading books, magazines, or newspapers? Who influenced you as a reader? You may be surprised to know that reading was a struggle during my formal learning years. The first positive memory I recall occurred during my first year of teaching when a veteran teacher introduced me to an array of read-aloud books. Reading aloud not only helped me manage a class of ornery boys but also lured me into the exciting world of print. Thirty-eight years later, I not only am thankful for the guidance of that caring teacher, but I also have had countless conversations with adults and students about turning points in their becoming readers.

I am finding that readers are born every day, often as the result of one caring individual. What I also am noticing is that student responses differ from adult reflections. Adults tend to view reading as a meaningful way to interact with other adults. They value the opportunity to read and share thoughts with friends. Personal selection of materials based on where they are in their lives is important to them. For example, new mothers may read and converse about babies, whereas adults in their fifties may read and reflect on retirement.

As I continue to interview students some still report that their turning points occurred as a result of teachers reading aloud favorite books, getting to select books of interest, reading and sharing with friends, or through independent reading time. Unfortunately, too many students still respond, "I read to get the assignment done," or "I read to please the teacher." Sometimes daringly honest students admit they don't bother to read the assignment because the following day the teacher will tell them what they need to know.

When reading is connected to students' lives, they enjoy the experience and are motivated to read. Turning points occur as memorable moments, created when the reader connects and interacts with the printed word. These experiences energize readers, causing them to uncover insights about themselves and the world. **Meaningful turning points have the potential to turn fledgling readers into life-long readers.**

Rationale

Since the first publication of *Teaching Reading in the Content Areas: If Not Me Then Who?* (1996) the focus on reading processes K-12 has continued to grow. All educators are aware of the national emphasis on standards, accountability, and high-stakes testing; the pressure to test well creates a greater demand for students to develop the advanced literacy skills required to master academic content subject matter. Societal and economic changes have also caused districts to emphasize literacy efforts. Employability rests on the ability to read; the ability to read develops good learners, earners, and citizens (Hirsch, 2004).

Yet many children do not read, or they don't read often enough. Some admit that they don't see reading as an important or meaningful part of their lives. In 2008, Americans spent an average of 1704 hours watching television, up from 1553 in 2001, 183 hours using the internet up from 125, 168 hours reading daily newspapers, down from 199, 117 hours reading magazines, down from 127, and 106 hours reading books, down 1 hour (Stevenson, 2008).

Is it any wonder that some children in school have a disinterest and difficulty with reading. How can one compare 1704 hours of watching TV to 168 hours (at best) of reading anything? Excuses for not reading are plentiful – "I am too busy to read," or "Reading is so slow and boring." Yet reading can change our lives by taking us to all parts of the world and teaching us things we never knew before. Why then is reading not revered as a critical ingredient for living a good life? Teacher Donalyn Miller, in *The Book Whisperer* (2009) emphasizes the importance of educators modeling the love of reading and showing students what it means to be a life-long reader. She incorporates activities such as using authentic materials, reading with and aloud to students, and discussing favorite selections to turn nonreaders into avid readers. Schools on the path to success for student learning are schools that recognize literacy as a necessary thread woven throughout all content area learning. They are schools that provide rich, literacy-based learning experiences resulting in increased thinking and learning for all students.

As educators examine educational practices and recognize reading as a key ingredient for student learning K-12, they are beginning to ask the right questions:
- How does the journey to become a strategic reader begin?
- How many minutes do students read during the school day?
- How are students allowed choice when it comes to what they read?
- How can narrative and informative text be used at all levels and in all content areas?
- Do students read in every lesson, integrating phonics and vocabulary?
- What opportunities are there for students to engage in independent reading?
- Are all teachers adequately equipped to address content area reading?

The purpose of *Strategic Reading in the Content Areas, 2nd Edition* is to address these questions and to outline how all classroom teachers can support K-12 students in becoming strategic readers.

Advancement in reading abilities will not come about through emphasis on reading instruction in isolation from the other work students do in school. Sending students to the "reading room" seldom addresses their inadequacies in reading a math word problem or understanding how to read science concepts. Teachers are discovering that teaching reading in their content areas not only increases student performance, but it also is essential to be successful in the world in which we live. Math authors (Chapter 6) state, "When students intentionally are taught the meaning of mathematical terms through the use of strategies they become strategic readers who can reason and communicate mathematically." Kevin Gerrity (Chapter 6) believes, "The integration of reading and music will augment the learning process and do much to produce musicians who have a greater appreciation and understanding of their work." Primary authors (Chapter 7) emphasize, "The focus during the primary years must be on both **learning to read** and **reading to learn**! A delicate balance between phonics instruction and modeling before, during, and after reading strategies promotes the development of strategic readers." The issue of students who snub reading yet spend hours online can be addressed through the appropriate use of digital media. Three sections in chapter 6 address online reading and provide meaningful ways to engage students as readers via the Internet.

Creating Communities of Readers and Learners

If we want to create a literate environment in which all teachers feel competent addressing reading problems and planning instruction to foster reading development, districts must invest in quality professional development. International Reading Association President Kathryn Au (2010) believes that professional development of teachers must be put at the top of the list. She also points out that a substantial amount of money has been invested in packaged programs with little success. A comprehensive professional development program must be sustained over time to impact student achievement.

As I work with teachers and principals across the country, I am witnessing professional development efforts that are making a difference. The Cedar Falls/ Waterloo, Iowa area educational agency invested in a three-year program to train teachers and principals from 26 school districts. Teachers and principals participated in large group training sessions, small group networking sessions, and classroom observation and coaching opportunities. Student performance not only increased on the state assessment but students also were reading more and enjoying it. Massive amounts of independent reading led to students participating in class discussions about their reading and increased vocabulary skills.

In some districts teachers and administrators have created professional learning communities to read, study, and implement ideas for developing strategic readers. Research indicates that when adults model the importance of reading, student reading increases. *Strategic Reading in the Content Areas: Practical Applications for Creating a Thinking Environment, 2ⁿᵈ Edition* incorporates a learning team format. It is my hope that teachers and principals will read, discuss the process activities, and ultimately will use new ideas with students. Effective professional development demands ongoing, long-term investments of time, energy, and effort from all staff members participating at all grade levels and across all content areas. Only then will students have the chance to excel as readers in all content areas.

Structure of the Book

So what will you find in this book? Chapter 1 provides you with the rationale for taking the time and energy to focus on developing strategic readers. Chapter 2 reviews the research supporting professional development for reading in the content areas. The research is organized into eight principles of learning and explains their connection to becoming a strategic learner and reader.

Chapter 3 delves into the title of the book *Strategic Reading in the Content Areas*. This chapter explains how to develop strategic readers, what strategic reading involves, and also provides a framework for strategic reading in all content areas. Chapter 4 revisits the importance of metacognition - "Thinking about your thinking" - during reading. Three metacognitive tools - questioning, talking, and writing - are described. To update yourself on the three interactive reading elements outlined in *Teaching Reading in the Content Areas: If Not Me Then Who?* proceed to chapter 5. There you will find research relating to the three interactive reading ingredients (reader, context, and text), as well as a multitude of examples provided by teachers with whom I have worked.

Chapters 6 and 7, written by classroom teachers, explore what it means to teach reading in specific content areas. Voices from the classroom include teachers who emphasize strategic reading through informative text with primary age children, teachers who focus on the needs of the English Language Learners, as well as teachers of content areas like science and social studies. They state why it is important that content teachers take responsibility for reading and provide examples for developing strategic readers. Two additional sections included in this edition are Strategic Reading and 21st Century Learners and Strategic Reading in Career and Technical Education. In recognition of the diversity of learners within the general classroom, a section entitled *Special Considerations for Developing Readers (Response to Intervention)* has been added to the core content areas in this edition.

Three reading staples, read-aloud, sustained silent reading (SSR), and family literacy, are explained in Chapter 8. Perhaps you are already a believer of strategic reading in the content areas and have been exploring the use of children's literature to motivate students to read. Your search for exciting literature selections has been made easier with Chapter 9, where you will find an annotated bibliography of more than 200 selections representing all content areas. Selections incorporated in the text as instructional examples are cited in chapter 10, p. 262. The Appendix also includes information on learning teams and contributors for chapters 6 and 7.

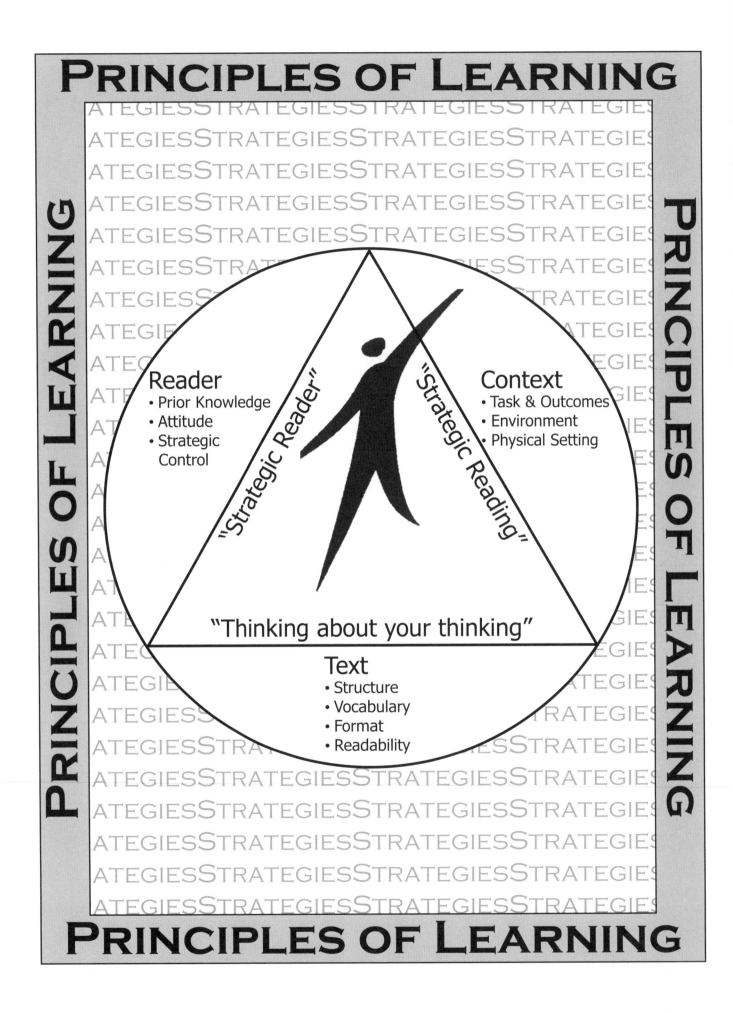

Chapter 2

Principles of Learning

"Learning Teams"

Notes

As a result of working through this chapter you will:
- Know the current research that is recognized as the foundation for learning
- Understand the connections between learning and strategic reading

Questions to ponder before, during, and after reading

Before reading – Quickly scan the chapter. What are your predictions about what you will learn in this chapter? What makes you think that?

During reading – How might this information support instruction in your classroom?

After reading – As you reflect on your current instructional practices, which of the principles of learning are your greatest strengths? Which ones stretch your thinking?

Process Activity

The process activity for studying the chapter on Principles of Learning is the Summary Wheel (Billmeyer, 2006b). The Summary Wheel teaches students how to organize key terms and ideas, to identify main ideas and supporting details, and to record their thoughts into meaningful, succinct summaries.

Directions:

1) Discuss what makes a good summary. *Summaries include only important information, combine ideas, add connective words for clarity and coherence, and use category terms instead of a list of words.* Review what a summary does not include. *Summaries do not include your opinion, material directly copied from the selection, or what you think the author should have said.*

2) Create a Summary Wheel (resembles a Pizza) on a piece of plain paper by drawing a large outer circle and an inner circle to form the crust. Next, divide the circle into 8 pieces and on the outer circle (pizza crust) record a key word(s) for each of the eight principles of learning, one principle per section.

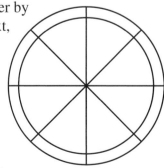

3) As you read each principle of learning, record your summary for that principle on the correct section (pizza piece).

4) Your learning team may choose to jigsaw the reading; each person reads and summarizes two or three principles of learning.

5) After each person has completed a summary, compare summaries with learning team members. How are they similar/different?

6) What ideas will you use from this study of the principles of learning?

7) Discuss the benefits of using the Summary Wheel strategy with your learning team. How might you use this strategy in your content area?

Chapter 2

Principles of Learning

The question is not, "Is it possible to educate all children well?" but rather, "Do we want to do it badly enough?"

- Deborah Meier

A Student-Centered Approach

Renowned educator Madeline Hunter defined teaching as a decision-making process; she emphasized that each learner, as well as each learning situation, is unique. Philosopher, John Dewey advocated a student-centered approach; student focused classrooms concentrate on the learning needs, abilities, and interests of students. Current research identifies key characteristics and generalizations about the learning process. A student-centered approach requires that educators understand how the varied perspectives and needs of students as readers and learners align with key principles of learning.

A student-centered approach stresses the development of strategic readers, readers who rely on their own minds as the primary source of thinking and learning. Because learning in each discipline is unique, students must be taught how to read to learn from content- specific text. Teachers can no longer tell students to open their books and begin reading; it is critical that students learn how to use strategies to extend meaning before, during, and after reading.

Research suggests that developing strategic readers begins with the implementation of the following eight principles:

1) Relies on cognitive and metacognitive abilities
2) Sets goals and reflects on progress
3) Links new information to prior knowledge
4) Works actively to construct meaning
5) Uses organizational patterns
6) Considers individual learning style
7) Collaborates with others to learn
8) Engages in three phases of thinking (Planning, Interaction, & Reflection)

When teachers incorporate these eight principles of learning students are provided with tools and opportunities to take responsibility for their own learning. These principles provide a framework that is important for creating a student-centered learning environment.

Principle 1: A Strategic Learner relies on cognitive and metacognitive abilities.

Metacognitive learners are aware of and have control over their cognitive abilities; they incorporate cognitive strategies before, during, and after learning. Strategic learners analyze their thinking and consciously expand their repertoire of abilities. For example, when solving a math problem the learner determines how to apply correct computational skills, or in science the learner frames scientific questions and draws conclusions based on substantial data. A strategic learner has the ability to recognize when there is a problem with learning and can use strategies to solve the problem.

One of the key differences between the thinking of adults and the thinking of children is in the area of metacognition. Students become effective adult thinkers when they develop metacognitive abilities. Becoming metacognitive requires explicit strategy instruction. Modeling, ongoing guidance, and opportunities for practice in applying self-monitoring strategies to academic tasks such as writing, reading, and problem solving help to develop strategic thinkers and confident learners. Processes to enhance students' mental engagement are critical to becoming a strategic learner.

Connection to Reading

Strategic readers possess well developed cognitive and metacogntive abilities. They consciously use strategies when reading **and** they constantly monitor their progress by "thinking about their thinking" as they read. For example, strategic readers know when their comprehension falters and are able to select from various methods to assist their understanding.

Chapter 4 elaborates on various methods for helping students be metacognitive. For example, they purposely ask themselves questions, talk with peers to clarify thinking about the meaning of key vocabulary related to the topic, or jot down important ideas.

Strategic readers have been taught specific cognitive strategies as well as how to be metacognitive. Teachers who model their own use of reading skills and self-monitoring thought processes help students understand the power of metacognitive abilities. The Think-Aloud strategy (see p. 135) is beneficial in helping the reader construct meaning from a difficult passage. Strategic readers not only have knowledge of cognitive strategies but also know how and when to use them; explicit teaching of reading skills such as questioning, making inferences, and drawing conclusions from text is key for developing metacognitive abilities. The use of student inventories listing strategies such as, *I make predictions before reading, I ask myself questions during reading*, or *I make connections to worldly applications* reminds the reader to incorporate important reading skills. Strategic control of the reading process results when readers recognize what they know, what they are still puzzled by, and can adjust their use of meaning-making skills.

Principle 2: A Strategic Learner sets goals and reflects on progress.

Strategic learners are goal-oriented people who regulate their own learning. They know that goal-oriented learners are more successful in life. People who set goals increase the likelihood of task completion; high quality goals lead to remarkable accomplishments.

Choice is an important aspect of goal setting; when students determine the goal, motivation and enthusiasm increase. Choice is especially important for students who believe they have little control over their learning. When goals are relevant to students needs and interests they work harder to accomplish them; they see connections between the efforts they put forth and the results. Goals are achieved when strategic learners continually reflect on their progress and make adjustments when necessary. Because reflection and self-assessment are fundamental to goal setting, most people learn from their failures as well as from their successes.

Connection to Reading

Strategic readers focus their reading through goal setting. They know individual goals are motivational, increasing their participation in the reading process. Readers who are independent and read to learn are goal-oriented, purposeful readers. Strategic readers determine what and how to read based on their purpose for reading. They intentionally use goal-setting strategies such as the K-W-L (see p. 110) and the DRTA (see p. 181) which ask readers to determine "what they want to learn" from their reading.

Collective classroom goals help to create a collaborative community of readers. When students see themselves as members of a learning community they work harder to accomplish class goals. Goals might be global in nature such as "to increase school-wide reading for adults and students," or "to incorporate a variety of print sources to encourage more reading," or they may be more task-specific such as "to expand my vocabulary knowledge of mammals," or "to ask myself more questions during reading." Strategic readers know goals are achieved when they continually reflect on their progress and make adjustments when necessary.

Principle 3: A Strategic Learner links new information to prior knowledge.

All new learning is based on prior knowledge; background knowledge refers to everything the learner knows or has experienced regarding a topic. Marzano (2004) emphasizes the strong relationship between student achievement and background knowledge. Because prior knowledge is learned rather than innate, educators must be willing to dedicate time and resources to develop background knowledge. A direct approach such as field trips or an indirect approach such as wide reading are productive avenues to enrich background knowledge.

Madeline Hunter talked about providing an anticipatory set at the beginning of a lesson to help students bring forward the appropriate prior knowledge. Let me illustrate with a simple example. As you read the passage below, use your prior knowledge to fill in the missing information.

> "The problems that confront p_____ in raising ch_____ from in_____ to adult life are not easy to s_____. Both fa_____ and m_____ meet with many di_____ in their concern for satisfactory pro_____ from the e_____ stage to later life. It is important that young ch_____ should have plenty of s_____ and good f_____ for healthy growth. B_____ and g_____ should not occupy the same b_____ or sleep in the same r_____. They are often afraid of the d_____."

Compare your responses to the answers provided below to see how well you did.

> "The problems that confront <u>poultrymen</u> in raising <u>chickens</u> from <u>incubation</u> to adult life are not easy to <u>summarize</u>. Both <u>farmers</u> and <u>merchants</u> meet with many <u>difficulties</u> in their concern for satisfactory <u>promotion</u> from the <u>egg</u> stage to later life. It is important that young <u>chicks</u> should have plenty of <u>sunshine</u> and good <u>feed</u> for healthy growth. <u>Banties</u> and <u>geese</u> should not occupy the same <u>barnyard</u> or sleep in the same <u>roost</u>. They are often afraid of the <u>dark</u>."

How many of you accessed the accurate prior knowledge for this task? Probably very few! Most likely you were thinking about parenting children. Unless prompted, you brought forward information most familiar to you (Billmeyer, 1996).

Knowing that learning can be difficult for some students, teachers must construct lessons that build upon their background knowledge. When planning lessons, it is important to determine the level and kinds of prior knowledge students must bring to the learning situation. As this exercise shows, it is important to capitalize on the "right" information in order for the learning to occur.

Connection to Reading

Strategic readers automatically bring forward their existing knowledge related to the topic when reading. They know that their previous experiences help to create reasons for reading. Knowing the purpose for reading directs attention during reading. Because attention is limited, readers cannot pay attention to everything they read (Lapp, Flood, and Farnan, 1996). Accessing prior knowledge helps the reader focus and direct attention to the most important information.

The information on the reader (see Chapter 5, p. 48), elaborates on the importance of background knowledge in comprehending and learning from text. Because prior knowledge influences how the text is understood, students must be taught how to use strategies to access prior experiences. There are a multitude of strategies that help students draw upon prior knowledge. Vocabulary strategies such as Concept Definition Mapping (see p. 202) or Frayer Model (see p. 122) help students relate new vocabulary to known concepts. Strategies can be open (examining any and all prior knowledge) or closed (focusing the student's thinking in a particular direction). PREP (Preview, Read, Examine, Prompt) (see p. 143) is an open-ended strategy, whereas the Anticipation Guide (see p. 127) directs students to focus on specific prior knowledge.

Principle 4: A Strategic Learner works actively to construct meaning.

Meaning is not created by a lecture or the words on the written page. Meaning is constructed when learners interact with what they hear or read. Information that is not meaningful is quickly forgotten. Think about a workshop you have attended where participants came from different organizations. You probably met many new people. How many people do you actually remember? Most likely very few, unless you had a meaningful interaction with them or a specific reason for recalling them.

What causes an experience to be meaningful? Being interested in the topic or having a need to know the content helps the learner construct meaning. In order to construct meaning, the learner must make connections, inferences, and interpretations about the topic. Strategic learners know that generating questions, talking with others, and reflective writing are powerful meaning-making tools.

Connection to Reading

Reading is thinking cued by text; the reader creates meaning as a result of the transaction between text and reader. Strategic readers know that reading has to make sense. It is more than simply moving one's eyes across a page of written symbols. Readers have their own mental maps of the world, and when they read they constantly compare their mental maps with what the author says. Thus, constructing meaning involves bringing forward the appropriate prior knowledge and using the necessary processing strategies.

To illustrate this point, read the following highlighted passage. As you read, analyze what your brain is doing to understand it and decide upon a title for the passage.

> *. . . Highly unsettling for some to come into close contact with them. Far worse to gain control over them and then to deliberately inflict pain on them. The revulsion caused by this punishment is so strong that many will not take part in it at all. Thus there exists a group of people who seem to revel in the contact and the punishment as well as the rewards associated with both. Then there is another group of people who shun the whole enterprise; contact, punishment, and rewards alike. Members of the first group share modes of talk, dress, and deportment. Members of the second group however are as varied as all humanity. Then there is a group of others not previously mentioned, for the sake of whose attention this activity*

is undertaken. They too harm their victims though they do it without intention of cruelty. They simply follow their own necessities, however, they may inflict the cruelest punishment of all. Sometimes but not always they themselves suffer as a result (Stiggins, 1991).

How did you do? If you had trouble understanding the author's message, why did you find it hard to comprehend? What strategies did you use to help your construct meaning while reading? When comparing your mental maps to the author's, did you notice the pronouns in the passage had no referents? This deprived you from using your prior knowledge to construct meaning. Would it help you construct meaning if you knew the passage was about fishing and using worms as bait? Read the passage again comparing what your brain is doing this time to the first time you read it.

Strategic readers intentionally use skills and strategies to assist their meaning-making process. They construct meaning before, during, and after reading a selection. For example, strategic readers bring prior knowledge to a conscious level before reading. As the information is encountered they discuss their ideas with others, question ideas that are not clear, and write down ideas in the margin or on post-it notes. After reading the selection they synthesize the author's ideas or reflect on new information learned.

Principle 5: A Strategic Learner uses organizational patterns.

Strategic learners know that organizing information is critical for thinking and learning. They know how to use organizational patterns to frame their thinking both "inside the head" as a conceptual framework and also "outside the head" with printed text. For example, a strategic learner could compare and contrast the similarities and differences between two or more items using the Venn diagram either mentally or on paper.

When students are taught how to use visual patterns to organize information retention increases. Visual organizers, such as semantic maps, story frames, webs, and flow charts graphically display thinking, patterns, and connections. Sorting information into like categories is helpful. For example, when studying vocabulary words to prepare for the SAT students may try to categorize words with familiar characteristics. Teaching students how to organize their thinking is a lifetime tool. When teachers continually model how to use different organizational patterns, students begin to use them as scaffolds for thinking, frameworks for accessing and retaining information, and a structure to transfer information from one situation to another.

Connection to Reading

Strategic readers analyze text structure; they know that narrative and informative structures require different thinking when reading. Reading a literary narrative text causes the reader to extract information about story elements such as beginning-middle-end, using that structure as scaffolding. Informative text often follows one of these common organizational patterns - cause/effect, compare/contrast, concept/definition, goal/action/outcome, problem/solution, proposition/support, and sequence.

Each organizational pattern (see p. **77**) has unique characteristics and frames thinking in a different way. Familiarity with these patterns helps maximize the learning of new concepts. Strategic readers use awareness of these organizational patterns as a scaffold when reading. Sometimes texts lack organization or cohesion, making it difficult for the reader to comprehend. When selections are written using an inconsiderate format, students must know how to discover an organizational pattern in order to derive meaning from the passage. Teaching students to use organizational patterns through ongoing modeling and practice creates strategic readers.

Principle 6: A Strategic Learner considers individual learning style.

Humans are born with the ability and desire to learn, but different people learn in different ways. Brain researchers believe their findings provide important implications for brain-compatible classrooms. For example, some students are holistic thinkers, seeing the whole picture concretely, while others are detail thinkers, seeing isolated pieces of information abstractly. People often refer to these two styles as "forest folks" and "tree folks." Teachers can use this discovery to work effectively with students.

Howard Gardner (1982) emphasizes teaching to multiple intelligences. He believes all students possess strengths, and it is important to determine their strengths and consciously teach to them. Tremendous variety also exists in the modes and speeds with which learners acquire knowledge. Auditory learners need to hear the ideas (often just a single time) and tend to process information quickly. Visual learners construct mental pictures or replay "movies" of experiences to help retrieve prior knowledge. Kinesthetic learners are physically active, often needing to move some part of the body in order to learn; they also tend to need more wait time to process information and construct responses.

How students demonstrate learning varies from one learner to the next; some prefer giving an oral presentation, others favor writing a research paper, some like composing and singing a lyric or rap. Teachers must be equipped with a storehouse of strategies and learning opportunities that focus on all intelligences to ensure successful learning.

Connection to Reading

What do you know about yourself as a reader? Where do you like to read, what are your routines? Do you read slowly, pondering ideas, characters, and words, or do you make movies in your head? Perhaps you are a fast reader, finding what you need and quickly moving on. Readers process text information differently.

Kinesthetic readers tend to be slow readers, emotionally connecting to text. They like to move their body as they read and may use their fingers to trace the text while reading. A preference to highlight, underline key ideas, or use post-it notes may signal a kinesthetic processor. Visual processors construct mental pictures as they read and replay movies of past experiences to retrieve prior knowledge; they may prefer graphic organizers to frame thinking during reading. Auditory processors are often characterized as fast readers and like to reread material aloud. They tend to process information quickly and need minimal wait time when answering questions or retrieving information.

It is not only important that teachers understand how students learn but also how to help students understand their own learning styles. Creating strategic readers involves modeling different reading styles and providing opportunities for students to capitalize on their learning preferences. Teaching students how to effectively use highlighters, to create graphic organizers, or to read information aloud plays to students' strengths. When students read difficult text they must be able to draw upon their strengths in order to comprehend text.

Principle 7: A Strategic Learner collaborates with others to learn.

Learning is a socially interactive process and students need to interact with one another in order to learn (Resnick, 1987). During workshops, participants comment on the benefits of collaborating with others to learn new strategies. Group work facilitates learning, and prepares learners for the real world where individuals often are required to work together.

Students who work together benefit by:
- Discovering different ways of thinking about a topic
- Gaining assistance in learning complex tasks
- Learning to listen to other students with respect and to build upon their ideas
- Finding out how to give as well as to receive feedback
- Learning to support their own assertions with evidence as well as to acknowledge different points of view

Connection to Reading

Strategic readers construct meaning both individually and socially. They collaborate with other readers to more fully understand an author's message or to gain different perspectives. Readers of all ages join book clubs because they like the social interaction and discovery involved in discussing a book. Classrooms that embrace collaborative learning teach students to be members of a learning community. When students work together they develop an appreciation for each other's talents and learn to value collaboration.

The **context** of the reading situation (see Chapter 5) emphasizes that a collaborative learning environment enhances comprehension. Classrooms include proficient readers, students who struggle as readers, and often special needs children; group work creates opportunities for all children to take leadership roles. Students learn to rely on their strengths and to feel good about their contributions to the group. When students assume teaching roles to help others read they become more responsible for their own learning. The Pairs Read (see p. 157) strategy is an effective way to foster a community of readers. Book talks, literature circles (see p. 220), and reader's workshop are other examples of activities that foster collaborative reading. When students discuss what they are reading with others, they understand the content better and can compare other students' information and beliefs with their own. Isn't that what the intellectual world is all about?

Principle 8: A Strategic Learner engages in three phases of thinking.

Successful learning involves three phases of thinking: before, during, and after learning.

- Phase 1 - "Planning" prepares and focuses the mind for learning
- Phase 2 - "Interaction" engages the mind mentally during learning
- Phase 3 - "Reflection" integrates, connects, and applies ideas after learning

Planning is considered the most important phase of the learning process because it sets the stage for learning. The learner is encouraged to analyze the task at hand and to identify approaches for learning. The more effective the "frontloading" the more successful students are.

The "during learning" phase requires students to use metacognitive strategies to think about and monitor their learning. Students frequently use graphic organizers or outlines to organize their thinking while learning. Teachers may stop the video or experiment to focus on specific thinking while students are learning. Researcher George Miller taught us that our working memory can hold seven plus or minus two ideas at one time. To capitalize on this information it is critical that students stop to monitor, consolidate, and summarize learning as it is taking place.

Typically, educational practices have focused students' thinking after learning has occurred. Without the planning and interaction, this is merely another "Pop Quiz." The purpose of reflection is to allow students to analyze, compare, and extend thinking about ideas stimulated in the planning or interaction phases of learning. A strategic learner understands the importance of thinking about and controlling the learning process during all three phases.

Connection to Reading

Strategic readers are not only aware of all three phases of thinking but constantly incorporate them. They know that reading comprehension begins before their eyes are on the page. Learning begins when the reader sets goals, activates prior knowledge, and makes predictions about the learning.

Strategic readers know that the purpose of the interaction is to monitor and adjust their thinking to achieve maximum understanding. If the passage is not making sense, they stop to reread it slower, or read it aloud, or look up a word, or jot notes in the margin. Guiding students to ask questions about what they are reading helps them to regulate their learning process. During reading, strategic readers are encouraged to compare what they are learning with what they already know about the subject and with what they predicted while previewing it. Strategic readers know if the learning process breaks down and how to use fix-it strategies to get back on track.

John Dewey said, "We learn when we reflect on what we have done." Strategic readers reflect on what they have read in order to determine if they have achieved the purpose, accomplished the assigned tasks, and integrated new information with previously learned information. They discover ways to extend what they've learned by applying the newly acquired knowledge to unique and/or new situations. The Role/Audience/Format/Topic (RAFT) writing strategy (see p. 190) helps students integrate new ideas into previously learned information. Journal writing can provide students with opportunities to reflect on what they have learned, as well as to develop as self-assessing readers.

Even though learning occurs in phases, it is important to remember that learning is not a linear process. Often strategies can be used in more than one phase. Strategic readers are aware of the three phases of thinking to learn, and they consciously self-assess how they are doing throughout learning.

Conclusion

As teachers examine the reading process within content areas, they will be able to make connections with the eight principles of learning and incorporate them into the decision-making process before, during, and after teaching. When all eight principles of learning are consciously incorporated to guide the reading process, students will benefit. Students will become strategic readers!

"Students can be valuable learning resources for one another. As members of a learning community, strategic readers work independently to formulate their own opinions and then share with group members creating an interdependent community of readers."

- Rachel Billmeyer

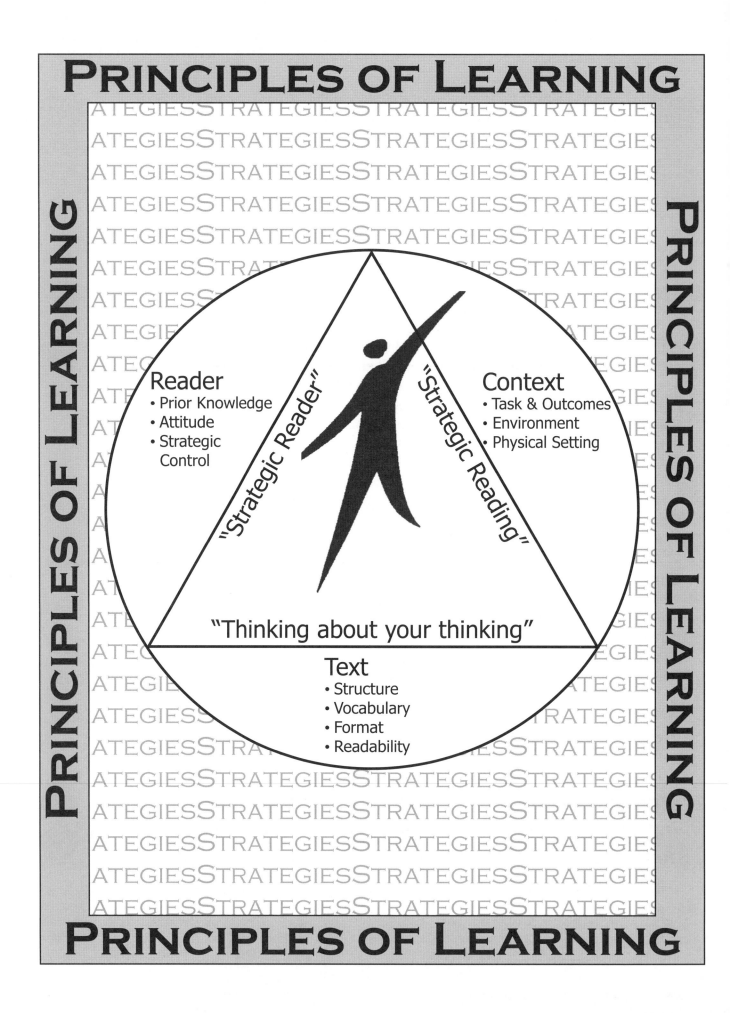

Chapter 3

Developing Strategic Readers

"Learning Teams"

As a result of working through this chapter you will:

- Define a strategic reader
- Describe strategic reading as it pertains to your content area
- Examine the traits and attributes of a strategic reader, relating them to your content area
- Determine how you can develop strategic readers in your content area

Questions to ponder before, during, and after reading

Before reading – What does the word "strategic" mean to you? When you think about strategic readers in your content area, how are they performing?

During Reading – How does this information compare to your original thinking? In what ways are you intentionally embedding strategic practices into your instruction?

After reading – What new "a-has" are you taking away from this reading? What new ideas will you add to your instructional repertoire for developing strategic readers?

Process Activity

The process activity for this chapter on strategic readers and strategic reading is the Give One to Get One (Billmeyer, 2006b) strategy. This strategy causes learners to think before, during, and after reading, creating a reflective community of learners. This process provides an opportunity for independent thinking, partner sharing, and then large group sharing. It also encourages active listening.

Directions:

1) Before reading the chapter, respond to the two questions on the top of page 20.
2) As you read the chapter (or after reading) record your thinking in the boxes, responding to each idea.
3) In a round-robin fashion, learning team members Give One to Get One by sharing recorded ideas. Group members listen, paraphrase, and inquire, asking questions to refine and elaborate thinking. Team members who have similar ideas then report to the entire team.
4) The process continues until all learning team members Give One to Get One, synthesize learnings, and determine next steps.

Chapter 3

Developing Strategic Readers

Give One to Get One

Before Reading

What reading behaviors cause students to be strategic readers in your content area?

What do you know about strategic reading in your content area?

I think the author wants us to believe/think...	Now that I have read this, I wonder...	I want to be sure that I remember...
I was confirmed in my thinking about...	One question I have is...	An interesting thought I have is...
A connection that I'm making with this information is...	Something I'm going to try in my classroom is...	Other...

⌘ ☐

Chapter 3

Developing Strategic Readers

No subject of study is more important than reading . . . all other intellectual powers depend on it. - Jacques Barzun

Reading can be a mystery; some students get it easily while others struggle. Years of focusing on literacy have taught me that readers are born every day. Readers are born when children of all ages have opportunities to read independently, can self-select materials, are read aloud to, read during the school day in all content areas, talk with others about what they read, and use instructional strategies that help them comprehend.

Our goal must be to develop strategic readers in all content areas–readers who engage in thinking as they read and have ongoing inner conversations that help them make sense of what they read. When approaching a passage strategic readers are equipped with instructional strategies they can draw upon to increase comprehension. This chapter will define what a strategic reader is, explain strategic reading, clarify the rationale for using strategies, and present a framework for strategic reading in the content areas.

What is a Strategic Reader?

Learning to read is a never-ending task because there are always new goals to reach, new horizons to explore, and new interests to expand. As Goethe said, "I have been learning to read all my life and I cannot yet say I have achieved the goal."

- Alberto Manguel

How would you define a strategic reader? What causes you to be one? Perhaps you set a purpose for reading, visualize as you read, or read with a pencil in hand. Maybe you like to do Internet searches for the best price when refinancing your home or buying a car. You would be classified as a strategic reader; you are focused and in charge of your reading. Strategic readers are active, independent thinkers, who read to learn.

A Strategic Reader works actively to construct meaning. Strategic readers are metacognitive; they think about text and are aware of their thinking as they read. They know that reading has to make sense, so they develop a toolkit of formal and informal strategies to assist comprehension. As readers in the content areas, strategic readers use strategies to focus thinking before, during, and after reading to make meaning from all kinds of texts. Strategic readers comprehend text by making connections to self, to other texts, and to the world, asking questions, determining importance, visualizing, making inferences, and synthesizing information (Keene & Zimmerman, 1997).

A Strategic Reader is independent. Becoming a reader is a life long process; new or unfamiliar reading experiences (such as Internet selections) require the use of various reading skills and competencies. Strategic readers are independent thinkers who know how to transfer reading skills from one situation to another (Palincsar and Brown, 1986). They use metacognitive processes to analyze the reading task, to make an appropriate plan for achieving the purpose, to monitor their understanding while reading, and, if necessary, to re-plan. If they struggle to meet their plan, they can independently adjust their approach through the use of fix-it strategies like rereading and questioning.

Strategic readers move from dependence to independence. We know that young readers rely on others to help them figure out the words, and to understand what the story means. Actually, most students must receive explicit instruction on how to think and read in each particular content area. For example, reading a spreadsheet requires different thinking than reading poetry and reading a math problem demands a different attention to details than does a biography of a president. Because learning in each content area is unique, students must be taught how to read by those who understand the purposes, concepts, formats, and syntax of the subject -- most likely their teachers. Teachers help students become independent readers when they ask them to reflect on and evaluate fix-it strategies to support or impede comprehension. Strategic readers know who they are as readers; they are equipped with an array of reading competencies to navigate and succeed in the world of information.

A Strategic Reader reads to learn. We live in an information age; staying on top of new information or data seems to be an impossible task. A friend recently purchased a new cell phone with all the fancy gadgets. She commented, "I'm constantly referring to the manual to figure out how to use it." Strategic readers know that reading to learn is essential; they value reading and read daily for information and pleasure. Reading from multiple sources causes a reader to think about a topic from different perspectives, thereby becoming more knowledgeable. Strategic readers regard book clubs, reading circles, and talking with friends about articles or books as important, worthwhile tasks.

Unfortunately, not all students realize the importance of reading to learn; far too often they rely on television and video for information and pleasure. The focus on reading has declined for children **and** adults. It is imperative that educators work to instill within each student the need (if not the passion) for reading. Massive amounts of voluntary reading must be integrated into the school day so students become curious knowledge-seekers. In summary, strategic readers continuously read to learn and learn to read because they know it opens many doors of learning and opportunities.

What is Strategic Reading?

What is reading? Take a minute to jot down your thoughts in the margin. If you ask students to define reading, their responses will range from knowing all of the letters, decoding the words and saying each word correctly, to understanding the main idea. If a student responds with "reading is thinking," that student has a good grasp of the reading process. How does your answer compare to the student's idea that reading is really thinking? More comprehensively, **reading is thinking cued by text**; reading involves not only decoding words but also understanding what words mean in a specific context.

Reading is clearly a three-pronged process, breaking the alphabetical code to figure out the words (grapho-phonics), understanding the way language works (syntax), and then thinking about the meaning embedded in the words (semantics). Effective reading instruction involves all three elements. Even young children understand how thinking changes when reading a fairy tale versus the school lunch menu. Decoding and comprehension must work in tandem. If the purpose for reading is not to think and understand the passage, then why bother reading at all? As you read this book you are engaging in strategic reading, you read with a purpose in mind, to gather information, to search for answers, and to compare or connect your reading with what you already know.

Strategic reading refers to thinking about reading in a manner that enhances learning and understanding (Harvey & Goudvis, 2000). The nature of how young people read and communicate is changing; digital technologies are revolutionizing how we read (Rooney, 2009). One size does not fit all; one text cannot meet the needs of all readers! As our reading world expands students must have access and exposure to multi-level reading materials, both narrative and informative, in all content areas. We can no longer rely on one textbook to provide all of the necessary information. If our goal is to develop strategic readers who understand, use, and appreciate the written word students must be offered opportunities to read from a variety of formats.

Why Strategic Reading in the Content Areas?

Learning new information has always been a major goal of education, but today with the information explosion and technological advances, the major goal has shifted. The focus can no longer be on acquiring and memorizing facts and trying to provide students all the information they will need to function in society (Rasinski & Padak, 2000). Living and working in society requires people to be capable and competent decision makers and problem solvers; people must be equipped with advanced literacy skills in order to cope with the vast amounts of information available on most topics. For example, having recently purchased kitchen appliances, I found that reading about the features of selected appliances on the Internet, in the newspaper, and from Consumer Report magazine helped me to decide which appliances to purchase. Students must become better strategic readers than ever before; they must become life-long readers who read to learn.

Reading in the content areas begins in the early years; even the youngest child can make inferences about ideas implied in the story *The Three Little Pigs* or draw conclusions about animals on the farm versus animals in the zoo (Vacca, 2002). We know that reading in each content area presents nuances and unique features; these features may be subtle but are nonetheless critical. A key challenge for many teachers is to articulate and make concrete the knowledge and skills they may take for granted but that many students need to be shown explicitly (Heller & Greenleaf, 2007). Too many students go through the motions of reading (word calling); they are skillful in the mechanics part. If students are to succeed in the content areas, teachers must demystify the reading that is unique to their discipline and teach students reading-to-learn skills needed for comprehending text. Chapters 6 and 7 presents nuances and examples for strategic reading in each content area.

Why a Strategic Reading Format?

Many of us remember receiving the assignment, *"Read the chapter and answer the questions at the end."* How many of us actually read the information for in-depth learning about the concept? Or did we simply take the easy way out - reading the questions and only the information necessary to answer the questions? If we want students to be motivated, interested, and independent learners in the content areas teaching practices must include significant amounts of interactive reading during the school day. The lecture-oriented philosophy of teaching, which often creates passive readers and learners who remain dependent on the teacher, must shift to incorporate literature circles, Socratic dialogues, and guided reading practices. The research emphasizes that when students are engaged in meaningful talking and/or writing activities comprehension increases. The Strategic Reading Format emphasizes the use of reading strategies that challenge students to think **before**, **during**, and **after** reading (Figure 1).

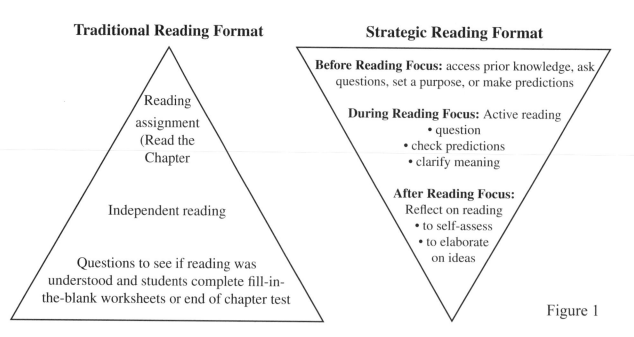

Traditional Reading Format

Reading assignment (Read the Chapter

Independent reading

Questions to see if reading was understood and students complete fill-in-the-blank worksheets or end of chapter test

Strategic Reading Format

Before Reading Focus: access prior knowledge, ask questions, set a purpose, or make predictions

During Reading Focus: Active reading
• question
• check predictions
• clarify meaning

After Reading Focus:
Reflect on reading
• to self-assess
• to elaborate on ideas

Figure 1

What Role Do Strategies Play?

Strategic reading requires that students learn to use and apply instructional strategies when reading narrative and informative text. The purpose of any strategy is to actively engage the mind when reading. For example, an Anticipation Guide causes a reader to make predictions about the topic before reading and to check for accuracy during reading. When readers understand the thinking involved within a strategy, they are able to adapt strategies to meet their content needs. For example, math teachers may change the **K-W-L** (What I **K**now-What I **W**ant to Know-What I **L**earned) strategy to **KNWS:**

K	N	W	S
What facts do I KNOW from the information in the problem?	Which information do I NOT need?	WHAT does the problem ask me to find?	What STRATEGY (operation) will I use to solve the problem?
Charlie's class has earned a pizza party because each student has read 5 books. Each will get 2 slices of pizza. There are 23 students & 1 teacher in the class-room. Each pizza is cut into 8 slices. How many pizzas should they order?	*Each student has read 5 books.*	*How many pizzas should they order?*	23+1 = 24 people 24x2 = 48 pieces 48÷8 = 6 pizzas

Selection of a strategy depends upon the type of thinking required for engagement and understanding and the needs of the readers. Strategies range on a continuum from quick thinking (tagging an idea with a Post-it note or rereading the paragraph) to in-depth thinking (completing a Learning Log Format or using Reciprocal Teaching). Strategic reading is possible when:

- Students are engaged in meaningful and purposeful work.
- Readers are explicitly taught how to use strategies and when to use them.
- Instruction of strategy use gradually moves from teacher-directed to student-initiated.

Explicit Strategy Instruction

Strategic learning is possible when the reader knows the task and the options for accomplishing it. Students who read strategically are flexible thinkers, knowing how to adapt their plans to incorporate different strategies. Helping students become strategic, progressing from novices to experts, necessitates instruction embracing three types of knowledge (Resnick, 1983; Paris, Lipson, & Wixson, 1994):

- *Declarative Knowledge.* Knowing **what** the strategy is
  Examples: I know that most stories incorporate story elements. I know that my comprehension goals change when reading a novel versus a newspaper.

- *Procedural Knowledge.* Knowing **how** to use the strategy
  Examples: I know how to skim the newspaper for a specific topic. I know how to determine an author's point of view.
- *Conditional Knowledge.* Knowing **when and why** to use a specific strategy
  Examples: I know to skim when I preview a selection or need to find a topic quickly. I know to re-read when I realize I am getting lost.

Declarative, procedural, and conditional knowledge are essential ingredients for strategic reading. Understanding all three forms of knowledge enables the reader to select appropriate behaviors to meet a specified purpose. For example, students may know that the SQ4R strategy (Robinson, 1961) means Survey, Question, Read, Recite, Review, and Reflect (declarative knowledge). But knowing what a strategy is does not mean knowing the procedure for using it. Students acquire procedural knowledge from modeling and guided practice in various situations. Only then do students know how to use the SQ4R strategy: asking themselves questions before reading each section in the chapter, reading with pencil in hand to answer the questions, and reflecting on what they have learned by revisiting each question.

Having declarative and procedural knowledge of the SQ4R strategy does not guarantee that a student can use the strategy appropriately as an independent reader. Not all situations require use of the SQ4R strategy; looking for a specific quotation requires skimming, or story mapping focuses on reading to detect story elements. Emphasizing the conditions under which a reader selects and uses a specific strategy is at the heart of strategic reading; strategic readers know when, how, and why to use a given strategy.

Are strategies necessary in all reading situations? Reading researchers, Ivey and Fisher (2006), believe strategies should be *transportable* and *transparent*. Transportable means that students can independently transfer a strategy learned in one situation to assist comprehension in another; transparent means that use of a strategy has become a natural way of thinking for the reader. When a reader decodes and comprehends a passage with little attention but yet understands the message, reading is being done automatically. In other words, information is acquired with little attention to processes. Unfortunately this is not the case for most students in content areas. As a result, modeling and applying strategies are especially important in the following reading situations:

- During initial acquisition of new skills
- When the content is expected to be difficult or challenging
- When emotions or stress impact or interfere with concentration and learning

Teacher-directed to Student-initiated Focus

Teachers help students become strategic readers by modeling and scaffolding the use of instructional strategies (versus merely assigning). For strategies to become transportable, students must also be taught to reflect on the benefits of using strategies to monitor reading comprehension. The purpose of any instructional strategy is to help students think in order to learn the content **AND** to learn about themselves as readers. We must constantly remind teachers that they **do not need to know as much about their students as readers as the students need to know about themselves.**

As students learn strategies it is important to analyze how well they are using them. The following four levels of reading proficiency illustrate how readers move from less to more sophisticated ways of monitoring their own thinking (Perkins and Swartz, 1992; Harvey & Goudvis, 2000):

- Tacit Readers lack awareness of how they think when they read.
- Aware Readers know they do not understand the passage but lack 'fix-it' strategies to repair the problem.
- Strategic Readers use 'fix-it' strategies to enhance understanding and to acquire knowledge; they monitor and revise meaning as needed.
- Reflective Readers are strategic thinkers who initiate and use strategies in a flexible manner; they self-assess and analyze how to revise the use of strategies.

For a student working as a Tacit Reader, teachers can use the Think-Aloud strategy to model how a reader thinks when reading. If a student is performing as an Aware Reader, the teacher might conduct class discussions that focus on students' awareness of their own performance. Another activity is the STOP – ACTION model in which the teacher reads authentic text (magazines), silently or orally, with small groups of students. Periodically, the teacher stops the students, asking them to share how they are constructing meaning, the kinds of comprehension difficulties they are experiencing, and how they are attempting to resolve them. Example statements:

> *"I am thinking that this is a really long sentence and I need to read it again so I know what it is saying."*
> *"I think I need to figure out the meaning of primitive because the word appears several times."*

Strategic Readers can independently transfer strategies from one situation to another. For example, they remember to read with a pencil in hand. They know that writing ideas in the margins or on sticky notes helps them keep track of their thinking and make meaning as they read. Reflective Strategic Readers know what strategies support or impede their comprehension and they self-assess their effectiveness through personal journal writing. Our overall goal is for students to assume primary responsibility for using strategies appropriately, for strategies to become transportable and transparent. The purpose is not to fill time with an activity; it is to help readers learn and apply strategies to aid comprehension. The final result is long-term efficiency!

Framework for Strategic Reading in the Content Areas

Traits of a Strategic Reader

Strategic readers engage in at least four different types of thinking when reading and reacting to text. (The connection can easily be made between Bloom's Taxonomy, a classification system describing different levels of thinking and various levels of thinking while reading.) The four reading traits are:

1) Reading the Lines for Recognition
2) Reading Inside the Lines for Meaning
3) Reading Between the Lines for Application
4) Reacting Beyond the Lines for Creation

Literacy scholars Luke and Freebody (1999) state that a passage beyond the literal statement of fact does not convey a neutral message nor is it bias free; rather it represents a particular point of view. Reading in all content areas should be tied to the world of work and to larger societal issues as students interact with text. Luke and Freebody emphasize that a critical reader must be proficient as: Code Breaker, Meaning Maker, Text User, and Text Critic.

Luke and Freebody's emphasis on developing critical readers closely matches the traits of strategic readers. Becoming a critical reader or becoming a strategic reader demands four types of thinking when reading and reacting to text. The four traits are interrelated but each possesses a distinct purpose; working toward mastery of each trait is essential for developing strategic readers. When teachers encourage students to process information learned through the four traits, students engage more deeply and thoroughly with text resulting in higher levels of understanding and learning (Pearson, Cervetti, & Tilson, 2008). The goal is to provide all students with rich literacy-based learning experiences, and this is possible if teachers create learning opportunities that incorporate the four traits of a strategic reader. The fun and excitement of reading and learning evolves, as students become text users and text critics.

Attributes of a Strategic Reader

Each reading trait (listed above) incorporates a series of reading attributes; reading attributes are cognitive skills that specify how to **think** when reading. For example, **making predictions** before reading is an attribute that causes the reader to construct meaning by forecasting the outcome of the selection, or **examining points of view** causes the reader to think from different perspectives during reading. Reading attributes are sometimes referred to as strategies, critical thinking skills, or reading skills. The reading attributes are extracted from years of research comparing successful and struggling readers. Successful readers use a vast array of reading attributes, such as questioning, inferring, and detecting bias. As students become strategic readers, they demonstrate mastery of reading attributes within the four traits.

Outlining the Traits and Attributes

This section explains each trait, cites specific reading attributes appropriate for narrative *(N)* or informative *(I)* text, and provides an instructional example. One could argue that all traits are applicable in both narrative and informative text. These distinctions are meant to indicate primary use. For a complete listing of the reading attributes within each of the four traits see *Capturing All of the Reader Through the Reading Assessment System* (2nd ed.) (Billmeyer, 2006a).

Trait 1: Reading the Lines for Recognition - "Code Breaker"

When Strategic Readers read silently or orally they decode the words, recognize the genre, and make use of the symbols, patterns, and text features. These acts build the foundation for comprehension and call upon the following attributes:

- Uses known words to figure out unfamiliar text *(N/I)*
- Attributes meaning to symbols *(I)*
- Decodes words using phonetic and structural analysis *(N/I)*
- Recognizes genre *(N)*
- Distinguishes organizational patterns of text *(N/I)*
- Distinguishes story elements *(N)*
- Overviews and makes use of text format and features (maps, charts, graphs, illustrations, and styles of type) to gain meaning *(N/I)*

Examples:

Figuring Out Unfamiliar Text

Students read an unfamiliar text, such as *Fall* by Jillian Cutting. Teacher prints sentences on separate sentence strips, omitting important vocabulary terms. Print vocabulary terms (falling, colors, play, winter, jack-o-lantern, Fall) on word cards. Students read cloze sentences and discuss the meaning with partners or small group. Students supply omitted word that makes sense in the cloze sentences and match vocabulary card to appropriate cloze sentence.

Use of Symbols for High School Music Performance

A high school music teacher teaches students about the following music symbols: key signature, meter or change of meter, repeat signs, tempo marking, and dynamic marking. As students prepare to sing musical selections for a performance, they are instructed to examine the entire selection for the music symbols.

Trait 2: Reading Inside the Lines for Meaning – "Meaning Maker"

Strategic Readers reflect on their own processing skills while reading. When readers are aware of and use reading strategies, they are able to monitor their understanding before, during, and after reading. Strategic Readers strive to achieve fluency and comprehension. The following attributes are applied:

- Learns new meanings for known words *(N/I)*
- Establishes purpose for reading *(N/I)*
- Builds on prior knowledge *(N/I)*

- Asks questions before, during, and after reading *(N/I)*
- Checks predetermined predictions during reading *(N/I)*
- Draws conclusions from text *(N/I)*
- Reflects on own reading process *(N/I)*

Examples:

Text Tagging with 2nd Graders

The Text-Tagging strategy (Billmeyer, 2006b) was used when reading an informative selection in the basal reading text. Before reading the selection, "Animals That Migrate," the teacher modeled the strategy using another nonfiction book about animals. The following text tagging code was written on the board.

   *   I already knew this.
   +   This is new information to me. I didn't know that.
   !   WOW! Awesome!
   ?   I don't get it.

As the selection was read to the students, the teacher stopped after each paragraph to discuss what she read. She tagged each idea with a small sticky note, wrote the symbol on the sticky note, and stuck the note on the correct spot in the paragraph. Students were given sticky notes to tag the selection while reading it independently. Students discussed how they tagged their selection and their reasons for tagging as they did. The Text Tagging strategy increased their engagement with the text, as well as their understanding of what they read.

Developed by Marilyn Rochford, Jefferson Elementary, Charles City, IA

Making and Retelling Meaningful Interpretations When Reading

Students were asked to preview the science selection, "Characteristics of Living Things," record their predictions, and share their predictions with a partner. Next, students read the selection, revised their predictions if necessary, and once again shared revised predictions with a partner. If necessary, students reread the text a third time until there was confidence of understanding. To demonstrate understanding, students created a graphic organizer or a diagram retelling the science selection so that someone new to the passage could understand it. Students explained the retelling to a partner and made comparisons; they referred to the text to check questionable interpretations and discussed the different formats for retelling.

Trait 3: Reading Between the Lines for Application – "Text User"

When Strategic Readers comprehend and interpret text, they apply their prior knowledge and skills to perform tasks, to revise text, and to answer questions using defensible sources. Making sense of the whole text comes from the ability to manipulate the parts. The following attributes are applied:

- Learns new words representing known and new concepts *(N/I)*
- Has knowledge of authors' styles *(N)*
- Connects interpretations to themes *(N)* - a main idea *(I)*
- Makes inferences and can document to support *(N/I)*
- Summarizes information read *(N/I)*
- Draws connections to world issues *(N/I)*
- Integrates new ideas, connecting them to a bigger picture *(N/I)*

Examples:

Facts + Background Knowledge and Opinions = Inference

During character education class, students were reading fables to learn about life lessons. Students were taught how to infer the life lesson embedded within the fable. The teacher read the fable, "The Hare and the Tortoise," aloud to the students and stopped to explain her thinking while reading. She explained how her brain paid attention to the facts in the story and made connections to her prior knowledge, experiences, and opinions. "I know that turtles move very slow and rabbits can run fast. The hare is acting boastful and rude to the turtle and those behaviors can get you into trouble. The hare brags that he will beat the turtle to the finish line but he ends up loosing the race. I can infer that the lesson in this fable is to go slow and to do your best." Working with a partner, students were asked to read a fable and infer the life lesson using the following format:

Fables and Life Lessons

Story Facts + My Experiences & Opinions = My Inference or Life Lesson

Pairs shared and compared their fable examples. Students discussed why their inferences may differ from those of other students.

Applying Art Principles to Character Analysis

The outcome for this high school project was to develop understanding of the arts as a tool for communicating ideas and feelings by creating a mask in clay that visually interpreted a character from children's literature. Students read a self-selected story and then chose a character to interpret. Each student completed a Character Analysis Graphic Organizer, listing six descriptive words to describe the character's traits. Students viewed examples of master works to identify and discuss visual interpretation in 2D and 3D work, including theatrical masks from a variety of cultures. They identified the use of color, texture, line, and shape to express feelings/mood and then created analog drawings. Students drew four thumbnail sketches of a mask and then used clay to create a final mask in the Greek theatre tradition to interpret their character. To summarize, students wrote a reflective analysis of their learnings.

Developed by Barbara Sampson, Lake Washington School District, Kirkland, WA

Trait 4: Reacting Beyond the Lines for Creation – "Text Critic"

Strategic Readers extend thinking when they evaluate what they have read by making critical, thoughtful judgments about the selection. Readers are encouraged to share their perspectives, ideas, opinions, and values. Readers create justifiable critiques to appraise the text's effectiveness and quality. The reader's perspective is valued in the process. They use the following attributes:

- Judges the effectiveness of word choice *(N/I)*
- Expresses opinions using supporting ideas *(N/I)*
- Uses information from multiple sources to produce new ideas *(I)*
- Challenges the text and author with questions *(N/I)*
- Shifts perspective to examine points of view *(N/I)*
- Recognizes cultural overtones and biases *(N/I)*
- Makes connections between text and own experiences, and other literature and the world *(N)*

Examples:

Questioning the Author

Primary age children were taught the Questioning the Author strategy (Beck, McKeown, Hamilton, & Kucan, 1997) in order to challenge what they read and to question what the author has written. The teacher read *The Big Orange Splot* by Daniel Pinkwater aloud and then led a discussion with the students. Students were asked questions such as:

- What does the author, Daniel Pinkwater, mean when he says, *My house is me and I am it. My house is where I like to be and it looks like all my dreams.?*
- Why did the author, Daniel Pinkwater, say, *He's got bees in his bonnet, bats in his belfry, and knots in his noodle.?*

Students drew a picture of their dream house and created one question for the author about their house.

Eighth Grade Social Studies

A class of eighth graders was divided into three groups to study the Civil War. Each group was assigned one of the following three novels:

- *Shades of Gray* by Carolyn Reeder (Southern Perspective)
- *Lottie's Courage* by Phyllis Hall Haislip (Slave Perspective)
- *Soldier's Heart* by Gary Paulsen (Northern Perspective)

As students read their novel, they periodically discussed ideas with other group members. After reading their novel, students individually completed the Thinking from Different Perspectives strategy (Billmeyer, 2006b). Upon completion, they discussed their ideas with group members who read the same book. The culminating activity was a class discussion with each group supporting their perspective and exploring the perspective of others.

Systematically Teaching the Traits and Attributes

Much has been learned since the inception of the four reading traits aligned with specific attributes. First, teachers, textbook authors, and literacy consultants interchange the term reading attributes with strategies, skills, critical thinking skills, or critical reading skills. Because **reading is thinking cued by text** the term attribute emphasizes how a reader thinks to engage in text, the emphasis is on thinking. Secondly, we know that elementary teachers spend time teaching the reading attributes during designated reading periods. However, this has not been the case for content area teaching. Lastly, after careful analysis, it is clear academic disciplines do incorporate specific reading attributes students must use in order to comprehend text within each area. Examples include:

Social studies textbooks identify the following reading attributes as important for reading history:	Science standards require students apply the following critical reading attributes:
• Identify cause and effect • Make predictions • Find main idea • Draw conclusions • Make inferences • Identify points of view • Identify bias	• Determine main idea • Draw conclusions • Make logical inferences • Identify fact and opinion • Recognize bias

Reading in math relies on the following reading attributes:
- Gather/identify critical facts
- Develop knowledge of vocabulary
- Access prior knowledge
- Generate conclusions
- Identify, sequence, and follow steps in directions
- Determine main idea
- Make inferences for logical reasoning

Reading in Vocational Education Classes require students to:
- Learn new meaning for known words
- Create visual images
- Determine main idea
- Distinguish text format and features

When teachers teach reading attributes they are in fact teaching reading within their content areas. When a science teacher models how to make logical inferences from a science experiment or a history teacher elicits predictions from students regarding outcomes of wars, they are helping students read and think as a scientist or a historian. The list of reading attributes above is not comprehensive; teachers are aware of other reading attributes essential to learning in their content area. Think about reading in your content area, what reading attributes could be added to the list above?

Teachers are beginning to realize the impact on student learning when traits and attributes are emphasized within their content areas. Some starting points for incorporating the traits and attributes of a strategic reader are:
- Read a passage aloud to your students and model the appropriate thinking for each trait.
  For example, a Code Breaker previews the entire selection to determine how to read it or a Meaning Maker thinks about prior experiences related to the topic.
- Link the 4 traits with Blooms Taxonomy to create lessons inclusive of different levels of thinking. For example, a lesson on Space could include the following activities:

    Code Breaker: Students cut out space pictures from a magazine and label each item or make a list of all the space words they know.

    Meaning Maker: Read about different astronauts and keep a journal of their space adventures. Explain the life of an astronaut in your journal. Explain how humans prepare to live in an alien environment. What are the risks?

    Text User: Create an application form for a person applying for the job of an astronaut. Make a list of questions you would like to ask an astronaut. What skills are critical for astronauts?

    Text Critic: Estimate how much money has been spent on the space program in the United States, use facts to discuss whether that was a wise use of money. What if that money had been spent on education or health care in our country?

〰️

- Determine which reading attributes/skills are incorporated in your content area. Introduce the selected reading attributes to students in context with a read aloud. For example, a high school social studies teacher selected eight reading attributes for focus first semester. To introduce the attributes to her students, she read *Faithful Elephants* aloud, stopping at appropriate times for students to respond to the designated reading attribute. Throughout the semester she selected strategies and activities that reinforced the identified reading attributes.

⌘

Targeting the Attributes – *Faithful Elephants* by Yukie Tsuchiya		
Predict what the story will be about based on the title. **Make Prediction**	What do you see/visualize from what I have read so far? **Visualize**	What was the perception of the elephants at this time? **Draw Conclusions from Text**
Revisit your prediction for accuracy and write what will happen next. **Check Prediction**	What theme is author Yukie Tsuchiya communicating to us? **Determine Theme**	What questions would you want to ask the author? **Challenge Author with Questions**

- Select instructional strategies or activities that align with the attributes emphasized in your content area(s). Examples:

⌘

Reading Trait	Reading Attribute	Strategy Option
Reading the Lines for Recognition "Be a Code Breaker"	Distinguishes organizational patterns	Thinking/writing Patterns
Reading Inside the Lines for Meaning "Be a Meaning Maker"	Establishes purpose for reading	Anticipation Guide
Reading Between the Lines for Application "Be a Text User"	Makes inferences and can document to support	Semantic Mapping
Reacting Beyond the Lines for Creation "Be a Text Critic"	Challenges the text and author with question	Questioning the Author

Understanding the reading traits and attributes inherent to your content area can assist in designing a meaningful unit of study in which students effectively read to learn. Reading strategies are incorporated and also can be used as assessment tools. For example, the planning process might proceed in the following manner:

1) Determine the standard or outcome for the unit
   Learning Target: Students will understand the concepts of courage, suffering, and leadership as they relate to military and civilian populations in the period of history surrounding World War II.
2) Select the reading trait matching the appropriate level of thinking and determine the specific attributes
   Reading Traits and Attributes: Reading Between the Lines for Application
   - Learns new words representing known and new concepts
   - Integrates new ideas, connecting them to a bigger picture

3) Create an assessment task to demonstrate learning
   <u>Assessment Task</u>: The learner will create a Character Analysis Map of a historical figure emulating courage, leadership, or suffering during World War II.
4) Select appropriate reading strategies which contain the reading attributes outlined
   <u>Reading Strategies</u>:
   - Concept Definition Map
   - Character Analysis Map
5) Create lessons which help students reach intended outcome
6) Teach the lessons
7) Assess students using the assessment task

Conclusion

Strategic reading in the content areas is critical for student success. To be a productive citizen in society people must be capable of handling, manipulating, and working with text. For this to occur, not only learning to read but also **reading to learn** must be at the top of each district and classroom agenda.

Strategic readers are created when we develop a common language for teaching and talking about strategic reading across all grade levels and in all content areas. When children come into the classroom knowing how to use strategies, teachers can extend rather than reinvent the wheel each time. They can focus on how to use the strategy for increasingly difficult content.

For strategies to transfer from one content area to another and from one level to the next, monitoring and assessment of strategy use are important. Once students learn strategies it is important to track how well they are using them and if they are using them independently. Performing a skill does not always mean that a reader did it intentionally or purposefully. Accidental responses are not considered strategic, perhaps lucky but not replicable. Just because students say they are using a strategy does not necessarily mean they are. It is important to check with readers to see what strategy they are using, how it is working, and why they are using it. Strategic readers know the benefit of using strategies; they use them purposefully and intentionally, and they monitor and assess their effectiveness.

When districts identify strategic reading as a major outcome and all teachers focus on developing strategic readers, the cumulative effect from kindergarten through high school and into life beyond is powerful.

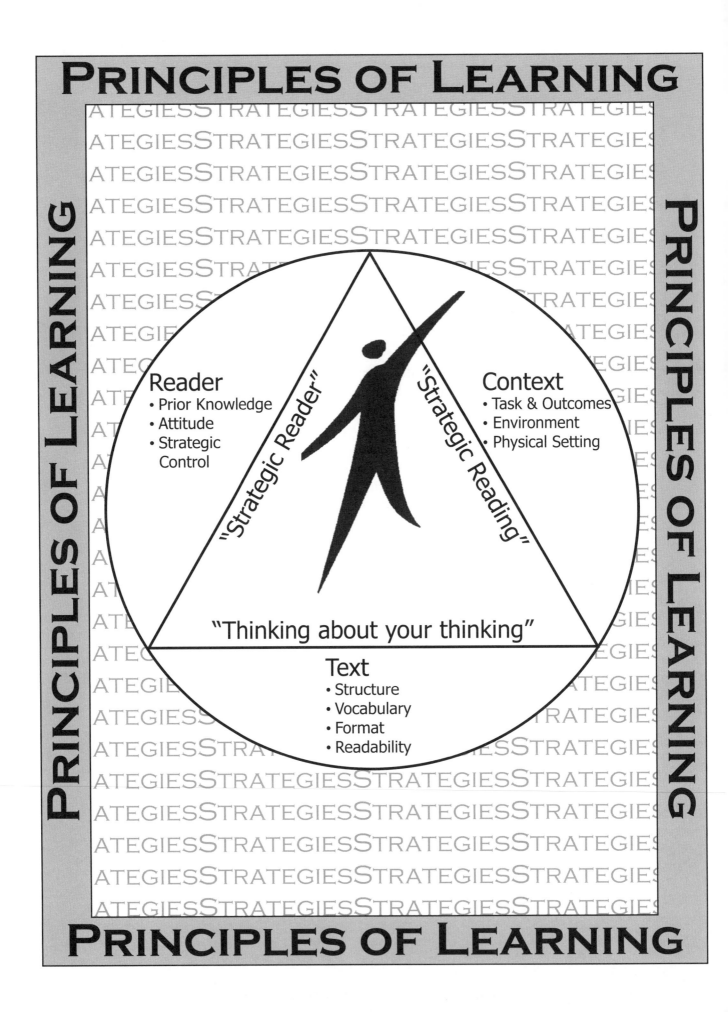

Chapter 4

Notes

Metacognition
"Thinking About Your Thinking"

"Learning Teams"

As a result of working through this chapter you will:
- Be able to explain metacognition
- Know how to help students become more metacognitive
- Understand the importance of metacognitive tools: questioning, talking, and writing

Questions to ponder before, during, and after reading

Before reading - What does metacognition mean? How do you teach your students to be metacognitive?

During reading - In what ways do you agree with the author? What differences do you have? What examples support your thinking?

After reading - In what ways might working with students to be more metacognitive strengthen their understanding of your content area?

Process Activity

The process activity for studying the chapter on Metacognition is the Read and Reflect strategy (Billmeyer, 2006b). This strategy helps readers practice communication tools that increase metacognitive thinking. Directions:

1) Select a partner and designate an "A" and a "B" person.
2) Preview the chapter on Metacognition pages 38 – 45 and converse about prior knowledge you bring to this topic.
3) Divide the chapter into four Read and Reflect sections: Introduction, Questioning, Talking, and Writing.
4) Both partners silently read the first section, Introduction through Helping Students Become Metacognitive pages, 38 – 39, highlighting key ideas.
5) Process the section in the following manner:
   "A" shares a key learning.
   "B" listens, paraphrases, and inquires. (Example, "You agree with the author's perspective. What connections are you making?")
6) Reverse roles and repeat the process with the first section.
   "B" shares a key learning.
   "A" listens, paraphrases, and inquires.
7) Continue the reading process with the three remaining sections: questioning, talking, and writing.
8) Reflect on overall learning about Metacognition, determine ideas for implementation, and discuss benefits of the Read and Reflect strategy.

Chapter 4

Metacognition
"Thinking About Your Thinking"

I thank the Lord for the brain He put in my head. Occasionally,
I love to just stand to one side and watch how it works.
- Richard Bolles

Introduction

Metacognition refers to the awareness and understanding of one's own learning process. Metacognition or "thinking about your own thinking" is at the heart of strategic reading. What we know today about strategic reading is a direct result of the research on metacognition. Strategic readers are metacognitive; they know how to approach a passage and take the necessary steps to comprehend what they read. They use fix-it strategies to get themselves out of jams when they struggle with difficult text (Santa & Alvermann, 1991).

Professor Henriksson (2001) offers the following examples from college students who struggle with metacognitive abilities:

> *Christianity was just another mystery cult until Jesus was born. The mother of Jesus was Mary, who was different from other women because of her immaculate contraption (p.23).*

> *Nineteenth-century America was an unequal society where only White males could download access to the power serge (p. 87).*

Henriksson's examples of students' work illustrate the ingenious ways students attempt to make sense of information they do not understand because they have no context or frame of reference for it. If all students were strategic readers equipped with metacognitive strategies, reading in the content areas would be more productive. Strategic readers realize that comprehension requires an interaction between the text and the reader; they have command of three critical areas: self-knowledge, task-knowledge, and self-monitoring.

Self-knowledge: "What do I know about myself as a reader?

In *Understanding by Design* (1998), Wiggins and McTighe describe one facet of understanding as "self-knowledge." Self-knowledge refers to the knowledge students have about themselves as learners and specifically, as readers. Strategic readers know how their patterns of thought and actions inform as well as affect understanding. They are aware of the attitudes and behaviors that affect their learning. For example, strategic readers examine their background knowledge, level of interest, and shortcomings when reading a particular selection. In other words, strategic readers analyze their reading abilities in relationship to the text.

Task-knowledge: "What is the task? Why am I reading this?"

Task-knowledge refers to analyzing the task and the text features and matching the task with appropriate strategies. Text features such as structure, vocabulary, format, and readability influence comprehension (see Chapter 5, Section 3). Strategic readers know how to prepare themselves for reading; they approach a narrative selection differently than an informative selection. They examine their prior knowledge about the topic and set a purpose for reading. Once strategic readers have analyzed the task, they scan their repertoire of strategies and select those appropriate for the situation.

Self-monitoring: "How do I monitor understanding as I read?"

Strategic readers actively monitor their comprehension before, during, and after reading (Baker and Brown, 1984). They use metacognitive strategies to facilitate active thinking and continuously check to see if they understand the author's message. Strategic readers are aware of their thinking as they read, selecting appropriate self-monitoring tools. Self-knowledge, task-knowledge, and self-monitoring work in concert when reading to learn.

Helping Students Become Metacognitive

To develop strategic readers, teachers need to teach students how to be aware of their thinking before, during, and after reading. Three metacognitive tools that support thinking during all three phases of thinking are questioning, talking, and writing. For example before reading, strategic readers preview the selection and create **questions** to focus thinking during reading. During reading they reread an unclear paragraph **thinking aloud,** or they use an organizer to **write** key ideas. After reading, they **discuss** interpretations with a peer and **record** impressions.

The use of a "Think Pad" is common practice in a middle school science class. Students are frequently asked to take a thinking break to record ideas during a read aloud, reactions during an experiment, or thoughts about a selection they're reading. What a powerful approach to help students understand that reading is thinking cued by text! To help students be metacognitive Ellen Billmeyer (my daughter) displays and refers to posters entitled "The Little Voice in My Head."

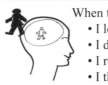

The little voice in my head helps me:	When the little voice in my head takes a walk:
• Ask questions	• I lose focus while I read
• Give opinions	• I don't care about what I'm reading
• Make connections	• I read a page and forget what was read
• Remember what I've read	• I think of other things

Reading strategies incorporate some form of questioning, talking, or writing; strategies such as Questioning the Author, Think-Alouds, and RAFT (Role, Audience, Format, Topic) incorporate one or more of the three metacognitive tools (see Chapter 6). Focusing on all three metacognitive tools pays dividends in the classroom.

〰〰〰

Metacognitive Tool – "Questioning"

Students do not take responsibility for their comprehension
when the teacher or the textbook is the "keeper of the questions."

- Hashey and Connors

Questioning is a powerful metacognitive tool to guide and monitor student learning. Rigby (1978) believes that self-questioning is one of the most potent cognitive tools for stimulating content learning because question-generation prompts readers to search for answers that are of interest to them. Everyone knows that young children thrive on asking questions, especially "why."

Research indicates that explicit training is a requirement for successful student generation of higher-level questions (Rosenshine, Meister, & Chapman, 1996). Higher-order questions extend learning because they require the reader to apply, analyze, synthesize, and evaluate information instead of simply recalling facts. Too often students have been given the assignment "Read the chapter and answer the questions at the end." Little attention has been given to questioning as an important metacognitive tool. As a result, students read passively with a goal to complete the assignment rather than to learn. Using higher-level questions makes reading an active process and prompts the reader to search the text and to have internal dialogue while reading.

A variety of different ways exist to teach students about the questioning process. For starters, students need to analyze the relationship between a question and an answer. Not all questions cause students to think in the same way. For example, compare what your brain does with each of these questions:

- Who was the first man to set foot on the moon? or When did Christopher Columbus discover America?
- How did Neil Armstrong's trip to the moon compare with Columbus' voyage to the new world?
- How might education be different if all of the money that was allocated to the space program had been directed to education?

As you read each question, perhaps you noticed your thinking process changed from searching for one right answer to comparing what the reader knows about the events, and finally (with the last question) to see that there are many possibilities and no right or wrong answer. Questions progressed from recall to analysis to evaluative, each requiring more think-time.

Reread the questions again to determine how the syntax of each question caused your brain to process as it did. For example, in the first question the word "who" signals to the brain there is one right answer or the word "if" in the last question signals many possibilities. Questions could be categorized into three types:

- Text explicit (answer explicitly stated in the text)
- Text implicit (answer implied within the text)
- Reader response (answer is found in the reader's head based on application of ideas read)

Teaching students thinking processes involved with questioning helps them to develop a deeper understanding of the questioning process. If we want students to develop higher-level questions, we have to teach them what these questions sound like and how they feel when responding. Once students understand the mental engagement required by the question, they must be taught how to develop their own questions. The instructional process involves three stages: identifying, classifying, and generating questions (Ciardiello, 1998). First, students are taught how to **identify** different types of questions, learning that key words or question stems signal certain types of questions. Teaching the Question/Answer Relationship strategy (Raphael, 1986) (see p. 173) through the use of cue cards is beneficial for developing questions. Cue card example:

Literal Questions (Memory) - Who, When, Where
Interpretive Questions (Application) - Draw Conclusions, Analyze, Predict
Evaluative Questions (Opinion) - Imagine, Speculate, Question the Author

The second stage of becoming an effective questioner is being able to **classify** questions into distinct categories. Students must be able to explain the differences among literal, interpretive, and evaluative questions before they are able to construct their own.

The last stage involves **student-generated** questions. After reading several chapters of *Holes* (Sachar, 1998) students were instructed to record questions about the book on individual strips of paper. Working in small groups, students shared their questions and recorded answers next to the questions. Next they organized their questions on a continuum from "skinny questions" to "fat questions." Skinny questions require a right/wrong answer, whereas fat questions require more thought, and allow for a variety of answers (Hashey and Connors, 2003).

←————————————————————————————→
Skinny Questions   Fat Questions

Once students learn that some questions beg to be answered while others bore the reader, they understand why questioning is an important metacognitive tool. Given ample practice, students will seek out high-level questions because they are more engaging. All students have the potential to learn how to think, reflect, and question in a competent manner. Low-achieving students benefit from the questioning process as much as those who may be labeled gifted. Too often the lower achieving student focuses only on the lower level basic questions, but current learning theory tells us that this view is too limiting (Palincsar & Klenk, 1991). Questions that cause readers to make connections to their own life by applying and comparing ideas provide the connections when learning the factual information. As stated earlier, without the high-order, connective thinking students struggle to understand or make sense of information because they have no context or frame of reference. Training all students to generate high-level questions helps all students learn how to think before, during, and after reading.

Metacognitive Tool - "Talking"

Free human dialogue . . . lies at the heart of education.

- Neil Postman

Graff (2003) believes that the talk about books and subjects is as important educationally as the books and subjects are themselves. In the real world, people who read will seek to discuss differing perceptions, debate whether the advice offered seems accurate, or analyze the author's viewpoint for bias. Students rarely are given the opportunity for academic dialogue about topics read; even today classrooms are too quiet, lacking the hum of ideas and student interaction.

Yet, students who were asked to explain their interpretations of information had higher reading scores than students not provided these opportunities. Based on the 1998 NAEP (National Assessment of Educational Progress) results, it appears that talking is an important ingredient for comprehension. Talking takes on a variety of formats including pair reading and exchanging ideas with a partner, participating in a book club discussion, rereading a paragraph aloud, or conducting a reflective conversation with a teammate.

Reflective conversations, sometimes referred to as metacognitive conversations, engage readers in dialogue with each other. Working in pairs, students coach each other's thinking about a selection read. The intent is to advance the reader's thinking about the topic to a higher level of understanding. The reader is not only encouraged to reflect on the topic, but also on the strategies used to make meaning during reading and the tools used for identifying and fixing comprehension problems. This nonjudgmental form of talking emphasizes the three phases of thinking outlined in the Principles of Learning (see Chapter 2, p. 8).

Phase 1 - "Planning" prepares the mind for reading. **Before reading** the coach stimulates the reader's thinking about the passage. Planning questions might include:
- What do you know about this topic?
- What is your purpose for reading this selection?

Phase 2 - "Interaction" engages the cognitive mind during reading. Reflective conversations **during reading** create an awareness of how the reader is thinking and what strategies are being used to monitor comprehension. Questions might include:
- What are you noticing about yourself as a reader while reading this selection?
- At this stage in reading, what questions would you like to ask the author?

Phase 3 - "Reflection" integrates, connects, and applies ideas after reading. Reflecting **after reading** focuses on two areas of thought: content and process. Questions include:
- How might you use ideas from the reading in your own life or for further learning?
- What successful reading strategies will you continue to use in future reading   endeavors?

For students to become proficient in the role as coach, modeling and practice are needed. Students are not familiar with this form of conversation, so modeling the process with a student produces the best results. Some teachers begin by listing sample questions on cue cards for students to use as they conduct the conversation.

The capacity to reflect in conversation is enhanced when students incorporate effective communication tools. Nonjudgmental verbal and nonverbal behaviors such as rapport, active listening, pausing, paraphrasing, and clarifying enhance thinking in conversation. Just as students were taught "eye-to-eye and knee-to-knee" when talking during a cooperative learning lesson, the same rapport building practice is essential during a reflective conversation.

Discussion is a structured form of talking in which groups of students share their ideas to refine thinking and explore comparable issues. Discussions allow readers to closely examine a topic by exchanging ideas and questions. Through discussion, students develop an awareness of their own beliefs and values. A sense of creative freedom evolves which encourages ownership of ideas and helps to build strategic readers. Two reading strategies that incorporate structured discussion are Reciprocal Teaching (see p. 214) and Literature Circles (see p. 220).

Talking causes the reader to be an active composer of meaning. When readers talk back to the text, they tap into the schema, making connections and organizing information. Strategic readers talk to stimulate their thinking and to extend and refine their understanding of content read. No matter the form, talking is a critical metacognitive tool to engage the mind of the reader.

Metacognitive Tool - "Writing"
Writing is the litmus paper of thought . . . the very center of school.
- Ted Sizer

Writing helps students connect the dots of knowledge, to find out what they know and what they don't know, and to make knowledge their own (Schmoker, 2006). Kuhrt and Farris (1990) stress that writing is the means by which students develop metacognitive awareness and eventually assume control over it. Students who write have tremendous advantages over those who do not; those who had more opportunities to write about information demonstrated the highest reading performance (NAEP, 1998). Reading and writing are connected – readers read writing; writers write reading. Strategic readers use writing to help them process what they read; when reading complicated text they reach for a pencil to make notes in the margin. We all have experienced writing our interpretations or reactions to something we have read; the writing deepened our understanding of the reading. Why? Writing is the visible surface of thinking. There are many benefits to linking reading and writing processes. Writing:

- Identifies "holes" in the learning.
- Provides the reader a visual structure for organizing thinking.
- Helps students determine key ideas as they reflect on what they have read.
- Creates an avenue for applying ideas from text to the reader's life.
- Helps students analyze different types of text to understand how they are organized. For example, to deepen the understanding of story elements in narrative text, students may apply them when writing their own short story.

Writing can take on a variety of formats, from production writing to informal writing. Production writing is a more elaborate, structured form of writing. Students read about a topic, progress through multiple drafts, and create a finished product to demonstrate understanding of the topic. Finished products are usually graded by the teacher and by the student using a scoring guide (rubric). Production writing examples include:

- Proposition/Support Outlines (see p. 180)
- RAFT writing strategy (see p. 190)
- Dear Author Letter – Students select an issue from the text they want to evaluate such as, The Treaty of Versailles or Global Warming in the 21st Century. They write a letter to the author expressing their opinions, raising questions, and suggesting alternatives regarding the issue. Students are encouraged to use personal knowledge, quotes, and primary sources.
- Language Experiences – Children create their own books about self-selected topics. They write their story or dictate their ideas for an adult to record. For example, students might write about "Family Traditions," or "Staying Fit in Junior High." Creating Graphic Novel books allows students to combine writing with their artistic talents. Student-developed books yield lots of meaningful material for students to read; authors read and reread their own drafts and take great pride in sharing their books with friends. These productions can even become part of the school library circulation.

Informal writing structures are appropriate for all content areas; they can be used before, during, and after reading to help students predict, clarify, organize, or summarize ideas. Informal writing formats are ongoing, brief, reflective, tentative, and exploratory in nature. Teachers incorporate different informal writing structures, such as "Think Pads" (discussed earlier in this chapter), content area learning logs (see Strategic Reading Journal, p. 136 and Learning Logs, p. 218), or writing-to-learn strategies (Billmeyer, 2006b). Fisher and Frey's work (2004) outlines a variety of writing-to-learn prompts such as:

- *Crystal Ball* asks students to predict what they think class will be about and to access their prior knowledge about the topic.
- *Take a Stand* requires students to clarify any confusing ideas or opinions about controversial ideas.
- *Yesterday's New* causes students to summarize the information presented in the previous class.

When readers keep track of their learning through writing they can revisit their thinking and chart their growth as learners, discovering what they know and what they do not know. Not all students are thrilled with more writing opportunities; they come with preconceived notions about writing and do not understand the benefits of writing-to-learn. To make informal writing a positive and productive experience, teachers should incorporate five key principles (Strong, et. al., 2002).

Model – Teachers who engage in journal writing and share their entries with students model the value of recording ideas to learn.

Criteria – Students who are provided criteria when writing are more successful in assessing their own writing. For example, when using a content area learning log, students may be asked to use specific vocabulary relating to the concept (see Strategic Reader Journal Scoring Guide p. 137).

Balance Assigned With Choice – Many students have not developed the habit of keeping a journal or log. Therefore, they need idea starters to jump-start their thinking. Starters can be open-ended or provocative stems specific to the topic they are reading. If the goal is for students to become independent keepers of their thinking through writing, it is necessary to occasionally allow them to decide how they want to respond. Open-ended starters include: "This is similar to what I know . . ." or "The big ideas seem to be . . ." Content specific stems: "What do you think caused Picasso to see and paint the world as he did?" or "Why do you think Shakespeare's poems and plays have been incorporated as essential high school reading for all students?"

Samples – To help students understand what reflective writing looks like, show them example journal entries from your own journal or sample writings from masters, such as Van Gogh or Churchill.

Feedback – Responding to student journal or learning log entries can promote more writing, as well as better writing. The type of feedback is of important consideration. If the goal is to create independent writers, the feedback needs to be in the form of reflective questions or comments. For example, "What else can you share about . . .?" or "What do you mean when you say . . .?" or "What questions are you asking yourself about . . .?"

Conclusion

Students' academic performance increases when they engage in meaningful questioning, talking, and writing activities. These metacognitive tools provide opportunities to reflect so students can become adept at monitoring, assessing, and improving their own performance as readers. To become a strategic reader means one is aware of oneself as a reader and knows fix-it strategies to solve problems that occur when reading. Metacognitive ability is developmental (Stewart and Tei, 1983). Older students tend to be more metacognitive and strategic when reading than are younger students. Readers with more experience use a broader repertoire of fix-it strategies to deal with comprehension problems. Knowing that metacognitive skills are developmental, it is critical that teachers actively teach and support younger students in the development of these skills. Teachers who help students acquire strategies as well as an understanding of when to use them enable students to become active, independent readers.

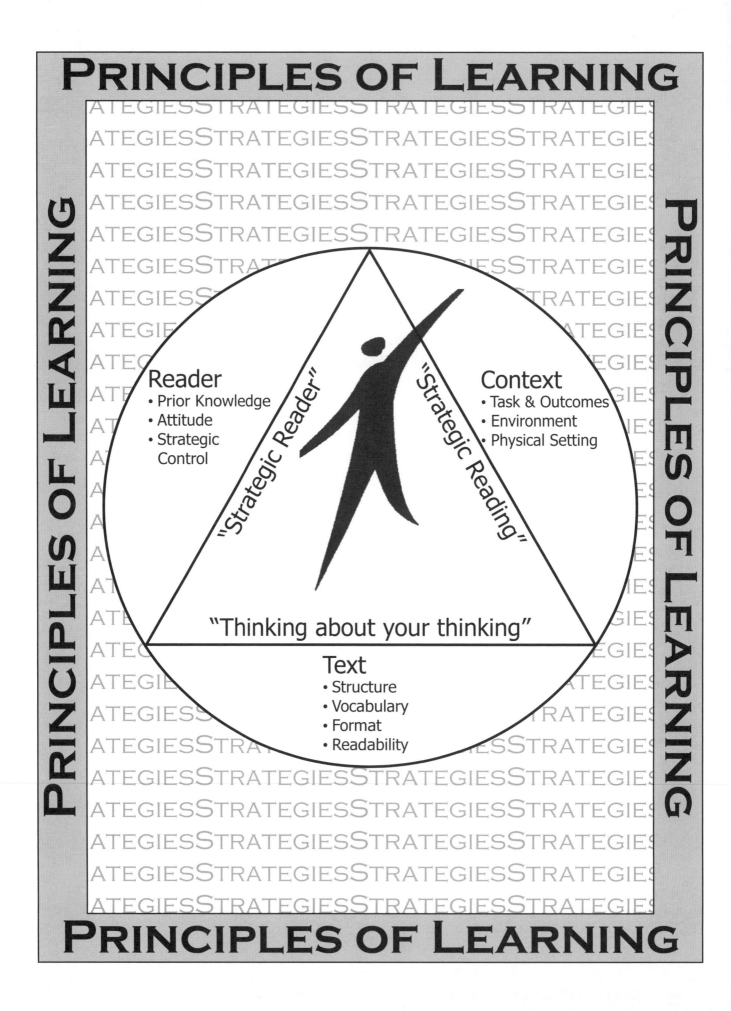

Chapter 5

Three Interactive Reading Ingredients

Introduction

Current reading research describes the reading process as an active and strategic process. Strategic reading in the content areas involves three interactive reading ingredients:

- What the **reader** brings to the reading situation

- The **context** of the reading situation

- The characteristics of the **text**

These interactive ingredients determine how the reader comprehends text. The section on **reader** focuses on prior knowledge, attitude, and strategic control of the reading process. Reading **context** examines the reading task and the expected outcomes, the environment, and the physical setting for reading. **Text** is comprised of four elements: structure, vocabulary, format, and readability. Comprehension is a dynamic interactive process of constructing meaning by combining the reader's existing knowledge with the text information within the context of the reading situation (Cook, 1989).

Chapter 5 is organized into three sections: Reader, Context, and Text. Learning team activities are included as follows:

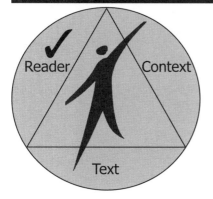

Chapter 5
Section 1

Reader

"Learning Teams"

☞ As a result of working through this section you will:
- Analyze the impact prior knowledge has on reading comprehension
- Study productive habits of mind and their role in developing strategic readers
- Discover ways to help readers gain control of their own reading processes

☯ ## Questions to ponder before, during, and after reading
Before reading - What would a struggling reader tell you about the reading process?
During reading - In what ways does this information reinforce and/or recharge your thinking? What aspects of this information caused you to revisit ideas you already knew?
After reading - Which habits of mind are critical for success in your classroom or content area? In what ways do students demonstrate productive habits of mind?

⌘ ## Process Activity
The Anticipation Guide strategy (Herber, 1978) has been selected to focus reading and discussion about the "Reader." This strategy causes the reader to formulate predictions about specific ideas related to the concept being studied. An Anticipation Guide is a great strategy to spark conversations before and after reading.

Use the following process to facilitate discussion with team members about the Reader.
1) Read the directions for completing the Anticipation Guide on page 49.
2) Complete the "Before You Read" portion by marking "agree" or "disagree."
3) Share marked responses and rationale with group members.
4) Read the information on Reader pages 50-55.
5) Complete both portions of the After Reading directions - by marking "agree" or "disagree" and recording brief evidence statements.
6) Conduct a team conversation comparing responses and explain changes you made. Discuss the evidence statements recorded, look for similarities and differences.

As a final debriefing exercise, dialogue about the following questions:
- What did the Anticipation Guide do for your thinking as you read the selection?
- What habits of mind does an anticipation guide establish?
- How might you use the Anticipation Guide in your content area?
- Under what conditions would you use the Anticipation Guide?

Anticipation Guide for Interactive Reading Ingredient Reader

Directions
On your own
Before Reading pages 50-55 read the 5 statements below and mark whether you agree or disagree with each statement.

Read pages 50-55.

After Reading return to the anticipation guide. Reread the statements and then mark if you agree or disagree with the statement. Have your thoughts changed as a result of reading the selection? Return to the selection, this time looking for evidence to support your agreement/disagreement. Write a brief summary statement in the space provided below.

Before You Read			*After You Read*	
Agree	Disagree		Agree	Disagree
____	____	1. Teachers, as experts in their content areas, know what areas of prior knowledge need to be activated to support student learning.	____	____
____	____	2. Pre-reading strategies benefit both struggling and accomplished readers.	____	____
____	____	3. Understanding productive habits of mind can encourage students to think about challenging situations in different ways.	____	____
____	____	4. Focusing on habits of mind can increase a student's chance of being a strategic reader.	____	____
____	____	5. It is necessary to discuss the benefits of using reading strategies with students.	____	____

After Reading: Find evidence from the selection and write a brief summary statement.

Evidence #1: _____

Evidence #2: _____

Evidence #3: _____

Evidence #4: _____

Evidence #5: _____

Interactive Reading Ingredient: Reader

Excellence is an art won by training and habituation. We are what we repeatedly do. Excellence, then, is not an act but a habit.

- Aristotle

The role of the reader is paramount in comprehending and learning from text. What the reader brings to the reading situation greatly impacts comprehension. In the past much emphasis for developing readers was associated with developing specific reading skills, applying phonics, citing the main idea, or making inferences. While these skills are important, the focus has expanded to include other reading aspects. The role of the reader focuses on three key elements: background knowledge, attitude, and strategic control of the reading process.

Background Knowledge

What students already know about the topic is one of the strongest indicators of how well they will learn new information about that topic (Marzano, 2004). Students who possess extensive background knowledge in a given area tend to learn new information readily and perform well. According to reading researchers Johnston and Pearson (1982), prior knowledge accounts for more variation in reading performance than either I.Q. or measured reading achievement. Prior knowledge greatly influences comprehension, the mental construction of what is on the page when correlated with what is already known. Because reading is thinking cued by text, the interaction between the reader and the text is key for constructing meaning. The more a student knows about a topic, the easier it is to derive meaning from new printed material on that topic.

The pre-reading phase is the perfect time to jumpstart thinking, to create interest, and to arouse curiosity about a topic of study. If you were going to assemble a thousand piece jigsaw puzzle would you study the picture on the box? Why study the picture? It seems obvious - to help you be successful when putting the puzzle together. You are doing what some teachers call "frontloading," starting the thinking process even before you open the box. Without the picture of the completed puzzle, you probably will struggle with the task. Many students have similar problems when they are assigned a task without preparation. Because teachers are experts in their content areas and aware of what needs to be learned, they know which areas of prior knowledge should be activated. Teachers must help students make the connections that will lead them to understanding.

Prior knowledge can be organized into three categories (Buehl, 2001):

- Knowledge about the topic and related concepts
- Knowledge about text structure and format
- Knowledge about the vocabulary

As students approach any unit of study it is important to assess their level of prior knowledge. The gap between what students know and what the passage presents helps teachers determine what instruction to provide during the pre-reading phase. Sometimes students have misconceptions about the topic, and if teachers are aware of students' inadequacies, they can focus particular attention on that area. Misconceptions can then be explored and approached from a different perspective. Helping students compare the differences between their misconceptions and the correct information enhances retention and understanding.

The second type of prior knowledge addresses text structure and format. When reading, the reader first determines the text structure. "Is this an informative selection or a narrative?" The reader's prior knowledge differs with each type of structure. When writing informative text, authors use organizational patterns, such as compare/contrast or problem/solution. Comprehension increases when students activate their prior knowledge about a particular pattern used. Format is another consideration when reading text. Internet reading (see Chapter 6) presents a variety of formats that are different from most textbook formats.

Vocabulary knowledge is synonymous with prior knowledge; teaching vocabulary is a powerful way to build background knowledge (Marzano, 2004). Teachers must help students make connections with critical terms relating to the topic and to familiarize them with the meaning of words in new contexts. A comprehensive instructional approach for vocabulary development (see Section 3c, p. 100) has the potential for dramatically increasing students' background knowledge.

Activating a student's prior knowledge about the topic, structure, and format of the text, as well as critical vocabulary enhances comprehension. Strategic readers ask themselves questions before reading.

- What do I know about the topic?
- What vocabulary is related to the topic?
- In past experiences, what has made me successful in reading this type of text?"

Such questions help the reader to prepare for reading and to retrieve pertinent background knowledge that is essential for new learning.

Attitude

Let me tell you the secret that led to my goal. My strength lies solely in my tenacity.

- Louis Pasteur

The purpose of reading instruction in the content areas is to develop strategic readers who are motivated to read and who possess positive attitudes about reading for information. Attitude refers to the mental dispositions a reader brings to the learning situation; students with a positive attitude are generally more successful. Research indicates that attitude and achievement are linked. When students repeatedly experience difficulty reading, their motivation to read wanes and negative attitudes develop toward reading and learning. Think about a topic you dislike or one that causes you to struggle as a reader–perhaps tax forms or a DVD program manual come to mind. Your attitude as a reader has a profound effect on your motivation to read and upon overall success.

Teachers comment that students are not motivated. Motivation is directly correlated to the success a person has in completing a task. The more students fail, the less likely they are to put forth effort because they anticipate failure. As a result they do not try, which comes across as being unmotivated. Attribution theory (Weiner, 1980) explains how people think regarding success or failure with a task. Success can be attributed to one of three items: ability, effort, or luck. Thinking goes something like this:

- *Ability*. I am or am not smart enough to do this task.
- *Effort*. My effort does or does not make a difference.
- *Luck*. My success or failure has nothing to do with me.

Successful students believe that effort makes a difference; poorly motivated students attribute failure to the lack of ability or not being lucky. Of the three items, the learner can control only effort. Teachers can help students understand the importance of effort by reinforcing effort every chance they get. Statements such as, *"You got a good grade because you spent time studying."* or *"Think about all you did to cause yourself to be successful."* reinforce a student's effort.

Attitude affects motivation, and motivation affects thinking about why we succeed or fail. A strategic reader knows mental habits influence thinking, comprehending, and learning. Art Costa and Bena Kallick (2000) identify sixteen habits of mind that are broad, enduring, and essential for students and adults. Once students learn these habits of mind they will be able to draw upon them when faced with challenging situations.

Sixteen Habits of Mind

- Gathering Data Through All Senses
- Listening With Understanding and Empathy
- Questioning and Posing Problems
- Applying Past Knowledge to New Situations
- Creating, Imagining, Innovating
- Taking Responsible Risks
- Responding with Wonderment and Awe
- Remaining Open to Continuous Learning

- Thinking Interdependently
- Finding Humor
- Thinking about Thinking
- Striving for Accuracy
- Persisting
- Thinking Flexibly
- Managing Impulsivity
- Thinking and Communicating with Clarity and Purpose

- Costa & Kallick, 2000

Strategic readers possess productive habits of mind; they are aware of their thinking, feelings, and behaviors as they read a passage. **Strategic readers know how to manage, monitor, and modify their thought patterns.**

Albert Einstein said, "The height of insanity is continuing to do the same thing and expecting a different result." If Einstein's statement is true, then it seems evident that the habits of mind need to be an integral part of the instructional process. Habits of mind are alterable, changeable; people can become more interdependent, flexible, or better listeners. Knowing and understanding productive habits of mind can encourage students to think about difficult situations in different ways.

Changing a habit requires a conscientious effort on the part of the learner. Because poor habits of mind lead to poor learning, it is important to actually teach specific mental dispositions. As teachers focus on content, it would be well also to focus on a habit of mind that will increase student success. They might ask themselves, "Which habits of mind will help students be more successful. Which habits will enhance my teaching performance?" Classroom examples for incorporating habits of mind include:

- When having difficulty understanding a selection, students use the Habit of Mind of *persisting* to find other strategies to help them understand the selection.
- Students use the habit of mind of *metacognition,* thinking about your thinking, as they read a selection. By doing this they know when "the little man inside their head" has gone for a walk and they are no longer understanding what they are reading.
- While reading a difficult science selection the teacher reminds students to *ask questions and to read for answers*.
- Before reading a selection in social studies, the teacher asks the students to think about what they already know from this period in history, reminding them that using the habit of mind *applying past knowledge to new situations* will help them discover meaning in text.
- When students read to finish a selection instead of reading to understand the teachers reminds them to *manage their impulsivity* by selecting reading strategies that help them comprehend the text.

Questions are another powerful vehicle to alert thinking about a habit of mind. For example, *In what ways have your emotions influenced your analysis of the story?* focuses on responding with wonderment and awe, or *How did the author cause you to think?* emphasizes thinking about thinking (Billmeyer, 2006b).

Investigating students' attitudes and interests is an important instructional step. Teachers at all grade levels use student observation, class discussions, private interviews, and written surveys to determine students' habits and perceptions about themselves as readers. Surveys are beneficial because students can monitor how attitudes change over time. Survey results enhance teachers' perception of students and can inform instruction in the following ways:

- Determine types of information or books to read aloud
- Determine selection of reading materials displayed in the classroom
- Guide individual students toward specific books, articles, or authors
- Determine which reading strategies to incorporate
- Group students according to interests for a project
- Share information when planning with other teachers or parents

Strategic Control of the Reading Process

Life can only be understood backwards, but it must be lived forwards.
- Soren Kierkegaard

As emphasized in Chapter 3, strategic readers are independent. In creating strategic readers it is important to relinquish teacher control of their reading processes. Strategic control means students know and understand themselves as readers. For this to occur, they must reflect on and evaluate their own work. An important reading attribute identified in *Capturing All of the Reader Through the Reading Assessment System* (Billmeyer, 2006a) is "*Reflects on own reading process.*" Reflective practices help teachers understand what students think of their work. Student reflection builds on two important aspects of learning: metacognition and responsibility (Harp, 1996).

Metacognition, thinking about your own thinking, occurs when students describe what goes on in their head as they think. Metacognitive students construct meaning from their experiences and work; they think about their thinking before, during, and after learning. Through self-evaluation practices students are taught to take a critical look at their work. When students are made aware and held accountable for their behaviors they develop a sense of **responsibility** for their own learning. Students exhibit an internal locus of control and begin to realize that their effort does make a difference.

Students gain knowledge about themselves as learners through reflection. Reflection can range from a simple conversation between the teacher and student, "*What did you learn about yourself as a reader when using the Anticipation Guide to study cell division?*" to formal writing activities, such as writing a letter to parents summarizing their learning. Other forms of reflection that develop strategic control of the reading process are:

- A checklist which focuses on before, during, and after reading skills

Before I Read I . . .	While I Read I . . .	After I Read I . . .
make predictions	check my predictions	analyze what I learned
think about what I know	ask questions to clarify	revisit new words
preview the materials		

- Reflective writing activities using sentence stems to jump-start thinking: *I selected this strategy because . . . I am learning to read different genres and . . . What I am learning about myself as a reader is . . .*
- A list of reading goals and reflection on their accomplishments

Art Costa and Bena Kallick (2000, p. 61) state, "To be reflective means to mentally wander through where you have been and to try to make some sense of it." When students reflect they will hear both internal and external voices of reflection. Internal refers to self-knowledge, while external voice comes from the comments and feedback of others. Examples to help students develop an internal voice include interviewing themselves about their experience or writing a letter to themselves citing what they are learning. External examples include conducting class meetings in which students share reflections about their learning or in small groups sharing "fix-it" strategies used when stuck in a reading assignment.

Reflection for adults and students is not necessarily an easy task; it is, rather, a learned behavior. When teachers model reflective practices, students begin to understand why reflection is important and how it leads to strategic control of the reading process. Students benefit from watching their teachers review, analyze, and self-evaluate their own work or perhaps through reading an entry recorded in their own learning journal.

The benefits of student reflection are many. Of most importance is helping students gain strategic control of their own reading process. A student's self-assessment informs the teacher when making instructional decisions as well as serves as feedback for parents. When the student, teacher, and parent communicate and collaborate, all three can work together to develop strategic readers.

Conclusion

Of the three interactive reading ingredients considered, **reader**, **context**, and **text**, by far the greatest potential for maximizing understanding lies with the **reader**. Texts vary with each encounter and contexts change not only with each reading task, but from classroom to workplace. As powerful as behavior appears, behavior is nothing more than the manifestation of one's thinking. Taking time to focus on the reader's mental disposition pays dividends. When a teacher invests time, energy, and expertise in developing confident and competent readers, students become strategic readers in content areas and more importantly in life.

Habit is a cable; we weave a thread of it each day, and at last we cannot break it.

- Horace Mann

Chapter 5
Section 2

Context

"Learning Teams"

As a result of working through this section you will:
- Understand what is meant by context as an interactive ingredient for reading
- Dialogue about ways teachers can consciously plan to address contexts

Questions to ponder before, during, and after reading

Before reading - What might students say about the reading assignments given to them, your classroom environment, and the physical setting and movement within your room?

During reading - How does the information in this section compare with your instructional practices?

After reading – Which components of this section will you consciously think about when integrating reading into your content area?

Process Activity

The process activity selected to study the interactive reading ingredient "Context" is Save the Last Word for Me (Vaughan & Estes, 1986). This strategy promotes thoughtful dialogue after reading a selection using a nonjudgmental format. Save the Last Word for Me causes readers to think from different perspectives and to connect ideas with prior experiences or knowledge.

Directions:
1) As you read the selection on Context use Post-it notes to mark three to five statements that you would like to discuss because:
   - You agree/disagree with the idea.
   - It contradicts what you know.
   - The idea intrigues you and you want to think about it.
   - The idea is something you would like to try.
2) After everyone is finished reading and marking their selection with Post-it notes, one team member begins by reading one marked statement but makes NO comment about the statement.
3) In a round-robin fashion, all group members respond to the statement. Using comments like, "I chose that statement as well. The reason I did was…." or "I did not choose that statement, but I think..."
4) When all group members have shared their response to the marked statement, the owner of the response now shares the "Last Word."
5) Repeat the process until all group members have had a chance to read their marked statement and have the "Last Word."

Interactive Reading Ingredient: Context

The greatest sign of success for a teacher... is to be able to say,
"The children are now working as if I did not exist."

- Maria Montessori

An integral part of the strategic reading process is the context in which reading occurs. Context includes three components – the task and expected outcomes, the environment, and the physical setting for reading. Research stresses the impact of context upon learning and identifies ways teachers can alter the context to improve student learning.

As Miller emphasizes in *The Book Whisper* (2009) no matter how dynamic and well planned a teacher's instruction might be, if the classroom culture is not a motivational, risk-taking environment for readers the instruction is doomed to fail. Creating a safe haven for learning has always been important but has become even more challenging because general education classrooms now include special needs children and children from different cultures. Full-inclusion classrooms are more prevalent; teachers need to focus on the context of the reading situation in order to develop all students as readers and learners.

Task and Expected Outcomes

Task and the expected outcomes refer to setting purpose and expectations, reading selections and student choice, and gradual release of strategy instruction. A student-centered curriculum, one that focuses on individual students' interest and abilities, begins with the teacher stating the task and its goals, how the task fits with previous learning, the expected outcomes, and why it is important. When students know the expectations they become engaged, motivated, and responsible learners.

Setting Purpose and Expectations

When students are assigned to read something, the first question often asked is, "Why should I read this?" Establishing a purpose for reading not only serves to motivate the reader, but also prepares the mind for reading. The purpose for reading helps students know what they are expected to do with the reading. For example, will they be expected to complete a project, use the information in a lab experiment or a class discussion, answer inferential questions, or write an essay? Unsuccessful readers often approach a reading activity with great anxiety. Knowing the purpose for reading and what the expected outcomes are will help to reduce that anxiety.

If teachers portray the attitude that all students can learn, students perform better. When teachers set high expectations for learning and support students as needed throughout learning tasks they help to develop independent learners who portray attitudes of "I can read this," "I'm responsible for my learning," and "I'm self-reliant" (Covey, 1989). Students who are expected to read every day and to be successful with reading tasks rise to the challenge. Motivation to read increases when students are allowed to self-select materials, are provided reading material at their level, and are engaged in high interest reading topics.

Reading Selections and Student Choice

If our goal is to create readers in all content areas, students must have opportunities to read interesting, varied materials (both narrative and informative) of appropriate difficulty during every class session. To accommodate the needs of diverse learners, students with different reading and comprehension levels, teachers must adapt textbooks. Adapting textbooks may involve offering supplementary texts that are more inspiring for students to read, making changes to the text by summarizing important content with bulleted points, or giving students strategies to learn the material in some other way (Kluth, 2005). For multi-level materials teachers can access content area websites such as, http://bensguide.gp.gov for social studies or www.chem4kids.com for science. Kluth's website, www.paulakluth.com, provides numerous ways to adapt textbooks for students with special needs. Teachers might consider soliciting help from the media specialist in selecting supplementary reading materials from the library for classroom use.

Digital media is a motivating way to translate learning goals and tasks of a student-driven curriculum into reality. For example, students used digital media to construct their community histories by interviewing community members and uploading them to an online wiki, converting the audio portion into downloadable podcasts, and engaging in Web-based text interviews (Weigel & Gardner, 2009). Reading online provides teachers with new ways of teaching and encourages readers to be purposeful, critical, and analytical about the information they encounter (Wolf & Barzillai, 2009).

Students need to make some of their own choices when pursuing learning goals as well as have opportunities to independently read self-selected materials. Reading researcher Brian Cambourne (1995) emphasizes that students who have no opportunity to make choices become disempowered, dependent learners. Students who choose their own reading material expend more effort in learning and understanding the material.

Gradual Release of Strategy Instruction

Content area teachers must spend time teaching students comprehension strategies for successful task completion and learning in their discipline. Consistent use of reading strategies builds confidence in the readers' attempts to unlock meaning. Purposeful instruction helps students learn how to apply and transfer strategies. The goal of strategy instruction is to gradually release responsibility from teacher to student through four phases of interrelated instruction; the *gradual release of responsibility model* helps teachers transition the responsibility for performing a task to the student's responsibility (Pearson & Gallagher, 1983; Fisher & Frey, 2003). The Text Tagging strategy (Billmeyer, 2006b) is used as an example for progressing through the four steps.

- Focused Instruction: model the strategy for the large group. "I'll do it and you watch." *The teacher demonstrates the Text Tagging strategy and models her metacognitive processes by reading and thinking aloud about where to tag ideas.*
- Guided Instruction: use the strategy in a large group setting with the teacher directly participating for direction and support. "I'll do it and you help me." *The teacher models the Text Tagging strategy with the large group but asks students to help determine where to tag ideas. Students share their thinking with a partner. Teacher elicits student responses.*
- Collaborative: expect students to use the strategy in small group settings with the teacher stepping back from direct participation in order to monitor the use of the strategy. The teacher monitors students' work both directly by observing students and indirectly by reviewing their work (logs, response journals, writing). "You do it and I'll help you." *Students work with a partner to use the Text Tagging strategy; they read a passage and share their thinking as they tag ideas.*
- Independence: expect each student to self-monitor, self-manage, and self-modify as they use the strategy independently. "You do it." *Students read an article or a section of the textbook and tags ideas as they read.*

Gradual release of responsibility may occur over a day, a week, a month, or a semester. The model is not linear; students move back and forth among the phases as they master strategies, skills, or encounter more complex material. The goal is for students to assume more responsibility for using the designated strategy as they work collaboratively with other students or independently.

Classroom Environment

Classroom environment includes a risk-taking intellectual climate, opportunities for social interaction, print rich setting, and response to student efforts. Environment has a significant impact on student achievement; when teachers provide a caring environment in which each student is valued, students are more motivated and learn more (Pratt, 2008). A student-centered environment that is supportive of diverse abilities and interests will certainly foster a literate environment.

Risk-taking Intellectual Climate

The foundation for a risk-taking intellectual climate is trust; establishing and maintaining trusting relationships with all students is one of the teacher's primary goals. Taking time to chat with students about personal interests, calling them by their first name or preferred nickname, greeting students as they enter or leave the classroom, honoring mistakes as new learning, being visible and accessible, sharing interests or hobbies, and making eye contact with them while teaching develops trust and fosters a positive learning climate. In a trusting climate students are more willing to ask questions or make hypotheses. Learning does not occur without a strong foundation of trust; effective teachers work to create, monitor, and maintain that environment.

All students need to feel a sense of emotional safety; teachers can create a healthy learning environment by making it clear that no form of put-down will be tolerated. Laughter and anxiety-free humor are key ingredients in a safe learning environment. When students engage in appropriate laughter, they feel more relaxed while learning and enjoy being in the class.

Opportunities for Social Interaction
Students need opportunities to interact socially with others about their reading. Social collaboration promotes achievement, higher-level cognition, and an intrinsic desire to read. Vygotsky (1986) believes that collaboration is a great way to enhance the learning process; knowledge is socially constructed through interactions with adults and peers.

As stated in Chapter 2, reading is essentially an act of human communication, requiring a setting for social interaction. How often do adults discuss a newspaper article or a recently read novel? Adults' talking about what they read is common practice; children need the same opportunity. A cooperative learning environment rather than a competitive one enhances comprehension. Readers who are struggling to comprehend **and** feel they are competing against others, experience stress. Struggling readers might believe that reading is a contest, and that they don't have the skills to adequately compete (Cook, 1989). They will do most anything to avoid embarrassment; the choices range from not reading at all to being disruptive, poor readers may find it easier and more rewarding to be a discipline problem.

Cooperative grouping practices have enormous implications for helping students feel comfortable about sharing their thinking. Students learn to rely on their strengths and feel good about their contributions to the group. Small group work creates opportunities for all children, including those with disabilities, to take leadership roles (Resinski and Padak, 2000). Strategies such as Reciprocal Teaching and Anticipation Guides are powerful for facilitating conversation between students in a cooperative group; students learn to assert, defend, and question their thinking while learning from one another.

Print Rich Setting
Brian Cambourne (1995) believes that students must be immersed in a positive, productive reading climate. Teachers must model the joy and satisfaction that can be found in reading. A print rich environment is one in which students have opportunities to read a wide variety of meaningful, relevant books and resources such as magazines, newspapers, charts, and pamphlets. Resources should be kept current and displayed in an inviting manner.

Readers read every day! Students should be given opportunities to read during each class period and/or throughout the day. When teachers talk with students about their reading preferences, the books they are reading, and the benefits of reading students thrive as readers. Students should be offered opportunities to share or "talk up" books or selections they have read and classrooms should include a special place where students can display messages or information about books or selections.

Response to Student Efforts

We have all heard the adages; *a half a loaf is better than none,* or *you catch more bees with honey than with vinegar.* When teachers focus on what students know instead of what they do not know and adapt their teaching to allow for student differences, students feel their efforts are on the right track and willingly pursue expectations. Students need nonthreatening, immediate, and specific feedback.

In a trusting environment, students will overtly "take a stab" at the answer even if they are not sure. They know that the teacher will help them out by providing more information, by redirecting thinking, or by dignifying the correct part of the response. By holding frequent conferences, requiring written responses about their reading, and discussing students' reading with them teachers can continually provide encouragement, guidance, and validation for their reading development (Miller, 2009).

Physical Setting for Reading

The physical setting for reading includes room arrangement and movement. The surroundings or environment in which one reads has an impact on comprehension. Where do you read insurance papers, lease agreements, or other business forms? Perhaps seated at the kitchen table with pen in hand. The room arrangement, the time of day, the noise level, and the type of lighting has a profound effect on student reading and learning.

Room Arrangement

Look into any classroom and watch the children at work; it does not take long to sense the atmosphere for learning. Are students seated at tables and chairs, at desks clustered into small groups, or in straight rows facing the teacher? The physical room arrangement conveys a message to the learner about overall learning expectations. If students are to communicate as members of a reading and learning community, it is important they have eye contact with other students as they express key ideas, interpretations, or judgments about the topics read.

Learners with disabilities often struggle to stay seated, to remain focused, and to engage in required work on assigned tasks (Kluth, 2006). Paying close attention to the physical setting for reading can make a difference. A variety of seating options can boost the educational experiences of all learners. Seating options in my daughter's 3rd grade full- inclusion classroom include large floor pillows, tables and chairs, individual desks with large exercise balls for chairs, and floor mats. The variety of seating choices positively affects students' learning, including her two students with Asperger syndrome.

Example of a 3rd grade classroom providing a variety of seating choices.

Students can be easily distracted when reading; side bar conversations, children playing outside the classroom window, or music playing can have a negative impact on reading comprehension. Some students, especially those with ADHD symptoms, cannot handle the movement and/or noise of students around them while reading. All students need to learn how to identify and take care of their needs as readers. Offering students a quiet area in the classroom to focus on the reading assignment positively effects learning.

Movement
To maximize learning the body needs to move; movement supplies oxygen to the brain, creating more alert, focused, and relaxed reading. Struggling readers cannot sit to read for an extended period of time; they must be provided meaningful ways to move during class. Collaborative structures such as learning buddies, offer students the opportunity to move and then to settle in for the task at hand. Some students need frequent movement and interaction. A middle school teacher provides students a question to discuss and then has them "talk and walk" with a partner. After three minutes of movement he asks the students to be seated and to discuss their conversations (Kluth, 2006).

Conclusion
The challenge in education is to create strategic readers in all content areas. To meet that challenge, it is imperative that educators give special attention to the context of the learning situation. Teachers need to consider a variety of contexts to facilitate a learning environment in which students will take risks; readers need to be guaranteed that reading is a rewarding and valuable experience. When the context of the reading situation is given special attention, students will gradually take control of their own learning, and teachers can concentrate on helping students master important content area concepts.

Chapter 5
Section 3

Text Overview

"Learning Teams"

As a result of working through this section you will:
- Understand the four elements of text: structure, vocabulary, format, and readability

Questions to ponder before, during, and after reading

Before reading - Scan the chapter looking for features such as headings and graphs. How does previewing the text enhance your understanding of the text you will read?

During reading - What insights are you developing as you consider the text(s) you ask students to read?

After reading - What new insights or learnings will enhance the use of any text in your content area?

Process Activity

The process activity to study the Text Overview is M.V.P. (Most Valuable Point) (Billmeyer, 2006b). This strategy causes the reader to select "the most valuable point" from the reading. After you have read each part of the text overview, (structure, vocabulary, format, and readability), record your Most Valuable Point for each section on the chart below. Exchange valuable points in a round-robin fashion with learning team members. Explain why it is a valuable point for you and what connections it is causing you to make or what questions it is raising in your mind.

Element	M.V.P. (Most Valuable Point)
Structure	
Vocabulary	
Format	
Readability	

Notes

Interactive Reading Ingredient: Text Overview

There is no such thing as a generic reader or a generic literary work; there are in reality only the potential millions of individual readers of individual literary works . . . The reading of any work of literature is, of necessity, an individual and unique occurrence involving the mind and emotions of some particular reader.
- Rosenblatt, 1938/1983

Learning from Text

Readers think and use text in different ways, depending on the type of text, the readers' prior knowledge, and the readers' purposes for reading. Text features, such as **structure, vocabulary, format,** and **readability**, are an integral part of the reading process and play a significant role in comprehension. The concept of **text** has expanded since the writing of *Teaching Reading in the Content Areas: If Not Me Then Who?*. Analyzing numerous textbooks, observing students as they interact with assigned selections, and reviewing current research have identified **format,** and **readability** as additional characteristics that impact reading comprehension. An overview of text structure and vocabulary is provided in this section with additional information on pages 73-107. A comprehensive explanation of text format and readability is provided in this section.

Structure and the Impact on Comprehension

Structure consists of two major components - the **type** of selection and how ideas in the selection are **organized**. The literature refers to two major writing types: narrative and informative. Each type requires a different thinking process when reading. For example, what do you know about yourself as a reader when reading a Jody Picoult novel or Poe's "Tell Tale Heart" as compared to reading the manual for a DVD player? Groundbreaking reading researcher Louise Rosenblatt (1978) distinguishes between narrative/literary and informative reading by explaining narrative reading as aesthetic, requiring a personal response, and informative reading as efferent, reading for information. Narrative reading (an assuming stance) involves experiencing the text through our senses—seeing, feeling, and thinking about the characters portrayed—as when reading a novel or short story. Efferent reading (meaning *to carry away*) focuses attention on ideas to be retained or information required to perform a task, such as reading a DVD manual. When people read for information, they may select parts of the text they need, rather than reading from beginning to end. An important point of distinction between an aesthetic read and an efferent read is that when reading a literary selection, **the reader focuses attention on what is being experienced *during* the reading, whereas an informative read focuses on what will be retained *after* the reading** (Rosenblatt, 1978).

Reading and understanding the difference between narrative and informative selections is important for readers of all ages. It is no secret that many students struggle to comprehend informative text; learning from text, especially informative text, is the cornerstone of the curriculum. While research stresses the importance of balance between narrative/literary and informative reading in the primary grades, studies have shown that only 3.6 minutes per day was spent on informative text-type activities and time was even more limited for children from classrooms in low socioeconomic areas (Duke, 2000). Students who are taught with only narrative become incompetent readers of informative text; they wait for the story to seize their interest when they should be focused on reading for main ideas and details. The journey of learning how to read and respond to informative text through the use of reading strategies must begin in the primary grades (Venezky, Kaestle, & Sum, 1987). Reading achievement of fourth graders improved when the diversity of their reading increased; they not only read stories but magazines, trade books, and newspapers (Campbell & Ashworth, 1995).

The second component of structure deals with how ideas are organized in a narrative versus other informative modes. For example, read the following selection entitled *Goldilocks and the Three Bears.*

Once upon a time there was a girl named Goldilocks who wandered through the forest. She entered an unfamiliar, empty house. First, she tasted a bowl of porridge that did not belong to her. Next, she sat in a chair and broke it. Finally, she slept in a bed that did not belong to her. In the end, the three bears caught her when they returned home. Goldilocks ran out of the house, scared to death.

Now read this favorite family recipe for *Banana Bread.*

2 C flour	3 ripe bananas
1 C sugar	1 C sour milk
1tsp. soda	½ C butter
¼ tsp. salt	2 eggs
½ C chopped walnuts	1 cup chocolate chips

Mix eggs and butter until creamy, add sugar. Mix dry ingredients and add to cream mixture with the cup of sour milk. Add smashed bananas, chopped walnuts, and chocolate chips. Pour into 2 greased and floured bread pans. Bake 30 – 45 minutes at 350`.

What did you notice about the organization of each selection? Perhaps, you thought the first one read like a story, the second a list of directions. Story grammar or elements constituting a beginning, middle, and end organize the writing of a narrative selection, whereas main ideas and supporting details provide the overarching structure of other informative texts. Strategic readers recognize the difference between informative and narrative text and learn the characteristics of both in order to increase comprehension.

Vocabulary and the Impact on Comprehension

Vocabulary knowledge is essential for comprehension of all spoken and written language. For example, have fun figuring out the meaning of the following passage.

> The terrified young actress thought that the *belligerent* director would whack her with a *ferule* if she annoyed the audience with her *borborygmus* while delivering the famous *soliloquy*, so she stood there wearing *galligaskins* wishing that a *jararacussu* would slip into the theater and bite the director, who would then become merely a harmless *apparition*.
>
> - Adapted from *Building Your Vocabulary*, Marvin Terban, 2002

How did you do? Perhaps you figured out some words from context; learning to infer the meaning of unknown words from context is an important part of vocabulary development. (Check your accuracy, definitions of italicized words are found on page 67.) This example helps us to understand why research emphasizes the high correlation between vocabulary knowledge and overall school achievement. If students are not readily familiar with words in print, they certainly will have trouble understanding what they read. Educators seem to know the importance of word knowledge when reading, yet studies indicate that there is little emphasis on the acquisition of vocabulary in school curricula (Biemiller, 2001; Marzano, 2004; Graves, 2006).

Word learning begins with young children; we have all experienced the laughter involved when a young child tries to use a new word. Oral language development is the foundation for reading comprehension; rich oral language experiences foster growth in children's knowledge of words and concepts. As students progress through the grades demands on vocabulary change from conversational to more technical, and terms are less familiar, more specialized, and abstract. Vocabulary makes each subject unique - think about the specialized words in music, social studies, sports, math, literature, science, or technology. If students are to become strategic readers, special emphasis must be given to vocabulary instruction in all content areas at all grade levels.

A robust approach to vocabulary development is essential at all grade levels and content areas if educators are serious about increasing student achievement. Review of the research clearly outlines a comprehensive word learning approach that includes:

- Indirect opportunities for vocabulary growth (extensive reading, read alouds, word-play)
- Direct instruction of critical words needed to understand the concept

It is no surprise that learning a word for future use requires multiple exposures in which students are actively engaged in meaningful learning processes. Vocabulary instruction in which critical terms are defined, illustrated, and/or explained through example affords students the opportunity to assimilate and elaborate on the meaning of new words and ultimately increase comprehension. Leading researchers on vocabulary development, Beck, McKeown, and Kucan (2002) have found that students become interested and enthusiastic about word learning in school and beyond when instruction is rich and lively (see Vocabulary Practices to Develop Strategic Readers p. 95).

Format and the Impact on Comprehension

Format refers to the physical layout of the printed material. Publishers organize books into sections such as table of contents, chapters, glossary, and use visual clues in the form of headings, captions, and graphics. The physical layout of a book can support or impede comprehension. Text format occurs both in whole book presentation and in chapter and page organization. When considering the format of a page, it is important to attend to white space; too much information on a page can be overwhelming for the reader. Size of print and length of paragraphs are important; some readers have a difficult time focusing or keeping their place when print is too small or paragraphs to long. Public libraries now have books available with larger print. Large print is not only easier to read but makes reading a more pleasant experience for beginning readers and those with aging eyes. It is important to evaluate the "considerateness" of the textbook students use to determine if it is written in a manner which helps students learn or if it places roadblocks to understanding.

Whole Book Presentation

Whole book presentation not only refers to the book title and overall appeal but also to organizational features, such as table of contents, index, glossary, references, and appendices. When purchasing a book for classroom use, begin by leafing through the book to see how it is organized and if the text accurately reflects the important ideas relating to the field of study. Read the short overview on the inside flap of the cover and check out the authors and their backgrounds. Typically, the greater the number of authors the more difficult the text; readers must adjust for different styles and voices more frequently. If the book is appealing, well organized, and includes the major topics, the probability of a sale increases. *USA Today* is, in part, a widely read newspaper because of the physical layout. The front page provides highlights for the other sections, articles are concise, graphics tend to be accurate and well placed, and the overall presentation is attractive. Readers not only deserve an appealing text, but with today's plethora of reading material, they demand it.

Chapter Organization

Informative text is organized by topic and supporting details. Authors use visual boldface headings, graphics, illustrations, and captions that signal importance in the text. Well-presented text is visually organized in a manner that facilitates the flow of the content. I recently attempted to read an eighth grade science book but struggled with the task. The overall book was full of charts, graphs, pictures, and boxes of activities. At first glance my eyes had difficulty focusing, trying to

belligerent – aggressive or hostile

borborygmus – rumbling sounds made in the stomach

soliloquy – speaking while alone to convey character's thoughts or ideas

apparition – a ghostly figure

ferule – cane or rod used for punishing children

galligaskins – loose fitting trousers

jararacussu – a snake from Brazil

decide where to begin reading. Secondly, the overuse of graphics and activities interfered with the flow of the passage, making it very difficult to read, much less comprehend.

Pictures, graphics, and captions should relate to the text and be displayed on the same page or at least close to where it is referenced. I recently previewed a new economics book for physical layout and noticed that "see Figure 2" was referenced two pages before the graphic was actually displayed in the book. When I located "Figure 2" the caption below the graphic read "Figure 1 and Figure 2." "Figure 1" was referenced four pages back in the text. Is Sherlock Holmes in your classroom? By contrast, examine this graphic explaining the periodic table. The graphic is in close proximity, and the explanation is written in a clear, concise manner.

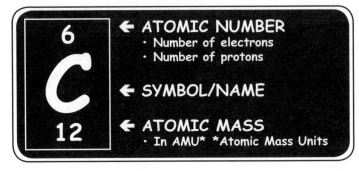

"Check out the blackboard. That box on the left has all of the information you need to know about one element. It tells you the mass of one atom, how many pieces are inside and where it should be placed on the PERIODIC TABLE."
- from Chem4Kids.com

Explicit instruction in the physical layout of the text increases reading comprehension. Doug Buehl (2001), reading specialist and author, refers to this practice as frontloading. He uses the strategy called Chapter Tours to guide readers through the text, highlighting special features. Some teachers use the Text Previewing strategy (Billmeyer, 2006b). If students are to be strategic readers, it is imperative that they be taught how to use the resources provided to them. Learning how to navigate text format must be an integral part of the instructional process.

Readability and the Impact on Comprehension

Readability refers to the reader's **mental ability** to connect with and make sense of the selection. Traditionally, readability implied formulas based on sentence length and vocabulary difficulty and did not consider other factors that might cause students difficulty in comprehending the selection. Webster defines readability as, "capable of being read easily; legible, pleasurable, or interesting to read." For our purposes, we will define readability as the ease with which a reader can access and comprehend printed material. When students approach a selection, they make mental connections between their prior knowledge and ideas in the passage. To emphasize the importance of readability, complete this activity.

1) First, read the following passage and determine the title. As you read, be aware of the connections you make to your prior knowledge.

Your first decision is to choose the size and shape you desire. Once you have made your selection, examine the general shape to determine where to start. The initial incision is always at the top, and you should continue until you can lift it cleanly. The removal of the interior portion can be fun, although some people regard this as the least enjoyable aspect. Once the shell is empty, you can begin to craft a personality. Some prefer a forbidding likeness, while others follow a more humorous direction. Finally, arrange for a source of illumination. Enjoy your results while you can, for your work will soon begin to sag. (Author Unknown)

2) Now that you have read the passage, answer the following questions. What mental connections did you make as you read this selection? What prior knowledge assisted your learning? How would you title it? What did you notice about the author's writing?

3) Reread the passage and think about Halloween.

4) After reading, answer the following questions. What mental connections did you make the second time? What prior knowledge helped you make those connections? Which reading encouraged visualization, why?

Readability speaks to three major components:
- Concept/topic presentation (How dense is it? Are there multiple concepts?)
- Author's writing (vocabulary, sentence length, syntax, and structure)
- Reader's prior knowledge

Just as in the section above on format, it is important to evaluate the overall readability of the text assigned to students.

Concept/Topic Presentation

How easy or difficult a selection is to read and understand is affected by the presentation of the concepts. When reading narrative text, students learn that the main idea is often presented at the beginning of a paragraph. However, when reading a science textbook, observations and data frequently are presented first and the paragraph may end with a concluding statement or main idea. For example, read the following paragraph taken from *What Your Sixth Grader Needs to Know* by E. D. Hirsch (1993, pp. 374-375).

There's an old saying: "A watched pot never boils." It means that if you are impatient for something to happen, it seems to take even longer. But water really does take a long time to boil. It takes only 100 calories of heat to bring a gram of water from 0° to the boiling temperature of 100°. But it takes 540 calories to change that water at 100° to steam at 100°. The amount of heat needed to change a gram of water at 100° from a liquid to a vapor is called "its heat of vaporization." Every liquid has a different heat of vaporization, but water has one of the highest.

The concluding statement "*Every liquid has a different heat of vaporization, but water has one of the highest.*" is at the end of the paragraph. Mentally connecting with the information in this paragraph can be very difficult for any reader, especially those who struggle when reading informative text. Many students may never read to the end of the paragraph to figure out the main idea.

All too often, they try to memorize the ideas presented at the beginning of the paragraph, assuming that's the important information.

Author's Writing

The author's style of writing is a major factor when it comes to the readability of text. As stated earlier, usually a textbook has multiple contributors. Teachers should check the number of authors included in the writing of their text and the background of each. Different writing styles and backgrounds of experiences cause the readability to change from section to section in a text. When reading text by a single author, the mind relies on past experience and becomes familiar with the format. However, when reading chapters in a textbook written by multiple contributors, the mind cannot rely on prior experience but must instead continually adjust for the unknown.

Reader's Prior Knowledge

Readability of text includes activating thinking about the topic before, during, and after reading. As demonstrated in the Halloween example, setting up the reader's prior knowledge is critical for comprehension. The reader has little control over the first two components of readability, concept/topic presentation and author's writing. However, the reader has control over accessing prior knowledge to increase readability of text. Prior knowledge has been addressed in Principles of Learning (see p. 10) and Section 1, Reader (see p. 48). This section discusses specific ideas to help students actively engage in the reading process, especially when the readability of the material is difficult.

Strategic reading in any content area requires that readers know how to sift and sort essential information as they read with a clear and engaging purpose. Learning how to read informative text begins in the earliest grades; teachers ensure active reading when they focus instruction on strategies such as, text previewing and use of manipulatives. Active reading does not mean rewriting the page on notebook paper, answering the questions at the back of the chapter, or filling-in-the-blank on worksheets that accompany the chapter. Instead, students must be taught how to mentally and physically work the material so the passage makes sense.

In *Strategies that Work* (Harvey & Goudris, 2000), the authors discuss the importance of previewing and highlighting the text to determine key ideas and critical information while reading. To overview means to skim or scan the selection before reading, much like the SQ3R strategy. As stated earlier, reading is **THINKING** cued by text; teaching students the process of previewing the text helps the reader mentally connect with the topic. The mind looks for familiar ideas and begins to assess what it knows or does not know about the topic. How do you overview an article before reading it? Perhaps you check the length, discover the author's background, read headings and subheadings in bold print, examine graphics, or read highlighted quotes taken from the article. Previewing the text before reading creates a mental scaffold needed for understanding.

Reading with a pen or highlighter (even sticky notes) in hand is a high priority when learning in any content area. Do you read with a pencil or highlighter in hand? What happens to your comprehension if those tools are removed during reading? Learning how to read using manipulatives piques readers' interest, helps them focus their minds, and can change reading attitudes, especially when the readability of the text is difficult. Many primary teachers model how to mark text with a highlighter or sticky notes when reading big books. Some sticky notes are transparent, making it easy for students to place them on top of the word or phrase in the text in order to jot personal connections.

High school teacher Cris Tovani (2000) believes there are many benefits for teaching students how to mark their text while reading. Marking text helps readers:

- Read with purpose
- Interact with the author's message
- Stay focused during reading
- Remember what they have read
- Reference ideas for discussion or written work

Highlighting involves reading the selection with neon pen in hand, thinking about it, and consciously deciding what is important and what is not. The reader need not remember everything. Guidelines for highlighting include:

- Highlight key words or phrases, not the entire sentence.
- Use different colors of highlighters to organize key learnings.
- Read the first and last sentence in the paragraph carefully. Typically, important information is related and needs to be highlighted.
- Use icons in the margin to trigger specific connections. For example, + means key idea to remember or ? means I have a question about this.
- Make notes in the margin about critical vocabulary words or key phrases.
- Check to see how much information has been highlighted. No more than one-half to one-third contains significant information.

Explicit instruction in how to preview materials and highlight is critical if students are to be successful with the task. Students forging into unknown content need assistance from the leader who knows the content, as well as the resource being used. After all, how many times have you reread information in the textbook you use? It is easy to assume students will figure it out but unfortunately many do not. Some teachers download textbook pages to the Smartboard, explain the purpose for reading, and then model how to highlight critical ideas specific to the content reading.

When students are not allowed to write in their books, teachers learn to improvise. Listed below are ways ingenious teachers help students actively engage in the reading process.

- Teach students to place plastic sleeves over the page (transparencies work) and then mark key ideas with overhead pens. A foreign language teacher recycled plastic sleeves to enable students to highlight in their textbook.
- Help struggling readers by making copies of specific chapters to highlight as they read.
- Teach students how to make a frame for the page using a blank sheet of copier paper. Place the one-inch frame on the page and write on the frame.
- Use highlighting tape. Pieces of the tape can be placed on 3x5 index cards for student use. Students can reuse the tape.

Thoughts About Difficult Textbooks

What can be done when teachers find their texts are "inconsiderate," making it difficult for students to be strategic readers? One possibility is to intentionally teach students effective strategies, such as those mentioned above, for learning from poorly written or organized text, as a lifelong skill. We all deal with "inconsiderate" text, tax forms or the small print on the back of a credit card statement come to mind. Another option used by numerous teachers is to provide students access and exposure to multi-level reading materials in all content areas. As much as we would like to have all students be able to make meaning sufficiently from one text, that will probably never happen. All of the strategy instruction in the world cannot compensate for texts that are too difficult for students to read.

Richard Allington (2002, p. 16) emphasizes, *You can't learn much from books you can't read.* Gay Ivey (2010, p. 20) argues, *You can't learn much from books that don't matter to you and you can't learn much from just one book.* Teaching students how to select resources that work for them is not only an important college skill but also a life-long skill. Supplementary materials such as magazines, newspapers, trade books, and children's literature are meaningful and interesting learning resources. Surrounding students with nonfiction trade books and other materials helps them build background knowledge and increases their understanding of difficult concepts. Chapter 9 provides examples of young adult and children's literature that can be used in all content areas at all grade levels.

Conclusion

Text features greatly influence reading comprehension; teachers need to examine text carefully for those features that help or hinder student learning. Teachers may fail to recognize how difficult a text is to understand because they are experts in their content. It is important to teach students to analyze a text for structure, vocabulary, format, and readability. Just as the quarterback takes time at the line of scrimmage to read the defense and predict outcomes before calling the football play, so too must the reader do an initial sweep through the text to set the stage for successful reading.

Chapter 5
Section 3a

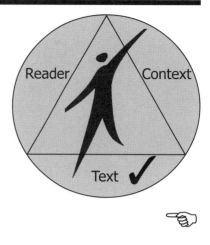

Informative Text

"Learning Teams"

As a result of working through this section you will:
- Learn about seven organizational patterns for informative text
- Consider how to teach organizational patterns to students

Questions to ponder before, during, and after reading
Before reading - How is reading informative text different from reading narrative text? How would you describe your thinking when reading both types of text?
During reading - As you consider your content area and the text that you have students read, what organizational patterns are most predominant?
After reading - How might organizational patterns be used as a reading tool?

Process Activity
Two process activities are included for the section on "Informative Text." You will find the first activity, Comparing Narrative and Informative Text, on pages 74 and 75. After you have completed the comparison activity, discuss the following questions:
- What prior knowledge did you find yourself using to complete this task?
- How would you describe the thought process you used to analyze each text?
- What are the major learnings you will carry forward from this activity?
- How might you use this type of activity with students?

The second process activity for studying informative text is the strategy called RAFT (Santa, 1988). RAFT (Role, Audience, Format, Topic) causes the reader to think about a topic from a different perspective, and then to write from that perspective. When readers examine text from different perspectives they think about the content in new and different ways. Select one idea from each section below, write your response, and share with colleagues on your team. Discuss benefits of the RAFT strategy.

Role	Audience	Format	Topic
A Student's Brain	Teacher	A thank-you note	Thank you Mr.___ for teaching me the organizational patterns for imformative text. They help me understand (subject/text) because...
Self	Your Students	A pledge	Things that I will do differently to help my students understand text structure...
Text	Student/Teacher	An "I'm misunderstood" plea	As I think about my text structure, I wish readers knew...

Notes

Comparing Informative and Narrative Text

Making meaning means making connections with experience. But just as experiences vary, so too can the kind of connections we make when we read.
- Peter Johnston

Introduction

Readers think and use text differently depending on the types of text and their purpose for reading. When students understand text structure, comprehension and retention of information increases. Two common text structures are informative (also known as expository) and narrative. Each type presents ideas and information in a different manner, causing the reader to think differently about the topic. For example, the following two passages speak to the same topic - electric shock therapy - but each is written with a different text structure. Read each passage and complete the Compare/Contrast activity provided.

Comparing Informative and Narrative Activity

- Read each passage and highlight the similarities and differences between the two structures
- Base the comparison on the selected characteristics:
  - *Emotional response*
  - *Type of thinking required*
  - *Benefits or results*
  - *Mental dispositions needed to comprehend each passage*
- Create a Venn diagram to display your thinking
- Summarize what you have learned

Comparing Informative and Narrative Text

Informative   **Narrative**

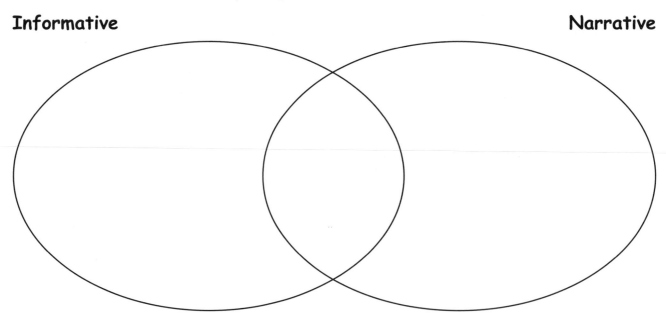

The following two selections speak to the same topic - electric shock therapy. Read each selection using the Compare/Contrast Activity on the previous page.

Informative Text

Holmberg discusses a number of biochemical and hormonal changes that have been reported in conjunction with Electric Shock Therapy. Hyperglycemia of one to several hours duration is a constant phenomenon. There is also an increase in nitrogen compounds, potassium, calcium, phosphorous, and steroids in the blood.

Holmberg also lists certain specific biochemical changes within the brain, and especially in the brain stem, which are increased but there is no change in the brain amine oxidase activity. The increase in serotonin is attributed to the electric stimulus and does not appear to be related to the intensity of the convulsion.

Some impairment of memory occurs almost constantly with EST. This impairment may range from a mild tendency to forget names or dates to a severe confusion. The amnesia may be both anterograde and retrograde. It is often disturbing to the patient and may continue for several weeks following the conclusion of treatment. The impairment of memory usually disappears within a month.

Depression-Causes and Treatment, Aaron T. Beck, M.D., pp. 306,307

Narrative Text

"Man, what they got going in there?" McMurphy asks Harding. "In there? Why, that's right, isn't it? You haven't heard the pleasure. Pity. An experience no human should be without." Harding laces his fingers behind his neck and leans back to look at the door. "That's the Shock Shop I was telling you about some time back, my friend, the EST, Electric-Shock Therapy. Those fortunate souls in there are being given a free trip to the moon. No, on second thought, it isn't completely free. You pay for the service with brain cells instead of money and everyone has simply billions of brain cells on deposit. You won't miss a few."

"I personally guarantee it. Completely painless. One flash and you're unconscious immediately. No gas, no needle, no sledgehammer. Absolutely painless. The thing is, no one ever wants another one. You ... change. You forget things. It's as if" - he presses his hands against his temples, shutting his eyes - "It's as if the jolt sets off a wild carnival wheel of images, emotions, memories. These wheels, you've seen them; the barker takes your bet and pushes a button. Clang! With light and sound and numbers round and round in a whirlwind, and maybe you win with what you have to play again. Pay the man for another spin, son, pay the man."

One Flew Over the Cuckoo's Nest, Ken Kesey, pp. 162, 164

⩘ Interactive Reading Ingredient: Informative Text

We are now at a point where we must educate our children in what no one knew yesterday, and prepare our schools for what no one knows yet.
- Margaret Mead

Take a minute to reread the informative selection about electric shock therapy on page 75. How would you describe informative writing; were you entertained or did you learn something new? Informative text is designed primarily to inform or persuade rather than to entertain the reader. Some adults just as some students prefer reading informative text; teachers create student interest in the topic of study by using both narrative and informative selections. You will find many useful ideas for helping students read different types of informative text in chapters 6 and 7. Comprehending informative text requires the use of various reading attributes or skills such as making inferences, drawing conclusions, or using organizational patterns as outlined in chapter 3. The purpose of this section is to outline with graphic examples seven organizational patterns used by authors to frame thinking when reading informative text. Graphic organizers are powerful learning tools; we have all heard the saying "a picture is worth a thousand words." Steps for teaching organizational patterns will also be discussed.

As stated earlier in this chapter, the goal of efferent reading is to gain knowledge about a specific topic to be used immediately or at another time. People frequently have different purposes for reading text of this nature, for example to discern food ingredients on a label, to choose generic versus label prescriptions, to determine the climate of a region for a future visit, or to select a mortgage package. We are surrounded by informative text; it helps us to understand the world in which we live. Specifically, we read informative text for information or perhaps to perform a task.

Reading for Information:
- Involves reading articles in magazines and newspapers, chapters in textbooks, entries in catalogues and encyclopedias, and books on specific topics
- Requires awareness of the features found in this type of text such as charts, footnotes, diagrams, subheadings, and tables
- Begins with a reader's overview of the selection to obtain general information (scanning an article to obtain information for a research paper)
- Involves understanding of information read, not necessarily application of ideas

Reading to Perform a Task:
- Involves reading directions for games, lab experiments, tax and insurance forms, bus and train schedules, directions for assembling a bike or toy, voter registration material, cooking, consumer warranties, and map reading to find a specific place
- Requires understanding the purposes and structures of documents
- Involves application of information read, not simply understanding
- Adapted from the Pennsylvania Reading Assessment

Seven Organizational Patterns to Frame Thinking

Main ideas and supporting details provide the overarching structure of an informative selection; authors of informative text organize the main ideas and subordinate details into different organizational patterns. Patterns, such as cause and effect, provide a mental scaffold for the reader, give coherence to the writing, and enhance comprehension. A graphic representation of the pattern can assist the note-taking process for the reader. When students understand the writing pattern used, they can develop an appropriate frame of mind for reading. For example, when reading a selection entitled *All Teachers Should Be Teachers of Reading* the reader recognizes an issue is being presented as a proposition, and information will be provided to support the proposition. If the reader understands the Proposition/Support frame, notes can be organized into five categories: facts, statistics, examples, expert authority, and logic and reasoning.

Jones, Palincsar, Ogle, and Carr (1987) explain different organizational patterns authors use to frame thinking when reading informative text.

- *Cause/Effect Frame* - establishes a causal relationship showing that things or events occur as a result of certain conditions.

CAUSE	EFFECT
Over thousands of years floods deposited new soil in the river valleys.	River valleys had rich soil that was good for farming.

- *Compare/Contrast Frame* - establishes a mental frame about multiple topics by highlighting the similarities and differences.

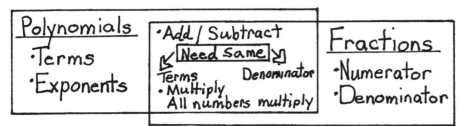

A student uses a Venn diagram to show the similarities and differences between polynomials and fractions.

- *Concept/Definition Frame* - highlights the importance of a specific concept by listing characteristics with examples.

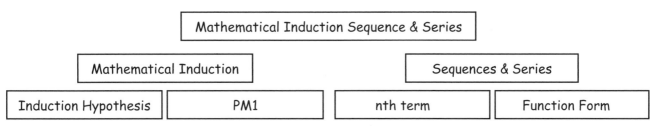

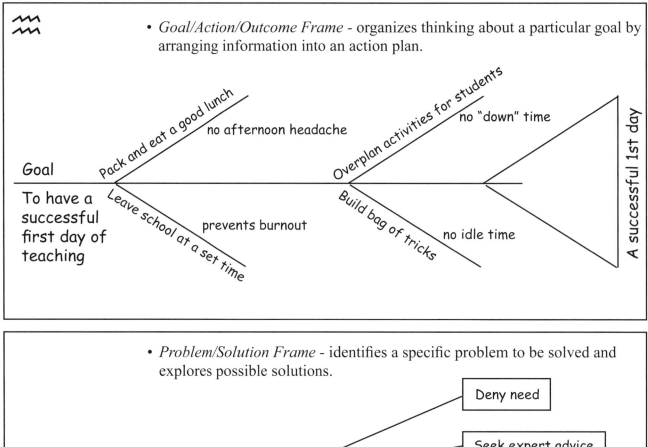

- *Goal/Action/Outcome Frame* - organizes thinking about a particular goal by arranging information into an action plan.

- *Problem/Solution Frame* - identifies a specific problem to be solved and explores possible solutions.

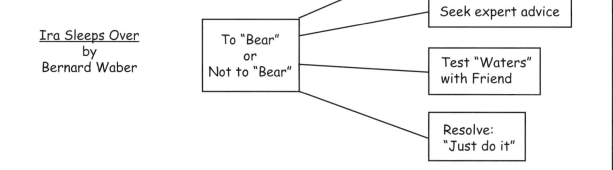

- *Proposition/Support Frame* - establishes a specific viewpoint about a topic, creates a hypothesis statement, and organizes categories of information that support and refute the statement.

Proposition	Proposition: Ranchers should not worry about threats from wolves.
Facts:	Facts: People are killing wolves for acts of eating their livestock.
Examples:	Examples: Biologists tried to save at least 100 wolves.
Expert Authority:	Expert Authority: Sharon Rose, US Fish, & Wildlife source.
Logic & Reasoning	Logic & Reasoning: Ranchers could get a fine of $50,000 if they shoot a wolf.

- *Sequence Frame* - arranges ideas or events into a series of events or a logical order.

A sequence story about a child's life.

Students who align their thinking with an organizational pattern when reading significantly increase understanding of the selection read because it:

- Helps discriminate between important and unimportant information
- Links new learning with prior knowledge
- Connects information from multiple sources
- Provides an organized structure for taking notes
- Assists with the development of questions to assist comprehension
- Serves as a study guide when preparing for a test

Once an organizational pattern is determined, the reader can mentally develop specific guiding questions to focus reading. Each pattern is accompanied with a set of guiding questions (see Figure 2, p. 80). For example, when a person reads a newspaper article about the number of teens using drugs and the effect this is having on our society, cause/effect questions can be developed. Some questions might be: What are some causes of high drug use? What are the important elements or factors that cause the high drug use? What are some effects of drug use on teens? In essence, readers must answer a set of relevant questions about the material, questions that relate directly to the purpose for reading the selection.

Authors use cue words or phrases that link one idea to another. These signal words serve as clues to the organizational pattern. Readers learn to identify cue words; they realize specific words alert them about what is to come when reading. For example, *in other words* is followed by a definition or example or *the difference between* signals a comparison of two ideas. Once readers become familiar with the cue words they can detect the nature of the text structure, as well as the specific organizational pattern being used (see Figure 3, p. 81).

Informative Text
Questions for Organizational Patters

Cause/Effect Frame
- What has happened?
- What causes this to happen?
- What is the effect?
- What are the important elements or factors that cause this effect?
- How do these factors or elements interrelate?
- Will this result always happen from these causes? Why or why not?
- How would the result change if the elements or factors are different?
- What is the cause/effect process the author is describing?
- Why did a cause/effect structure emerge?

Compare/Contrast Frame
- What elements/concepts are being compared and contrasted?
- What categories of characteristics or attributes are used to compare and contrast these things?
- How are the things alike or similar?
- How are the things not alike or different?
- What are the most important qualities or attributes that make them different?
- In terms of the qualities that are most important, are these things more alike, or more different?
- What can we conclude about these things or items?
- Why is the author comparing/contrasting these things?
- Why did the comparison/contrast structure emerge?

Concept/Definition Frame
- What is the concept?
- To what category does it belong?
- What are its official characteristics/attributes?
- How does it work?
- What does it do?
- What are some of its functions?
- What are examples of it?
- What are examples of things that share some but not all of its characteristics/attributes?

Goal/Action/Outcome Frame
- Who are the people or forces involved?
- What are they trying to do or achieve? What is their goal?
- What actions help them achieve their goal?
- What are the effects of their actions? What happens?2
- Were these actions successful for achieving their goal?
- Are there unexpected outcomes from their actions?
- Would other actions have been effective? Could they have done something else?

Problem/Solution Frame
- What is the problem?
- Who has the problem?
- What is causing the problem?
- What are the effects of the problem?
- Who is trying to solve the problem?
- What solutions are recommended or attempted?
- What results from these solutions?
- Is the problem solved? Do any new problems develop because of the solutions?

Proposition/Support Frame
- What is the subject being described?
- What are the facts?
- What statistics support the proposition?
- Who are expert authorities on the topic?
- What examples are explained to support the proposition?
- Does the proposition make sense, is it logical?

Sequence Frame
- What is being described in sequence?
- How does a chronological pattern emerge?
- What are the major steps/events in this sequence?
- Why is the sequence important?

Figure 2

Informative Text
Que Words for Organizational Patters

Cause/Effect	*Compare/Contrast*	*Sequence*
because	different from	before
since	same as	next
consequently	similar to	then
this led to	as opposed to	first
so that	instead of	second
nevertheless	although	initially
accordingly	however	begins with
because of	similarly	after
as a result of	as well as	when
in order to	either…or	finally
may be due to	and yet	preceding
if…then	on the other hand	following
therefore	not only…but also	on (date)
consequently	the difference between	not long after
for this reason	unless	now

Concept/Definition	*Goal/Action/Outcome*
characteristics	achieve
attributes	possibility
examples	plan
category	outcomes
one function	steps taken
the way it works	results

Problem/Solution	*Proposition/Support*
needs to be improved	statistically
the question is	expert said (quotes)
the issue is	examples to support
one answer is	fact(s)
one reason for that	inquiring
a possibility	logically

Figure 3

Teaching Organizational Patterns

Strategic readers are independent; they use organizational patterns to focus their thinking and read with an *active* mind. Readers know that more than one organizational pattern can be used to read and interpret a selection. For example, when reading an article about drugs, one reader might use the cause/effect frame while another reads using the problem/solution frame. As a result, teachers may need to alert students to a specific organizational pattern needed when reading an assigned selection. Knowing that the readability of some textbooks is difficult, it is especially important that an organizational pattern be identified to help students be more successful when reading. To ensure that all seven organizational frames

〰〰

are taught, it is important that teachers communicate with one another regarding introducing, teaching, and applying each pattern. Strategic reading requires students be adept in using all seven organizational patterns.

Organizational patterns are not only helpful for reading; they also organize thinking for writing. Many state assessments incorporate a section that requires students to construct a written response using different organizational patterns. Guided instruction with meaningful practice is key for student success. The following steps are helpful for teaching students how to use organizational patterns when reading and writing.

⌘

1) Explain the concept of organizational patterns and the purpose for using them when reading and writing.
2) Select a specific organizational pattern and describe its purpose and structure. Explain when writers might use it. Share cue words, questions for the selected pattern, and an example of a graphic representation.
3) Model how to use the organizational pattern, first with familiar, less complex information and then with new, more complex material. Consider using a literature selection found in Chapter 9. Using chart paper or a white board, show students how to use a graphic representation, such as a Venn diagram for compare/contrast, for taking notes when reading. (Remember to match the graphic organizer to the structure of the text and/or required response.)
4) Teach students how to use the organizational pattern first with familiar information and then with new material. Have students locate examples in trade books, magazines, textbooks, or newspapers. Instruct students to identify cue words, answer questions for the selected pattern, and create a graphic representation.
5) Model how to use an organizational pattern when writing. Show students how to incorporate the appropriate signal words that cue the reader. Working in small groups, assign students a writing activity using the organizational pattern. Students select a topic, gather information, and organize the information using a graphic representation. Remind them to incorporate the appropriate signal words.
6) Reflect on the use of the organizational pattern by sharing examples and benefits.
7) Repeat the process for each organizational pattern so that students may become proficient in recognizing and using all frames when reading and writing in any content area.

Conclusions

If students are to become strategic readers, it is critical that they be taught how to read, comprehend, and learn from informative text. Ensuring comprehension of informative text involves explicit strategy instruction that facilitates the readers' interaction with the text, as well as the students' interactions with the teacher. Active, well-crafted instruction consists of showing students how to use strategies that strategic readers employ rather than merely assigning or telling them what to do. Students must be shown how to solve a task cognitively in order for them to understand the thinking involved in the strategy. The age-old assignment of "read the chapter and answer the questions at the end" must be replaced with "let me demonstrate how to use this strategy to guide your thinking before, during, and after reading this passage on Human Infectious Disease."

Chapter 5
Section 3b

Narrative Text

"Learning Teams"

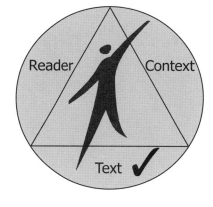

As a result of working through this section you will:
- Become aware of the thinking required to read literary narrative text
- Analyze current practices for teaching narrative text
- Develop a lesson/unit with this information in mind

Questions to ponder before, during, and after reading

Before reading - What do you know about the differences between narrative text and informative text? How does thinking differ when reading each text?

During reading - As you reflect on your reading of literary narrative text, in what ways do you like to share your interests and thinking with another person? How does this compare with the way you were taught/teach?

After reading - In what ways did this section stretch your thinking about your current practices for teaching narrative text? As you consider the instructional practices included, which ones are you going to try with your students?

Process Activity

The activity to study "Narrative Text" is called Cooperative Retelling (Billmeyer, 2006b). This strategy requires readers to predict the content of a passage, read the passage, and then retell it in their own words. Sharing the predictions and retellings in a learning team enhances all members' understanding of the selection. Directions:

Prepare
1) Before reading narrative text, think about the title and sub-headings.
2) List words and phrases you might expect to find in the selection.
3) Share your perceptions with your learning team.

Read
1) Read pages 84-92 with the intent of retelling, think about how you might retell the information to your students to help them understand the kind of thinking required when reading literary narrative text.
2) Without looking at the text, quickly write your own retell of the selection.

Share and Compare
1) Share retellings looking for similarities, differences, and confusions. Inquire: How did you decide what to include, what to leave out? What was confusing?

Write a Collaborative Retelling
1) Return to your notes and write the best possible retelling of narrative text. Share it with your students. Develop a lesson with this information in mind.

Notes

Interactive Reading Ingredient: Narrative Text

Unfortunately . . . literature is treated more like information to be memorized and tested than an experience to be enjoyed and appreciated.

- Dugan, 1997

I remember receiving a phone call from my sister; when I answered she was on the other end crying. I gasped, "What's the matter?" fearing the worst. She responded, "Have you read *My Sister's Keeper*?" And do you know I did not respond with, "Who is the main character?," "What is the setting?," or "How is the setting critical to the theme?" Rather, I asked inquisitively, "No, what happened, why are you crying?" Good readers read and respond!!! Real world readers seek opportunities to construct meaning and personally connect with ideas; they speak of what captivates them, rings true, stirs their soul, or challenges their preconceptions. Nancy Atwell confides that it was "adults gossiping about books" that finally made a reader of her in her twenties. She wanted to gossip with the best of them.

Sometime ago an article appeared in the local paper about Toni Morrison discussing her novel, *Love*, with the Mocha Moms, an organization for at-home parents of color. This multigenerational novel explores many kinds of love, such as parental and romantic love, or love as control, desire, or connection. Toni's opening question to the circle of people was, "What did you think?" The Mocha Moms had many responses, which included, "It made me reflect on my own life, and I knew certain events could have been me." "I took so many ideas from your novel and applied them to my own life." As they revealed their personal thoughts they frequently referred to their marked up copy of the novel. One simple non-directive question brought a plethora of responses. The readers connected the text to their experiences, to other texts, and to their knowledge of the world.

If "gossiping" and "a simple question" motivate adults to read and respond, why would this approach not be beneficial for our students? As Dugan's quote implies, the reading of a literary selection is a boring, arduous task for many students. If our goal is to create students who read and even love to read, we have to figure out ways to incorporate book gossip and/or open-ended questions to foster enthusiastic conversations in our classrooms. Once readers are accustomed to questions like Toni Morrison's, "What did you think?" they will stop focusing on "What color is the red pony?" and begin to search for meaning.

The Book Whisperer (Miller, 2009), a phenomenal read, influenced and confirmed my thinking about creating thoughtful, life-long readers. Classroom teacher Miller explains how she immerses her students in actual reading (40 books per year) versus mindless reading lessons formerly used in hopes of raising test scores. Her story reveals mindful, purposeful, and practical practices for teaching children rather than teaching books or stories. Other researchers, such as Fisher,

Ivey, Calkins, Schmoker, and Dobbertin (see Chapter 6) reveal classroom-shaking ideas for promoting authentic literacy. This section on narrative text will expound on their thoughts, as well as provide a plethora of examples used by excellent classroom teachers. Throughout this section you will read compelling practices that motivate and inspire students to read more and to love reading long after they leave our classrooms (and even raise test scores). The information in this section is designed to cause you to reflect upon and refine your literacy practices.

Defining Narrative Text

Literacy narrative text is designed primarily to entertain the reader. **The purpose of a literary selection is to elicit reader response based on experience** (Rosenblatt, 1978). When reading a story, the reader ideally should experience emotional and intellectual involvement as well as making connections with the characters and events in the story; my sister and the Mocha Moms mentioned earlier model the value of personal connections. Narrative text has an underlying time sequence (not always chronological) and is organized as a story; it includes imaginary stories (fiction, fables, tales, poems) and true stories (autobiographies, biographies, histories, and memoirs) (Rasinski and Padak, 2000). Specifically, reading a literary passage involves:

- Exploring the human condition and the interplay among emotions, events, and possibilities
- Engaging in vicarious experiences through the text
- Knowing what and how an author might write and forming expectations of how the text will be organized and presented
- Responding as a text critic to the deeper meanings (themes) of literature

The structural pattern of narrative text is called story grammar or story elements. A typical story is organized around setting, characters, problem or goal, events related to the problem or goal, solution or resolution, and theme. Story plot can consist of a single episode such as in the short story, "Papa's Parrot" by Cynthia Rylant in *Every Living Thing* or plot can be complex, consisting of many episodes with multiple settings, such as Mitch Albom's *Tuesdays with Morrie*. The difference between action (what happens?) and plot (what causes this to happen?) can be clearly illustrated:

　　Action. The King died, and then the Queen died.
　　Plot. The King died, and then the Queen died of grief.

Just as with informative text, questions serve as a guide to focus thinking about narrative text story elements. Each story element is accompanied with a set of guiding questions (see Figure 4, p. 86). The purpose of any question is to stimulate thinking, causing the reader to analyze and debate issues when reading a literary selection. Far too many classrooms, according to Schmoker (2007), drill students on the story elements, not only ruining the story but the love of reading. Ivey and Fisher (2006) stress the importance of teaching literary elements to impact comprehension and ultimately for use in writing a story.

As Dobbertin stresses, her major role as a high school English teacher is to help students actively think about what they read in authentic ways. Through the use of meaning-making strategies she helps students personally connect with the words on the page. This interplay between the reader and text is crucial for creating motivated, strategic readers who are proficient as *text users* and *text critics* outlined in Chapter 3. As we know, it's often the instructional approach that makes the difference for either motivating a reader to push ahead to the next chapter or boring a reader to a grinding halt.

Narrative Text
Questions for Story Elements

Setting
- Where does the story take place?
- When does the story take place?
- Why did the author select the setting?
- How might the setting have been different?
- How is the setting similar to other selections?
- How does this setting make you feel?

Problem/Goal
- What is the major problem/goal?
- What is the relationship between the problem and the main character?
- What advice would you give the characters?
- How is the setting related to the problem?
- How would you relate to the problem?

Characters
- Who are the characters in the story?
- Do the characters seem real? Why?
- Which character is most important? Why?
- Which character did you enjoy the most? Why?
- How would you describe each of the main characters?
- Which character would you want to be like?
- Which characters evoke negative feelings (disgust, fear, distrust) in you? Why?

Solution/Resolution
- How is the problem solved/goal achieved?
- What are other ways of solving the issue?
- How might you change the resolution?
- Is the outcome just or fair?
- In what other ways could the story have ended?

Event
- What important events take place in the story?
- What is the starting point for those events?
- How does each event connect to the problem?
- What is the result of the events?
- What role did major characters have in the events?
- What is the main course of action?
- Which part of the story is most interesting?

Theme
- What does the story mean to you in addition to what it tells?
- What is most memorable?
- What is the author trying to say to you?
- What do you see in the story regardless of what the author may have meant?
- What is the moral of the story?
- Why would someone else want to read this book?

Figure 4

K-12 Reading Trends

The trend at all levels of education - elementary, middle, and high school - is to broaden the scope of literature used, as well as to incorporate meaningful and authentic literacy practices. The emphasis has been to make literature more engaging and relevant to **all** students, to use children and young adult literature to enhance reading and learning, as well as to help integrate the curriculum. For example, teachers are balancing the types of literature offered between selections that cause students to reflect on their own lives and those that broaden students' knowledge about life. Personal reflection selections include *Loser* or *Stargirl* by Spinelli and *Speak* or *Twisted* by Laurie Halse Anderson. Experience broadening selections include *Tuck Everlasing* by Natalie Babbitt and *To Kill a Mockingbird* by Harper Lee.

A literature approach that is more engaging and relevant to **all learners** involves the use of an abundance of trade books that represent diversity in topics, culture, and authors, as well as in levels of difficulty. Ivey and Fisher (2006) stress four reasons for including informative text in addition to literary narrative as an option in ELA classrooms:

- Many students (especially boys) prefer informative texts.
- Informative texts permeate the world, in school, at home, and at work.
- Informative texts serve as models for writing students will be expected to do.
- Many state standards focus on informative reading and writing.

Take a minute to reflect on the reading habits of your male students. Do they read? Do they like to read? What do they like to read? It is no secret that male readers (even very young boys) are different from female readers; many prefer reading informative to narrative text. My grandchildren, twins – Grace and Grant, offer a great example; Grace at the age of two knew all of the fairy princesses and Grant knew the car symbols. Grant had little interest in a fairy tale and today, at age five, prefers informative text. Research indicates that there is a male reading "crisis," crisis not being too strong a term, especially for low-income, black, and Hispanic boys (King & Gurian, 2006; Newkirk, 2006; Perkins-Gough, 2006; Sheppard, 2006; Tyre, 2008). Boys at all grades must be offered the opportunity frequently to make their own reading choices, especially those selections that count for a grade. **Allowing boys choice is far preferable to their not reading at all.**

Due to the diversity of readers within any classroom more teachers are using graphic novels to expand student literacy skills. Graphic novels are not a traditional genre of literature but present stories that feature different genres. For example, *Ethel and Ernest: A True Story* is a biography about the life of Raymond Brigg's parents. This form of text is great for helping English language learners, motivating male readers, and assisting gifted and talented students (Carter, 2009). Teachers can team with art teachers to instruct students on writing their own graphic novels. Comic Book Creator or Microsoft Word are used to create meaningful and engaging stories students love to read and reread (see Graphic Novel titles page 240).

Literature also serves as a vehicle for integrating the curriculum. Teachers save teaching time and impact learning when they combine concepts/themes instead of teaching concepts in isolation (O'Neil, 1994). Teachers from different content areas work together to teach concepts in subjects such as, music, art, English, science, social studies, and math. For example, an English teacher co-teaches with a trigonometry teacher incorporating the selection *Rocket Boys*. Students use trigonometric functions to estimate how high the rocket will go and how fast the rocket will accelerate in its flight. When studying ancient Egypt in social studies, sixth graders read *The Egyptian Cinderella* to learn about the lifestyles and traditions of the ancient Egyptian people. The concept of slavery is studied through music and art in an eighth grade classroom by incorporating *Follow the Drinking Gourd* and *The Middle Passage: White Ships/Black Cargo*.

Focus on Elementary
Literature-based and guided reading approaches are emphasized at the elementary level. Active reading, moving from decoders to critical thinkers, reading real-life material, both fiction and nonfiction, and reading a large percentage of the school day are emphasized. Allington (2001) insists that students must be provided opportunities to read and reread for critical thinking purposes from the moment they learn to decode the simplest text. Guided reading affords teachers the opportunity to carefully observe readers in the act of reading; small groups facilitate conversations that help students make connections between texts and readers, as well as offer opportunities to introduce and reinforce reading skills and strategies. While children must learn skills such as sound-letter relationships and vocabulary words, skills are most effectively taught during the act of reading. When skills are taught in isolation (often with worksheets) they become ends in themselves and children read to figure out phonics instead of to understand a story. For some children skill development is an important part of learning to read, but effective skill development requires an authentic book in hand and comes with practice. Lining up the shortening, sugar, eggs, flour, nuts, and chips on the counter in no way equals eating a freshly baked Toll House Cookie.

Lucy Calkins (1994), well known for her work in literacy education, has stated numerous times that children spend an extremely short amount of time actually reading during a two and a half hour time set aside for reading instruction. She asks a valid question, "What are the other students doing when not engaged in small group work with the teacher?" In my daughter's primary classroom students not working with her in guided reading spend time at various reading centers. Choices range from engaging in reading to self, reading to someone using the Pairs Read strategy (Billmeyer, 2006b), listening to a self-selected story on a CD or tape, writing stories, cartoons, or poems, or playing vocabulary games. Students are engaged in meaningful and authentic reading activities. Miller (2009, p. 51) believes, *No matter how long students spend engaged in direct reading instruction, without time to apply what they learn in the context of real reading events, students will never build capacity as readers.*

Focus on Secondary
Literacy approaches at the upper elementary through secondary level are
changing; deemphasizing the whole class novel is high on the priority list.
One size does not fit all! Fisher and Ivey (2007) argue that a whole class
novel approach has inherent problems, such as books are too difficult or not
interesting, it is hard to locate one book that addresses the needs of all students,
life experiences, which enable one to make sense of a text, vary too much, and
laborious activities over one novel take too much time and reduce comprehension.

One might ask, why has the age-old practice of everyone reading the same book
hung on so long even we know the approach has many flaws? Miller (2009)
believes it is because teachers teach how they were taught. After all, didn't many
of us read the same book and do the same activities when we were in school?
She goes on to say what is even more disheartening is that many students expect
nothing more; for them school is all about reading assigned selections they do
not understand or care about and completing endless activities. Unfortunately,
reading more than a few books is not possible because the assigned units take so
long to complete. Frequently the excuse surfaces that state standards require a
continual diet of predetermined books. But one can survey standards from many
states and discover that no particular book or author is mentioned as required
reading for any test. Rather, standards focus on knowledge of a wide range of
genres, and students are expected to speak, read, and write about a variety of
literary devices, texts, and authors (Schmoker, 2006; Ivey & Fisher, 2006).

Using the whole-class novel approach does not create life-long readers. How
many of your friends read as a result of their school reading experiences? It is a
known fact that the more time students spend reading independently, the broader
their knowledge base, and the better they test. Allington's (2001)
research found that as early as 1ˢᵗ grade, the highest achieving
classrooms spent as much as 70 percent of class time reading.
Still, districts are slow to adopt the philosophy of more reading.
For example, some states are setting a standard that each student in
grades 6 through 12 read 25 books per year across all subject areas.
As stated earlier, Miller requires her students to read 40 books
per year. Districts are also turning to more in-class reading and
discussion of what is being read. As a matter of fact, teachers have
commented that the more students read and discuss in school the
more they read at home (even without being assigned).

Miller's 40 Book Requirements
Poetry anthologies 5
Traditional literature 5
Realistic fiction 5
Historical fiction 2
Fantasy 4
Science fiction 2
Mystery 2
Informational 4
Biography/autobiography/memoir 2
Chapter-book choice 9

Read and Respond Options to Create Life-long Readers

Instructional practices are changing from a "text-centered" approach in which
the reader is a passive recipient, to a "student-centered" approach in which the
reader actively responds to and interprets selections. Dobbertin emphasizes
that the teacher's role has changed from one of literary expert to that of process
modeler, facilitator, and coach. Instead of assigning students to read and then
checking their understanding through low-level questions, the teacher plans for

and provides a variety of before-, during-, and after-reading experiences that give all students both access to complex text and metacognitive awareness of effective reading strategies. Our goal must be to create critical, enthusiastic, and life-long readers.

Instead of focusing on one book teachers are selecting a theme central to the standards and then choosing a variety of books related to the theme (Fisher and Ivey, 2007). Themes might include culture, ethnicity, feminism, power, or connections to the wider world. Incorporating a broader range of literature to motivate students to read allows teachers opportunities to offer students choice in selecting books they read. Students just as adults respond positively to choice. A wide range of genres allows teachers to design instruction around district mandates and/or state standards, as well as give students a chance to select a book that speaks to them. Guiding or essential questions about the targeted concept are useful for monitoring student progress. Such questions can be an integral part of a group discussion or incorporated within the activities explained below.

Literature Circles, or book discussion groups, focus teaching on a central theme and offer students choice of different selections to reach the goal. This form of in-class reading and response is the catalyst for purposeful, meaningful, and authentic reading experiences. Mini-lessons, an integral component of the Literature Circle approach, are brief and target the students' current needs as readers and responders. Talking about books is vital to a reading community; these conversations develop relationships among students and the teacher (see Chapter 7 for information on Literature Circles, p. 220).

Janet Allen's (2000) **Book Pass** is a popular method for selecting books to read. Students preview a book by reading the jacket and a few pages in the book; they record the title, author, a few notes about the book in their book log, and assign a 1-5 rating indicating their interest in the book. When time is called students pass the book they were previewing to the next student and the previewing process continues until most books have been previewed. Students turn in their top three choices to the teacher and book groups are formed based on choices, reading levels, student capabilities, group dynamics, and number of books available. Well-supplied libraries and knowledgeable, willing librarians are essential for assisting classroom teachers with book selection.

"Wait a minute." I can hear you saying, "I can't possibly read and develop activities for dozens of books." Remember Toni Morrison's question, "What did you think?" What a great time to listen. A "student-centered" approach in which the reader actively responds to and interprets the selection must also take a new look at how students are asked to comment upon what they have read. Recently I was asked to share my philosophy on book reports. I responded with a couple of questions – Why do teachers assign book reports? Do book reports increase students desire to read? In regard to why teachers assign book reports, the response alluded to the need for accountability or evidence students had read an assigned book. But does assigning a book report guarantee that students are actually reading? How many readers have faked a book report? The second question caused quite a stir; teachers admitted they did not really think about increasing students' desire to read. Sad but true! If our goal is to create students who read and even love to read, ways of responding to what they read must also change. Traditional practices of assigning and reporting via a book report must give way to thoughtful and purposeful reading and responding methods; practices that grow readers. The remainder of this section shares a variety of options from which to select; ideas gleaned from many insightful teachers.

One alternative to the dreaded book report is a **Book Review**. How many book reviews have you read to help you select a book? For adult readers reading a review is common practice; students like it too. This activity adapted from Miller's version was first choice for responding to selections when reading with my grandchildren this summer. They wrote the book review on a large lined Post-it note and placed it inside the book jacket. Sharing book reviews with their friends and parents increased their desire to read. This builds reader confidence as well. *I can figure out the story myself. I don't need others to tell me!* Consider the criteria listed in the box for Book Reviews.

> **Book Review Criteria**
> - Name of book and author
> - Personal reactions and opinions
> - Quotes from the book
> - Cliffhanger questions
> - Information about the author
> - Awards the author and the book have won
> - Books by the same author
> - Quotes from famous writers and reviewers
> - Recommended reading age
> - Book club questions

> **Book Review Example**
> *Hooray for Fly Guy* is a funny book by Tedd Arnold. He has written a lot of Fly Guy books. His books make me laugh because they are about a pet fly that helps his friend Buzz. Fly Guy helped Buzz win the football game. Tedd Arnold writes a lot of books for children. He won the "Theodore Seuss Geisel Honor" for his book *Hi! Fly Guy*. He draws the pictures in his books too. Where do you think Tedd Arnold went to college? Read *Hooray for Fly Guy* to find out.

Response Journals encourage the reader to react, respond, and extend thinking about a story. Students not only record the books they are reading but capture thoughts and reactions about topics, authors, and genres. Journal entries can be open or closed. An open entry encourages readers to write whatever they want about what they read; a closed entry focuses the reader to respond in specific ways, such as answering essential questions about the targeted theme, plot summaries, impact major and minor characters had on story development, or evaluative responses that question the author. Dobbertin explains a Learning Log for reluctant and struggling readers on page 218. High school teacher Cris Tovani incorporates an Inner Voice Sheet to elicit reader response.

> ***Inner Voice Form***
> Name: Title of Book:
>
> Think about the conversation you have going on in your head while reading your book. Record your inner thoughts in the boxes below. It is important you write four entries from four different pages. Analyze the conversation in your head to determine if it is helping you construct meaning while reading or if the inner voice distracts you from making meaning. If you use a reading strategy include that in the box, too.
>
> Inner Voice on page _____   Inner Voice on page _____
> Inner Voice on page _____   Inner Voice on page _____

Character Quotations provide an opportunity for readers to analyze favorite characters in a story. To gain a greater insight into a particular character, students study quotes spoken by the character within the story. People tend to remember people by what they say. For example, who comes to mind when hearing - "Ask not what your country can do for you, ask what you can do for your country." Character Quotations can be used to introduce characters, as well as to focus thinking during reading.

As a pre-reading activity, students independently or organized into small groups, receive a quotation to study. After reading the quote they predict what the character will be like by listing qualities and traits. Groups share their quote and prediction with the class. Each group may study the same character or a different one. As students read the novel they collect information about their character. As a concluding activity, students generate a personality profile. Through Character Quotations students learn to analyze the development of a specific character, which ultimately helps them when writing their own stories.

Reader's Theater is an enjoyable and pleasurable way for students to respond to their reading. Students work in groups using only their voices and expressions to perform a story or a key segment of a story for an audience. The cast reads aloud from the script, enabling the audience to visualize the action while students bring characters to life through their voices. Reader's Theater is a valuable activity for all ages, increasing fluency and causing comprehension to soar. As the performing students become characters, they grow to understand the thoughts and feelings portrayed in the story. Eager tenth graders used the activity as they read *Oedipus Rex* to highlight the importance of plot and suspense when reading the play. High school teachers use Reader's Theater to teach *Pax Romana* and *Julius Caesar* or to turn primary source documents used in social studies into Reader's Theater scripts. Selections used for primary Reader's Theater might include: *Piggy Pie*, *Paper Bag Princess*, actually any text that has copious dialogue is suitable.

Conclusion
Students become readers by **reading**! While reader response is a critical component of the reading process, the focus needs to be on reading rather than reporting out on reading. Knowing there are many response activities available, an important rule of thumb is that **the "response to reading" should take less time than the "eyes on the page**!" Student-centered practices which open doors to an abundance of reading result in confident, engaged, and enthusiastic readers. Researcher and policy leader, Richard Elmore (2002), believes it is time to "examine the wallpaper" - to analyze institutional policies and classroom practices that are entrenched in culture or tradition to determine if they have a positive impact on student learning. If we desire higher achieving students literary practices must be examined; educators can no longer afford to look at the old wallpaper of unsuccessful practices steeped in tradition. As Schmoker (2006, p.50) states, "Such a change would transform average schools into intellectually vibrant places that prepare students for college, for life, and the life of the mind."

Chapter 5
Section 3c

Vocabulary Practices
to Develop Strategic Readers

"Learning Teams"

As a result of working through this section you will:
- Understand the rationale and the research for vocabulary development
- Examine effective vocabulary instructional practices

Questions to ponder before, during, and after reading

Before reading - What are your beliefs regarding vocabulary development? What are your current practices regarding vocabulary development?

During reading - What questions does this information raise for you about vocabulary instruction? How does the information compare to your current teaching practices for vocabulary development?

After reading - What ideas were reinforced? What do you better understand about vocabulary instruction? What ideas will you incorporate into your teaching?

Process Activity

The process activity for studying Vocabulary Practices to Develop Strategic Readers is the Learning Log Format (Billmeyer, 2006b) located on page 94. This strategy causes the reader to focus on specific reading attributes and to monitor comprehension before, during, and after reading. After completing the learning log, use your written thoughts as a springboard for discussion in your learning team. Directions:

1) Record your prior knowledge about vocabulary development.
2) Read the selection, jotting down questions that surface as you read.
3) After reading, record conclusions you're drawing about vocabulary practices.
4) Record the connections you are making as a result of reading this information.

Possible discussion questions for the learning team:
- What questions surfaced about vocabulary practices? Brainstorm possible answers.
- What conclusions are you drawing and what prompted them?
- If your learning team is a content department, discuss how this information might be used to teach vocabulary in your content area. If you are a cross-discipline learning team, what are the implications for your team, for your school?

Learning Log Format

Concept: Vocabulary Practices to Develop Strategic Readers

Pages:

Builds on prior knowledge What are your experiences for vocabulary development within your teaching area?	*Asks questions before and during reading* What questions are surfacing about vocabulary development?
Draws conclusions from text What conclusions are you making about vocabulary development within your teaching area?	*Makes connections between text, own experiences, and other sources* What connections are you making to your experiences or to other things you have read for developing vocabulary?

Vocabulary Practices to Develop Strategic Readers

Give a person a fish and he eats today, teach him to fish and he eats for a lifetime.

- Chinese Proverb

Introduction

What goes through your mind when you hear someone speak using precise vocabulary? An expansive and articulate vocabulary is the hallmark of an educated person. Typically people are impressed thinking the speaker must be quite intelligent. Anderson and Freebody (1981) emphasize the strong correlation between vocabulary knowledge and general intelligence.

So, what is vocabulary? Vocabulary refers to the understanding of words used when communicating (listening, speaking, reading, and writing); words are labels connected with packets of knowledge stored in permanent memory (Marzano, 2004). For example, when hearing the word *dog* we may link it to our stored chunk of knowledge about dogs, or we may think in idiomatic terms, a person can "dog-it," or the car may be a real dog.

One of the earliest findings in reading research is the strong correlation between vocabulary knowledge and reading comprehension (Davis, 1944; National Reading Panel, 2000). Strategic readers not only know how to recognize words but also understand what they mean so they can use them in listening, speaking, reading, and writing situations. Marzano (2004) emphasizes a strong link between vocabulary knowledge and background knowledge; what students already know about a topic is one of the strongest indicators of how well they will learn new information. Conversely, teaching vocabulary is a powerful way to build background knowledge. This section will highlight the research on vocabulary development, explain critical components of vocabulary development, and outline research-based concept and word learning practices for indirect and direct vocabulary learning.

What Research Tells Us About Vocabulary Development

The relationship between vocabulary knowledge and academic achievement is well established; vocabulary deficiencies tend to be a primary cause of academic failure. Anderson and Freebody (1981) emphasize the strong relationship between vocabulary and general intelligence, and Jenkins, Stein, and Wysocki (1984) state that word knowledge is one of the best indicators of verbal intelligence. Individual differences in vocabulary size are strongly correlated with socioeconomic background; preschoolers with limited vocabulary skills begin their schooling drastically behind children entering with more advanced vocabularies. First graders from higher-income backgrounds often possess twice the vocabulary of children from lower-income settings (Graves & Slater, 1987). The vocabulary gap of disadvantaged students grades 3 through 12 continues to widen over time. For example, high-achieving high school seniors may know four times as many words as their low-achieving peers (Penno, Wilkinson, &

Moore, 2002; Beck & McKeown, 1991). The more words we know, the more words we have access to.

We know that academic achievement is profoundly dependent on vocabulary knowledge; however vocabulary instruction does not seem to play a major role in classrooms today. Studies find that basal reading programs do not incorporate strong and sustained approaches to vocabulary development (Walsh, 2003; Graves, 2006). As a matter of fact, many of the words emphasized in basal programs are words children already know, words such as, baby, happy, talk, or words that are easily learned from context (Beck, McKeown, & Kucan, 2002). The emphasis on vocabulary instruction in the academic subjects such as math, social studies or science fairs no better. Word learning in the content areas typically consists of providing students with definitions or assigning words to be learned; this ineffective approach does not lead to a "web" of understanding (Graves, 2006). Also, the focus with any vocabulary method tends to be on learning words for a particular lesson; there seems to be little emphasis on learning words for life-long use. **The goal of any word learning approach must be to build extensive vocabularies for both in and out of school.**

Without effective vocabulary instruction strategic reading becomes a laborious and frustrating (if not impossible) task, especially for the struggling reader. While attaining an adequate vocabulary can be a challenging task, it is not impossible. Research suggests that a gap in vocabulary development does not necessarily mean a cognitive deficit, but can be related to prior experiences and instruction (Blachowicz & Fisher, 2004). **When children with limited vocabularies are placed in optimal conditions that emphasize meaningful word learning approaches, academic achievement soars.** Vocabulary development must be frequent and robust because vocabulary knowledge is cumulative. The more words you know, the more quickly you learn new words!

Six Critical Components of Vocabulary Development

Research from the past 20 years has broadened and deepened our understanding of what vocabulary learning and teaching should look like. We now have a clear picture of what a comprehensive approach for word learning should include. Effective vocabulary development incorporates six components: language interactions, multiple exposures to words, learning words in context, using nonlinguistic representations, focusing on critical words, and using a meaningful and active process.

• Vocabulary development incorporates language interactions.
Researcher, Gerald Graff (2003) believes that *the talk about books is as important educationally as are the books themselves*. The most meaningful use of vocabulary today is through speaking. Language interactions serve as a strong foundation for vocabulary development; ongoing conversations with people about field trips, games, and books are productive ways to introduce students to new words, ideas, and concepts. Students of all ages need to hear words used in a

wide variety of situations, as well as engage in frequent discussions in which they interact with other mature language users in real-life situations (Graves, 2006). Research indicates that when students discuss terms that are critical to the subject matter content, they not only develop a deeper understanding of the words but also remember them for future use (Marzano, 2004).

For the young child, oral language comprehension is the foundation for reading comprehension; rich oral language experiences foster growth in children's knowledge of words and concepts. Younger and less able readers require a steady diet of oral language activities and opportunities to learn word meanings (Biemiller, 2001). Conversation that is cognitively challenging using a wide variety of vocabulary is correlated with children's literacy development (Dickinson, Cote, & Smith, 1993). For example, exposure to the vocabulary used in the *Fancy Nancy* books by Jane O'Connor is an excellent way to incorporate cognitively challenging vocabulary for the young child.

In the early stages of reading there are limitations on the amount and complexity of what children can read independently, as a result vocabulary is not expanded from those materials. The reading vocabulary of young children does not catch up to their speaking vocabulary until 7th or 8th grade; vocabulary development cannot be put on hold until the reading vocabulary catches up with the speaking vocabulary (Nevills & Wolfe, 2009). Reading aloud nonfiction books introduces a wide array of words representing concepts students will read in later grades.

Oral language experiences prepare readers for the language encountered in text. During the primary years teachers have the opportunity to build the foundation for the vocabulary and concepts needed to understand the increasingly difficult texts children encounter (see p. 201). Word knowledge in kindergarten and first grade is a significant predictor of reading comprehension in middle and high school grades (Graves 2006).

• Vocabulary development demands multiple exposures to words.
How many times do you have to see or hear a new word before you actually remember it for future use? Most people require multiple exposures. Regardless of whether it is through conversation, reading, or writing the average student must be exposed to a new word from 6-14 times for competent, frequent use to occur (Jenkins, Stein, & Wysocki, 1984; Moats, 1998; Marzano, 2004). While 12 exposures are enough for most readers, some children need to use a word 20 times or more before they can remember or attach meaning to it. Word learning ranges on a continuum of no knowledge to thorough understanding of how to use the word. There are four levels of word knowledge:
  • *Unknown* - I have never seen this word.
  • *Familiar* - I have seen this word but need to think about what it means.
  • *Recognized* - I automatically know what this word means.
  • *In-depth* - I have extensive knowledge about this word and can use it in my listening, speaking, reading, and writing.

Knowing the importance of multiple exposures for learning words, research indicates that interacting with the words in a variety of ways enhances word learning. Teachers should vary the types of interactions students have with vocabulary terms using both receptive (reading and listening) and expressive (speaking and listening) language. Words walls (see below) provide ongoing support for vocabulary development.

• Vocabulary development incorporates learning words in context.
Context clues are hints about the meaning of an unknown word. These clues are found within the word, the phrase, or in surrounding sentences or pictures.

Word Walls - "Out of sight, out of mind." Because words need to be used at least six times before students internalize their meanings, words can be displayed on a word wall. Teachers record new or interesting words on butcher paper hung to the wall. Words can be organized into categories according to a theme, concept, story, or letter patterns. Words Walls provide quick and easy access for students when speaking, during writing activities, when defining other words, or as a reference. If students are listening for new words, they can suggest additions to the word wall.

Learning to infer the meaning of unknown words from context is an important part of vocabulary development. Students learn more words in context when the context is sufficiently challenging; learning new words from context is affected by ability level, grade level, and density of the text. Due to more extensive background knowledge, higher ability readers have a greater chance of learning words in context than do lower-ability students, who often need a more explicit approach. Older students typically benefit from context word learning more than younger age students.

If there are too many new words and the concept is unfamiliar the chances of learning new words from context are minimal (Marzano, 2004). In the content areas multi-level text featuring fewer unknown words better facilitates learning from context. Teaching word parts, such as prefixes, suffixes, and roots is a powerful way to help students learn the meaning of new words in context. These must be taught for transfer to new, unfamiliar words. Consider creating a word wall, described earlier in this section, listing prefixes (un-, re-, in-, dis-) and/or suffixes (less, ness, ful). Challenge students to add words to the list, and to use the words when speaking and writing.

• Vocabulary development incorporates nonlinguistic representation of words.
Take a minute to think about a memorable experience from the past! What goes on in your brain as you revisit ideas? Perhaps you relive through mental pictures. Research continually reveals that the brain loves pictures; for information to be stored in permanent memory it must have linguistic and nonlinguistic representations. Sketching or representing the meaning of a word with a symbol or an organizer has positive effects on word learning (Sadoski & Paivio, 2004). According to Marzano (2004, p. 73), *Nonlinguistically based techniques produced vocabulary gains that were 37 percentile points higher than those produced by having students review definitions, and 21 percentile points higher*

than those produced by having students generate sentences that demonstrated an understanding of the vocabulary words. A helpful and humorous book for SAT review, *Picture These SAT Words* (Geer & Geer, 2008), uses cartoons to focus on word meanings and their usage. To maximize vocabulary development, students should be encouraged to elaborate on their understanding of words using pictures, organizers, and symbols.

• Vocabulary development focuses on learning critical words.

So how many ideas can you remember at one time? When do you revert to making a list? A well-known finding is that the brain remembers seven plus or minus two ideas. It is not unusual for content area texts to incorporate an abundance of new vocabulary. For example, a 2009 biology text includes a sixteen-page chapter titled *Birds and Mammals* that introduces 30 new words (maybe more for some students). Typically not all of those words are necessary to understand the topic. Content area words can be organized into two categories:

- Critical words – Words students must know to understand the concept.
- Embellish the meaning words – Words that are nice to know but not essential.

For example, *molting*, *preening*, and *migration* are critical terms when learning about birds; *archaeopteryx* is a nice to know word but not essential to learning the concept.

When planning a unit of study, teachers can brainstorm possible words students will encounter and then categorize them. For example, students were reading *The Diary of Anne Frank* as part of a unit on the Holocaust; words were organized into the following categories. Teachers selected vocabulary strategies to support students' acquisition of the critical words.

Critical/Must Know Words	Embellish Meaning/Nice to Know Words
Holocaust	Dr. Josef Mengele
Nazi	Kristallnacht
Hitler	Hitler Youth
Jews	Axis Powers
Nuremburg Laws	Allied Powers

Learning vocabulary in the content areas can be a challenging task. When vocabulary instruction focuses on the **critical words** needed to understand the concept students score 33% higher on tests than students with no focused instruction (Marzano, 2004). This dramatic difference indicates that instruction focusing on the critical words can have a profound effect on students' abilities to learn that content.

• Vocabulary development must be an active and meaningful process

Many adults remember being assigned long lists of words to define and memorize. Usually the assignment involved looking the words up in the dictionary or glossary, writing the definitions, and using the words in sentences. Once the assignment was complete, the words were forgotten. Research indicates that students who receive no instruction on difficult words score the same on comprehension tests as students who receive ineffective instruction (Nagy, 1988/89). The dictionary approach as a sole device to word learning has minimal impact on students' reading comprehension; a dictionary uses vague language due to space restrictions (McKeown, 1993) and building knowledge requires more than knowing word definitions. For example, the dictionary meaning for *commotion* is *a condition of turbulent motion*. Based only on this definition, how equipped are you to use the word *commotion* when speaking or writing?

Unfortunately, current instructional approaches for vocabulary often stem from past practice. Students must move beyond a superficial, definitional word learning approach to an active and meaningful process, one that creates motivated word learners who internalize word meanings. Successful vocabulary instruction requires interacting with new words by activating prior knowledge, attaching personal meaning, and restating dictionary definitions based on how a person really uses the word when talking. When conversational descriptions, explanations, and examples of terms stemming from students' own lives are used vocabulary development soars which means achievement soars (Marzano, 2009). An active and meaningful process for teaching the word *commotion* might sound something like this. "Remember when Tom dropped the guinea pig during science class and you started screaming and running around trying to catch it? Well, *commotion* means something that is noisy and confusing. People in the hallway heard a *commotion* in our room." Then ask students to draw a picture of *commotion* and/or place the word and picture on the word wall.

A Comprehensive Approach for Promoting Vocabulary Growth

The goal of any comprehensive approach for promoting vocabulary growth is to develop strategic readers, students who are enthralled, independent word learners and knowledge seekers. **The research and criteria for vocabulary development pleads with educators to incorporate efficient, effective, and robust vocabulary practices at all levels and in all content areas.**

So, what is a word; and what does word learning involve? As stated earlier, words are labels connected with packets of knowledge stored in long-term memory. Words can be classified as receptive (reading and listening) and expressive (writing and speaking). Receptive vocabulary refers to words we hear used by others, while expressive vocabulary refers to our use of words. Word learning practices focus on receptive oral (words we hear) and written (word we read) and on expressive oral (words we speak) and written (words we write) (Graves, 2006). Thus, vocabulary knowledge can soar when emphasis is placed on listening, reading, speaking, and writing vocabularies.

Word learning can be incidental, as well as intentional; most vocabulary is learned indirectly, but some vocabulary must be taught directly. Struggling learners particularly benefit from vocabulary instruction. No matter how old we are we learn new words indirectly through our life experiences, real or vicarious. Focusing on vocabulary related to student experiences in and out of school (field trip to a museum, guest speaker, vacation, learning centers, or a class or individual project) is a meaningful way to increase vocabulary. Direct vocabulary instruction refers to students being explicitly taught both individual words and word-learning strategies; strategies teach students how to comprehend words when reading and use them when writing. This section will outline approaches for indirect and direct word learning opportunities.

Indirect Opportunities for Vocabulary Growth

A major goal of indirect opportunities for vocabulary growth is to help students become independent word learners. As described in Chapter 3, strategic readers are independent; they know how to figure out the meaning of unknown words on their own. Opportunities for indirect vocabulary growth are numerous; three ways to increase word learning are by reading extensively, being read to by others, and creating word conscious learners.

• Reading Extensively

Strategic readers read extensively; wide reading is the largest source of vocabulary growth, especially for older and more able readers. Exposure to concepts in books and other written materials (newspapers, magazines, brochures) is essential for word learning. When students read on a wide variety of topics they are introduced to many new words and concepts, acquire new labels for experiences they read about, and rise to new levels of understanding. Researchers, Cunningham and Stanovich (1998), estimated that 5th graders who engaged in 10 minutes of reading a day read 622,000 more words each year than students who do no independent reading. Think of the advantage for some students when they have a teacher who values reading and incorporates numerous opportunities for independent reading!

Some teachers lament that they do not have time for independent reading, they feel overwhelmed to cover the curriculum. Once teachers make the time to incorporate independent reading they are amazed with the positive results. One teacher during a training commented to another, "Try free reading. You will like it!" She went on to explain how she begins each class with five minutes of independent reading and was pleasantly surprised how reading prepared students for class, increased their interest in the topics they studied, and created an overall community of readers and learners. Other teachers encourage all students to carry a book, magazine, or newspaper in their backpack for free reading once they have completed an assigned activity. Some schools embrace a school-wide extensive reading approach called SSR (Sustained Silent Reading) (see Chapter 8 p. 228).

As stated earlier, it takes repeated encounters with a word before students really own it for future use. To increase the likelihood of ongoing use of the words encountered during independent reading teachers incorporate book talks and/or vocabulary notebooks.

Book Talks – Students love to talk; people love to talk. During book talks students exchange ideas pertaining to the author's use of words, the words they found interesting or puzzling, or unique words used to describe characters. Third grade teacher Ellen Billmeyer teaches her students to be Word Detectives when reading narrative or informative text. While reading independently, students generate two questions and two vocabulary words they will discuss with group members. Word choice is a compelling way to build interest for word learning.

Vocabulary Notebook - A meaningful way for students to keep track of self-selected and assigned words is in a vocabulary notebook or journal. Students can record how the word was used in different contexts, sketch what it means, and provide meaningful examples that link to their lives. Through the use of a notebook students can manage, explore, and review important concepts learned throughout a course of study, the year, or life. Journals can also encourage pairs of students to select and study interesting words from their readings. This example is from a 9th grader using the SAW (Student Action Words) Notebook strategy (Billmeyer, 2006b).

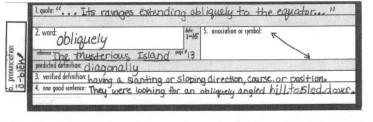

• Being Read to By Others

Reading aloud to children is another powerful way to expand vocabulary (see p. 226). Students of **all** ages can learn words from hearing texts of various kinds read to them. Teachers can expose children to literature that expands their vocabularies by reading aloud selections that might be too difficult for many of the students to read independently. Reading interesting informational material can introduce new words to struggling readers with limited vocabulary, as well as help them get a jump-start on content area concepts they will learn. Optimal reading aloud practices involve conversations about new or interesting words before, during, and/or after reading the selection; all students must be engaged in discussing the new terms and concepts so they can make connections to their prior knowledge and experiences.

Multiple and meaningful exposures to the same book, story, or poem can also help cement word meanings. A powerful way to build vocabularies of less advantaged learners is to employ interactive oral reading; read a selection aloud periodically stopping to discuss individual words or phrases. A primary example (see below) of interactive oral reading producing substantial vocabulary growth comes from the work of Biemiller (2003).

Interactive Oral Reading - The process involves reading a story without interruption; then reading the same story three more times on consecutive days stopping so children can explain and discuss targeted words and finally, recording them on chart paper or a word wall for more in-depth learning. The study stresses the need for three interactive readings in which children (not the teacher) engage in word discussion.

• Create Word Conscious Learners

Oliver Wendell Homes once said, "Once the mind is stretched by a new idea it never goes back to its original dimension." That quote speaks to the powerful outcome of creating word conscious students. We have all heard unfamiliar words used in conversation and pondered the meaning once the chat ended. Research indicates the brain is curious and has a need to know or figure out different or unfamiliar information. Word conscious learners have an awareness of and an interest in new words, their meanings, and their power; students begin to take notice of words they read, hear, and those they write or speak (Armbuster, Lehr, & Osborn, 2001; Graves, 2006).

When teachers focus on creating word conscious learners many students for the first time are actually motivated to learn new words. Traditional practices have done little to cause students to be word learners; past results at best focused on a passing acquaintance with words. Motivation is everything; if students are to achieve academically, they must be motivated to learn and use many new words. There are numerous ways to create word conscious students. Below are three K-12 examples for you to try; brainstorm more options with your colleagues.

Word Play and Books – Highlight the use of interesting words in text, point out how authors arrange words to create varied effects, and discuss how the writer's choice of words enhances meaning, promotes curiosity, or creates feelings. Introduce students to books that focus on word play. Books by Fred Gwynne, *The King Who Rained* and *Chocolate Moose for Dinner*, or the *Amelia Bedelia* books by Peggy Parish focus on hilarious wordplay and zany humor that keeps children of all ages in stitches. *Get Thee to a Punnery* by ingenious author Richard Lederer offers a humorous use of words representing more than one possible meaning for most content areas. For example, complete the sentences using the following math or science terms: addition, atom, catalyst, and centigrade.

You keep track of cows and bulls on a _____.   This priceless book is a first _____.

Eve's husband was _____.   A nickel a grade is more expensive than a _____.

Teacher Language - Modeling the use of new or unique vocabulary words is a powerful learning tool. Words can be linked to a known synonym or antonym, as well as used in a variety of settings. A middle school principal developed the habit of using interesting words in conversation as he spoke with students in the hall. Students were curious enough to find out the meanings of words used and also began using the words in their conversations. Examples include **Prudent** *Priscilla kept her vocab box in a vault so nobody would steal it*, or *Our middle school dances are usually a pretty* **convivial** *place.*

Word Games – Word games are a powerful instructional word-learning device (Marzano, 2004; Covington, 1992). Word games are a meaningful and enjoyable way to expand vocabulary; games can challenge a student's capacity, yet allow the student to be in control of how much challenge is appropriate. Some benefits of word games are: language interaction is encouraged, words are used in different contexts, and words can be analyzed from different perspectives. Word games used by teachers are Scrabble, Boggle, Scatagories, Apples to Apples, Pictionary, and Balderdash.

The overall goal of word consciousness is to highlight, celebrate, and kindle children's interest in words. Teachers at all levels need to be a positive role model by demonstrating an interest and enthusiasm for word learning. For example, some teachers introduce new words from a novel or an article they are reading. A few minutes of "word-play" each day is a motivating, yet a simple way to expand vocabulary and improve comprehension. As a result, students develop an appreciation for words and make an investment in word learning because they believe it is a worthwhile endeavor (Scott & Nagy, 2004).

Direct Opportunities for Vocabulary Growth

Direct instruction helps students learn words not yet part of their background or words representing complex concepts in the content areas. Direct instruction involves teaching both individual words and word learning strategies. This

~~~~
~~~~

section focuses on word selection, different levels of word learning, and a sequential process for teaching individual words.

• Selecting vocabulary words for direct instruction

Teachers cannot directly teach all the words in a text or in a unit of study for several reasons: the text may have too many unknown words, students can understand most texts without knowing the meaning of every word, and students need opportunities to independently use word-learning strategies to figure out the meaning of unknown words. As a matter of fact, pre-teaching all unknown words before reading can create lazy readers, students who memorize the teacher's definitions rather than read to extract meaning from text (Armbruster & Nagy, 1992). One common approach is to pre-teach those critical words students do not know but will need to understand the meaning of the concept and to **highlight** words that might cause students difficulty during reading but are not essential for understanding the concept. The FORECAST strategy (see pp. 134) provides a sneak preview of key words in a meaningful way before reading.

Research suggests selecting from three types of words for instruction: critical words, useful words, and specialized words (Beck & McKeown, 1985; National Reading Panel, 2000; Vacca & Vacca, 2001). As stated earlier in this section, **critical** words (including technical vocabulary) are words students must know to understand concepts when reading in the content areas. Critical vocabulary is essential for developing background knowledge that helps students succeed in all disciplines. **Useful** words are new terms students are likely to see and use again and again. For example, the word *fragment* is more useful than *fractal*. Vocabulary researchers Beck, McKeown, and Kucan (2002) call these words *tier two words*, high frequency words used by mature language users and those terms students will encounter in the texts they read throughout their schooling. And finally, **specialized** vocabulary represents words with multiple meanings, such as a line in math or a line of people, matter in science or dealing with a matter, and words used in idiomatic expressions. For example, "chip off the old block" or "drawing a blank" may require direct instruction. Students benefit academically when instruction focuses on word learning before, during, and after reading.

Word selection is not an easy task; teachers should feel free to use their best judgment based on student needs and the demands of the reading selection. Graves (2006) provides four helpful questions to consider for word selection:

- Is understanding the word critical for understanding the selection in which it appears? When studying photosynthesis students must know the meaning of chlorophyll.
- How useful is the word beyond this particular reading selection?
- Can students use context clues or structural analysis skills to figure out the meaning of the word? If so, provide them the opportunity to do so.
- Can this word be used to further students' understanding of context, structural analysis, or dictionary skills ultimately helping them become

independent word learners. For example, teaching the word *insatiable* to focus on the commonly used prefix *in-*.

Teachers frequently ask how many words they should teach at one time. Of course the answer will vary based on the difficulty of the words, student capability, and the current vocabulary load in other areas. The human brain can remember seven plus or minus two ideas, so a rule of thumb is to carefully select up to nine words to teach. Once teachers have selected specific words to teach they must consider the different levels of word learning they want students to achieve. (See Marzano's (2004) K-12 comprehensive list of vocabulary terms.)

• **Different levels of word learning**

Another factor to consider with direct instruction is the level of word knowledge students need to achieve. As stated earlier, word learning ranges on a continuum of no knowledge to in-depth understanding of how to use the word when speaking and writing. Word learning is multidimensional; different types of words require different types of instruction. A goal of any vocabulary approach is to introduce, reinforce, clarify, and extend word meanings. Effective vocabulary instruction introduces new words and also elaborates on the meaning of known words. Students who know the meaning of lukewarm water stretch their vocabulary when introduced to the word *tepid*. Vocabulary acquisition proceeds in the following manner (Billmeyer, 2006a; Graves, 2006):

- Reads known words automatically
- Uses known words to figure out unfamiliar text
- Learns new meanings for known words
- Learns new words representing known and new concepts
- Infers nuances of meaning in words
- Judges the effectiveness of word choice

For example, knowing the word *fair* assists the reader when reading, *This rule is unfair* or *fair to middling*. Another meaning for *fair* is *the gathering of people to sell something*, such as a *book fair*. Another meaning of fair is light and bright – *We have a fair day* or *She has fair hair*. A nuance refers to a slight degree of difference in meaning. Examples of nuances are slang and idioms. Fair used in the word *fair shake* is slang for *a fair chance*. Judging the effectiveness of word choice is, *He got a fair shake when he tried out for the soccer team. The coach was fair in selecting team members.* Students performing as talented writers are astute at judging the effectiveness of word choice.

One of the most challenging types of word study is learning new words representing new concepts; reading in the content areas typically involves this type of word learning. For example, when students learn about *mores* and *civilization* they may be learning both new concepts and new words. Learning words and concepts in science, math, and social studies can be challenging because a major concept is frequently associated with other new concepts. The concept of *desert* is associated with other concepts like *plateau*, *mesa*, and *cactus* or the concept of *symmetry* is related to *proportion* or *balance*.

The Frayer Model (Frayer, Frederick, and Klausmeier, 1969) is an excellent strategy for teaching new words representing known and new concepts. This popular and powerful strategy uses a graphic organizer divided into four components for recording information related to the concept (see page 177).

Frayer Model Study

Using a cooperative jigsaw process, a physics teacher organized students into small groups assigning each group three critical words to learn; later they would teach the three words to students from other groups so students learned all nine new words. Each student used 3x5 cards to create a Frayer Model for each word; the nonlinguistic representation was drawn on the back of the card. When all group members were ready to teach their new words to other group members the teacher reorganized groups. Students created a Frayer Model on a 3x5 cards for the other six new words. Students developed a word bank of cards throughout the semester; they used them for Word Sorts and to review for tests.

Because word learning is multifaceted, an instructional plan needs to consider the different levels of vocabulary development. Giving students multiple opportunities to learn and use known, and especially new, words allows them to develop an expanded permanent vocabulary. Vocabulary strategies (Billmeyer, 2006b) provide students the opportunity to apply new words in meaningful ways. Researchers suggest a sequential approach for teaching words.

• A sequential process for teaching individual words

As stated earlier, a critical component of word learning is that it be an active and meaningful process in which students elaborate on the meaning of new words, this does not imply rote memorization of definitions. Teachers are embracing a five-step process for learning new words.

Step 1 – Define the word associating the meaning with personal experiences or **"student-friendly" explanations**. For example, the dictionary defines *ambition* as *eager desire for success or power*. A student-friendly definition – *describes someone who really wants to be successful when trying something*.

Step 2 – Provide **meaningful and relevant examples** - Linking an example with the word advances the student's thinking from knowledge to a comprehension level. Examples are a powerful propellant to learning; students actually personalize the definition. *Peter's ambition to be starting goalkeeper on the soccer team caused him to practice many hours daily.*

Step 3 – Students **restate the meaning of the word using their own words** and provide examples from their own lives. Personalizing the definition causes students to actively process the meaning of the word, storing it in long-term memory.

Step 4 – **Draw/sketch** what the word means - Sketching the meaning of a word encourages deep processing; this action requires more mental effort and creativity.

Step 5 – Provide an **antonym** – Antonyms are words that are opposite in meaning and help students distinguish examples from non-examples. Deciding on an antonym for a word is not an easy, or in some cases not even a possible task. An antonym for *ambitious* is *unmotivated*.

Chapters 6 and 7 incorporate a variety of vocabulary strategies for all content areas. Learning new words is a process. Students cannot use a strategy for each new word. Our goal must be to create independent learners who mentally incorporate the five-step process when learning new words.

Students must not only know how to read words but they must also use them when speaking and writing. The Wordsplash strategy provides students meaningful practice using words when writing and speaking.

Wordsplash - Words pertaining to a unit of study are organized in random fashion on a sheet of paper. Students read the words to determine what the unit will be about, what they already know about the topic, and/or to summarize what they learned. They write a paragraph or two using the appropriate words and then exchange them with a partner. Read the Wordsplash below and summarize what you are learning about vocabulary development. Exchange your ideas with a colleague.

multiple exposures	dictionary	critical words	word parts
nonlinguistic representations	word conscious	wide reading	direct
language interactions	context clues	read aloud	indirect

As a final note, coordination of effort among teachers for teaching vocabulary is important. Cross-grade level planning helps ensure that critical words are taught across the content areas so students are offered numerous opportunities to retain new words. Focusing on the same strategies across grade levels ensures two things: students know strategies are important and necessary to increase learning and teachers do not have to spend as much time teaching the strategies. Instead, teachers can expend energy on adapting the selected strategies to meet their content area and student needs.

Conclusion

The ultimate goal for word learning is to develop strategic readers who are capable of dealing with unfamiliar words **during** the act of reading; they know how to make appropriate and flexible use of vocabulary strategies. When adults read an article no one introduces new vocabulary words up front, they know how to figure them out during the act of reading. Word learning is a complex task; students deserve a comprehensive approach to vocabulary development that incorporates the six components for vocabulary development, as well as both indirect and direct word learning approaches. Focusing on all approaches to word learning has potential for causing students to be successful, resourceful, and independent learners in all content areas.

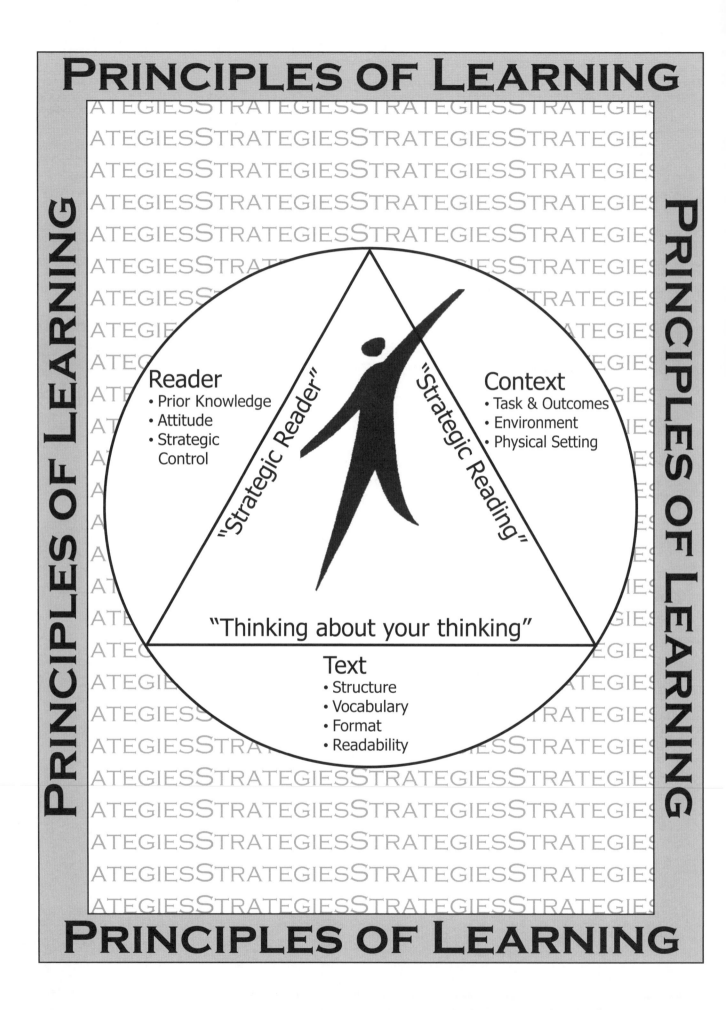

Chapter 6

Notes

Voices from the Classroom

The idea that reading instruction and subject matter instruction should be integrated is an old one in education, but there is little indication that such integration occurs often in practice.
- Becoming a Nation of Readers

Introduction

Since the 1998 publication of *Teaching Reading in the Content Areas: If Not Me Then Who?* much has been learned about reading in the content areas. With a focus on comprehension, the text posited that if teachers used appropriate strategies, students would comprehend. Yet, students still struggle, and teachers still are asking, "How do I get students to understand what they are reading in my subject?" This question has led us to believe that more is needed.

As a result, teachers are refining and recognizing unique reading processes for their disciplines and beginning to understand the specific thinking required for comprehension in their content area. Even as teachers are feeling the pressure for content coverage and success on high-stakes testing, more teachers are taking time to teach students how to strategically read subject area content and adapting strategies to fit. Teachers are accepting that the resource teacher or the language arts teacher cannot be held responsible for teaching students to read in all content areas. Reading a novel or poem in English is very different from reading a biology text in science or comprehending an equation in math.

Researchers have identified positive effects on student achievement when teachers engage students in classroom conversation about how to read in different subject areas (Schoenback, Braunger, Greenleaf, and Litman, 2003). Metacognitive (thinking about your thinking) conversations help the covert reading process become overt. When teachers become more aware of the wide array of literacies and strategies they apply in their content area, they can open up powerful resources for students and other teachers. The intent of this chapter is to initiate metacognitive conversations.

Teachers from content areas have shared their knowledge and experiences about teaching reading in their subject. Their writing includes some of the following:
- Rationale
- Issues and Nuances (slight degrees specific to the particular content area)
- Learner Considerations
- Text Considerations
- Teacher Considerations/Instructional Practices
- Special Considerations for Developing Readers (Response to Intervention)
- Conclusions: Implementing an Integrated Approach

Chapter 6

Voices from the Classroom

"Learning Teams"

As a result of working through this chapter you will:
- Understand what strategic reading looks like in different content areas
- Think metacognitively about teaching reading in your content area

Questions to ponder before, during, and after reading

The before, during, and after questions are incorporated into the strategy. The learning team process for this section is a modified K-W-L, a K-W-L-A (What do you Know? Want to learn? What have you learned? What additions would you make?) The K-W-L strategy is a learner-driven strategy because it asks the learner to generate questions for which they are interested in finding the answers. Use the template below for your note taking needs.

K   What do you already know about helping students become strategic readers in your content area? What challenges do you see students facing when reading to learn in _____?

W   What questions are you seeking answers to regarding strategic reading in your content area?

L   What did you learn or what new insights did you gain from this reading? From your dialogue with team members?

A   What additions would you make to the information that you read?

KWLA

K – What do I already know about teaching reading in my content area?	W- What questions do I have about teaching reading in my content area?	L – What did I learn from the reading and/or my colleagues?	A – What additions would I make to the information provided?

Strategic Reading and 21ˢᵗ Century Learners

Author, Pam Krambeck

Rationale

Instruction in reading is evolving; teaching reading across all content areas offers an opportunity to address the skills and strategies considered essential to 21ˢᵗ Century readers. Different sources report varying statistics but everyone from Gallup to the Kaiser Family Foundation is reporting increased time with on-line reading and text. Educators who have an understanding of 21ˢᵗ Century skills can "retool" their strategies and techniques to address reading instruction for 21ˢᵗ Century learners.

Reading within content areas often involves reading for learning and discovery. Where do students start when faced with information overload? Consider these statistics cited by researchers Fisch and McLeod (2010) and the widely popular "Did You Know" video and web site:

- Over 1,000,000 books are published worldwide every year (source: UNESCO Institute for Statistics numbers).
- Americans have access to 1,000,000,000,000 web pages (source: http://csrc.nist.gov).
- Newspaper circulation is down 7 million over the last 25 years (source: http://www.nationmaster.com).
- In the last 5 years (2004-2009) readers of online newspaper are up 30 million (source: http://www.nationmaster.com).
- Wikipedia was launched in 2001, it now features over 13 million articles in more than 200 languages. Like it or not, people are using Wikipedia (source: http://www.wikipedia.com).

The Partnership for 21ˢᵗ Century Skills has emerged as an advocacy leader, and the skills outlined in its framework are the ones most widely communicated and accepted nationwide. The framework includes:

- Life and Career Skills
- Learning and Innovation Skills
- Information, Media, and Technology Skills
- Core Subjects & 21ˢᵗ Century Themes

The strategic reading format wraps itself nicely around the 21ˢᵗ Century Framework as illustrated in Figure 5. Consider the following bands of the Framework and the role that strategic reading plays in the development and nurturing of the skills addressed.

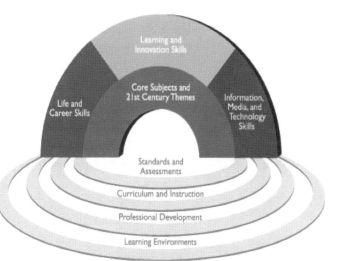

Framework from the Partnership for 21ˢᵗ Century Skill
Source: http://www.21stcenturyskills.org

Figure 5

Life and Career Skills: The Partnership for 21st Century Skills outlines one band of the arch as life and career skills. Businesses need individuals who are well versed in reading for content and knowledge in a variety of texts, especially informative text. Teaching organizational patterns and attention to cue words will assist students when they apply knowledge of reading informational text into their chosen career path which may take the form of planning a heart healthy menu in a culinary arts career or testing a blood sample in a health and science career. Reading with a purpose, reading for meaning, and decoding text are life and career skills for 21st Century learners.

Learning and Innovation Skills: Included within this arch of the framework are the areas of collaboration, communication, and critical thinking. Strategic readers read for meaning (critical thinking), process and reflect on their reading (communication), and communicate the meaning of their reading to others (collaboration). The use of technology driven communication and collaboration tools is an area that educators need to explore and integrate into their plans for developing strategic readers. Tools such as on-line discussion forums, blogs, and wikis are available free of charge and can be integrated into reading and writing instruction. These tools will engage students in the communication and collaboration associated with reflective reading and processing.

Information, Media, and Technology Skills: Information, media, and technology skills form yet another arch in the 21st Century framework. 21st Century readers find code breaking skills essential when processing on-line information that is targeted at wide, diverse audiences, often times above the students reading level. On-line information requires students to read for meaning and to function as text critics in order to process and garner meaning from a variety of text formats.

Reading and 21st Century Skills are intertwined with numerous strategies that will support both strategic reading and the inclusion of skills that address success in the 21st Century. Use the strategies shared in this section as a springboard for your own ideas and adapt them to your curricular area. Become familiar with the 21st Century Framework and use it as a basis for "retooling" reading instruction to develop strategies that develop and nurture strategic readers.

Issues and Nuances of 21st Century Readers

Jukes and McCain (2008) summarized findings on 21st Century students and their learning styles; results pertinent to reading in the content area are included in the table (Figure 6).

Students of the 21st Century have a preferred reading style that tends to gravitate toward on-line resources with multimedia offerings and hyperlinked text when researching and reading for school related topics. With this in mind, it becomes apparent that educators need to provide reading strategies for students as they process on-line text.

21st Century students prefer:	Educators prefer:
• information that is received quickly from multiple sources with important information bulleted for quick scans	• slow and controlled release of information from controlled sources—often a textbook
• multi-tasking and parallel processing of information	• singular processing and single or limited tasking
• processing pictures, sounds, color, and video before text	• concentrating on text before pictures, sounds and video
• random access to hyper-linked multimedia information	• linear, logical sequencing of information
• collaborating and networking simultaneously with others to process information	• independent work by students before they begin discussing and interacting with other students
• information that is formatted in an "F" pattern on the page or screen	• information that is formatted in a "Z" pattern on the page or screen

Figure 6

With on-line resources, students must be taught strategies to decode words, make use of charts, graphs, pictures, and multimedia on the page. Because of the mixed page formats, various genres, and varied reading levels, added importance should be given to teaching students strategies for pre-reading, during reading, and post-reading reflection.

On-line reading has changed the eye tracking habits of learners who read large amounts of information on-line. Eye tracking patterns of the past followed the Gutenberg Z pattern where readers read left to right, returned to the left forming a "Z" pattern. However, recent eye-tracking studies (Quinn & Stark-Adam, 2008) show that readers processing on-line text start their scanning with a fixation in the upper left corner of the page

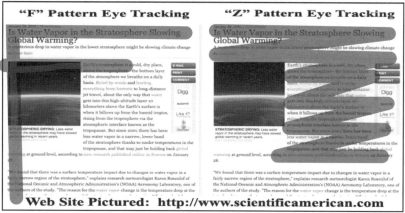

Examples of F and Z eye tracking patterns using the Scientific America web site, www.scientificamerican.com.

forming a "Z" pattern and then proceed along the left area of the page forming a "F" pattern.

Text Considerations

Readers of the 21st Century have grown up reading web pages. Research studies from the early days of monochrome monitors found that there was not a huge difference in speed and comprehension between on-screen reading and reading from paper (Dillon,1992). The only clear difference cited in the early research was related to skimming text where paper became the clear winner. Later studies are however less definitive. Nielsen and Pernice (2007) found in their most recent research that on-screen reading is 25 percent slower than reading on paper because of the many visual distractions and options available to the reader, for example, graphics, visuals, pop-ups, and clicking on text. Eye-screen distances and positioning before the computer as well as visual information processing factors such as visual tracking, lighting, eye fatigue, and print size can affect readability and therefore must be taken into consideration. When working with students who are reading vast amounts of on-line text a number of strategies can be utilized to assist with eye fatigue and readability:

- Choose a default font designed for screen reading such as: Verdana, Trebuchet, or Georgia.
- Design on-line reading activities of not more than 30 minutes.
- Know how to adjust monitor settings (brightness, contrast, focus).
- Minimize reflections from windows, lighting, and other light sources.

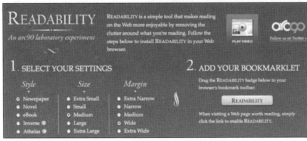

Screen capture of the Readability web site: http://lap.arc90.com/experiments/readability.

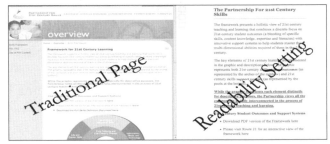

Examples of a traditional web page and a page using the readability web site to control the font style, size, and margin settings.

Readability Issues and Distractions Related to Online Text
Some educators, depending on the needs of their students, use a web tool called "Readability" that allows computer users to add a readability button to their web browser. They simply click to display the web page with a certain style, size, and margin that will improve the readability of the web page.

Web Browser Settings
It is important to show students how to change the default web browser setting for fonts, font sizes, and styles when they will be reading passages on-line.

Windows Internet Explorer:
Step 1: Click to access the items in the *Tools Menu*
Step 2: Select *Internet Options* from the items in the *Tools Menu*
Step 3: Click the *General Tab* and under *Appearance* you will find the *Default Fonts Menu*

Macintosh Firefox Settings:
Step #1: From the *Firefox Menu* in the top left corner select *Preferences*
Step #2: From the *Preferences* menu select the *Content Tab*
Step #3: Make changes to the default web browser fonts in this menu

Learn the settings for the web browsers your students are using and have them add these settings to their planners, class notes, or on-line discussion forums. Students can even text the settings to each other for saving on their cell phones so that they have the preferred reader settings for their web browser anytime, anywhere.

Online Readers Become Text Critiques

Student readers in the 21st century are reading content that is targeted to a wide audience with different reading levels. This requires a repertoire of skills that include interpreting visual clues and processing nonlinear ideas. Many teachers are still teaching reading using only traditional texts, applying teaching methods they were taught prior to the influx of on-line reading and digital text. Billmeyer (2006a) identifies four traits of strategic readers: **code breaker, meaning maker, text user, and text critic.** It is critical that these be taught to online text readers.

In addition to the traditionally code breaking tools such as using surrounding words and images on the page, students should be taught assistive tools available with on-line text such as right clicking a word to activate built in dictionaries, word look-up in Google, and accessing a thesaurus. Many computers also have text to speech features that allow students to hear words spoken for correct pronunciation. Turn on audio accessibility features with these links:

- Microsoft accessibility features: http://www.microsoft.com/enable/
- Apple accessibility features: http://www.apple.com/accessibility/

Meaning making, text user, and text critique skills can take on a new dimension when viewing through the lens of 21st Century Skills. Introducing a classroom blog for reading reflection and comments will promote making meaning from the text and text critiquing. Students who may not be willing to raise their hand in class or write three paragraphs summarizing the text will process their reading by commenting on a classmates blog or defend their interpretation of the text that was read on a class discussion board. Below are two **free** education sites that allow teachers to create a classroom blog site for reading reflection:

- EduBlog: http://edublogs.org/
- Blogger: http://www.blogger.com/

Strategies to Extend Strategic Reading for 21st Century Learners

The **Word Sift** (Wientjes, 2010) before reading strategy will activate prior knowledge, familiarize students with key vocabulary terms, help students become familiar with the text and generate questions about the reading.

Step 1: Have students copy and paste the on-line text they are about to read into the URL address field on the web site http://www.wordsift.com.

Step 2: Once the text is pasted into the rectangle, have the students click the "SIFT" button.

Step 3: The text is "sifted" with the most used words showing up larger and the once-used words showing up much smaller. Words can be sorted from common to rare or rare to common.

Step 4: A visual thesaurus is available on the page. When students click on a word in the sifted work area, a visual thesaurus allows them to explore synonymous words.

Step 5: As students highlight words in the text by clicking on them, pictures and images are made available at the bottom of the screen to visually represent the word.

Step 6: Students can click on the "Create Workspace" button to drag words and pictures together forming a visual picture of the text they will be reading.

This pre-reading strategy allows students to visually picture the text they will be reading, aids in vocabulary development, and visually brings key concepts that will be covered to the students' attention using larger print.

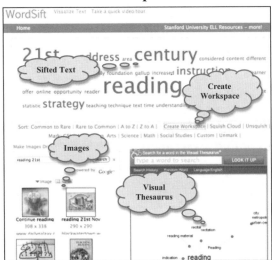

Screen capture of the WordSift web site with descriptors for the page layout.

RGB Notetaking (McKenzie, 1998) strategy works great for note taking and processing on-line text. The idea presented below reflects "my spin" on the original idea.

Rule 1: All information/notes from on-line reading is pasted into a word processing document (such as Microsoft Word)—pictures, text, and other entries.

Rule 2: Students may copy as much as they want from their online reading but it always goes in **"black ink."**

Rule 3: The entire web address of the on-line text must be "pasted" into a word processing document page in **"red ink."**

Rule 4: For every paragraph of **"black ink"** that students copy, they must write at least one original sentence in their own words with **"green ink"** that captures the main idea presented.

Rule 5: Only the **"green ink"** becomes a part of the students' writing or project.

Rule 6: All **"red ink"** becomes a list of resources cited.

Following the above rules for notetaking and processing text, students may use the "green text" (green signifying new growth) for their projects.

Conclusions: Implementing an Integrated Approach

Teaching reading to 21st Century readers requires an understanding of the 21st Century Framework and the incorporation of technology tools into the strategic reading process. Understanding the 21st Century Framework and how it "fits" with teaching strategic readers allows teachers to address on-line reading, as well as assist students in their efforts to find meaning from text in all areas of instruction.

Strategic Reading in Art
Authors, Cindy Cronn and C. J. Potter

Rationale

The integration of reading with art may seem a new idea to some, but in reality this concept is anything but new. Imagine if you will, the first time a human being picked up a tool – perhaps it was piece of charcoal or simply a stick lying in the sand—and made a mark with it. We can almost be certain that it gave him or her pleasure, and that s/he did it again and again—playfully, at first, but eventually with a sense of purpose. In time it surely would have become apparent that these marks could create patterns or designs… and then shapes. We could venture to guess that the first *shape* was a circle, since we know this is an important step in a child's development in the "scribble stage." Art is communication. Strategic reading in art involves *uncovering* the deep understandings that are foundational to the human creative experience, as well as the content understandings of the visual arts.

Creating marks and shapes that have meaning attached is writing, is it not? And when one person understands the meaning in the marks and shapes that another has made, that, of course, is what we call reading. In our classrooms today the natural connections to be made between reading, writing, and art are too valuable to ignore. Comprehension in reading can be broadened by using art in the process, and likewise, giving students opportunities to strengthen their reading skills will enhance their learning in art. Chapter 3 states that, "A Strategic Reader works actively to construct meaning" (p. 3). In relation to **the arts** this means *constructing meaning* about the creation, criticism, and analysis of the artistic process.

Issues and Nuances When Reading in Art

Comprehension is, after all, the key to learning in *every* subject. If we are to teach young artists to create art that expresses ideas or feelings articulately, we must also teach them to comprehend the meaning to be found in works of art made by others. The critical process (describing, analyzing, and interpreting works of art) is itself a form of reading.

Reading in the traditional sense of the word is a necessary part of learning in art; every discipline has a vocabulary that is content based. Art vocabulary goes beyond knowing the elements of art and the principles of design; it must include multilevel concepts such as "perspective" and others as specific as "graffito" or "intaglio." But art teachers have an edge, if we only will use it! When students are intrigued by a work of art or a particular style or culture, it becomes natural for them to want to know more about the person or people who created the work, the process that was used, and where the ideas for this piece came from. We have the wonderful advantage of being able to *entice* students to read — to present "opportunities" instead of merely assignments.

Doubtful? Picture the expressions on the faces of art students when you send them out with a list of terms to define and memorize for tomorrow's quiz. Now compare that to the expression on the faces of those who have just seen reproductions of pots made by Maria Martinez. Can you imagine a pottery class where no one would say, "How did she *do* that?" A perfect follow up statement is, "I'm so glad you asked, we'll find the answers to your questions in a reading about Maria Martinez. You'll find words like matte finish, burnishing, pueblo, and traditional motifs that will help you understand how she did that."

Viewing a work of art without considering its conception, creation, and analysis is like moving one's eyes across a page to merely read words. Without comprehension, the act is meaningless. Reading about art can be a wonderful opportunity to immerse students in independent reading. Artist journals, narratives about patrons of the arts, art history texts, news articles about current events related to the arts, as well as artistic criticism/ analysis provide learners with multiple entry points into the artistic process.

Learner Considerations

What does the **Reader** /art student bring to the learning experience? The answer to this question, in every case, is *a great deal*. The problem is how to find out what this means for each student; it's not the same for any two students. Having a frequently changed display of art in the room provides opportunities for students to study and comment on what they see. A poster featuring Klaus Oldenburg's giant *Baseball Bat* or Luis Jimenez's *Vaquero*, or one of Arcimboldo's faces made of fruits and vegetables does more to get students talking about art than the traditional portraits and still life paintings we often see. A single piece of paper with no more than a half dozen questions can be placed alongside the reproduction, (large, bold print with lots of white space) challenging the viewer to find out more (about why a giant baseball bat is standing up on the street in Chicago, or what Arcimboldo could have been *thinking* when he plastered a king's face with fruit and vegetables!). Add a reference at the bottom so students can explore answers to these questions. Art, like reading, is about making meaning from visual cues.

The use of journals/sketchbooks provides artists with an important tool that is authentically used "in the field." Documentation of ideas, collection of inspiring words or images, as well as artistic processes can be "captured" in journals. A teacher in a 9th grade Humanities class displays excerpts of her students' journals on the wall and begins class with a quote that is attributed to a young artist.

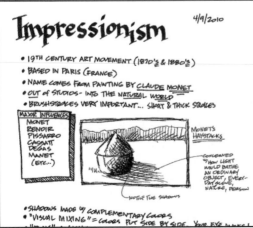

A sampling from a student's journal to document reading connections.

Text Considerations

Text structure is an important element of reading. Perhaps more than in any other discipline, it is important in art class for the teacher to *guide* students in their reading assignments – to identify key vocabulary words, to point out how the headings are the key to what information is included, to focus on illustrations, and to link predictions to those illustrations before reading. Why is this so important? Partly because students *expect* reading assignments in their other classes; they thought art was about making and doing…so you may need to change attitudes. Also, there is your own need to have students *get* the needed information so they can succeed in the projects and discussions that are vital to objectives in art. A myriad of text features (photos, captions, tables, labels, maps) are found in the reading associated with art history; they should be used to help readers construct meaning, read to learn, and become increasingly independent readers.

Teacher Considerations/Instructional Practices

In Chapter 3 a *traditional reading format* was compared with a *strategic reading format*. This model can be extended to provide the *art reader* with foci before, during, and after reading purposes. Instructional planning can stem from the strategic reading format (Figure 7); this model provides purpose for reading and learning, as well as encourages thinking before, during, and after learning.

Strategic Reading Format for Art

Thinking Phase	Type of Thinking
Before Reading Focus	• Access prior knowledge • Set purpose for reading • Determine how this art/ work or creative process relates to what we previously studied
During Reading Focus	• Question the intent of the artist • Validate notions • Look inside the creative process/divergent thinking process • Compare illustrations with informative text
After Reading Focus	• Articulate understandings • Analyze how work "fits into" history/ time period • Organize schema

Figure 7

The strategic reading format for art provides a structure for designing lessons and activities that can engage students in meaningful reading experiences to learn about the world of art. It is through planning and purposeful reading that teachers help young artists be practitioners, critics, or designers, and to understand the work of other artists. What follows are a variety of strategies that emphasize all three reading phases as well as different reading skills teachers can use to create strategic readers in art.

Reading Lenses - To engage readers before reading, teachers can use a **Reading Lens** (Figure 8) approach; students are provided with a purpose for reading and questions to keep them focused. For example, an entire class may be reading about Michelangelo and his body of work, yet students may choose one of the following "lenses" for analyzing the text.

Lens	Purpose for Reading	Focus Questions for Lens
The Artist	Analyze the process that Michelangelo went through to decide if this project/ commission would be artistically, financially, and socially feasible.	• Does this project further my body of work? • How do I decide if I can do this commissioned piece of work? • Is art still art if I sell it?
Patron of the Arts	Articulate reasons that this work should / should not be purchased by an individual, community, or institution. Study the ways in which those with financial wealth support the arts. Prioritize works of art that you would support through your purchase or donation.	• Can this work become part of history with my help? • What art is worth preserving? • Can thoughts and ideas be communicated through the arts? Can my purchase benefit others?
Community Member	Distinguish between art and design. View projects that could be become part of the community (for examples, displayed in public places, museums, sculptures, architecture).	• What is art? • Is there a difference between functional art (architecture, for example) and art "for arts sake"?

Figure 8

Read and Respond: Students not only need to view pieces of art but also must read about the work of art and the artist to fully appreciate the masterpiece. The following read and respond format encourages meaningful interactions between the reader and the work of art and the text:

- Read and/or listen to text related to art.
- View the art.
- Make meaningful connections related to the art form.
- Write individual responses about the information shared and the art form.

An example might be a quote from Vincent van Gogh's letters to Theo or a few lines of comment on Picasso's *Guernica,* followed by a question such as "Have you ever had feelings similar to this?" or "What image in this painting is most disturbing to you?" or "What was Picasso's purpose in creating an ugly painting?"

News Corner: Devote a small section of bulletin board, chalkboard, or wall (perhaps near the door to the classroom) to display magazine and newspaper articles about artists and art-related topics. Most major newspapers carry articles weekly about exhibit openings, museum events, and such. Make the display eye-catching so students will stop to take a look and make casual comments about events or articles, hopefully leading to students' interest in reading.

Strategies to Extend Strategic Reading in Art

Effective reading strategies in art range from a short verbal outline of what students should look for in the assigned passages to informational paragraph frames, and graphic organizers. Instructional strategies help students construct meaning as they read and sort out the most important points.

Graphic Organizers help the reader focus on, analyze, and think about the necessary information (for examples of graphic organizers, see p. 77). After reading about art from two different movements, a student could use a Venn diagram to record the similarities and differences found. Graphic organizers work well as note-taking devices when introducing key concepts. Students might assist in filling in information on a white board or chart paper, or an organizer could be given to students to use in taking notes when reading an assignment.

A **Concept Map** is another form of graphic organizer; it highlights the important ideas about a specific concept by listing examples. The concept map organizer in this case highlights broad concepts under study.

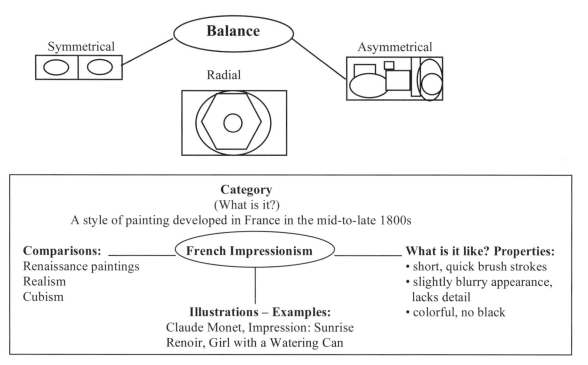

Examples of concept maps for Balance and French Impressionism.

Vocabulary development is critical to creating strategic readers; it is also a huge part of teaching art effectively, yet is often overlooked in the interest of time for hands-on art production. To benefit from reading assignments, to appreciate and find meaning in the works of artists, or to participate in discussions on art issues, students must have the vocabulary at their disposal. Effective vocabulary strategies for art are Frayer Model and Word Walls.

The **Frayer Model** (Frayer, Frederick, Klausmeier, 1969) causes the reader to focus on definition, characteristics, examples, and non-examples of the concept being studied. Students can use the form as a note-taking device when reading about an art movement or historic period. The Frayer Model can also be used to analyze group thinking after viewing reproductions of works. The Frayer Model can be completed on an overhead or chart paper. This model can be easily modified (using technology) to differentiate for high readiness learners, as well as to provide different points of view for reading.

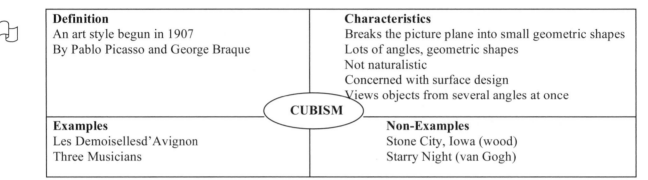

Definition	Characteristics
An art style begun in 1907	Breaks the picture plane into small geometric shapes
By Pablo Picasso and George Braque	Lots of angles, geometric shapes
	Not naturalistic
	Concerned with surface design
	Views objects from several angles at once
	CUBISM
Examples	**Non-Examples**
Les Demoisellesd'Avignon	Stone City, Iowa (wood)
Three Musicians	Starry Night (van Gogh)

Example of a Frayer Model for the concept of Cubism.

Conclusions: Implementing an Integrated Approach

The very definition of "strategic" implies that planning and foresight are involved. Yet we as teachers are sometimes guilty of trying a little of this and a little of that, and then – not surprisingly – finding that the so-called strategies we heard about didn't have a great effect on student learning. Used systematically (*strategically*), however, they will become part of the routine of your classroom and be seen as a useful learning tool by students. The goal is to have readers use these strategies independently and when reading is not directed by others.

It is extremely important that art teachers begin the year with strategic reading processes, introducing them gradually as they become appropriate. They need to be seen as "the way things are done" in this class. Graphic organizers can be a normal part of presenting lesson material and of students' assignments. Using the word "reflection" in conversations about art encourages students to be introspective. Encourage students to contribute to the News Corner or suggest topics to examine briefly in Read and Respond assignments.

Comprehension is foundational to the creative process, and when we have students engage in the arts we give them an invitation to be strategic readers - and to uncover connections to a brand new way of thinking.

Strategic Reading in Career and Technical Education
Authors, Shawna Gareau-Kurtz, Deb Schwartz, and Lindsey Post

Rationale

Reading is a critical skill for Career and Technical Education (CTE) students, many who go on to employment or technical colleges. Our students find that as technology changes, they need to read to remain current in their profession. In CTE, the vocabulary encountered is often unfamiliar because of its technical nature. Therefore, in addition to teaching the hands-on skills that students need to succeed on the job, today's CTE teachers also need to equip students with reading strategies to comprehend the complicated texts, concepts, and vocabulary of a particular trade or career.

Issues and Nuances When Reading in Career & Technical Education

The International Center for Leadership in Education conducted a study showing that a large number of entry-level jobs have higher reading requirements than those required for high school graduation. The real world requires substantially higher reading proficiency levels than most students possess (Daggett, 2004). The most critical skill needed as a technician is technical reading.

When integrating strategic reading into CTE, it is important whenever possible to select materials at the correct reading level. In order to keep current with their career area, students are expected to read technical manuals, trade journals and newspapers. Typically, such sources are written at a higher level than many students are able to read independently. As a result, strategy instruction is critical.

Learner Considerations

Students enroll in CTE for a number of reasons. Some are interested in the business world and in becoming successful whether as a cosmetologist or an entrepreneur. Others choose technical education because their aptitudes lie in the area of applied science…they are hands-on people. No matter what their motivation for entering the field, students find that once they get there, their learning has only begun. Teaching students how to read, understand, and interpret information as it applies to careers and technology is not only appropriate but essential. These skills determine students' future success.

Text Considerations

There are many considerations when looking at text for students in CTE. Of all of the factors that affect student success in reading and understanding a text, readability should be considered first. Readability includes the physical aspects of the text and the complexity of words and sentences in relationship to the reading ability of the reader (Johnson, 1998). There are several online sites that can help you determine the readability level of your students' texts. Using a variety of leveled texts, if available or a variety of articles at different levels can help students who are not equipped with strategies for determining meaning. This is where reading strategies can be introduced to help students make meaning out of difficult texts. Students benefit from a "toolbox of strategies" for reading.

An important understanding for CTE students is the difference between informative and narrative text. Informative, "real-world," factual texts such as the newspaper, trade-related articles, and technical manuals are primary texts for students in CTE. While narrative (story) selections are read in their entirety from beginning to end, informative texts are frequently read selectively. We typically read the parts that are of interest or meet our needs (Duke, 2004). For this reason, students should be taught to preview their textbooks to determine what information is of importance. In addition, the content should be up-to-date, have vocabulary that is easily understood and defined, and have reading and writing intertwined within the suggested activities.

Teacher Considerations

The CTE teacher's role is to teach students how to utilize resources just as they would in the workplace. Since we cannot possibly teach students everything that they need to know about their careers, students should be able to locate information efficiently and use it for a purpose — to solve a problem or troubleshoot. If teachers can provide students with the tools to read through complex technical material and locate information, they will create independent, life-long readers.

In order to help students practice these skills, Career and Technical teachers might consider creating situations or problems that require students to find information. Instead of giving students the answers as they hit stumbling blocks, teachers should model where to go to find the information they need to solve the problem. For example, when teaching students about tables in a word processing application, start by teaching concepts about raw data and how data is more useful when it is organized in some fashion. Give students some raw data or have them collect it and organize it into a draft table. Once they have learned this "big idea," they can teach themselves the table-making actions by looking in their computer manuals, by using "Help," or by using the wizards that are built into the program.

Instructional Practices

Am I an *English* teacher? Five years ago, this is the question that we heard so many of our CTE teachers asking. Career and Technical Educators now see the importance of teaching *literacy* skills to help students learn their course content. We understand the differences between teaching English and teaching students to be more strategic users of our course content. Welding teacher Michele Robbins says, "Finding ways for literacy strategies to appear seamless and support the content, not add to the coursework students already struggle with, is the biggest challenge."

Historically CTE has been thought of as the place to teach students the technical "hands-on" skills needed to be successful in the workplace. Over the past decade CTE has changed. The workplace is telling us that if students can "read to learn" they will be more successful in the 21st century. The *transferrable* skills of being a strategic reader are the tools that will allow students in Career and Technical fields to adapt to changes in our industries. Teachers need to give CTE students the *tools* they need to be independent readers who are able to use data to interpret messages from coworkers and customers, follow instructions, complete procedures, make decisions, and solve problems.

When you teach students to be strategic readers of text the quality of learning, understanding, and application of the content will increase. Therefore it is imperative that we analyze our curriculum to determine what is essential, focusing on those skills that will transfer to the workplace and to life. This is a challenge for CTE with industry standards that require a great deal of technical knowledge and skills to be integrated into our curriculums. We need to decide what the essential exit skills are and focus on teaching those well instead of covering every page of our textbook.

Strategies to Extend Reading in Career & Technical Education

Teaching literacy is equivalent to good teaching. All CTE teachers should be asking themselves the questions, "What are my essential objectives? "How will I engage my students in this material?" We want our students to know how to locate, read, and interpret text to access information.

The text we encounter in CTE classes relies heavily on charts and graphs to convey meaning to its readers. In Walt Burrows Information Technology Essentials class, he begins a lesson on reading a chart of Wireless Ethernet Standards from CISCO Networking Academy with a previewing task to get students to notice certain features about the chart (code breaking) such as the chart title, the column and row headings, symbols, and abbreviations.

Wireless Ethernet Standards

	Bandwidth	Frequency	Range	Interoperability
802.11a	Up to 54 Mbps	5 GHz band	100 feet (30 meters)	Not interoperable with 802.11b, 802.11g, or 802.11n
802.11b	Up to 11 Mbps	2.4 GHz band	100 feet (30 meters)	Interoperable with 802.11g
802.11g	Up to 54 Mbps	2.4 GHz band	100 feet (30 meters)	Interoperable with 802.11b
802.11n (Pre-standard)	Up to 540 Mbps	2.4 GHz band	164 feet (50 meters)	Interoperable with 802.11b and 802.11g
802.15.1 Bluetooth	Up to 2 Mbps	2.4 GHz band or 5 GHz band	30 feet (10 meters)	Not interoperable with any other 802.11

Example of a chart used in an Information Technology course.

He also asks them to preview the vocabulary in the chart by listing words that they have never heard, that they've heard but cannot define, and words that they know. As students read the chart, Mr. Burrows asks them to text-tag by underlining words and abbreviations that they know and annotating definitions in the margins,

Previewing Content Vocabulary

I've never heard these words or abbreviations:
I've heard these words but don't know what they mean:
I know what these words mean:

Example of an organizer for previewing content vocabulary.

and making a question mark by words and/or abbreviations that they do not know and creating questions in the margins about these terms (meaning-maker).

After they text-tag the chart, Mr. Burrows reviews some of the words/abbreviations the students already know, fills in some of the missing definitions, and clears up misunderstandings. To assess, Mr. Burrows presents a simulated problem that requires students to apply the information found in the chart to a real-world application. They might be asked to demonstrate their knowledge and understanding of the charts' application by describing which protocol they would have to use when designing a network with a given bandwidth (text-user).

PREVIEWING Electrode VOCABULARY

Based on the title, list the words I would expect to read in this chapter

SMAW	**F1, F2, F3, F4**
Electrodes	**flux**
Ground	**Vertical**
Position	

I've never heard the word . . . Put a line through
I know the word . . . Circle
I've heard the word, but I don't know what it means . . . Underline it

Vocabulary

Groups	Groove welds	Iron-powder-based fluxes
F1	Fillet welds	Position
F2	Root welds	Flat
F3	Weld beads	Overhead
F4	High deposition	Horizontal
Medium penetration	Cellulose based fluxes	Vertical
Low penetration	Rutile-based fluxes	Slag
High penetration	Mineral-based fluxes	Polarities

Another example of before, during, and after reading occurs in Michele Robbins Welding classroom. Ms. Robbins selects one and a half pages of text on "electrode selection." Before they read the text, the students are asked to look at the title and list words that they might expect to see in the reading. They are then given a teacher-created list of vocabulary words that will be found in the excerpt. The students are asked to put a line through the words that they have never heard of, circle the words that they already know, and underline the words that they have heard of but cannot define.

As the students read the text, Ms. Robbins asks them to **text-tag** using "X Marks the Spot," to help make meaning (Stephens and Brown, 2005).

X means "*I've found a key point.*" **!** means "*I've found some interesting, new information.*" **?** means "*This is confusing; I have a question about what it means.*"

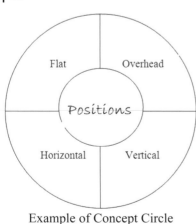

Example of Concept Circle connecting vocabulary about welding positions.

After they've read and text-tagged, Ms. Robbins uses **Concept Circles** (Allen, 2007) to help them make connections. She gives them a box to insert a key word or phrase to help them find the connection and asks them to write about what each word means in relationship to the concept word. They then link the words to each other while circling and connecting to the overall concept. The example shows how one student connected the welding positions that he read about in the text.

Students in trade classes often have a high level of interest in the content area. CTE teachers can use this to their advantage by teaching new strategies in conjunction with high-interest texts. Consider the example of an Automotive Collision Repair class learning about the difference between aftermarket parts and original equipment manufacturer (OEM) parts. Students might have a vague opinion on this often-debated issue, but they probably have not done any independent research on the subject.

Before reading about this debate, the use of an **Anticipation Guide** helps to clarify students' preconceptions about the topic. By evaluating whether they agree or disagree with a series of statements, students are primed to be "meaning makers" as they read text that challenges their prior knowledge of the debate.

Anticipation Guide: Aftermarket Parts vs. OEMs

Before Reading: Check One		Example Statements	**After** Reading: Check One	
Agree	Disagree		Agree	Disagree
		Aftermarket parts are just as safe and effective as original equipment manufacturer OEM parts.		
		The customer has the right to know whether an aftermarket part or an OEM part is being used in his/her car repair.		
		It is OK for insurance companies to push for the use of aftermarket parts if it saves the customer some money.		

Example of an Anticipation Guide used in an Automotive Collision class.

Once students have accessed prior knowledge on the topic, they are ready to look at new reading material. Dan Boyler, Joe Alati, and Eric DiGiulio, CTE teachers use a series of short articles to get students to examine both sides of the issue. They support their students in being strategic readers by having them apply the **Text Tagging** strategy (Billmeyer, 2006b). Some of the articles are clearly in favor of the use of aftermarket parts, some are clearly against, and some show both sides of the issue. Students might take notes in the margins to "hold onto their thinking" (Tovani, 2004). Or, they might use a simple coding system to label key ideas. Either way, the purpose for reading is clear to students before the reading begins. They know what they are looking for in the text and how to respond when they find it.

Symbol	Meaning
+	*In favor of the use of aftermarket parts*
-	*Against the use of aftermarket parts*
?	*I don't understand what the author is saying here*
!	*This causes me to change my mind about one of my answers on the anticipation guide*

Example of coding key ideas in articles or text.

The final part of this series asks students to become "Text Users" and "Text Critics." One way to do this with a pro/con topic is to have students synthesize what they have learned by participating in a formal debate. Preparation for the debate includes returning to the anticipation guide and completing the "After Reading" column. Students should evaluate whether their opinions have changed and why. They will also need to evaluate the sources they read in order to determine which articles were the most convincing, which seemed to include a hidden agenda, and which make weak arguments. Additional preparation for a debate might include completing a position statement with points of evidence from the text. As students become Text Critics, a debate is the perfect format for developing the attribute of "expressing opinions using supporting ideas."

The ultimate purpose for conducting a debate is to prepare students to conduct a well-informed, thoughtful conversation with a customer about the benefits and drawbacks of aftermarket parts. Being able to perform in a classroom is important, but being able to be a successful "Text User" in a live shop with customers who depend on your knowledge is a huge incentive to students. The authentic audience they will be facing in a few years motivates them to use a combination of strategies while reading to learn.

The field of Family and Consumer Science, like many other CTE classes, focuses heavily on process-based and step-by-step tasks. Texts such as recipes ask students to break down a job into smaller parts that must be followed with a degree of precision. The vocabulary in such texts is highly specialized and is often the 'make or break' factor for students in determining whether the text is interesting or frustrating and particularly whether the product edible. Therefore, vocabulary instruction is an ideal before reading task when supporting students with the "Code Breaker" stage of reading comprehension.

A simple recipe for a Fresh Berry Tart might include a dozen or more vocabulary words that are either unfamiliar to students, or are familiar only in a different context. Students who have limited experience with baking might assume that "flute" refers to a musical instrument instead of the shape of a piecrust, for example. Using a **Categories and Labels** strategy (Allen, 2007) students try to sort words according to their type in order to get a broader picture of the word's context. The dictionary definition of the word is not yet important; the goal is to start building a map of relationships among words to increase comprehension. Research shows that identifying similarities and differences in this way has the highest effect size on achievement gains among a group of nine instructional strategies (Marzano, 2001). Students come up with the category names independently and place the words into columns according to those categories.

Vocabulary Words		
scant	das	strain
level	preserves	currant
flute	hull	invert
Category Name: **Measuring**	Category Name: **Action to take**	Category Name: **Ingredients**
scant	*flute*	*preserves*
dash	*hull*	*currant*
level	*invert*	
	strain	

Example of an organizer for categorizing and labeling vocabulary.

While reading the recipe, students should work together to locate the vocabulary words and define them based on context clues. The strategic reading attribute of "learning new meanings for known words" is especially relevant here as students realize that a "dash" is not a race in this context, and "preserve" acts as a noun instead of a verb. When helping students become aware of context clues, model the following:

- Determine the part of speech of the unknown word (verb, noun, adjective) by reading the sentences aloud
- Examine the words right before and right after the unknown word for clues to its meaning
- Pay attention to prefixes and suffixes in the unknown word
- Check to see if an example of the word is given later (It might become clear what "preserves" are if the recipe suggests strawberry preserves.)

Students are almost ready to tackle the recipe. In order to check for understanding and support students further in becoming "Text Users," the teacher might have students summarize the new information by completing a process flow chart. If students can explain what they have read in their own words, they are ready to apply a new skill/idea that came from a challenging text. A flow chart would not only create a visual of the recipe but would also allow students to review their newly learned vocabulary words. Once students have mastered the vocabulary of a new recipe and have used comprehension strategies to "see" the process, they are set up for success in applying what they have learned.

Conclusions: Implementing an Integrated Approach

Teachers who create a long-range literacy plan using instructional strategies will produce strategic readers and learners. Essential components of a long-range plan for strategic reading include:

- Providing opportunities for students to interact with text
- Exposing students to a variety of technical resources
- Determining the essential curriculum concepts and skills
- Providing reading materials at varied reading levels
- Creating a literacy-rich environment
- Teaching strategies that will help students be life-long learners

The ultimate goal is to provide CTE students with the tools needed to be successful in the workplace. Our information-based society demands high reading proficiency levels. Teaching reading strategies in CTE is an effective way of raising literacy levels of students not only in the classroom but in the real world as well. One of the greatest gifts teachers can give students is the ability to comprehend and apply the content area material they read and the ability to transfer knowledge and skills to future learning.

Strategic Reading in English/Language Arts

Author, Cheryl Becker Dobbertin

Rationale

Perhaps more than any other content area, English/Language Arts (ELA) teachers need their students to be proficient and confident readers. Our most fervent hope is that our students come to discover what we have discovered, that reading opens countless doors, that the whole world is available within the pages of books. Perhaps you made these discoveries on your own. Maybe you were such a good reader from the beginning that you "automatically" brought a wealth of prior knowledge and an active, thinking reading style to your more challenging texts. But not all of our students are like that. If we truly want to give them the gift of great books, we have to help them understand more about the way reading works.

Teaching reading in ELA makes it possible for students to tackle and enjoy *Macbeth* without having to depend on the teacher for translation. It makes it possible to recapture students who can read but may be choosing not to. Teaching reading in ELA makes it possible for students who have never enjoyed a book to take that first step toward life-long literacy.

Issues and Nuances When Reading in English/Language Arts

As students move through the grades, it becomes increasingly likely that they will be asked to read a book in ELA class that they have not chosen themselves and/or that may be too difficult for them. In chapter 3, a Strategic Reader is defined as one who works actively to construct meaning, is independent, and reads to learn. ELA teachers are especially suited to creating the conditions through which strategic readers can be developed. We can use strategies to make sure students thoughtfully engage in before, during, and after reading experiences that will help them to become interested and active readers. Consider this example. Students in a fifth grade ELA class are working with the novel *Tuck Everlasting* by Natalie Babbitt. The teacher wants students to discuss their reading, but finds that they are only sharing the answers to the comprehension questions in the study guide she's designed. Then the teacher remembers a new strategy she recently heard about – **Save the Last Word for Me** (Vaughan and Estes, 1986).

The teacher shakes up her classroom by asking her students to read not to answer the questions in their study guides (in fact, she doesn't assign the study guide with the next chunk of reading), but with the goal of being able to talk with their friends about their reactions to and questions about the Tuck family's unusual circumstances. She asks students to put a sticky note in their books at the place where they find something they want to talk about, suggesting that students "stick" places where they are surprised or intrigued, where they are confused, or where they see that author Natalie Babbitt has written a passage in a way that helps the reader understand the Tuck family's perspective.

After students finish their assigned reading and "sticky note sticking," the teacher shows her students the places that *she's* marked in her copy of the book, then models for students how she transfers small but significant sections of her marked passages onto 3 x 5 cards. She asks the students to write a sentence or two from the part they indicated with their sticky notes on 3 x 5 cards. Then the teacher models how she recorded her own questions and reactions to the passages she's selected on the back of her 3 x 5 cards, and asks her students to do the same. The teacher collects the cards to check her students' comprehension of their reading.

The next day, the teacher assigns her students to small groups, strategically putting students together who seem to have similar ideas that they want to discuss or question. She returns the cards to the students and puts the directions for the discussion activity up on the overhead:

- One person keeps time and another makes sure the group stays focused.
- Everyone needs to pick out one card that you think will be interesting to your group.
- Your group needs a volunteer to go first. The volunteer shares ONLY the passage from the book (the front of the card) – NOT his or her reaction on the back (yet!). After the volunteer tells his/her passage, that person has to keep quiet for awhile!
- All group members have a conversation about the passage that was read by the volunteer. Each group member must participate. This conversation should last at least two minutes.
- When all group members have said something, the volunteer who offered the passage can say what he/she wrote on the back on the card. That's the "last word" on that passage.
- Another person then shares a passage from his/her card and the group follows the process above until all group members have had the chance to offer a passage for discussion and have "the last word."

The teacher meets with a small group of students who seem to be confused about the text or had a difficult time selecting passages for their 3 x 5 cards while the rest of the class works in their small groups. The teacher is very pleased to see most of her students engaged in animated conversation while she has the opportunity to work more directly with the smaller group not yet ready for independent conversation. As the lesson closes, the teacher asks her students to tell her what they did to make the discussion work well in their groups. She and the class develop an anchor chart of the "Good Practices in Group Discussion" such as "pick something that's important to talk about (not little things, but big things) and "listen to what the people say so you can add on."

In subsequent lessons, the teacher increases the amount of time students are expected to discuss to four minutes and notices that her students get better and better at selecting passages worthy of discussion. By employing the Save the Last Word strategy, this teacher has greatly increased meaningful student engagement.

Learner Considerations

One of the first big "ahas" I had as a secondary English teacher is what, exactly, reading *is*. I used to think that if I could hear students saying the words aloud, and they said them right, then they were reading. Kids who stumbled over words or read without inflection were poor readers; kids who read fluently aloud were good readers. While there's some truth in that statement, I quickly came to the realization that plenty of students who could say the words had no idea what they were reading. At the same time, some of the students who were struggling with the words were able to insightfully interpret and analyze. I began to realize that becoming literate is not a linear process – first you say the words, then you think about their meaning, then you write – but an interrelated, circuitous process.

I began to learn more about what happens in the brain as a strategic reader reads. In *Capturing All of the Reader Through the Reading Assessment System* (2006a) Billmeyer describes the attributes of a strategic reader (see p. 34). Yes, good readers "decode the words, recognize the genre and make use of symbols, patterns, and text features." But they do much more. They "reflect on their own processing skills while reading." They "monitor understanding before, during, and after reading." Strategic readers are active thinkers.

What I began to realize was that my biggest challenge was **not** so much to teach my students how to get words off of the page but to teach them to *think about* those words and do something important with them, to really engage in "meaning-making and meaning-using." Ultimately I came to the following conclusions:

What "assigning reading" looks like.	What "teaching reading" looks like.
• Text is chosen for the reader based on external criteria (from a list or curriculum). • The amount of reading to be completed in a certain time period is pre-determined by the teacher and is designed to move students through the reading in an orderly fashion. • Student is expected to do the bulk of his or her read independently, often outside of school. • The student is expected to "get" the meaning of text without any explicit strategy use. • Comprehension is measured through a series of questions, often pre-determined by the teacher. • Discussion and reflection are based on the teacher developed questions.	• Student chooses text and/or teacher chooses text based on reader's interests and/or reading level. • The amount of reading to be completed in a certain time period is based on what the student can do well. • Student completes the bulk of the reading with the support of a reading "coach" – his or her teacher during the school day. • Teacher models his/her thinking and the use of strategies so that students see what strategic readers do. • Comprehension is measured by collecting students' reactions and questions – prompted and collected through well-designed strategies. • Discussion/reflection involve both the meaning of the text and the effectiveness of strategies.

Text Considerations

Much of the text in ELA is pre-determined by district curriculum guides, often with certain novels assigned to particular grade levels. As our classrooms become increasingly heterogeneous, this presents a complex challenge. *The Scarlet Letter* may be the eleventh grade text, but there will undoubtedly be many students who do not read at an eleventh grade level. Depending on a district's policies, English teachers may or may not be able to, or even feel that they want to, move away from the assigned text. In these situations, it is the teachers' responsibility to recognize the difficulty of the text they are asking students to read and the mismatch between students' reading capacity and the level of the text. It's important for teachers to realize that when they make the choice to use text that's challenging for their readers, that they have created a learning scenario that won't necessarily develop all students' *reading skills*, but could help all students build *cultural knowledge*, depending on how students are supported.

When teachers make the choice to teach a book or short story because it is part of our common cultural knowledge, they must take the time to build students' background knowledge so that readers are better prepared to make connections and make meaning of the text. For example, students who understand the Jim Crow laws, school segregation, and the social class structure of the deep South during the Great Depression are better prepared to understand some of the more subtle racial overtones surrounding Calpurnia in *To Kill a Mockingbird*.

A terrific strategy for accessing, assessing, and building students' background knowledge is **Carousel Brainstorming** (Billmeyer, 2006b). In this strategy, small groups of students rotate around the room responding to questions or adding ideas to charts posted on the walls or centered on groups of desks. Each group uses its own color marker so the teacher can track which group contributed what thinking. To get students ready to read about the trial in *To Kill a Mockingbird*, for example, the teacher might post charts that say "lawyer," "jury," "judge," "defendant," "accuser," "innocent until proven guilty." Each group of students would start at one of the charts and are given 2 minutes to write everything they know about that idea. Then they rotate, read what was written on the chart by the previous group, and add *new* thinking to the chart for 2 minutes. With each rotation, students have to dig deeper into their background knowledge for new information, or "twists" on the information already stated. For example, students might start out writing "always true" on the "innocent until proven guilty" chart, but then additional groups might add "sometimes not true because people get falsely accused," and "also some judges are bad" – all key ideas that will come into play during Tom Robinson's trial.

Teacher Considerations/Instructional Practices

In an ELA classroom dedicated to developing strategic readers, the teacher's role changes from that of literature expert to that of process modeler, facilitator, and coach. Instead of assigning students to read and then checking their understanding through questioning or quizzes, the teacher plans for and provides a variety of before-, during-, and after-reading experiences that give all students both access to complex text and metacognitive awareness of effective reading strategies. There's a shift in focus in assessment as well. Students and teachers focus on how to make meaning rather than solely on if the "right" meaning was drawn from the text. Teachers and students engage in conversation not only about what is happening in the novel or other literature that they're reading, but how they are going about determining what's happening and what it means.

As described in chapter 3, strategic readers develop four traits and corresponding attributes. It is important that while developing instructional plans and selecting strategies that teachers balance their approach to ensure that students develop in all four ways – as "code breakers," as "meaning makers," as "text users," and as "text critics." Interestingly, these four reading traits are mirrored in some of the national standards of teaching ELA as developed by the National Council of Teachers of English (http://www.ncte.org/standards).

Helping Students become "Code Breakers" in English/Language Arts.
When Strategic Readers read silently or orally they decode the words, recognize the genre, and make use of the symbols, patterns, and text features. These acts build the foundation for comprehension.

The **Forecast** strategy (Billmeyer, 2006b) is one that English/Language Arts teachers can use regularly to help introduce students to new words and to prepare them to "break the code" of challenging text. A teacher used Forecast to prepare students to read *Out of the Dust* (Hesse, 2005). The teacher chose the words "desperate, grit, plowing, civil," and "riled." The teacher started with desperate, and posted the following on the board "d_ _ _ _ _ _ _ _" (9). Students were told they would be learning new words that had to do with the Dust Bowl, a time in America's history when many families suffered tremendously because great dust storms covered their homes and farmlands. "The families felt terrible, they didn't have anything to eat and their crops weren't growing, so they became very worried about what to do. What's a word that begins with "d" that means so worried you don't know what to do, so worried you almost give up hope?" The students conferred with each other and offered "downcast," "denied," and "desperate." The teacher asked the students to look at the number of spaces (9) and talk with each other about what the word might be. Hands went up all over the classroom – "desperate!" The teacher revealed all of the words this way, with some, like "riled," she had to give all of the letters and students still didn't know it; with others, like "plowing," the students got the word in three letters. After all of the words were revealed, the teacher asked the students to predict what they thought would happen in the first chapter of their new book. Then they read, looking for the new words and to confirm or deny their predictions about the first chapter.

Helping Students Become "Meaning Makers" in English/Language Arts.
Strategic Readers reflect on their own processing skills while reading. When

readers are aware of and use reading strategies, they are able to monitor their understanding before, during, and after reading.

One of the most powerful strategies in helping students become meaning makers is the "**Think-Aloud**" (Davey, 1983). When ELA teachers think-aloud, they are opening a window into their minds and letting students see inside. Students literally watch teachers make sense of text. Teachers are modeling the attributes of strategic readers – making connections, summarizing, drawing conclusions, and monitoring understanding – processes that are usually invisible to students. Rather than telling students what is known about a particular selection, teachers show students how they came to know. Here's an example.

> "So far, I know that these boys are trapped on this island and there is starting to be some trouble among them (modeling accessing prior knowledge). Last night I was thinking about *The Lord of the Flies* while I was watching *Survivor* on Television (making connections). It's interesting to think about how little societies are formed when people are together in unusual circumstances. You can see it happening on *Survivor* – how some people take on the leadership role, some are lazy. Anyway, I wonder if the producers of *Survivor* did any thinking about *The Lord of the Flies* when they designed the show? (asking questions). I'm going to keep trying to see parallels between the show and the book (setting purpose). (Continue reading.)

> (Stop reading to think-aloud.) "You know that little section seems to be telling me something (monitoring comprehension). I can see the child throwing the rocks – wanting to throw the rocks at the other kid but there's almost like an invisible force stopping him (visualizing). That force is civilization, all of those rules that we live by, even though our natural instincts are to do something else, something meaner (drawing conclusions). That's what Golding means by "parents and school and policemen and the law" (checking, adding support details). Those things are what keep us from becoming the crueler beings that we might be otherwise."

You might already do those things in front of your students, probably without thinking about it too much. But in a strategic classroom, the teacher does think about it and *is very purposeful in it*. There's a difference between talking with kids about a book and helping them see you using strategies – I would often stop my Think-Aloud and ask students to tell me what attributes of a strategic reader they saw me displaying. They would know how to label those attributes because we have discussed them and monitored them together.

Another important way to focus students on the process of strategic reading is by replacing traditional study guides with Strategic Reading Journals (Figure 9). Instead of answering teacher-designed questions to show comprehension and in order to practice important reading strategies, students ask their own questions prior to reading, keep track of their connections and reactions during reading, and summarize and evaluate after reading. I evaluate their journals using a scoring guide (Figure 10) that honors insightful thinking over "right answers."

Example

Name _____

Book _____ **pp.** _____ **to pp.** _____

Strategic Reading Journal: *Romeo and Juliet*

Before Reading:	So far in the play Romeo has been so silly and impulsive. He drops Roslyn after knowing Juliet for about two seconds. He doesn't really love Juliet, but she thinks he does. I think they are going to get into some kind of trouble because Romeo can't be trusted and Juliet is so swept away that she doesn't know it.
• Write down what you're trying to find out. • Brainstorm what you already know. • Predict what you thing will happen in this section. • Ask yourself a question.	

	Passages	Reactions
During Reading: • Mark the places in the text that jump out at you – you're surprised, you connect to the text or something you already know, you're confused – with a sticky note. • Jot on the sticky (if necessary so that you remember what your reaction was. • Copy the passages later (enough so that I can find what you're referring to). • Note your reactions, ideas, connections, questions, in the column next to the copied passage. — This reminds me of … — I was thinking about… — Now I know that … — That explains why …	"What's in a name? That which we call a rose by any other name would smell as sweet."	That's really true, but still, they can't pretend that it doesn't matter that their families hate each other. Their parents aren't going to let them be together. Also, I don't think that if you've been told you're supposed to hate someone your whole life that you can fall in love with that person just by looking at them.

After Reading:	They're getting married! That's so ridiculous! What is Shakespeare trying to say about love? Maybe he thinks that you can know right away. I just don't agree with that. Or maybe you're supposed to follow your heart no matter what your family or friends think that's a theme in other things we have read. I think that Romeo is just pressuring her so that he can get what he wants. Look at how fast he dumped Roslyn.
• Answer the question you asked yourself in the beginning. • Summarize what happened or key points in a paragraph or outline. • Tell why what happened is important.	

Figure 9

Strategic Reading Journal Scoring Guide

Criteria	Emerging Reader	Developing Reader	Engaging Reader	Expanding Reader
Before Reading • Sets or acknowledges purpose for reading • Makes predictions about the text • Brainstorms what is already known about the topic/genre • Develops guiding question(s)	You spent a small amount of time with pre-reading work.	Your pre-reading work is done, but it shows little planning for reading.	You complete pre-reading work well enough for me to see you actually put some thought into what you're about to read.	Your pre-reading work is insightful, detailed, and enables me to see your unique point of view on what you're about to read.
During Reading • Makes text-to-text, text-to-self, text-to-world connections • Reacts to ideas • Identifies tools the author is using to create the story • Asks questions • Monitors comprehension and uses strategies when necessary	Your work is too brief to show understanding. You select minor or trivial passages for comment/reaction/connection.	Your work in the response column shows a surface level reaction to the text. You identified something that confused you, but you don't tell me about how you got "unconfused." You can identify a literary element or technique but have trouble explaining the significance of it.	You select appropriate passages for comment/reaction/connection. Your work in the response column shows a clear reaction to the text. You have made a good attempt to identify and explain the significance of a literary element or technique.	You select significant passages for comment/reaction/connection. Your work in the response column shows an insightful reaction to the text. You have told me about something that confused you and how you got "unconfused." You have correctly identified and explained the significance of a literary element or technique.
After Reading • Clarifies understanding • Summarizes and/or generalizes about the reading • Reaches conclusions about the reading	Your post-reading work is too brief to show understanding.	Your post-reading work is done, but it reveals very little about what you "got" from this section of your book.	You complete post-reading work well enough for me to see you actually put some thought into what you read and why it's important.	Your post-reading work is insightful, detailed, and enables me to see your unique point of view on what you read.

Figure 10

Helping Students Become "Text Users" & "Text Critics" in English/ Language Arts

When Strategic Readers comprehend and interpret text, they apply their prior knowledge and skills to perform tasks. Strategic Readers also extend thinking when they evaluate what they have read by making critical, thoughtful judgments about the selection. The **Reading from Different Perspectives** strategy (Billmeyer, 2006a) is particularly effective in helping students shift perspectives and examine different points of view on events and characters. Students take on a certain perspective or role from which to examine and interpret an event or character. For example, readers might consider the death of Romeo and Juliet from a variety of perspectives (which may or may not be explicitly stated in the text): the Nurse, the Friar, the townspeople of Verona, and Mayor of Mantua (yes, I know he's not actually in the play – but for a strong student, it's a great abstract task to think about how a character not even present might react based on their background knowledge!). Students might be given a graphic organizer like this:

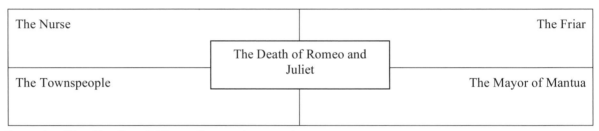

The Nurse		The Friar
	The Death of Romeo and Juliet	
The Townspeople		The Mayor of Mantua

Example of Reading from Different Perspective organizer.

Students would read the end of the tragedy, focusing specifically on how their chosen person (perspective) might or did react to the deaths of the young lovers. When students have completed their reading, inferring, and note taking, they would meet in mixed group perspectives to share their thinking, discussing why some characters might be sad, others guilt-ridden, and others relieved that perhaps the feud is over. Then the teacher might introduce a provocative question, which students would discuss from their chosen perspectives. In this case, students could be asked, "Could Romeo and Juliet's deaths be seen as a good thing?" The Nurse might express an adamant "no," but the townspeople might say "yes."

Special Considerations for Developing Readers (Response to Intervention)

Often teachers ask, "What strategies are most important for struggling readers to use in ELA?" The answer is at the same time both complicated and simple. The real key to helping struggling readers learn more about how to read well isn't simply a matter of choosing the right strategy for them to learn; it's the level of explicitness with which they learn it. All students benefit from being taught strategies to help them organize their thinking about text. Struggling readers benefit from learning not only about strategies, but the *thinking* that strategies help them develop.

Consider the following examples. In the "Tier 1" scenario, the teacher employs the **Summary Wheel** strategy (Billmeyer, 2006b) to help all students determine important ideas from non-fiction text. Note how in the "Tier 2" scenario the teacher goes much more deeply into the thinking students are expected to do.

Tier 1: Model and Cue For All Students	Tier 2: Demystify the Reading Process For Some Students
In Mr. Phelps' English class, he introduces students to the Summary Wheel as a way of collecting key facts from a non-fiction article about the Puritans they are reading in preparation for their study of The Crucible. He shows students the Summary Wheel graphic organizer, as well as a completed model. He reads a brief section of text and shows students how he selects details and puts them in a "slice" of the Summary Wheel.	During period 5, Mrs. King works with seven 10th graders who all have difficulty capturing important details from non-fiction text. Mrs. King has been using the Summary Wheel with her class for about two months.
Then Mr. Phelps organizes students into heterogeneous teams so that each group has a combination of above grade level readers, grade level readers, and below grade level readers. He asks students to work in their groups to read and use the Summary Wheel on the article.	"Remember," Mrs. King reminds her group, "the Summary Wheel is designed to help us determine important ideas and synthesize. These are the skills we're working on."
	Mrs. King distributes a Summary Wheel that has four topics already filled in the "crusts" and a non-fiction article about the lifestyles of the Puritans that's at a reading level her group can read with fluency. She asks one student to read the first two paragraphs aloud and the rest of the class to listen and underline key ideas that might go into the first pizza slice.
When students are finished, Mr. Phelps allows students to use their Summary Wheels to take a short quiz on the content of the article.	"Ok," she says when the reading is over. "Who can share an important detail for that first wedge?"
	"Puritans were really afraid that they weren't going to go to heaven," says a student.

Conclusions: Implementing an Integrated Approach

Beginning of the Year: Getting started with Strategic Reading in ELA involves talking with students about what reading *is* and what good readers *do*. Your struggling readers may not know that reading is thinking. They may believe that some people just "get it," and others "don't." Take the mystery out of reading, begin with a Think-Aloud, modeling and labeling for your students what good readers do. Once students have the words to describe how their brains think while reading, ask them to begin recording their thoughts by using Strategic Reading Journals.

Then: As students gain confidence showing their thinking, you'll want to transition to increasingly complex strategies such as Carousel Brainstorming, Forecast, Save the Last Word for Me, that help students make richer and deeper connections to the literature they are exploring.

When You've Got Them Thinking and Sharing: Finally, you will have created a literary community in which students are unafraid to take risks, express opinions, and back up those opinions with evidence from the text. Now it's time for strategies such as Reading from Different Perspectives.

Strategic Reading in Foreign Language
Authors, Pat Branson and Janine Theiler

Rationale

The ability to read strategically opens the door to a wealth of opportunities for the foreign language learner. Foreign language students who are strategic readers can access literature, periodicals, professional publications, and scientific or technical journals written in the second language. With the ever-increasing accessibility of technology, there is daily opportunity for students to encounter their second language via e-mail, text messaging, Facebook pages, and blogs. For foreign language students to take full advantage of the text-based opportunities available to them, they must be able to read strategically. A strategic reader approaches each of these opportunities with confidence, makes meaning of the text, and successfully engages in the reading process.

Foreign language learners in the United States are primarily at the high school level, with approximately 91% of high schools providing foreign language instruction compared to only 25% of elementary schools (Rhodes & Pufahl, 2009). This is unfortunate from a proficiency standpoint, as the typical high school student will attain only novice-level proficiency after two years of foreign language study, and four years of study may result in intermediate levels of proficiency (ACTFL, 1998). With the vast majority of foreign language learners in our classrooms being classified as "beginners" it is logical to emphasize the issues and nuances specific to them while also allowing for the development of a general picture of the foreign language classroom.

Issues and Nuances when Reading in a Foreign Language

The old paradigm of foreign language reading theory and methodology was derived from studies on reading in the native language. While there was logic to this reliance on the native language research, there has been also a need for knowledge specific to reading in a foreign language. Issues and nuances tend to appear in one of two categories: reader variables and text variables. A brief overview of these variables will aid the foreign language teacher in better understanding the challenges facing the student hoping to become a strategic reader of a foreign language.

Text Considerations - Reader and Text Variables

Reading in one's native language is a complex task. Reading in a foreign language is all the more difficult. Native language readers begin their exploration of the reading process with five years of acquired oral language. They have an extensive vocabulary, syntactical, and lexical base upon which to rely when they begin reading. Foreign language readers, on the other hand, begin with an empty slate for oral and written language. They must learn the reading process simultaneously with the acquisition of oral language.

Current knowledge of how the brain processes information assists us in developing a better understanding of this picture. Most brain processing models emphasize a limited capacity for actively processing information. For efficient processing during complex activities (such as reading), some of the basics (such as vocabulary recognition) must be automatic, not attention demanding. For beginning foreign language learners, vocabulary recognition is not automatic, an inordinate amount of attention is placed on basic processes, and students find themselves frustrated and unable to engage in the reading process. As stressed in chapter 3, reading is thinking cued by text; reading involves not only decoding words but also understanding what words mean in a specific context. Foreign language students often experience a cognitive "short circuit" when decoding words for the reading selection (Taillefer, 1996).

Many researchers hold to the existence of a "language threshold," a certain level of vocabulary that must be established before students are able to transfer reading skills from a native language to a foreign language text. Until that "language threshold" is established, the limited capacity of beginning learners "short circuits" their ability to operate at higher levels of thinking (Clarke, 1979). These theories stress the importance of scaffolded lesson planning for strategic reading in the foreign language, emphasizing awareness of reader and text variables that might interfere with cognitive load.

A reader's level of comprehension of text is determined by how well reader variables interact with text variables (Figure 11). Student and text variables to consider when planning a reading activity include:

Reader Variables	Text Variables
• Interest in text • Purpose for reading text (student and teacher purpose may be different) • Student knowledge of text (familiar story) • Student knowledge of context (general topical awareness) • Awareness of reading processes and reading strategies • Student proficiency in language • Student cultural familiarity	• Genre of text • Length of text • Grammatical, syntactical, and lexical complexity • Level of vocabulary • Repetition (vocabulary, syntax) • Cultural references

Figure 11

The student's level of proficiency should determine the choice of the text. At the beginning level, choices are often determined by strict curriculum guides that require work with texts such as menus, train schedules, advertisements, and other concrete, functional pieces from everyday life. While ignoring the above choices would be a disservice to our students, we might consider supplementing curriculum with authentic texts, easily accessible via the Internet. Student-generated texts such as journals, letters, conversations, and poems also might increase intrinsic motivation on the part of students. A Mexican wedding invitation provides meaningful text. Students can be asked, in the target language what the item is and what clues they used to help them decide. They can then identify parents of the bride and groom, as well as where and when the event is to take place. A cultural discussion of names can ensue such as, What will be the family name of a future child? or What do the abbreviations and symbols mean?

When choosing text outside of the prescribed curriculum, difficulty seems to be the primary factor considered by teachers. While intuition tells us to progress from easy to more difficult texts, this is not entirely supported in the research base. There is evidence of successful use of authentic novels after students have had very little foreign language experience (for examples, see Maxim, 2002). While this information seems to clash with the previous discussion of "threshold capacity," "short circuiting," and "cognitive load," the apparent contradiction is clarified when one realizes that the aforementioned theories address independent reading, done without guidance and beyond the classroom and with no teacher to scaffold the experience. Full knowledge and awareness of reader variables and confounding text prepares the teacher to scaffold the reading experience so that cognitive load is not exceeded.

Teacher Considerations

When planning for a successful reading experience the following considerations hold potential for improving comprehension. Establishing clearly defined teaching objectives and carefully aligning strategies will help to ensure a successful strategic reading experience. For example, if students will be asked to scan a text, then language proficiency is not as important and not as much time needs to be spent on vocabulary input activities. If students will be asked to make meaning of a text, then pre-reading activities focused on vocabulary acquisition are essential.

Pair and group-work allows students to pool their background knowledge on context, vocabulary, and strategies. Cognitive load is reduced when students are allowed to rely on the knowledge and skills of others as well as on their own, whereas independent learning may lead to cognitive overload if students lack the skills or knowledge necessary for a task.

Using and evaluating strategies may involve discussions in English instead of the foreign language. Allowing students to interact in their native language when exploring a text (or preparing to read) may lower cognitive load and allow them to better focus on the actual reading process or text content. The level of critical thinking that is required of students when they reflect on and discuss the purpose of a text, reading processes, and the use of strategies may not happen as easily or as quickly if students are required to speak only using the foreign language.

Strategies to Extend Strategic Reading in Foreign Language

As a result of the delicate interaction between the reader and the text, second language teachers must walk a fine line between challenging students appropriately and overwhelming them. Students need to have success with reading in the second language if we are to expect them to persist with the difficult, but not impossible, task of reading in the second language (Barnett, 1988). As indicated in chapter 3, understanding the "what, how, when, and why" of strategy use is a critical component in becoming a strategic reader. This does not differ when reading in the foreign language, as was emphasized when Anderson (1991) closely analyzed both highly successful and less successful foreign language readers in their strategy utilization. He had expected to find the highly successful foreign language readers using more or different strategies, but he was surprised to find that they were using the same strategies as less successful readers. Anderson surmised that the less successful readers, while using the same strategies, were not able to apply them strategically. They knew the "what" and the "when," but they were not confident with the "how" or "why." If we are to guide our students toward successful strategic reading, they must be given the "what, when, how, and why" of strategy use.

Each of these types of knowledge may be purposefully integrated into any lesson involving the reading of a foreign language text while simultaneously scaffolding the experience such that it remains within the cognitive processing load of the reader. Moeller (2007) recognizes three distinct phases in reading and applies different strategies for each phase. In the pre-reading phase, the teacher introduces the text with the twofold purpose of captivating student interest while providing them with the background knowledge necessary for success when reading. In the second phase the teacher scaffolds and guides reading followed by close analysis of the text. The third phase requires the student to move beyond the text, often doing so in an independent manner that requires the integration of previous knowledge and skills with the text.

When referring to the Strategic Reading Format explained in chapter 3 (p. 24), there is clear alignment between the inverted pyramid format and Moeller's 3-stage plan for foreign language readers. Because of this close alignment, a series of practical applications for the foreign language classroom will be presented within the Strategic Reading Format framework.

Before Reading: Pre-reading
The **PREP (Preview, Read, Examine, Prompt)** strategy (Langer, 1981) activates prior knowledge, encourages questioning for clarity, and promotes meaningful class discussion.

1) Preview: During this step the teacher introduces the text to the students by having them examine the title, pictures, graphics, and headings. Students should scan the text for cognates and familiar words. Then have the students read either the first and last sentences or the first and last paragraphs, depending on the length of the text and the proficiency level of the students. Have students create a list of questions that they plan to have answered through reading the text. This helps to support learning about vocabulary and grammatical structures that they will encounter in listening or may try to use orally or in writing. For example, in a beginning level Spanish course students generated questions about a menu.

Examples:
What does "propina" mean and why is it at the bottom of the menu?
How do I know if I would want to eat these things?
How would I know if I would eat here at all?
Do they have the same categories on their menus as we do?

Beginning with such easily identified clues can help develop beginners' confidence in their capacity to make meaning out of a text. A menu is a simple form of text. It is basically a list of words belonging to a single category. When applying the PREP strategy to more complex text it is important to use a familiar story or poem. Students do not have to struggle to understand the story; they can focus their energy learning the second language.

2) Read: During this step students read the selection and answer the questions they generated. Teachers should reassure students that they can use resources like dictionaries, vocabulary work from previous lessons, or textbooks to find answers within a reasonable time frame. Students may have a tendency to persevere in finding the meaning of every word; reassure them that they only need to answer the questions they generated. The task of reading in the second language can be overwhelming to the kind of mind that wants to always have the one right answer.

3) Examine: This step causes the students to examine their responses for quality, understanding, and clarity. It is important for the teacher to interact with students as they refine their note taking on the text. The teacher could circulate throughout the class and offer feedback on what students are writing, and where and how they are finding answers.

4) Prompt: This last step helps students to encounter the learning from the text in another context. This is the time when a word with more than one meaning, like "comida," and the dangers of ignoring context can be discussed. For example, the teacher could have an overhead of the menu and take students' interpretations of the text and write them on the board. Student questions could be posted around the room and students could write answers to the questions and present them to the class. Providing students an opportunity to share and discuss their answers with the group increases their chances of understanding and using the language well into the future.

The **Prevoke/Vocabogram** strategy (Rasinski & Padak, 2000) helps the reader develop vocabulary and prediction skills. Prior to the activity, the teacher determines the essential vocabulary for the reading selection. Students work in groups and each group receives a few of the vocabulary words/expressions. They must "teach" their peer groups the new words without using native language words. Once all vocabulary words have been addressed, each group receives an envelope containing all new words/expressions on individual slips of paper. Groups work independently to categorize the vocabulary, and a class discussion ensues concerning the different categories and connections among the vocabulary words. Finally, based on the discussion of vocabulary categorization, students are encouraged to make a prediction about the content of the text.

During Reading: Active Reading

Checking predictions might be informally combined with a **Character Map** (Billmeyer, 2006b) during the active reading process. A Character Map is a graphic organizer that invites students to write down what they have concluded about a character in a story, magazine or newspaper article. Prior to reading the story or shortly after beginning the story, each student chooses a character and notes predictions concerning facts, traits, properties, or qualities about the character. During the reading of the text, this list might be updated or changed as students check and expand upon their predictions. Finally, students might use butcher paper and markers to create an outline of their body, creating a comprehensive visual representation of the character. Time should be allotted for students to share the final product.

Click or Clunk (Clark, 2009) is an activity which can be used during reading at any level. As the students read they record ideas, words or phrases that they understand or that "click" with them in the *click* column. In the *clunk* column, students will record ideas, words or phrases about which they have questions – things that "clunk" them. When students seem to be accumulating several "clunks", the teacher may choose to pause reading and have students engage in a **Paired Verbal Fluency** (Billmeyer, 2006b) activity. Students are placed in pairs. They nominate who is "partner # 1" and "partner # 2" in each pair, and pairs are told that there will be three rounds of uninterrupted pair discussion (in their first language). At the word "go", partner # 1 speaks for 60 seconds about what has "clicked" and what has "clunked". At the word "switch", partner # 2 will then have 60 seconds to respond to partner # 1 or share his/her own "clicks" and "clunks". This is repeated for a set of 45 seconds (45 seconds for each partner) and a set of 30 seconds. After the completion of three rounds, the teacher may choose to have students share their "click or clunk" discussion in groups, or a class discussion might ensue.

After Reading: Reflect on Reading

Taking the time to assess student understanding of both content and process after reading is key to long term literacy skills for second language learners. Moeller (2007) would have students reflect on reading by acting as "text critics," going beyond the text. Students may be asked to write a new ending for the story or retell the story from a different viewpoint. For example, in the fairy tale "Red Riding Hood," students could retell the story from the point of view of the wolf, the grandmother, or the hunter.

Strategic readers reflect on the effectiveness of the strategy used. Holding students accountable for their reflections is an important choice for teachers to make. Students know that we assess what we value, and we value what we assess. Consider having students record in their journal an assessment of which strategies worked best and why.

The **Pinwheel Discovery** strategy (Billmeyer, 2006b) lends itself well to post-reading reflection. Prior to the activity, the teacher prepares a series of questions or prompts about the text, about strategies utilized during the reading process, or about what works best for students as readers of a foreign language. The best questions or prompts for this activity are those that promote discussion, are broad, and allow for personalized responses. Example questions include: How would you describe two main characters from the story? or How did you determine the meaning of new vocabulary words? or What would you have done differently if you were the story's villain? If a question or prompt warrants defending ideas, teachers may ask that students support their ideas by referring to the text. Because the objective of this strategy is to review the content of the text while simultaneously reinforcing reading strategies, teachers will most often conduct this activity in the first language. To begin the activity, the teacher asks half of the class to form a circle and face outwards. The other half is told to match up with students in the circle and face them. The end result is an "inner/outer" circle of students facing each other. The teacher explains that pairs will have one minute to discuss the question that is posed to them. A question is posed, and pairs discuss. After one minute, the teacher instructs only the outer circle to move one person to the right, a move resulting in new pairs. The teacher might pose a new question or the same question. Posing the same question allows for reliance on knowledge gleaned during the previous conversation. This process continues for several questions; conclude with a class discussion to graphically organize ideas discovered during the Pinwheel Discovery conversations.

Conclusions: Implementing an Integrated Approach

While reader variables and text variables may differ slightly when reading in a native or foreign language, most strategies that are effective in making meaning of a first language can be adapted to reading in the second language. With the careful integration of these strategies and meticulous scaffolding of instruction, foreign language teachers can become strategic reading facilitators for the many minds that enter their classrooms. It is understandably difficult for teachers to surrender instructional time to teaching and assessing the application and effectiveness of reading strategies, but when faced with doubts, foreign language teachers must recall the power and potential of reading in a second language. The ability to read strategically will essentially unlock an entire world of new resources, experiences, and possibilities for our foreign language learners.

Strategic Reading and the Internet

Author, Lindsey Post

Rationale

In the last fifteen years, the Internet has gone from being an anomaly in the classroom to being an expected part of a school experience. The incredible speed at which this change has occurred results in not only ever-growing opportunities, but also in potential learning gaps for both students and teachers. Teachers need to make it a priority to stay current.

The Internet is a tool that can be utilized by *all* content area teachers to enrich and expand resources beyond the walls of the classroom. Students in classes ranging from algebra to welding technology can benefit from using the Internet in the classroom. Therefore, teachers in *all* content areas should strive to help students become strategic readers on the Internet.

Issues and Nuances When Reading on the Internet

While early research looked to establish links between online and offline reading strategies, it has become clear that a simple transfer of traditional strategies to a digital environment is not the most effective way to support our students (Leu & Zawilinski, 2007; McVerry, Zawilinski, & O'Byrne, 2009). Recent research shows that students who excel at offline reading comprehension do not necessarily excel at online reading comprehension, and vice versa (Leu et al., 2007). There are distinct demands on a person when reading online which require a set of skills and strategies not often taught in a school setting. A good starting point for recognizing these differences is the strategy described below.

Compare and Contrast Strategy: When explicitly teaching online reading comprehension for the first time, students benefit from experiencing the difference between online and offline research. Using a Venn diagram or a simple T-Chart, select a topic relevant to the content area and design a series of questions for students to answer. Have them start either at the computer, or with a traditional print text. Twenty minutes into the activity, have them switch texts and continue to search for answers. The important piece is the reflection afterwards. Use a Think-Pair-Share to facilitate a discussion using questions like the ones below. Once students have experienced some of the differences in the two modes, they are ready to learn concrete strategies to improve their searching, reading, and comprehending capabilities online. Questions include:

- What was easier about using the print text? What was more difficult?
- What was easier about using the Internet? What was more difficult?
- Which was better organized?
- Which had the greater amount of information?
- Which one was written more recently?
- Can you identify the author of each source?
- Which one did you prefer using? Why?

Learner Considerations

Today's students have grown up with computers in their schools and, often, in their homes. They have not had to learn as adults the language of email and search engines. They do not remember life before cell phones and iPods. Because of this, many teachers assume that students do not need extensive support with Internet-related reading skills. In nearly all cases this is untrue.

In 2007 I was curious about my own students' perceptions of what is "out there" on the Internet. I was shocked to learn that given the statement, "All of the information found on the Internet is reliable," 50% of my high school students responded either "agree" or "neutral." Half of my students did not understand that there is unreliable information on the Internet! At the same time, 90% of these same students reported that they turn first to the Internet when faced with a research task. Instead of assuming that our students are tech savvy because of the number of gadgets they carry or the speed with which they text message their friends, teachers need to incorporate direct instruction in online reading.

Text Considerations

As mentioned above, reading online and reading offline place different types of demands on our students. Coiro (2003) outlines some of the most significant differences between reading comprehension when it comes to traditional print texts versus reading on the Internet. If we are going to help students read to learn on the Internet, both teacher and students need to understand how this list impacts a person's online reading experience. Online texts have the following qualities that print-based texts usually do not:

- A lack of consistency in format from site to site and page to page
- The absence of "quality control" on the Internet at large
- An overwhelming volume of information available at any given time
- Frequent digital manipulation/distortion of images
- Hidden agendas or bias found with more frequency than in print-based text

Teacher Considerations

One of the major obstacles in guiding students toward successful online comprehension is the fact that many teachers themselves are intimidated by teaching others how to effectively read on the Internet. As a result, some teachers rely exclusively on the "just tell them where to look" method of conducting research. This may mean book-marking certain approved sites for students to search, or using school-purchased databases at the exclusion of other options. While databases are an excellent source of information, this section will focus primarily on strategies for using search engines and locating, evaluating, and reading the results on those pages. Searching the web is a life-long skill that students can use in any situation. Chapter 3 emphasizes that strategic readers are independent readers. The strategies outlined here are ones that students can use long after class has ended, and they only require an Internet connection.

Instructional Practices

When it comes to reading on the Internet, three main areas of instruction often give students trouble. These areas are:

a. Locating relevant information - (Becoming a Meaning Maker and a Text Critic)
b. Critically evaluating Internet texts - (Becoming a Text Critic)
c. Synthesizing information - (Becoming a Text User)

The next section outlines specific strategies to use/adapt in the content area classroom for each of these three areas.

Strategies to Extend Strategic Reading on the Internet
A. Setting a Purpose and Locating Relevant Information

When students are locating information on the Internet, a familiar search engine such as Google.com is often their first (and only!) stop. Because search engines are user-friendly and intuitive, direct instruction in using this tool is often overlooked in the classroom. However, a few lessons dedicated to supporting students with this skill will assist in online comprehension. In fact, Henry (2006) calls locating information a "gate-keeping" skill that determines which students are able to succeed with online comprehension and which ones struggle.

Boolean Operators: One way to improve search engine results is to use Boolean operators. Boolean logic is named for mathematician George Boole, and has far-reaching applications in math and science. In searching the Internet, these words (or their symbolic equivalent) inform the search engine what relationships you want to establish among the keywords you use in a query. See the examples below for ways to apply Boolean operators in conducting more efficient searches.

	AND (+)	NOT (-)	OR (|)
What it Does	Narrows the search by returning documents containing both words	Narrows the search by excluding documents containing keywords	Broadens the search to return documents containing either word
When to Use It	Use AND (or the + sign) when you have more than one keyword that must appear in your search results.	Use the – sign when your topic might bring keywords to mind that you do not wish to see in your search results.	Use OR (or the | sign) when you are not sure which keyword will produce the results you are looking for.
Example	colleges + scholarships	colleges -fraternities	colleges	universities

Explanation of Boolean operators

(Two notes: It is important that there *not* be a space between the exclusion operator and the following keyword. Notice that there is a space on either side of the + sign and the | sign, but not after the – sign. Also, most search engines now assume the operator AND if you are searching for more than one term, so that {college AND scholarships} is equivalent to typing {college scholarships}.)

One student in an electrical trades class was interested in learning more about a career as a lineman. A simple Google search for {lineman} resulted in over four million pages, many of them related to the football position and not the electrical career. As this student was not at all interested in football, he used the Boolean operator NOT to narrow his search. By typing {lineman –football} he narrowed his results to about 1.5 million pages. While this is still an enormous number of options, all of them related to his future career instead of football.

Google.com also offers an advanced search link to the right of the query box (http://www.google.com/advanced_search?hl=en). It uses Boolean logic to build a search in a format that might be appealing to students learning this skill.

Quotation Marks: Another simple strategy for supporting students in more productive searches includes the use of quotation marks. Quotation marks around a query tell the search engine to return documents containing an exact phrase. This is particularly useful when searching for lyrics, quotes, sayings, slogans, or phrases that need to be found verbatim. Search engines work by building a list of all the words and phrases in each document on the web. Therefore, if you are looking for a phrase or question that you would like to see word-for-word in a document or forum, using a longer phrase or question with quotation marks increases the likelihood of finding exactly what you are looking for. See the scavenger hunt below for an example of how to combine Boolean operators with quotation marks for an even more specific search.

Scavenger Hunt: Once the teacher has modeled the first two strategies, an effective guided practice tool is an online scavenger hunt. For this activity, give students specific questions to answer and let them come up with the query that they think will lead them to the answers. Encourage students to combine Boolean operators with the use of quotation marks.

Question	Answer	Strategy Used
Who wrote the book that starts with the line: 124 was spiteful?	Toni Morrison	I combined the Boolean operator + with the use of quotation marks: "124 was spiteful" + author

An example of an organizer used for a Boolean operator scavenger hunt.

This activity helps readers become Meaning Makers in two ways. First, the teacher models setting a clear purpose for online reading by giving specific questions that need specific answers. This will soon become the independent reader's job, but it is important to emphasize that success in online reading starts with having a clear goal in mind. Second, by asking students to be metacognitive about the process they used for searching, students are developing the attribute of reflecting on the reading process. More examples of tutorials and scavenger hunt questions (including the one above) can be found at the 21st Century Information Literacy Project http://21cif.com/tutorials/challenge.

B. Critically Evaluating Internet Texts

To help students develop the attributes of a Text Critic, there is no better place to practice than online. A key component of online reading comprehension is the ability to evaluate material for credibility and reliability. Teaching students to take time for critically evaluating websites and discouraging the passive click-and-print method of "research" is difficult but well worth the effort.

Hoax Sites: A good place to start (particularly with students who believe that everything on the Internet is reliable) is to show examples of websites that look legit but are most certainly not reliable. One popular such hoax site is devoted to the cause of saving the "Endangered Pacific Northwest Tree Octopus." Teachers often use this site (http://zapatopi.net/treeoctopus) as a starting point for examining students' perceptions about content on the Internet.

Screen shot of a popular hoax site: http://zapatopi.net/treeoctopus.

Students may argue that the site looks professional, that it includes pictures, that it was recently updated, and that it has working links. However, after using a few of the strategies below, it becomes clear that this site is a hoax.

Strategies for Digging Deeper when Examining the Credibility of Websites

Strategy	Application
• Locate the author/owner of a website using easywhois.com.	• An easywhois.com search reveals that the Tree Octopus domain name zaptopi.net is registered to Kevin Fraites. A next step would be to conduct a Google search to determine if this person is an animal expert, if he is affiliated with professional organizations, or if his credentials can be found.
• Check the URL for a clue about who created the site. Was it an organization (.org), a company (.com), or a government institution (.gov)?	• Because some of these domains can be purchased by anyone (.com and .net, for example), they may or may not be less reliable that those that cannot be purchased by the general public (.edu and .gov, for example).
• Corroborate material by conducting additional searches and comparing claims about the topic or person you are researching.	• Additional searches for the "Pacific Northwest Tree Octopus" bring up pages for collections of hoax sites, as well as teacher blogs and lesson plans that use this site to teach website evaluation.
• Look to see when the website was last updated.	• This will often be located at the very bottom of the site. On the Tree Octopus site, there are recent updates in the "news" column on the left, causing some students to think the site is reliable.
• Check external links to see which types of sites are linking to the one you are evaluating.	• Use a search engine to check external links. Type link: followed by the URL of your site without any spaces. For the Tree Octopus site, type link http://zapatopi.net/treeoctopus/. There are no links from credible sites related to endangered species.
• Look for author bias and hidden agendas by examining point of view, loaded words, opinions, and exaggerations.	• Ask yourself questions such as: Who stands to benefit from people viewing this website? Do others writing about this topic have the same views? Are these mostly facts or opinions? Do the creators of this website hope that I will buy something as a result of reading?

C. Synthesizing Information

After students have strengthened their skills as Text Critics and made judgments about the sites that they will use and the ones they will reject, they need to be able to function as Text Users. Part of what makes Internet research so complicated is the fact that the non-linear structure of the text makes it possible to jump from page to page without seeing the larger picture of what you are researching. Links to other sites can be both useful and distracting as topics and formats change with the click of a mouse. For this reason, students need support sorting what they have read online and how it connects to their purpose for reading, a synthesis chart provides structure.

Synthesis Chart

My Topic: *A Raisin in the Sun*				
My Purpose: To find background information about the play's first Broadway production				
Website	**Author**	**Last Updated**	**Main Idea**	**Three Details**
http://www.npr.org/ programs /morning/features/ patc/raisin/	National Public Radio Interviewer, Cheryl Corley	March 11, 2002	Despite an uncertain start, the play exceeded expectations and has an important place in the history of theater.	1. It was a struggle to raise the money to get the play produced in the first place. 2. The preview shows were not very well received. 3. Once on Broadway, the reviews were wonderful. It won awards and drew African Americans to the theatre for the first time.

Example of a synthesis chart used to record key information about a particular website.

Keeping track of what information was found where and how it relates to a larger purpose helps students to make connections among various sources and start to form a big-picture understanding of a concept.

Conclusions: Implementing an Integrated Approach

Using search engines to research a content area topic is one of the most common uses of the Internet in classrooms. By applying a few simple reading strategies, both students and teachers can improve the quality of their searches and their comprehension of the text that results.

Of crucial importance in this area of literacy learning is the fact that access to explicit instruction in online reading comprehension will narrow growing achievement gaps in our schools. That is, those who lack access to the Internet in their homes and under-funded schools are falling behind in terms of literacy learning in the 21st century. Because these skills do not appear on the standardized tests tied to federal funding, the temptation may be to overlook Internet literacy in favor of more traditional, "testable" skills (Leu & Zawilinski, 2007). However, we do our students a disservice if this becomes the attitude of classroom teachers. The Internet is much more than just a technological tool for teaching content area material. It is an opportunity to open doors for all of our students as they prepare to be leaders in the 21st century.

Strategic Reading in Mathematics

Authors, Abdelhafid Djemil and Elizabeth Scheppers

Rationale

Language skills are given high visibility in the National Council of teachers of Mathematics (NCTM) standards. The 2000 standards include a mathematics process strand specific to communication, requiring that students be able to explain a problem and its solution orally and in written form. Also, NCTM expects students to hold discussions on mathematical ideas, controlling terminology and developing precision of language as they solve problems.

Research indicates that students have to understand vocabulary in various contexts as well as in those used specifically for mathematics in order to be successful in mathematics. The complexity of terms and their various meanings reflected in high stakes tests influence a student's outcome in math (Pierce & Fontaine, 2009). Even high achievers in math sometimes find their cognitive engagement disorganized when solving complex math problems. In addition, many students rush to answer a math problem while ignoring the meaning of the problem or the goal of the question. In most situations, students perceive incorrectly that the answer has more importance than the mathematical process (Yang & Lin, 2008). When students intentionally are taught the meaning of mathematical terms through the use of strategies they become strategic readers who can reason and communicate mathematically.

Issues and Nuances When Reading in Mathematic

Because standardized assessments are considered the means to evaluate and measure learning, they influence math literacy in several domains. Standardized tests have added reading and interpreting various types of math problems, analyzing and applying appropriate strategies, and then performing the calculations necessary to solve the problem. Students not only have to answer the problem, they are also required to use numbers, symbols, and mathematical vocabulary to explain how they solved the problem. The example problem below, taken from the June 2007 New York State Integrated Algebra I Regents' exam, illustrates these demands:

> *At the end of week one, a stock had increased in value from $5.75 a share to $7.50 a share. Find the percent of increase at the end of week one to the nearest tenth of a percent. At the end of week two, the same stock had decreased in value from $7.50 to $5.75. Is the percent of decrease at the end of week two the same as the percent of increase at the end of week one? Justify your answer.*

To gain the full credit of 3 points, the answer has to be 30.4, with adequate work shown, and the answer "no," as well as an appropriate justification. In other types of problems, students are allowed to use any strategy to solve the problem, but in other cases students are not.

When assessing students' conceptual understanding of a problem, their precise interpretation of the problem to mathematical language is expected. The focus is on the comprehension of the problem as well as on the process used to find the correct solution. As a result, students must be able to read, understand, interpret, analyze, synthesize, and even create their own problems. Efficacious math teachers must take on the challenge of creating a toolbox of strategies to help their students become math readers and writers (Demski, 2009).

Text Considerations

Reading and understanding in mathematics involves many different skills, often applied within the same math text. The use of mathematical symbols interchangeably with concepts and processes increases the difficulty for the non-literate math student. Math textbooks are not designed with novice mathematicians in mind. To understand the critical role of vocabulary and concept development in math, consider this problem taken from an Algebra 1 textbook:

The reciprocal function is an example of a relation called inverse variation. In inverse variation, as one variable gets larger, the other variable gets smaller. A formula called the Rule of 72 is an inverse variation used to approximate how fast money will double when it is invested at a given compound interest rate. The number of years (y) to double an investment is equal to 72 divided by the annual interest rate (r) expressed as a percent.

$$y = {}^{72}/_r$$

For a student to comprehend this problem, vocabulary needs to be understood – reciprocal, function, relation, inverse, variation, variable, formula, approximate, double, invested, compound interest, rate, annual interest, and percent. In addition, the student must be able to make the necessary connections –vocabulary to vocabulary, vocabulary to major concepts, and vocabulary to symbolic representation. After making meaning of these related concepts, the student must organize the information in such a manner that it not only makes sense, but that it can be retrieved whenever reference is made to any one of the concepts.

The Math Reader

We know that good readers make connections to their prior knowledge when reading new information. These connections determine how the data is stored and how it is retrieved. These connections are the key to helping struggling readers understand the concepts embedded in math text. Good readers also interact with the text being read – questioning as they read, recognizing confusion and rereading as needed, and reflecting and checking back to ensure understanding. Math readers must learn to use these same strategies when reading any mathematical text and reasoning through problem solving.

When reading math problems, students must be able to evaluate the information and determine what is relevant to solving the problem. Additionally, the math reader must determine what solution the problem demands, assessing which problem-solving strategy is appropriate, applying that strategy, and then determining if the answer makes sense. To ensure transfer of the information learned from solving problems, students must be able to accurately verbalize their thinking with correct numbers, symbols, and mathematical vocabulary.

For example, Troy answers the math assessment for 3rd graders as follows:
Problem
Culley left his house at 5:05 P.M. for football practice. Football practice started at 5:15 P.M., and lasted 1 hour and 20 minutes. What time was practice over?
Answer
- To solve this problem correctly, Troy, a 3rd grader determined that *Culley left his house at 5:05 P.M. for football practice* is not needed to solve the problem because it doesn't matter when he left his house.
- The answer is figuring out the end time. *What time was practice over?*
- Possible strategies for solving the problem include: *Using a clock manipulative or adding 5:15 + 1:20 = 6:35.*
- The last step in solving the problem is to determine if the answer makes sense. Troy said, "My answer makes sense because I started with 5:15, added an hour on it to make 6:15, and then I added 20 minutes."

When students cannot associate a word to a symbol or a mathematical sentence with a known action, the terminology becomes unrecognizable and understanding becomes a challenge. Even though students come to an answer in different ways the reasoning behind their final answer must be logical.

The Math Teacher
Math teachers stimulate students' thinking and reasoning while bringing the abstract to a more concrete level through the use of manipulatives and real-life situations. Math teachers help students understand mathematical concepts when they focus instruction on mathematical terms and symbols, as well as how and when they should be used (Buehl & Fives, 2009). If students do not fully understand the content, will they ever be able to use mathematics independently to reason through problems or to make connections to other concepts? It then becomes a wise instructional choice to teach the math reader the strategies necessary to gain and sustain content knowledge.

Strategies to Extend Strategic Reading in Math
The following is a sampling of possible strategies for the math classroom. The goal of each strategy is to stimulate students' mathematical thinking and increase learning.

K-N-L (What I **K**now, What I **N**eed to Know, and What I **L**earned About the Process) is an adaptation of the commonly used K-W-L; it can be used prior to reading, during read, and after reading to check new knowledge. The K and N columns provide ample opportunity for students to pull up prior knowledge, to set a purpose for reading, and to identify pertinent information that may be gained from reading. With the spiral curriculum of mathematics, this helps students make connections between what they already know and what they are learning through this new topic. It is suggested that teachers use K-N-L first as a whole group activity. It may also be used as an independent activity to assess student knowledge and learning. An alternative approach to the K-N-L is the K-N-W-S explained in chapter 3 page 25.

K-N-L Topic: Algebraic Equations
Goals/Objectives:
- Students will identify variables and use variables in writing algebraic expressions.
- Students will write and solve algebraic equations to solve problems.

What I **Know**	What I **Need** to Know	What I **Learned**
A variable is a letter that stands for a number. Algebra involves using letters in place of numbers.	*What is the difference between an expression and an equation? How do I find out what number a variable is? Can a variable be different numbers? How will this Help me solve problems?*	

Example of the K-W-L strategy adapted for teaching algebraic equations in mathematics.

Vocabulary Writing in Math
Learning math often has been equated to learning a new language, and no wonder with the vocabulary-dense text and conceptual context within which vocabulary is presented. One way to help students assimilate mathematical language is to have them create their own vocabulary journal. Another way is to have a word wall bank where students write the new words on posters and hang them on the classroom walls.

Word	Picture	Definition
yard	*ft ft ft*	*A standard unit of measure made up of three feet. It is smaller than a meter.*

Example of an entry in a student's mathematical journal.

During Reading
The **Think-Aloud** (Davey, 1983) strategy can be used for either text passages or problem solving passages. The teacher pauses during reading in order to share her thinking as she reads. Think-aloud examples include strategies used to attack unknown concepts or terms or strategies to synthesize the information in the passage. The teacher can include personal connections or visualizations that occur during reading.

Three Phases of a Think-Aloud

Phase 1	Teacher models think-aloud
	Students listen
	Zero interaction
Phase 2	Teacher reads story problem and stops often
	Students express the thoughts that occur at teacher designated spots
	Teacher controlled interaction
Phase 3	Teacher reads story problem
	Students signal stopping point to express thoughts occurring
	Student controlled interaction

Example of the three phases of a think-aloud in math indicating who is in control during each phase.

Post-it Notes: Students are typically not allowed to write in textbooks, and if they were allowed to highlight and write in the margins, many would not know what was important to highlight. The Post-it Notes strategy forces students to identify only those facts, definitions, or concepts that are important. It also compels students who use all of the Post-its before they finish reading the passage to reread and prioritize the important ideas.

Begin by determining the facts, concepts, or definitions students must take away from the given math text. Share with the class those concepts seen as "need to know" ideas. Instruct students that Post-it notes may be moved as students change their thinking of what is most important to take away from the text. Model the process projecting the pages on a large screen with students working with a partner. Conclude with a large group discussion sharing definitions, facts, or concepts which were marked and why they marked them; lead the group to consensus on "need to know" ideas.

The **Pairs Read** (Billmeyer, 2006b) strategy addresses the needs of the auditory learner. The strategy provides development of listening skills and reading comprehension. Each partner takes a turn reading aloud the part assigned (or a story problem). While one partner reads, the other partner reads quietly knowing that once the passage has been read aloud, it will be his turn to summarize the main idea or if a story problem the information necessary to solve the problem. After the listener paraphrases main ideas or information needed to solve the problem, the pair writes a summary statement or solves the problem. They switch roles and move to the next part/story problem.

After Reading
A **Word Sort** asks students to classify vocabulary terms into groups, reinforcing meanings and connections, and aiding in understanding the major concepts. A Word Sort can be an open sort (no categories provided) or a closed sort (teacher identifies the categories). An open sort provides a higher level of cognition for the students, as they have to see connections, develop the groups, and classify the terms accordingly. A sort can be done either as a small group activity, partner activity, or independent work. If the goal is to quickly review and assess individual student learning, individual work with teacher observation is more appropriate. This activity allows teachers to see what learners have learned or need to learn; it can be used effectively at any point during instruction.

Open Sort Example: Sort the vocabulary words into similar categories.

| product | factor | sum | addend | multiplication | |
| division | addition | subtraction | array | quotient | difference |

One student created a word sort using the following categories.

Operation	Answer	Other
multiplication	difference	array
division	product	factor
subtraction	sum	addend
addition	quotient	

Explain how and why you sorted the words the way you did. For Example:

I sorted my groups by operation, answer, and other. I used Operation because it's the type of operation you do to solve a math answer. I sorted it by Answer because those are four words that mean the same as the answer. I sorted it by Other because the other words don't fit in the other categories.

Problem Solving/Process Writing in Math
While the reading strategies can help students understand the problem, they will not always provide students with the means for solving the problem. To do this, teachers need to understand what is going on with students' thought processes. Using a T Chart enables a teacher to witness the thought process the student has while completing the problem. The problem solving steps are generally universal:
- Understand the problem – What is it asking?
- Plan a strategy – What will you do to solve it?
- Solve it – Carry out the plan.
- Verify the solution – Does the answer make sense?

The reading strategies can be incorporated to help students with understanding the problem and choosing a strategy. Writing can help students with their thought processes, and help teachers with assessing those thought processes throughout the solving and verifying stages. Consider this logic example:

Ronnie, Robbie, and Roberta are seated in three chairs in a row from left to right. Robbie is not in the last chair. Ronnie is sitting directly to the left of Roberta. Write each name below the appropriate chair.

Solve	**My Thoughts**
Ronnie, Roberta, Robbie	*Ronnie and Roberta have to be in that order, but this cannot be right because the clue says Robbie is not in the last chair.*
Robbie, Ronnie, Roberta	*This meets all of the criteria in the clues, so this must be the solution.*

On the standardized tests, when students are asked to explain their reasoning, the thoughts expressed in the My Thoughts column can easily be translated into the student's reasoning.

Special Considerations for Developing Readers (Response to Intervention)

Some students come to math having a difficult time reading and understanding any text, while other students mainly have trouble deciphering the language used in mathematics. Students who struggle in math typically have trouble reading a story problem for meaning, arriving at a reasonable answer, and reading to understand mathematical concepts outlined in a text.

Reading a Story Problem

When students have difficulty understanding a story problem, rewrite the problem into bulleted ideas instead of paragraph form. For example:

> *Josh was planning a summer vegetable garden. He bought 24 feet of fencing to surround the garden. Before planting his garden, he wanted to draw the different options of his garden design to be able to plant the most vegetables. Design all the possible ways to create a garden using 24 feet of fencing and what are the dimensions. What is the area of each of the different garden designs? What is the most efficient use of the space to plant the most vegetables? Justify your answer.*

Rewrite the problem breaking it up to different tasks. Students see the tasks as an organized list, checking off each item as they complete the problem.

> *Josh was planning a summer vegetable garden. He bought 24 feet of fencing to surround the garden. Before planting his garden, he wanted to draw the different options of his garden design to be able to plant the most vegetables.*
> - Design all the possible ways to create a garden using 24 feet of fencing and determine the dimensions.
> - What are the areas of each of the different garden designs?
> - What is the most efficient use of the space to plant the most vegetables?
> - Justify your answer.

Next, the student can highlight the pertinent information to be able to solve the problem. They would look for the math terms as well as the numbers needed such as *24 feet of fencing, dimensions, area of garden,* and *efficient use of space.*

Arriving at a Reasonable Answer

When students have difficulty arriving at a reasonable answer, the teacher can give them three possible answers from which to choose. The students will then talk to their classmates about each possible answer and whether or not it is reasonable. Three possible answers from the above problem would be:
- A rectangular garden with a length of 10 feet and a width of 2 feet.
- A triangular garden with each side being 8 feet long.
- A rectangular garden with a length of 8 feet and a width of 4 feet.

After discussing the possible answers with classmates, students will use the Problem Solving/Process Writing in Math strategy to justify their answer, verifying their thought process.

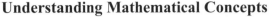

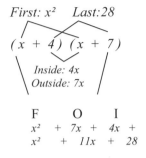

First: x^2 Last: 28

$(x + 4)(x + 7)$

Inside: $4x$
Outside: $7x$

F   O   I   L
x^2 + $7x$ + $4x$ + 28
x^2 + $11x$ + 28

Example of factoring two polynomials using the FOIL method.

Understanding Mathematical Concepts

When students have difficulty reading to understand mathematical concepts outlined in a text they need to read one section at a time, explain how the example supports the text on the page, and then create another example to connect their learning. For example, when multiplying binomials taught in an algebra textbook, it looks as follows:

A popular mnemonic device for multiplying two binomials mentally is called the FOIL method.
- *Multiply the First terms*
- *Multiply the Outside terms*
- *Multiply the Inside terms, Add the outside and inside products.*
- *Multiply the Last terms*

Students will read step one in the FOIL method Multiply the First terms. Using the example, the student explains how it supports the explanation. They might say, "I know that the first term in (x + 4) is x and the first term in (x + 7) is x. I need to multiply x times x and that equals x^2." Students will then create their own example explaining their connection to the concept, "(2x + 9) (4x + 8) if I multiply the first terms in each of the binomials, I would get 2x times 4x which equals $8x^2$."

Conclusions: Implementing an Integrated Approach

Strategies are selected to match content and purpose; teachers may refer to the following guide for implementation of the various strategies. While this chart is set as a guide for planning literacy integration into mathematics instruction, it is not a time frame with deadlines to be met. Introduction of various strategies will vary according to students' needs. It is important to continue to review and use previously learned strategies throughout the year.

	Strategy	Purpose
First Trimester	• K-N-L • Think-Aloud • Vocabulary Writing	• Supports activating prior knowledge • Supports metacognitive processes • Supports vocabulary development in math
Second Trimester	• Word Sorts • Pairs Read • Post-it Notes	• Supports vocabulary development • Supports student interaction with text • Supports reading for key ideas

Third Trimester	• Interactive Note Taking
	• Problem Solving/
	  Process Writing
		• Supports student writing
		• Supports reading comprehension
		  from informative text

Reading can no longer be viewed as skills taught in isolation; it is the common thread that unites all content areas. Reading in math presents special challenges for students, because math language is precise and compact, and authors assume that readers have background knowledge about the content presented. For student success, teachers must help students learn how to comprehend mathematical text. Strategy instruction in mathematics will create strategic readers who know how to use strategies as powerful tools, ultimately developing independent math learners.

Strategic Reading in Music

Author, Kevin Gerrity

History and Rationale

For years, content area teachers have held positive views toward the teaching of reading. Recent studies have confirmed this belief and suggest that more content specialists, including music teachers, are actively integrating reading into daily instruction (Gillespie & Rasinski, 1988; Wilson, 1995; Gerber & Gerrity, 2007). Some music specialists, however, still debate the value and/or need for reading instruction in their subject area (Swiggum, 1993). This debate stems from the performance-based nature of the music classroom. Ensembles like choir, orchestra, and band are rarely characterized as courses that require students to engage with traditional printed texts. Likewise, exemplary general music courses stress comprehensive musicianship and activity-based learning. In music, students must listen, perform, and create. Experiencing music in each of these ways remains essential. While students can certainly read to learn about music, this is not considered a strong model within music education. Unfortunately, this type of "content" approach, often achieved through silent sustained reading (SSR) mandates in every class, does not account for subjects' unique characteristics. This has been especially troubling to music educators who continue to observe the marginalization of their subject in this era of *No Child Left Behind* (Gerrity, 2009). Understandably, "many music educators believe that abandoning musical content to emphasize reading instruction devalues music and weakens its place in the core curriculum" (Gerber & Gerrity, 2007, p. 74). Despite continued efforts, many music specialists and other secondary school teachers continue to see themselves as teachers of their specific content rather than teachers of reading (Mraz, Rickelman & Vacca, 2009).

Although a purely "content" approach may lack appeal to a great number of music educators, a strategic approach toward the integration of reading and music may offer teachers greater possibilities, flexibility, and success. Indeed, students improve both their reading and music skills when reading strategies are utilized for the teaching of music. Music educators will appreciate specific suggestions for planning and implementing a strategically integrated course of music and reading. Understanding the need for reading instruction and being armed with practical teaching strategies, music educators will feel more comfortable in accepting their role as teachers of reading.

Issues and Nuances When Reading Music

Reading music notation and reading text require the same thought processes. Both expect students to decode a series of visual prompts, generate meaning, and incorporate that meaning into their knowledge base for future application. Sullivan (1979), Taylor (1981) and Tucker (1981) have conducted meta-analyses of research that confirm this notion and outline even more commonalities between music reading and text reading. Therefore, the traits and attributes of a strategic reader, outlined by Billmeyer in *Capturing all of the Reader Through the Reading Assessment System* (2006a), can also be used to describe a strategic reader of music. Defining strategic readers of music and text in similar terms is a necessary first step toward developing processes and strategies that will benefit both the reading and musicianship skills of students.

Traits and Attributes of a Strategic Reader of Music
TRAIT 1: Reading the Lines for Recognition
"Code Breaker"
When strategic readers of music perform alone or with others, they attribute meaning to symbols, read known rhythms and pitches automatically, and use what is known to decipher and perform unfamiliar musical passages. They recognize genre and begin to distinguish form and other organizational patterns within the music. These acts build the foundation for comprehension and are essential for an accurate performance.

Musicians assign meaning to all the symbols they encounter in a composition. These symbols may be thought of as the vocabulary of music. As students increase their music vocabulary and recognize musical symbols on sight, they will become better at the art of making music. This strongly suggests a need for educators to adopt strategies that will reinforce music vocabulary. A popular strategy among many language arts and reading teachers is the **Frayer Model**, which may be an ideal choice for music educators. It allows students to develop their understanding of concepts by studying them in a relational manner. This is accomplished by examining what the concept looks like, discussing the meaning, and providing aural examples of the specified concept. The following example may represent a music student's completed model for the concept of staccato.

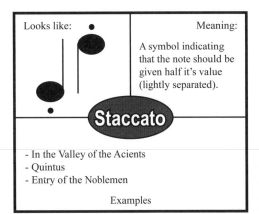

Example of a Frayer Model adapted to incorporate both aural and visual aspects to accommodate a greater number of students' learning styles.

Individual students can reference these models as they investigate if a new composition incorporates the concept of staccato or any other chosen concept. Using the examples to remind them of how they have performed that concept in previously studied music, the student will be more likely to accurately read and perform the concept in the new composition.

TRAIT 1: Suggestions for Teachers

In addition to having students complete their own Frayer models for various musical concepts, words, or symbols, teachers might also consider generating group models with students that can then be posted throughout the room. This will ensure that students have the same information for any given concept, which could be easily referenced in teaching and learning situations. Likewise, establishing a **Word Wall** will provide students with a visual representation of the many musical concepts, words, and symbols that they learn over time. If maintained, a Word Wall can become the basis for curriculum planning and assessment and an illustrative tool for parent-teacher and/or administrative conferences.

Another suggestion for teachers would be to rethink the traditional view of music literacy. Many music specialists perceive the labeling of pitches, rhythmic counting, and/or fingerings/bowings as the mark of a weak musician. Yet, reading and language arts teachers regularly encourage students to use many decoding strategies. For instance, phonemes can be likened to pitches and chunking can be applied to various rhythmic patterns. If instructors allow their students to label the pitches of a musical excerpt, locate and identify dynamic markings, or apply rhythmic counting in problematic measures, over time, these strategies certainly will improve students' music-reading and performance skills. Students should be encouraged to use as many strategies as possible as they strive to improve performance and comprehension.

TRAIT 2: Reading Inside the Lines for Meaning
"Music Maker"
Strategic readers of music reflect on their own processing skills while performing. When musicians are aware of and use strategies, they are able to monitor their understanding before, during, and after a performance. Strategic readers of music strive to achieve fluency and comprehension in each performance.

Once musicians master the art of "code breaking," they find themselves in a much better position to accurately and artfully perform music. However, this represents only the first step in developing students' music reading and comprehension skills. To continue their development, strategic music readers will make use of learning strategies before, during and after a performance. Historically, music educators have done well to arm their students with strategies they might use during performance. Tapping one's foot and subdividing to maintain pulse and vertical alignment, following a conductor's gestures for the proper interpretation of dynamics and style, and listening across the ensemble to maintain good balance and intonation represent common strategies that most, if not all directors regularly use with their students. However, musicians will also benefit from using learning strategies before and after a performance.

One such strategy to be explored by student musicians and educators is a sight-reading or pre-reading plan. Lautzenheiser and colleagues (2000) advocate an example of this strategy in the popular band method *Essential Elements 2000*. The **STARS strategy** methodically guides students through the exploration of a new composition. STARS is an acronym for **S**harps and flats (key signature), **T**ime signature and tempo, **A**ccidentals, **R**hythms, and **S**igns and symbols. Using a sight-reading or pre-reading plan allows students to gain valuable information about a composition prior to its performance. Furthermore, this information can be easily incorporated into any number of graphic organizers that students can refer to as they get ready to practice or perform the piece. A semantic map of Ed Huckeby's "Blue Lake Reflections" is provided as an example.

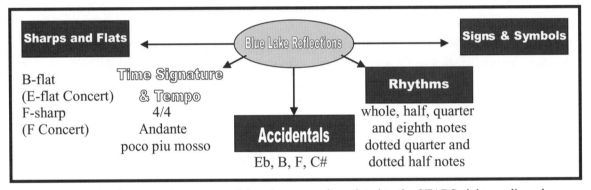

Example of a semantic map organizing the categories related to the STARS sight-reading plan.

Semantic maps, like other graphic organizers, are visual tools that help musicians activate their prior knowledge and recognize the important components of a piece of music. Pre-reading plans and semantic maps are widely used by language arts and reading teachers. When music educators embrace these strategies and embed them in instruction, the similarities between text-reading and music-reading processes become apparent to the students.

TRAIT 2: Suggestions for Teachers
In addition to exploring the musical content of a selection, pre-reading plans may also be utilized to investigate a composition's thematic content. Few would argue that a choir's performance is not enhanced if they possess background knowledge about the origin and purpose of the spirituals they sing. Similarly, a band will enhance its performance of a composition about the Civil War if the students and director investigate what is known about that period in our history and the music that defines it. Choosing to utilize pre-reading methodologies in exploring thematic content not only represents a concerted effort toward increasing both the reading and musicianship skills among students, but might also allow teachers to more easily address the historical/cultural component of the National Standards for Music Education.

Another widely used strategy that music teachers might utilize in addressing Trait 2 is the KWL. Having students articulate all that they know and all that they wish to learn in a specific piece of music is itself a formative assessment. Just as a

Word Wall might provide a foundation for curriculum development, a KWL can essentially act as a musical IEP, pointing students toward the content on which they need to focus. Then, in reflecting on what it is they have learned from the performance a particular piece, the learning gleaned from the experience is more likely to be retained and applied to future performances.

TRAIT 3: Reading Between the Lines for Application
"Music User"

When strategic readers of music comprehend and interpret music notation, they apply their prior knowledge and skills in the performance of a piece of music and are able to answer questions about that composition using defensible sources. Making sense of the whole composition comes from the ability to manipulate the parts.

Music overflows with nuance. As musicians' knowledge increases and their performance skills are honed, they will begin to seek out and exploit many of these musical intricacies. For example, a pianist may begin to incorporate turns and other melodic embellishments when performing the keyboard works of Johann Sebastian Bach. A cellist might explore his use of vibrato when performing a particularly expressive passage. Choirs can employ rubato to manipulate the steady pulse of a song to increase its dramatic effect. And a band will stylistically swing the eighth notes when performing a work by Duke Ellington. In every case, students apply what they know about music to create new concepts and interpretations. And, as students will discover, these new concepts and interpretations are justified by accepted performance practice or historical reference. Through exploration, students become equipped with the proper knowledge to justify future performance decisions of similar works.

By examining nuances, musicians begin to fully recognize a composer's intent and the meaning conveyed by the composition. This may serve to open a dialogue among students as they debate how the expressive qualities of a piece of music support its intent. Initiating these discussions provides students with another outlet for applying their musical knowledge. To do so, educators may wish to have their students complete or construct a musical map for each composition they choose for study or performance. Musical maps, similar to the **Story Maps** used by language arts teachers for exploring narrative texts, are another type of graphic organizer that can serve as visual representations for any musical composition. A map illustrates the composition's form and outlines its sequence of musical events. Certainly a map will help students recognize the structure of a composition, and over time, a wider variety of organizational patterns. However, it may also serve to enhance performance. Maps can tell students which musical forces are utilized throughout the piece and the relationship they have to one another. This is important information needed by students and directors as they work to improve the balance and intonation of the ensemble. Whether teacher-provided or student-generated, maps will help students enhance their musicianship skills while reinforcing a process common to the reading classroom. An example of a musical map for Robert Smith's "At the Crossroads" follows:

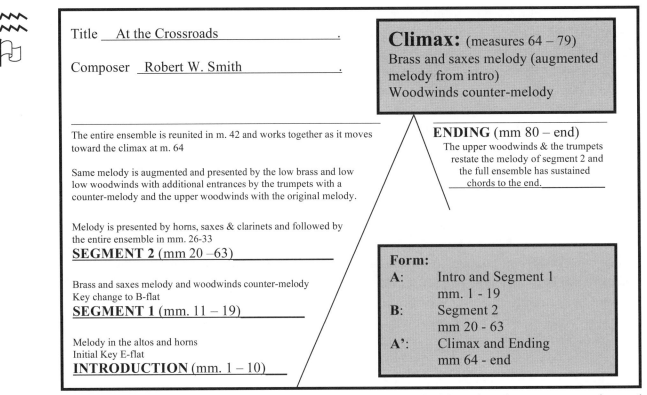

Title __At the Crossroads__ .

Composer __Robert W. Smith__ .

The entire ensemble is reunited in m. 42 and works together as it moves toward the climax at m. 64

Same melody is augmented and presented by the low brass and low low woodwinds with additional entrances by the trumpets with a counter-melody and the upper woodwinds with the original melody.

Melody is presented by horns, saxes & clarinets and followed by the entire ensemble in mm. 26-33
SEGMENT 2 (mm 20 –63)

Brass and saxes melody and woodwinds counter-melody
Key change to B-flat
SEGMENT 1 (mm. 11 – 19)

Melody in the altos and horns
Initial Key E-flat
INTRODUCTION (mm. 1 – 10)

Climax: (measures 64 – 79)
Brass and saxes melody (augmented melody from intro)
Woodwinds counter-melody

ENDING (mm 80 – end)
The upper woodwinds & the trumpets restate the melody of segment 2 and the full ensemble has sustained chords to the end.

Form:
A: Intro and Segment 1
 mm. 1 - 19
B: Segment 2
 mm 20 - 63
A': Climax and Ending
 mm 64 - end

Example a musical map highlighting the concepts of musical form, key change, augmentation, and musical climax.

TRAIT 3: Suggestions for Teachers

As a discussion strategy, maps can be utilized in both music-reading and text-reading situations and will surely increase student understanding and performance. Besides illustrating form and providing information that can improve performance, maps may also be employed to aid students in determining more subtle patterns of construction like phrasing, melodic treatments (augmentation or diminution), rhythmic treatments (ostinato), or foundational motives. Students can then make sense of the whole composition by understanding how the composer has manipulated its parts. Students will be more likely to recognize a variety of organizational patterns presented in compositions and less likely to allow such treatments to hinder or diminish performance.

The more music that is examined, the more refined students' perceptual skills will become. Active listening lessons, then, can be utilized to expose students to a greater number and variety of musical compositions. Students can identify musical concepts and employ a discussion strategy to help them articulate an understanding of the piece and/or the writer's compositional choices. To draw comparisons between the music students listen to and the music they ultimately perform, teachers may wish to use the **Venn diagram**. In doing so, teachers can keep students focused on performance goals while exploring a broad array of musics. For example, a Venn diagram created to explore the relationship between Pachelbel's *Kanon* and Blues Traveler's *The Hook* may instill a greater appreciation and understanding of Baroque music among middle-level general music students. Adolescent learners may be more likely to sing the familiar bass line of *Kanon* when it is revealed in other, more popular tunes.

TRAIT 4: Reacting Beyond the Lines for Creation
"Music Critic"

Strategic readers of music extend their thinking when they evaluate their performance by making critical and thoughtful judgments. Music readers are encouraged to share their perspectives, ideas, opinions and values. Music readers create justifiable critiques to appraise a composition's effectiveness and quality. Therefore, the musician's perspective is valued in the process.

Thinking about one's performance is the mark of a true musician. The critical evaluations and judgments one makes about an individual performance represent deliberate steps in monitoring personal learning. To encourage thoughtful reflection and critical evaluation among students, teachers might use the **Collaborative Summarizing** strategy. In this process, students work individually, in small groups, and as a whole ensemble to accurately describe a performance. Beginning at the individual level, students are asked to generate three positive aspects of their performance and three areas that may need further attention. Next, students are asked to reach consensus and agree upon three positive and three negative aspects of the performance of their section (for example, clarinets, altos, or violins). And finally, the whole group evaluates its performance and determines its areas of strength and weakness. After the initial read of a piece, a completed summary might look like the following.

Individual	Section	Ensemble
Positives I made it through the piece. I performed the right notes & rhythms. I attempted to perform the dynamics.	Positives We made it through the piece. We performed the right notes & rhythms. We performed our solo section well.	Positives We made it through the piece. We attempted to perform the dynamics. Our notes and rhythms were mostly correct, and we changed keys well.
Needs my attention I struggled with the tempo of the piece. I can tell that I was out of tune at times. I forgot to repeat the marked segment.	Needs our attention We are generally too loud. We tend to go out of tune at louder dynamic levels.	Needs everyone's attention We didn't always line up vertically. The balance of the ensemble suffered. At times you couldn't hear the melody.

This summary illustrates a means for students to thoughtfully reflect on a performance and affirms that success for the larger ensemble begins with the individual.

Offering students time to reflect on the positive and negative aspects of a performance encourages them to create their own strategies to aid in rectifying performance deficiencies. Indeed, once students have identified performance areas that need attention, they may use their knowledge of all the traits to compose or arrange practice exercises, more achievable/advanced alternatives to a particular musical phrase, and/or original etudes that focus on specific musical content. Considering that composing and arranging is arguably the least addressed National Standards for music education, the strategies outlined here may offer teachers a practical way to incorporate the standard, improve musicianship, and enhance students' reading skills.

TRAIT 4: Suggestions for Teachers

In addition to self-evaluation, students might also choose to critique the performance of another individual or group. Such actions demand that students possess a great deal of knowledge about music. The opinions they express must be supported by defensible observations and facts. To expand on an earlier example, students must recognize that the melodic embellishments a pianist performs, although unappreciated and absent in the musical score, may very well be appropriate performance practice. Similarly, students should expect to hear a band swing the eighth notes when performing certain types of jazz music. Although it may not be easy, processing and making sense of the complex and multi-layered nature of music will allow students to develop individual internal standards to analyze musical performances, to draw comparisons to their own performances, and expand their musical knowledge in ways that might otherwise be left unexplored.

Finally, as students become more skillful at appraising the quality of musical performance, they will begin to pose challenging questions to the composer and his or her composition. Doing so is evidence that students have a firm grasp of this music reading trait. The ability to interact with music literature, determine its strengths and weaknesses, and evaluate its relevance for student learning demands some of the highest levels of thinking from all our student musicians. Yet, many students of music are never elevated to these heights. Too often, music instructors become bogged down in a hand out the music, practice the music, perform the music rut (Duke, 1984). By recognizing the important role that each reading trait plays in the nurturing of musicians, music educators will be able to plan and implement teaching strategies that can lead to increased musical development, enhanced performances, and improved reading skills among students.

Considerations for Learners, Texts, and Teachers

As with print text, reading music is a life-long process of acquiring knowledge. Therefore, a person's age, background, and prior experience with music will determine the level at which he or she will be able to decode, perform, and draw meaning from musical texts. These characteristics must be considered by music educators if they are to select appropriate literature for student exploration. Failure to do so may lead to student frustration, decreased comprehension, and less than desirable performances. Of course, even the most carefully selected literature will not always meet the needs of every musician in the ensemble. For this reason, instructors should compile a relatively significant library of solo and chamber music that encompasses a wide range of musical styles and difficulty levels. Students can then choose to borrow these materials to supplement the music being explored by the whole. Being able to choose their own materials has motivated many English language arts students to continue to read and develop their comprehension skills, especially those students struggling with reading (Mathison, 1989). Musicians may react in similar ways. Offering students a varied repertoire of solo and chamber music will enable struggling musicians to explore more level-appropriate literature. Also, the more advanced students may continue to sharpen their musicianship and performance skills through the exploration of more musically challenging compositions.

It is important to note that the similarities between music reading and text reading expressed in these pages revolve around process and strategies. What we teach is not as important as how we teach. Ultimately, a perfect performance of the ideal piece becomes meaningless if students cannot transfer learnings to a new, unfamiliar composition. Likewise, a fluent oration by a language reader is diminished if he or she fails to understand the meaning of the words. To have the greatest impact on product, whatever it may be, students and teachers must strive to improve their processes. Such is the rationale behind many *Response to Intervention* (RTI) initiatives across our country. Measuring the effectiveness of strategies to improve student understanding has helped teachers identify unique processes that resonate with individual students. Knowledge of the teaching and learning strategies expressed here, then, may provide music teachers with additional ways in which to differentiate instruction for students who may be struggling with reading and/or musicianship skills.

Conclusions: Implementing an Integrated Approach

Music educators are beginning to blend reading instruction with musical content. For those who fear they must choose reading instruction over music, the focused, strategic approach outlined here may provide a better model than many other "content" approaches that are currently in place in our nation's schools. The process outlined here represents a systematic way in which music educators can go about creating and implementing a strategically integrated course in music. By focusing on one trait at a time, educators can develop appropriate strategies to help students navigate each of the four reading traits. Once a trait positively affects the students' skills, knowledge, and performance, educators sustain learning by directing their students to the exploration of the next trait in the sequence. Exploring all the traits of a strategic reader will provide students with several learning experiences that will undoubtedly nurture their growth into strategic readers while at the same time improving students' musicianship skills.

Reading can no longer be viewed as a skill taught in isolation. It is the common thread that unites all of education's content areas and the undeniable foundation of education's promise. If we are to succeed in our endeavor to create a culture of strategic readers, content-area specialists must do their part. By adopting a strategic approach, music educators will be able to reinforce students' reading comprehension skills while exploring musical content. This is content reading. Certainly all teachers feel a connection and obligation to their own content area. But, we remain, above all, teachers of children. And, *...to suffer children to read without understanding is one of the most flagrant cases of incompetent teaching...* - Horace Mann, 1845

Strategic Reading in Physical Education and Health

Authors, Casie Onken

Rationale

Many students look forward to participating in Physical Education. It is an opportunity for them to put down pen or pencil, close the heavy textbook, and burn off some energy. Although PE may not be your typical environment reading is a good way to get students to learn about the body and how physical activity is an essential part of lifelong fitness and a healthy lifestyle. The secret to reading in PE is to not let students realize they are doing it.

Nuances When Reading in Physical Education and Health

How am I going to implement reading when I only have the students for 30 minutes? Not to mention the fact that I have no desks and or chalkboard, and the students have their back packs with writing utensils and paper in the lockers or back in their classrooms. Since you only have the students for 30 minutes, by the time you get them organized, papers and pencils handed out, and get them quiet, it will be time to leave, and they didn't even break a sweat. When students walk into a PE classroom and are greeted with pens and papers they become resistant; they want to move. The lack of motivation to read in PE and resistance by the student is what poses the greatest challenge for PE teachers.

Teacher Considerations

Reading in physical education must be quick, focused, and implemented without stopping the physical aspect of the class. Since there are no assigned texts, teachers need to rely on other resources to enhance reading. This can be used to the teacher's advantage. Given that students need to become independent readers, using resources such as directions to a game, the proper techniques of a fitness activity, the physical benefits of the task performed, and/or articles related to physical fitness can help students to obtain the knowledge they need individually. These types of resources help bring the classroom and the real world together with a realistic connection that motivates students.

Strategies to Extend Reading in Physical Education and Health

Creativity and Personal Interest: Group students (teacher selected or student selected) no larger than four per group and have them create their own ideas about the concept. For example: If you taught a unit on aerobic fitness – have students write an aerobic routine and present it to the class.   If you have completed a unit on dance have the students create and perform a dance or if you taught a unit on team sports have them create a game that involves teamwork. Give them time in class to prepare and have all necessary equipment available, including paper, pencils, markers, and tape. Identify and post specific criteria that the students must meet. A research day in the library helps to promote ideas. If students have the opportunity to put their own thoughts and ideas into reading they are more motivated to do it.

Reading as They Walk into the Gym: Posting newspaper articles featuring current fitness ideas and trends is an easy way to implement reading into the PE classroom. Write the activity for the day on the board and group assignments for the class period. Students will get used to coming into the gym and reading the board. Instead of you sharing the class events students are responsible for reading the board, and becoming independent readers. How many times have you seen someone turn first to the sports page in the newspaper? Why not post the sports section where students can read it if they have a couple of extra minutes? After all, it's prep for lifelong reading.

Example of daily objectives, list of teams, PE news articles, and current grades.

Station Work: A common instructional technique in PE is Station Work. Stations provide a quick change of environment for the students while giving them a chance to work on specific individual skills. Posting specific instructions at each station is an excellent way to implement reading into PE resulting in independent readers and learners. For example, if you are teaching a basketball unit and one of the stations is *passing* you can identify different types of passes and their descriptions, students must read the description to complete the station.

Passing	**3 Point Shots**
Chest Pass • 2 handed pass • Start at chest throw towards partner's chest Bounce Pass • 1 or 2 handed • Bounce 1x to partner's waist	• Feet must be behind 3-point line • Rotate from different angles • See who can make the most in your group

Examples of station descriptions, students read the directions and work on the specific skill.

Instructional Packets: Providing a variety of reading packets for units and activities is a simple way to incorporate reading and is also a way to differentiate instruction for students with various learning styles. You may have each student read the packet to him/herself, have a pair and share, or the teacher may read the instructions out loud while the students follow. After each specific instruction is given the teacher should provide a visual example or have a student give a visual demonstration of the described activity.

If you were using this idea in a Weight Training class you could hand the student a packet that describes a lift, read through the description, show the class an example, and then have the students practice before moving onto the next activity. Once you have explained the packet to the students post it on a bulletin board so the students can refer to the instructions as needed.

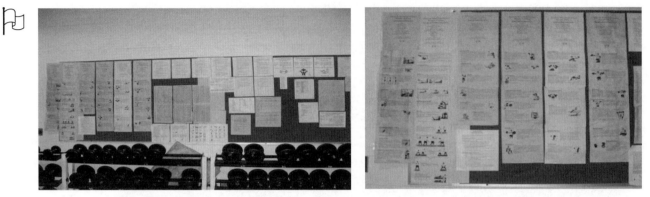

Example of a weight room, lifts taught in class with written descriptions of proper form and technique as well as a visual aid to remind students of the lift.

Sequencing: Students consistently use sequencing while working on activities in PE. For example, when playing soccer the players must start in the middle with players on both sides. The ball is then kicked and play begins. The game continues with the sequence being determined by goals and penalties as well as time. Baseball has an obvious sequence of going from first, to second, third, and finally home, not to mention outs and innings.

Students' skills in sequencing may be used in the interpretation of games. Have the students take notes as they watch a film of an athletic event. This can be by quarters or even minutes. Have students work in pairs and add the commentary to the film. When showing the film have the students critique the work and discuss how the dialogue fits with the plays and what makes it difficult for sportscasters to follow along with the action and be accurate. This activity reinforces main ideas and details, critical thinking and reading skills, and will make students better consumers of sports reporting in newspapers and magazines.

Not only can sequencing be used while playing the game, it can also be used as a form of evaluation. For example, students place the following events in order:

Jane steps up to the plate with a bat.   Jane runs to 2nd.
Paul throws the ball over the plate.   Jane runs to 1st.
Jane misses the ball.   Jane swings and hits the ball.

Cause and Effect: Cause and Effect is inherent to physical education. If you don't do something correctly you may be hurt. If you are in shape you perform better. If you know the rules, you or your team is not penalized.

Reading directions for an activity in physical education is not only a literacy skill it is also a safety necessity. Students can easily show through the use of a cause and effect diagram the necessity of following the rules.

- Have students read directions for the activity that you are going to play.
- After students read the directions break them into groups of 3 or 4 and have them create a cause and effect chart that describes the possibility of events that could happen when playing the activity.

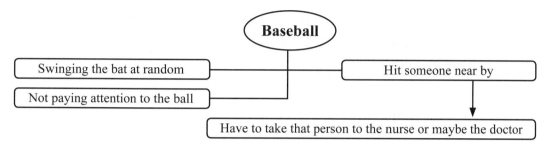

Example of cause/effect graphic for following the rules.

Word Walls: Reading can be learned and supported in all environments. If the gym and dressing room wall have only "Go Team" or "Place Wet Towels Here" signs, huge opportunities are being overlooked.

Students can create a Word Wall of important words that they deal with in PE and Health. They then write the word on one paper and the definition and or drawing of the word on the other. These are placed on the wall for future review. An example is fairness, nutrition, and success. Word Walls in the gym and locker room are powerful. They show the students the importance of words and impact thinking, participation, and performance.

Help Score Some Points: Another way to encourage vocabulary exploration is to have students take the first fifteen minutes during class to focus on sports vocabulary development. As students enter have them read the sports page and write down unfamiliar words specific to athletics on slips of paper. After ten minutes of reading collect unfamiliar words written on slips of paper. Next, divide the class into teams and randomly draw out the unfamiliar terms from a container. If the team can come up with the correct explanation of the term, they receive points; if not, the term goes to the other team for a chance to get points. Encourage team members to reference the sports page for actual use of the word. If no team gives the correct answer, the teacher uses it in a sentence and helps teams understand the meaning using context clues. You can also use just one word a day and the group who knows the meaning gets to be first at the day's activity.

Question/Answer Relationship (QAR): The Question/Answer Relationship (QAR) (Raphael, 1986) strategy supports comprehension in a number of ways. It helps students make connections between their prior knowledge and the information presented in the text, as well as develop and refine questioning skills at various cognitive levels. Four types of questions (or prompts) are used as part of the QAR strategy: right there, think and search, author and you, and on my own. Questions can be asked of students while waiting in line, exiting the gym after play, or recorded on chart paper and displayed on the gym wall.

Right There Questions	• What is flexibility and stretching? • When did American football and rugby originate?
Think and Search Questions	• What are important stretching habits everyone should develop? • How would you compare and contrast the game of American football and that of rugby? (The game known as "football" in other parts of the world?)
Author and You Questions	• How did the information presented on stretching and flexibility compare to what you already knew? • What questions would you ask of an American Pro football player?
On My Own Questions	• What role can a sports trainer play in helping someone with stretching and flexibility? • How would the fitness of people be different if rugby was more popular than football?

Example of QAR questions for flexibility and football versus rugby.

Mystery Athlete: Type out a clue to an athlete and post that clue every day in the gym. At the end of the week whoever can correctly identify the athlete is rewarded. This is a clever way to involve all students in reading without specifically telling them to read. This can also encourage students to discuss who the mystery person is with others such as parents and teachers. For example,

1. In three years I won 31 games and lost 30.
2. I discovered a lump on my arm that increased in size.
3. I began playing with the Padres and was traded to the Giants.
4. I broke my arm while pitching in a game.
5. I was diagnosed with cancer in 1988.
   Answer: Dave Dravecky

Pairs Share: Students in today's society are aware of body image and the controversy that surrounds it, from obesity to anorexia in children. One important exercise that will benefit all students is to cut out articles from various health magazines, like *Shape* or *Fitness,* and have the students read individually an article of their choice. During reading, students identify the main topic and supporting details of the article. In small groups, students then share this information with each other. This provides an opportunity to share in a secure small environment, as well as a chance to share in a large group, generating a lot of discussion. The teacher can ask one or two students to list big ideas on chart paper for all to see, read, and remember.

Read Aloud: Reading aloud to the students helps develop listening skills and expand understanding. You have the opportunity to give them examples of sportsmanship as well as behavior. The book *Chicken Soup for the Teenage Soul* (Canfield, Hansen, Kirberger, 1997) has great short entries that can cause students to think about their behavior as well as what others go through. This could be accomplished while waiting for students to get into squads at the beginning of class, or it could be used as a cool down session at the end of class. Students could be invited to bring short pieces to read to class. You could also use a tape recorder to record stories; this would allow students to listen to the stories as you continue to maintain the structure of your class.

Two Things at Once: When athletic equipment is used, such as a treadmill or exercise bike, take a Sports Illustrated for Kids and laminate the pages. This will give students something to read as they exercise. Explain that this is something adults do as they exercise, it is fun and they can do two things at once.

Incorporate Math Reading: The reading of charts, graphs, and statistics is critical in our world. Use the statistics in the sports section of the newspaper, and have the students compare two teams. Have them elaborate on the comparison of the numbers by giving their opinion as to the ability of the team when looking at the statistics. When students have a purpose for reading numbers, they are more able to make sense of them. Incorporate math reading into PE by calculating:

- BMI (Body Mass Index)
- Target Heart Zone
- Percentage Programs
- Scoring Sports (bowling, golf)

Conclusions: Implementing an Integrated Approach

As educators, we realize that the learner does not typically associate reading with PE activities. Therefore, we need to model the importance of reading. Class time is limited, but reading can be incorporated in quick focused ways. The goal is not to replace physical activities with reading for students need to be active, but to make reading an integral part of your class. As a society of overweight individuals, students must learn how to live a healthy and active life.

Many students who dislike reading will read in PE and health because they enjoy reading the sports page, fitness magazines, and about sports figures. Reading in PE and health is one way to entice students to read and to show them how reading influences their daily lives.

Strategic Reading in Science
Authors, Jody Bintz and Elizabeth Smallwood

Rationale

An effective science program integrates reading, writing, hands-on activities, and student discourse. These components focus on the big ideas of science to create a rich learning environment (Bybee, 2002). One of the goals for science teachers is to help students read to learn. Toward this end, students must learn to interact with text by accessing prior knowledge, asking questions of the text, and thinking critically about the content.

The National Science Education Standards (NSES) emphasize the development of students' abilities to do inquiry, as well as acquire understandings about the work and habits of scientists. A number of parallels exist between skills needed to do inquiry and skills used in reading to learn science (see Figure 12).

Inquiry Skills (Bybee, 2002)	Reading Skills (Billmeyer & Barton, 1998)
• Learner poses a question.	• Reader asks questions of the text.
• Learner determines what constitutes evidence and collects it.	• Reader establishes a purpose for reading and consciously plans for the reading task.
• Learner formulates explanation after summarizing evidence.	• Reader analyzes information against prior knowledge, makes inferences, and draws conclusions.
• Learner independently examines other resources and connects to explanations.	• Reader extends and refines new learning to deepen understanding of the information.
• Learner forms reasonable and logical arguments to communicate explanations.	• Reader communicates understanding through discussion and reflective writing.

Figure 12

Issues and Nuances When Reading in Science

A major issue when learning science is detecting misconceptions. Teachers must discover what preconceptions students hold about a science concept. Preconceptions may be a naïve understanding of a concept or they may be firmly held misconceptions - inconsistencies between student understanding and scientific principles. Activating prior knowledge serves to both address students' preconceptions and give students the framework to add new information as they read.

For students to be able to look for and resolve inconsistencies as they read, they must first know that it is possible for their thinking to be inconsistent with scientific principles. This may seem obvious, yet students often discard logically presented and valid information in favor of their current understanding. The process of overcoming this challenge begins with students' recognition of their prior knowledge and where their current understanding falls short of the scientific principles. Initially, it was observed in science that strongly held misconceptions prevented accurate knowledge to penetrate.

Strategies help students surface their preconceptions and recognize inconsistencies in their understanding. When teachers select and use these strategies, the goal is two-fold: learning in the moment to understand the concept and learning for the long run to achieve science literacy. Whether the task involves manipulating equipment or reading a passage, the skills parallel the traits of a strategic reader outlined in chapter 3. When reading in science the "code breaker" takes in the information, follows directions, and collects information. The "meaning maker" asks questions and makes predictions while drawing conclusions from the text or activity. The "text user" evaluates ideas and makes connections between known information and newly discovered information. Lastly, the culmination of the event, the "text critic" takes the new experience and integrates it into the bigger picture or worldly view of science. These skills are integral to the work of scientists and to the development of science literacy. Focusing on the development of strategic reading skills helps students not only understand a text or interpret a set of laboratory instructions, but to develop the skills necessary for life-long learning in science.

The Frayer Model (Frayer, Frederick, & Klausmeier, 1969) helps the reader activate prior knowledge, build vocabulary, and develop conceptual understanding by identifying characteristics, examples, and non-examples. In the example that follows, the teacher prompted the student to define the term, list characteristics and give examples and non-examples of matter. Students working in small groups were each given a common text to read on the nature of matter; they added to or edited their original ideas. Students shared their ideas in small groups and created a group model to share. Teacher prompting brought students to a clearer understanding of matter and allowed them to edit their original ideas, eliminating misconceptions and adding new information. Using the skills of a strategic reader, students were able to work on their prior knowledge, identifying and adjusting misconceptions, and making meaning from a scientific text. (Edited ideas by the students are in parentheses, italics, or have a single strikethrough.)

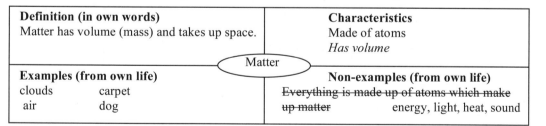

Example of accessing prior knowledge about the concept of matter using the Frayer Model.

Learner Considerations

Creating a learning environment in which students are actively involved in talking and writing about important science concepts is emphasized by the NSES teaching standards (NSES, 1996). Designing an environment for scientific reading entails establishing an atmosphere conducive to sharing ideas, skepticism, and questioning. To actively engage in these activities, students must feel safe and be willing to take risks.

Through the use of strategies, students develop important skills that help them feel more confident in taking the risk of sharing their ideas. For example, the **Think**, **Ink**, **Pair**, **Share** strategy (Billmeyer, 2006b) requires students to read an assigned passage, think about a substantive question posed by the teacher, record ideas, and share with a partner.

Think	Why does the temperature of a boiling liquid remain constant? What happens to the energy?
Ink	
Pair	
Share	

Example of a reading strategy that requires students to think about and respond to a scientific question.

Text Considerations

Reading from a variety of sources is essential to the environment for scientific reading. Common sources include textbooks, trade books, journal articles, web-based text, electronic sources such as CD-ROM, the Internet, blogs, and peer-authored text. The use of a variety of resources provides:

- The experiences necessary to understand science content
- Current information based on the exponential growth in science knowledge
- A context for developing the skills needed to learn about science beyond the classroom

Science textbooks are notorious for formats that are complex. A single page may include text, inset scenarios, problem sets using combinations of words and symbols, graphs and tables, and diagrams with captions. Strategic readers are able to take advantage of these various types of visual tools, but struggling readers may miss key features (Yore, et. al., 2003). Teachers can guide students in making sense of what they see on the page using a thinking aloud technique.

Science textbooks not only use complex formats but also are written using a different organizational pattern. In science text, the main idea is often found at the end of the paragraph as a conclusion after details have been outlined. Other types of text frequently have the main ideas at the beginning of the paragraph. Teachers can make students aware of the possibility and point out specific examples. Scientists have data gathering minds, which eventually draw conclusions; **text** is a reflection of scientific **thinking**.

Common organizational patterns found in science text include compare/contrast, concept/definition, problem/solution, proposition/support, and cause/effect (see Informative Text, p. 77). Reading with a specific organizational pattern in mind helps students make sense of the text. To identify organizational patterns and select the appropriate strategy, teachers (and students) may look for clues in the form of cue words or phrases in the text. The following table includes examples of science topics, the potential organizational patterns that may be used in text, and strategies to help students understand the text.

Examples or Topics in Text	Potential Organizational Patterns	Potential Strategies
Mitosis and Meiosis Clouds	Compare/Contrast	Semantic Mapping Venn Diagram
Sound States of Matter	Concept/Definition	Concept Definition Map
Scientific Studies	Proposition/Support	Proposition/Support Outline
Pollution Population	Problem/Solution or Cause/Effect	Problem/Solution Summarizing Cause/Effect Summarizing

Table of scientific topics, organizational patterns, and possible strategies to assist understanding of text.

Aligning the purpose for using a particular strategy to the needs of the learner, the knowledge or skills to be learned, and the nature of the text is critical to a successful reading experience for students. The strategies included in this section provide specific examples of this type of alignment.

Teacher Considerations and Instructional Practices

Strategies are used to help students construct meaning from text, organize their ideas, store them for retrieval, and facilitate application and transfer—in short, to help them learn science. The strategies, including reading attributes and processes, also need to be learned to help students become life long science learners and strategic readers.

The model for teaching the skills and processes includes three basic components: 1) teacher modeling, 2) guided practice, and 3) independent practice. During the modeling, teachers may describe how it can help students learn, provide written steps or graphics, and relate the strategy to other skills or processes. As students move to guided practice, they can think aloud individually or in small groups. The teacher monitors the student discussions and student products, providing prompts and identifying common errors in the process. Independent practice can occur in class and as part of homework. The results of strategy use will inform instruction, provide information for rich classroom discussions, and result in written work for assessment purposes.

Reading in science, as in any content area, requires the reader to think; reading is thinking. When students read in science it is important to determine how students must think. Developing the attributes of a critical reader can help students be successful in understanding the text. Critical reading attributes include identifying the author's purpose, recognizing bias, making logical inferences, drawing conclusions, and identifying fact and opinion (Billmeyer, 2006a). Reading from a variety of sources helps students fully understand and develop the habits of a scientist and develop the attributes of a critical reader.

Specific strategies can be used to help students develop the attributes of a strategic reader and achieve science literacy. For example, the Proposition/Support Outline (Santa, 1988; Buehl, 2001) strategy emphasizes the following reading attributes: identify the author's purpose, recognize bias, make logical inferences, and identify fact and opinion. The Proposition/Support Outline can be applied to a journal article or to passages similar to those included in standardized tests.

For example, students were asked to read the article, "Studies Show Students Need To Sleep Late: Night Owls Versus Early Birds," and then assigned the following task: *Write a letter to your principal arguing for or against the proposition that classes at your school should begin and end much later in the day.* Be sure to give detailed reasons to support your argument and make it convincing.

Proposition/Support Outline

Topic: Sleep Patterns
Proposition: Schools should change their daily schedules.
1. What facts, information, or evidence is presented that leads to a claim?
    a. Adults and children have different sleep patterns.
    b. Teenagers' hormones and energy levels are lowest between 9 am and 12 noon.
    c. Teenagers go to bed later at night and get up later in the morning.
2. What expert authority does the author cite?
    a. Hormones related to energy levels—Journal of Medicine
3. What logic or reasoning does the author present to support this claim?
    a. A later start and dismissal would allow students to be more attentive and increase learning.

Summary Statement: Schools should change the daily schedule so that school begins later in the morning and gets out later in the afternoon because adults and teenagers have different sleep patterns. Teenagers tend to be "night owls." The Journal of Medicine announced the results of several studies showing that the levels of teenagers' growth hormones are related to their energy levels. Since their hormones and energy levels are lowest in the morning from 9 am to 12 noon, school should start later. If the school day were to begin at about 12 noon, more of the school day would occur when students are more attentive and able to learn.

Example taken from eighth grade released NAEP test item http://nces.ed.gov/.

Strategies to Extend Strategic Reading in Science
Before Reading

The **Anticipation Guide** (Herber, 1978) is a powerful strategy for detecting misconceptions. Teachers identify important concepts from the text and use their knowledge of student misconceptions to develop statements. For example, statements 2 and 3 in the following Anticipation Guide get at predicted student misconceptions about photosynthesis.

Anticipation Guide - Photosynthesis

Directions: Before you read the section on photosynthesis, read the statements and mark true or false. After you read the chapter, reread the statements. Using your new knowledge, mark the statements again as true or false. Write the page number where you found the answer and a summary statement from the text to support your answer. Reflect and write about your learning as a conclusion to this activity.

Before Reading			After Reading	
True	False		True	False
_____	_____	1. I think sunlight is the source of energy plants use to make food. On page _____ the text says...	_____	_____
_____	_____	2. I think plants get the food they need to survive and grow from the soil. On page _____ the text says...	_____	_____
_____	_____	3. I think plants, like trees, are made up mostly of water and nutrients from the soil. On page _____ the text says...	_____	_____

I learned that...

Example of an anticipation guide detecting misconceptions about photosynthesis.

A **Directed Reading/Thinking Activity** (DRTA) (Moore, Readence, and Rickelman, 1982) can be used to help students approach text that addresses common misconceptions. Using the reading strategy along with a series of activities designed to surface preconceptions and challenge misconceptions, helps students learn to access prior knowledge and approach text with purpose, with questions, and with the expectation of learning.

The scenario and DRTA shown below could be used when the text includes diagrams of ice skaters to help students understand Newton's Third Law. Students are asked to predict what would happen to each skater if they both "push off" one another and then what would happen if only one "pushes off" the other. Driver's (1994) data indicates that most students correctly described the result when both "push off" one another, but that fewer than half of students correctly described the result when only one "pushes off" the other. The activity described below provide a learning experience to address students' misconceptions.

Scenario - Before *reading* about Newton's Third Law and studying the typical skater diagram, students *make, record and talk about their predictions* based on "what if" statements. What if both skaters push off one another? What if one skater pushes off the other? What if one skater has twice the mass of the other? Teachers could then use momentum carts, put students on roller blades (carefully!), or take advantage of video to set up a *discrepant event*. Students could then *talk* and *write* about their observations and be encouraged to ask additional *questions*. The temptation is to repeat the same words or event. A powerful alternative is to let the students respond because the discrepant event will change the thinking of some students. Let them make their case! Take advantage of the opportunity and have students *read* selected passages using a DRTA.

DRTA—Directed Reading/Thinking Activity
What I Know I Know - If the skaters both push off each other, they both move backward.
What I Think I Know - If one skater pushes off the other, then the skater who pushes moves backward.
What I Think I'll Learn - If I'm right.
What I Know I Learned - If one skater pushes off the other, then both skaters move backward away from each other.

Example of the DRTA strategy to help students understand Newton's Third Law.

After reading the text, students complete the "What I know I Learned" section. Allowing students to pair and share ideas enhances the learning process.

During Reading
The **Question-Answer Relationship** (QAR) (Raphael, 1986) strategy supports comprehension in a number of ways. It helps students make connections between their prior knowledge and the information presented in the text. It helps both teachers and students develop and refine questioning skills at various cognitive

levels. Four types of questions (or prompts) are used as part of the QAR strategy: right there, think and search, author and you, and on my own.

Right There Questions	• What is "normal" science according to Kuhn? • What do scientists do with the prevailing theory and novel findings during this time of "normal" science?
Think and Search Questions	• How is a paradigm shift-shift in understanding-represented in the visual representation? • How do the animated representations help communicate Chen's ideas?
Author and You Questions	• How does the information presented by the author, Ivars Peterson, compare to what you understand about the nature of science? • What questions would you ask of Dr. Chen?
On My Own Questions	• What can you do to deepen your understanding of the nature of science? • What is your prior experience with mathematical models and how they are used to make predictions or explain phenomena?

Questions based on the article *Mapping Scientific Frontiers* taken from www.sciencenews.org.

After Reading

Vocabulary development is a special concern in science. Students in typical science classes are constantly exposed to many new words. It's not unusual for a student in middle school to encounter 20 to 25 bolded words in a given chapter in their textbook—fewer for elementary students and more for high school students. Pruning the vocabulary highlights the "Must Know Words" (see Vocabulary p. 99), helping students develop the vocabulary needed to communicate about important science concepts. Students need to know that not all science words are of equal importance. Vocabulary strategies enhance the learning of critical words.

Mind Sketching (Billmeyer, 2006b) encourages students to associate a picture with the meaning of a word or concept. This activates the creative part of the brain and encourages students to think in pictures. Students write definitions in their own words and sketch the meaning of the word.

One caution, some science words have multiple meanings either in relationship to everyday language (light, glass) or across various science domains (plasma, nucleus). For example, work has an everyday meaning and a science meaning. If students' prior knowledge about work is based in something done for a paycheck, then it may be difficult to shift thinking to work as a force applied over a distance. Teachers may want to use care when students are sketching terms that fall within this category.

The Mind Sketching strategy was used when studying electricity. Students completed a hands-on investigation in which they were asked to get the bulb to light given wires, a bulb, battery, and switch. Students created the sketches and wrote definitions in their own words using the text as a resource.

Student Summary:
A circuit has to be a complete circle or it will not work. You have to have a battery, wire, and light bulb. Connect the two wires to the separate end[s] of the battery, then put wires on two different part[s] of the bulb.

Teacher Note:
This fourth grade student draws a picture of and describes a complete circuit involving a light bulb, wires, and battery and in the second case, also includes a switch.

The student work resulted from hands-on activities and reading about electricity. Notice the student writes about and draws the critical factor of connecting the wires to two different parts of the bulb base. Not all students captured this idea in their definitions or drawings.

Example of a student response for the Mind Sketching strategy about electricity.

Concept Definition Mapping (Schwartz & Raphael, 1985) is a visual representation of the meaning of vocabulary terms. Using the strategy helps students organize their thinking and internalize the meaning of vocabulary terms in ways not possible when students simply copy the definition from the text or glossary. The strategy works well with vocabulary of dense concepts.

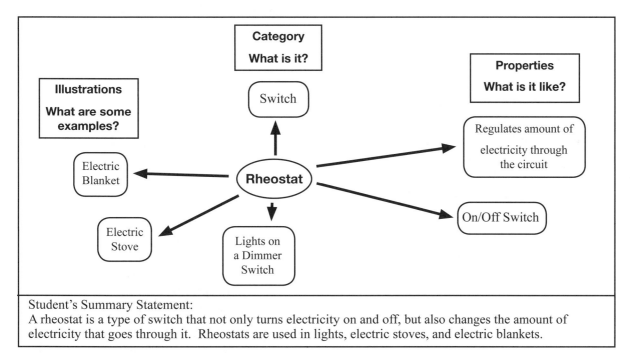

Student's Summary Statement:
A rheostat is a type of switch that not only turns electricity on and off, but also changes the amount of electricity that goes through it. Rheostats are used in lights, electric stoves, and electric blankets.

Example of a student's understanding of the word *rheostat* using the Concept Definition Map strategy.

Understanding of the difference between **relevant** and **irrelevant knowledge** (Bransford, et. al., 2001) is a key to using this strategy. Relevant knowledge helps students understand the concept. When using the Concept Definition Map strategy help students think about non-examples that are *relevant* to the concept. For example, if the topic is minerals, examples might include dolomite or feldspar. Relevant non-examples might be sedimentary rock or igneous rock. Irrelevant non-examples are clouds or erosion.

Special Considerations for Developing Readers (Response to Intervention)

Some students enter a science classroom well grounded in the use of literacy skills, for others the deficit of strategic reading skills compounds the difficulty of mastering new science content. To help students in developing literacy skills and mastery of science content teachers can employ differentiated strategies; by using different tiers of instruction all students advance their science knowledge. Consider the following example. In an environmental science class students were studying the Great Lakes, specifically concerns for environmental health of all the Great Lakes. Students were placed in small groups of mixed reading abilities. A folder was given to each group containing a variety of articles discussing different health issues for the lakes. Students passed the folder, each member **self-selecting** an article to read and then sharing main ideas extracted from the article with group members. Each group created a graphic organizer on poster paper representing the information read from all articles. Posters were displayed in the classroom and shared with the entire class.

For many students this sounds like a simple assignment but struggling readers need special assistance. It is important that teachers provide struggling learners that extra help, allowing them to reach the same success as their peers. One way to provide additional support is by doing the following.

• Before handing out the folder of articles select an article at the appropriate reading level for the struggling student within the particular group and write that student's name on the article. When handing the folder to the group first give it to the struggling child so she can privately select the article with her name on it. The teacher would have previously worked with this student in a small group setting providing support for mastery of reading strategies and science concepts. During that time, they would have agreed on cues to support her during group work situations, such as name on the article.

• At the beginning of the year, the class was taught the **Focused Reading** strategy (Billmeyer, 2006b); while reading students draw icons near an idea which represent certain ideas. Icons included: ✱ = an important idea, ∿ = supporting details, ☹ = unfamiliar vocabulary, ☺ = interesting idea, and **?** = confusing information. Icons the class agreed to use were displayed on a wall chart hanging in the classroom. Before reading the self-selected article students were reminded to use the Focused Reading strategy. As students read their self-selected articles, the teacher roamed to support struggling readers. For example, when the teacher noticed a big question mark in the margin on one struggling student's article, she quietly discussed the unfamiliar information with the student.

By employing these strategies struggling readers are able to build their strategic reading skills, be a successful and active group member, and gain new science knowledge. Differentiating reading strategies, allowing students to self-select reading material, and incorporating group work helps all students develop strategic reading skills on a personal level.

Conclusions: Implementing an Integrated Approach

Strategies are selected to match content and purpose. Teachers may refer to the following guide for implementation of the various strategies; one caveat to consider though is that each student varies from the norm. While this chart is set as a guide for planning literacy integration into science instruction, it is by no means to be considered a time frame with certain deadlines to be met. Considerations of the time frame and introduction of various strategies will change from year to year and from student to student. It is important to continue to review and use previously learned strategies throughout the year.

	Strategy	Purpose
First Trimester	• Think, Ink, Pair, Share • Anticipation Guide • Focused Reading	• Supports learning as a social process • Supports accurate learning • Supports metacognitive processes
Second Trimester	• Frayer Model • QAR • Proposition/Support Outlines	• Supports vocabulary development • Supports student interaction with text • Supports student writing
Third Trimester	• Concept Definition Mapping • DRTA • Mind Sketching	• Supports vocabulary development • Supports reading comprehension from informative text • Supports vocabulary and metacognition

Life as a science teacher would be so much easier if teaching were telling - if all students walked into our classrooms with a wide range of characteristics which included life experience, adequate prior knowledge (not misconceptions), appropriate motivation, and a plethora of independent learning strategies. And "If wishes were horses, beggars would ride." The exciting news is that we know more about learning and effective instruction than ever before. We have the benefit of a multitude of resources that help define the big ideas of science and a wide variety of strategies to teach scientific concepts. When students learn and apply strategies to enhance science literacy, we are enabling them to continue to learn about science through reading.

Strategic Reading in Social Studies
Authors, Ellen Billmeyer and Tim Dobbertin

Rationale

Just this past week, while talking with a colleague, a conversation regarding reading and social studies arose. She shared that once a week her seventh grade social studies students are required to select an article from a newspaper, local or national, and to read it looking for the main idea. This is a common assignment at the secondary level and is perceived by many teachers as a great way to expose their students to current events. Yet many students struggle with this type of text-based assignment, regardless of their grade level, because they don't understand what they are reading. The likely reason is that no one ever taught them how to read newspaper stories effectively.

During our conversation, the question "why teach reading in Social Studies?" echoed in my mind. To many the logical answer is, "because reading needs to be incorporated into all content areas." However, it is not that simple; just reading the text is not enough. It is important to teach students how to read to understand, and how to interpret information, the hallmarks of strategic reading. When teachers understand how to teach reading and use appropriate reading strategies, students become strategic readers who grasp the full meaning of the text.

High school teachers report that it is an ongoing challenge to help students who struggle with reading, much less comprehension of what they have read. Few secondary teachers see themselves as being responsible for teaching their students how to read effectively. Isn't that the job of elementary teachers? Few content area teachers have been taught how to teach reading, and besides, who has time to teach reading when they have all this content to cover by the end of the year? The problem with this thinking is that reading is a primary vehicle through which secondary social studies teachers transmit information. Poor readers are practically guaranteed a failing grade, even if they understand most of the course content that they hear.

Issues and Nuances When Reading in Social Studies

Many social studies teachers use textbooks, and textbooks are formatted in similar ways. They begin with a table of contents, a glossary, and end with an index and/or a bibliography. Typically the author focuses each chapter on one economic, political, geographical, or historical concept and provides students with numerous detailed facts and new vocabulary. High school textbooks sometimes integrate social, economic, and political concepts within a chapter; this can be confusing to students who are used to encountering one idea at a time. Chapters typically end by asking the students to answer questions and mindlessly recite facts. Because these questions usually are at the knowledge or comprehension level, they require little depth of understanding. These questions rarely have any relation to the students' everyday lives, and the information becomes a stream of meaningless facts.

A big flaw in many social studies texts is their lack of structures to engage prior knowledge. The information is often something that occurred long ago or far away, and most students do not see any direct correlation to their lives. This makes creating and activating prior knowledge essential for the reader to grasp the concepts and information from new material. It is up to teachers to encourage them to see the purpose in reading, no matter the content or the context. For example, while studying the American Revolution, a teacher might have the students focus on the abuses of citizens that lead to the revolution. This helps them achieve a sense of understanding prior to reading.

The **Anticipation Guide** (Herber, 1978) is an excellent social studies strategy because it helps build background knowledge prior to reading. To use an Anticipation Guide, first determine the concept, and then select four to six essential ideas students must understand. Write the ideas as statements, using one of the following formats: agree/disagree, fact/opinion, or true/false. Before reading the selection, students independently or with a partner respond to each statement. After students have responded to the statements, conduct a class discussion about their responses. Students then read the selection, looking for information to support their ideas. After reading, students reread each statement and change any answers. Working in small groups or as a large group students discuss their findings. Some teachers ask students to record which page they found evidence to support or refute the statement.

		Concept – The Cold War		
Before	**Reading**		**After**	**Reading**
<u>**Agree**</u>	<u>**Disagree**</u>		<u>**Agree**</u>	<u>**Disagree**</u>
_____	_____	1. The Cold War was a war based on the differing political and economic values of countries.	_____	_____
_____	_____	2. The Marshall Plan supported a democratic way of life for all people living in Europe.	_____	_____
_____	_____	3. NATO and the Warsaw Pact basically were the same thing.	_____	_____

Example of an anticipation guide to focus thinking when reading about the Cold War.

When teaching social studies, it is important to take the learners' needs into consideration. For example, a 7th grade class this year is of high academic ability, so the text is slightly below their interest level. As a result several students tend to get off task. To address this discrepancy, children's books related to the same topic are incorporated to draw out different ideas and opinions. Favorite selections are *Faithful Elephants* by Yukio Tsuchiya, *Tiger Woman* by Laurence Yep, *The Empty Pot* by Demi, *Lon Po Po* by Ed Young, *People* by Peter Spier, and *Grandfather Tang's Story* by Ann Tompert. (See Chapter 9 for more ideas.) These books relate to civilizations or geography, past and present. They serve to captivate and engage students, provoke their curiosity, and help them to formulate predictions about the upcoming information. Teachers also use children's literature with reluctant or struggling readers to compensate for a text that is too difficult.

For high school students another great way to integrate content area reading in social studies is through historical fiction. Students could read the novel, *A Family Apart,* to learn about the impacts of the depression or *Across Five Aprils* when studying the Civil War. Prior to reading, the teacher might have students make predictions based on the front cover or the brief explanation on the back. As students read the book, they can use the **Text Tagging** (Billmeyer, 2006b) strategy tagging or marking specific ideas with an icon or sticky note.

Example Icons (you can create your own also)	
!	I already knew this.
+	This is new information to me and something I want to remember.
?	I am confused by this information.
☺	Wow, how cool!

To enhance understanding, some students record their own ideas on the Post-it notes. The Text Tagging strategy allows students to flip back through the book and quickly remember their thoughts as they read. This strategy can also be used when students are reading textbooks.

While textbook publishers are beginning to include more instructional tips for teachers and students for reading and understanding text and primary source materials, they are no substitute for teachers creating relevant tasks that cause students to interact with the words through **meaningful** strategies, conversations, questions, projects, and writing activities. Remember, the textbook is not the curriculum, it is a tool that is used to teach the curriculum when it best meets the needs of your students.

Text Considerations

Social studies content at each grade level is determined by district curriculum guidelines. For example, fourth grade commonly studies the state in which they live; 8th grade usually entails the study of the history and geography of the United States; 12th grade is some combination of how Government functions and Economics. Regardless of the content or grade level, the main source of social studies knowledge comes from informative text. Most textbooks contain an overload of information and without the use of interactive strategies, students have a hard time grasping the main idea, identifying important concepts, and determining what information is important and what is not.

Textbook companies target the most populous states in the country. Textbooks tend to include concepts and topics that are emphasized by those state standards and exclude some content called for by smaller markets. This can leave large gaps in curriculum areas required by certain states or regions. It is important for teachers to know their curriculum and supplement their textbooks when necessary. For example, if you discover that none of the famous people, events, or maps from you region are included, you will need to supplement.

With the advent of the Internet, primary sources and other historical materials are now accessible to almost everyone. Teachers should use their textbooks as just one resource that can be used when it meets the instructional needs of students. Supplementing textbooks with engaging primary sources and interesting articles will build engagement among the students.

Teacher Considerations/Instructional Practices

The teacher first needs to determine the important concepts to be learned, sifting through what is found in a textbook, supplementing as necessary. The teacher then needs to help students determine which facts correlate with the important concepts and how to make them meaningful. It is essential that teachers be aware of students' reading abilities and that texts are matched to the students' academic levels. With teacher intervention and strategies, students can learn effectively. Use of ongoing formative assessment of student reading ability will assure that teachers know what type of interventions to use for their students.

A strategy to use when you want students to gain a deeper understanding of a topic is to compare the similarities and contrast the differences between two geographical or historical areas. During a unit on Ancient China, students created a Venn diagram for two of the five ancient civilizations they had previously studied. Students individually recorded similarities and differences between the two civilizations they gleaned from the readings; this was followed by a class discussion of recorded ideas. Students discovered that all five civilizations shared the following characteristics: a fertile river valley, a formal government, and a social system. A **Venn diagram** class composite was created and ideas from the diagram were used to make predictions about the upcoming chapter. This approach provided students review, created background knowledge, and caused students to anticipate learning.

Venn Diagram

EGYPT
- The Nile is the longest river in the world.
- Egypt was divided into two parts, Lower and Upper.
- Egypt had Pharaohs for their rulers.
- They believed the God Ra gave life to their people.

BOTH
- Used water to help them transport goods.
- Relied on the weather for their crops.
- Had a type of social and government system.

MESOPOTAMIA
- This was a region surrounded by two rivers, the Euphrates and the Tigris.
- Mesopotamia means "Land between two rivers."
- The Mesopotamians invented the wheel for vehicles and pottery.

Example of a Venn diagram comparing and contrasting two ancient civilizations.

Strategies to Extend Strategic Reading in Social Studies

All reading strategies can be applied in social studies. In fact, some students are probably already using them and may not even be aware of it. However, struggling readers do not know that in order to understand what they have read, **they need to think**. Effective strategies cause students to think before, during, and after reading. The strategies in this section incorporate reading processes frequently suggested in social studies textbooks, including activating prior knowledge and experiences, using organizational patterns and structures, synthesizing and summarizing, and evaluating sources, issues, and trends.

Before Reading

Forecast (Billmeyer, 2006b) is a vocabulary strategy that engages all students in a meaningful way, causing the reader to access prior experiences about the topic. It can be used at all grade levels. The teacher previews the selected reading and determines three to six unfamiliar or interesting vocabulary words or phrases. Each word is represented on the board by placing spaces on the board, one for each letter in the word, _ _ _ _ _ _ (6). Once the students see how many letters are in the mystery word, the teacher gives clues regarding the word's meaning.

Concept – Human Rights and Democratic Ideals
    Words: Democracy, Protection, Ethnic Cleansing, Cultures, Children's Rights
      D   **E**   **_**   —   —   —   —   —   —   (9)

Example clues to share with the students for Democracy
    1. This word is an antonym of monarchy or dictatorship.
    2. This is a philosophy of government.
    3. When someone has a say in what occurs in his or her country, it is called a _____.

If students need additional help, place a few letters in the blanks, allow them to use resources, or to work with a partner. Ask students to pay close attention to the meaning of the forecasted words as they read.

During Reading

Questioning the Author (Beck, McKeown, Hamilton, & Kucan, 1997) is a strategy that helps students construct meaning while coping with challenging text. The strategy helps students analyze what the author is saying rather than accepting just what the textbook states.   A benefit of Questioning the Author is that it keeps the reader's mind actively engaged during reading, seeking clarity by asking author queries while reading. Queries differ from questions in that they are not asked specifically about the information, but rather about the author's meaning or intentions.

> *Adolf Hitler or the incarnation of absolute evil; this is how future generations will remember the all-powerful Führer of the criminal Third Reich. Compared with him, his peers Mussolini and Franco were novices. Under his hypnotic gaze, humanity crossed a threshold from which one could see the abyss.*
> — Elie Wiesel – Commentary on the Holocaust

Author Queries:
- What is the author trying to say?
- What does the author think we already know?
- What do you think the author wants us to think, feel, or do?
- What would you like to ask the author?

After Reading

The **RAFT (Role, Audience, Format, Topic)** (Santa, 1988) is a reading and writing strategy that incorporates imagination and creativity. Students write from a specific viewpoint to an audience about a historical topic. After selecting a reading passage, the teacher first determines the important ideas students need to understand and remember. The topics for writing pertain to those key ideas. For example, write about the frustrations that faced the American colonists just prior to the Declaration of Independence or identify the positive societal changes resulting from the 1960s Civil Rights Movement. Then select unique writing formats, such as a diary entry or a commencement speech. Determine audiences for whom students can write, such as grandchildren or the current graduating class. Finally, brainstorm possible roles students can assume when writing, such as a colonist or Martin Luther King's son.

ROLE	AUDIENCE	FORMAT	TOPIC
Maya Angelou	Public	Talk Show	Impact of Abuse
President Obama	High School Students	Persuasive Speech	Rationale for continuing the war in Afghanistan
US Citizen	Congress	Letter	Telemarketers vs. First Amendment

The RAFT strategy requires students to write about social studies topics in a meaningful way.

The **Cause and Effect** organizational pattern helps students summarize and review main ideas. This thinking pattern causes students to clarify what they have read, as well as check their understanding. Teacher prepared Cause statements (including page numbers) were given to students; students read a selection appropriate for their reading level to find the Effects. Once students completed their Cause/Effect chart they were paired with another student to compare ideas.

CAUSE	EFFECT
Over thousands of years, floods deposited new soil in the river valleys. (p. 119)	*River valleys became a great area to farm because of their rich soil.*
German settlers planted different crops on their land each year. (p. 120)	*The Germans planted different crops to help the soil stay fertile.*
Farmers grew more wheat than they needed. (p. 120)	*The farmers grew more wheat than was needed, they traded their wheat for manufactured goods.*

Example of a cause/effect graphic organizer explaining how the German settlers farmed the land.

Special Considerations for Developing Readers (Response to Intervention)

Social studies books incorporate numerous facts with details; they assume the reader has the prior knowledge necessary to link the facts with the overarching concept. An overload of new vocabulary and difficult, unfamiliar concepts causes learners to flounder. This passage, found in a sixth grade textbook entitled "World," is an example of the density of concepts and unfamiliar vocabulary:

By the early 1900's, however, change had come to China. Britain had seized control of Hong Kong, and forced China to open its markets to trade. Japan had taken over the island of Taiwan. Britain and other nations also set up zones within China that were subject to their laws, rather than China's.

In the high school textbook, *Holt World History: The Human Journey* (2003), Chapter 34 is "Latin America Since 1945." Nowhere does the textbook explicitly state the countries included in Latin America. One opening paragraph states:

One reason that Latin American economies were unstable was their basis in monoculture. In other words, almost every country in the region relied on just one or two crops or minerals for exporting. Venezuela and Mexico relied on oil; Colombia and Central American nations relied on coffee (p. 911).

After reading this passage the reader might assume there are four countries included in Latin America, but what about the Caribbean and South America? The reader might wonder too, "What does Latin America really mean?" or "Are there other elements to monoculture other than economics?"

To help students comprehend a difficult passage, it is imperative that they build background information and be given ample opportunities to discuss ideas with other students. For example, students might use the **L.E.T.S. Connect** strategy (Billmeyer, 2006b) where students read the passage together, stop after each paragraph, and say to their neighbor, "The main idea in this paragraph is . . ." and then clear up misconceptions. Students also benefit from the **MVP (Most Valuable Points)** strategy (Billmeyer, 2006b). Students complete a MVP Card while pair-reading the selected pages. They then can share their card orally with the class and give reasons why they feel their points are essential. Because content can be interpreted in a variety of different ways, students need to share their perceptions and ideas for clarification and to personalize the information.

In meeting struggling readers' needs in the social studies classroom, it is important to know something about their reading levels. Teachers do this through formative assessments – looking at their work to determine what students do well and what they are struggling with. Then teachers could group students for reading assignments and provide each group with appropriately scaffold text.

Example: In United States History students are often assigned to read "The Declaration of Independence" in order to list what grievances the colonists had for breaking away from the British Empire and the type of government they wanted to form. In a classroom attempting to meet the needs of struggling readers, students might work together in homogenous groups based on their reading level. Below-grade readers might be given a plain-English version of the document written at an 8th grade level, at-grade readers would get an annotated copy of the original document, and above-grade readers would receive the original document itself. All groups have the same task and are expected to produce the same product, all are successful because they had access to the same concepts and information.

Conclusions: Implementing an Integrated Approach

The key to using any strategy in any subject is making sure that they are purposeful and effective. Teachers often find it difficult to assess and understand new material. As a result, strategies may be thrown into the curriculum without a clear purpose or outcome. Strategies need to be thought about in advance and the objective predetermined. A key question might be "What must students know and understand before they leave, and how will the strategy help them accomplish this?" Consider the following plan for implementing strategies.

Start of the year

If strategies are in place and taught from the beginning, students will become accustomed to them and will eventually be able to apply them independently. Get to know your students as readers right away. This is an excellent time to use text preview to gauge your students' understanding of how textbooks work. Begin to use strategies to build background knowledge prior to reading about new concepts. One strategy to start with is Forecast, a perfect way to introduce students to a new way of making meaning of the endless stream of vocabulary words. Use graphic organizers to teach students how to understand relationships between important vocabulary words and concepts.

Middle of the year

When expectations are understood and more basic strategies have been used, (Venn diagrams, KWL charts) it is a good time to introduce more complex strategies, such as the Cause and Effect strategy. This strategy requires students to review their most recent reading, going back to examine thoughts that were recorded during Text Tagging to determine the initial cause and the long-term effects. Also by mid-year you will have a good sense of which students need interventions such as additional background building, opportunities to connect with a partner during reading using the L.E.T.S. Connect strategy.

End of the year

The goal for the year is to allow students to take control over some of the strategies that have been introduced. Teachers are always looking for ways to engage their students, and what better opportunity than to allow them to help decide how they learn. Have students develop their own graphic organizer, create their own Forecast problems, or R.A.F.T.'s. This is an excellent opportunity to create ownership in what is being learned.

First Trimester	Strategy	Purpose
	• Text Previewing • Anticipation Guide • Forecast • MVP	• Understands how textbooks work • Builds prior knowledge • Introduces critical vocabulary words • Supports main idea and summarizing
Second Trimester	• Venn Diagrams • Text Tagging • L.E.T.S. Connect	• Supports compare & contrast thinking • Supports student interaction with text • Promotes comprehension during reading
Third Trimester	• Cause and Effect • Question the Author • RAFT	• Supports summarizing and review main idea • Helps students become text critics • Supports creative thinking & student writing

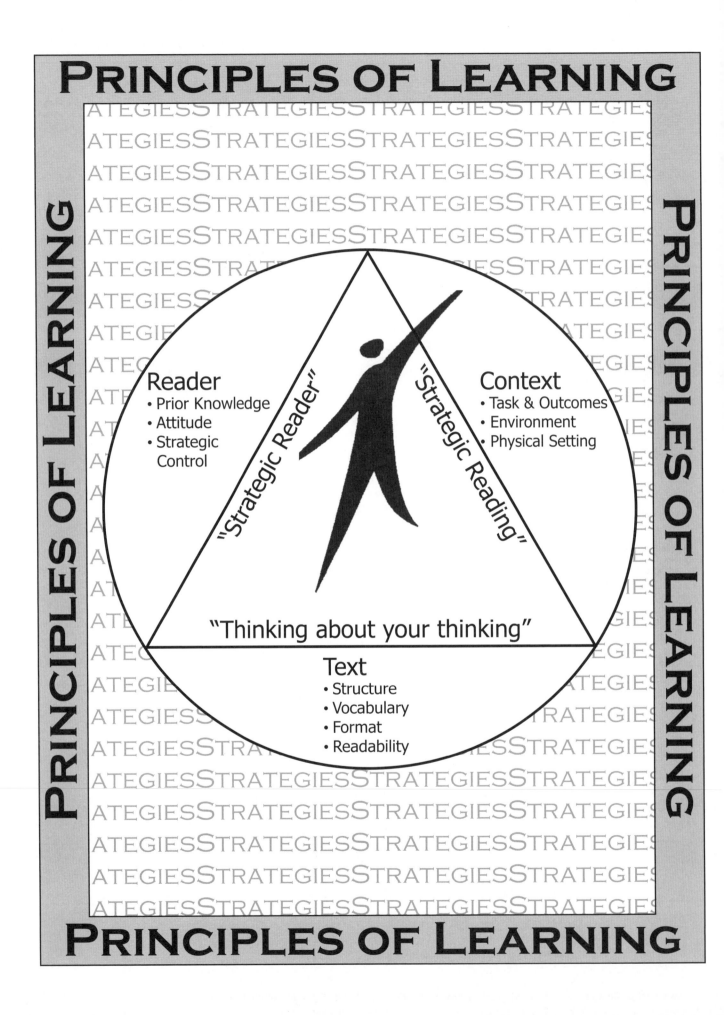

Chapter 7

Notes

More Voices from the Classroom

*The kids in our classroom are infinitely more significant than
the subject matter we're teaching them.*
- Meladee McCarty, *Chicken Soup for the Teacher's Soul*

Reading is key to learning in all content areas. This chapter features the thinking and inspired work of teachers who represent four unique teaching and learning situations. Each section highlights key strategies; additional examples are found in Chapter 6. Good instruction demands that teachers adapt strategies for their own learners and content.

Strategic Reading and the Young Child - Effective instruction for beginning readers consists of a balanced approach, focusing on word recognition and comprehension of meaningful text. Snow (2002) states that when children are not challenged to read for meaning (comprehension) in the early grades they hit a "comprehension wall" in the fourth grade, a wall that becomes nearly impossible to knock down. It is imperative that early reading instruction not only incorporates "learning to read" approaches but also "reading to learn" strategies.

Strategic Reading and the English Language Learner - As our nation becomes increasingly diverse, many teachers encounter English Language Learners (1 in 10 students in 2006 according to NCELA). Teaching non-native speakers to speak and read English is an arduous task. ELLs benefit from high expectations, not from a simplified curriculum. Teachers must understand the learning needs of ELLs in order to offer them a quality education.

Strategic Reading and the Special Education Learner - Working with the special education student requires a patient, highly efficacious teacher. Many special education students are struggling readers; perhaps that is why they are labeled for special education. Helping them develop skills and a willingness to read is critical not only with the special education teacher but for all teachers who impact their lives.

Strategic Reading and the Reluctant Reader - Working with a reluctant and/or struggling reader is a task few teachers envy. Students who progress from year to year always struggling as a reader, failing to understand the comprehension process, can become huge discipline problems. The job of any teacher, especially secondary reading teachers, is a monumental task because they are being called upon to "save the students" so they can go into the world as readers and productive citizens.

〰〰〰

Chapter 7

More Voices from the Classroom

"Learning Teams"

As a result of working through this chapter you will:
- Understand what strategic reading looks like in your teaching area
- Think metacognitively about teaching reading in your unique situation

Questions to ponder before, during, and after reading

The before, during, and after questions are incorporated into the strategy. The learning team process for this section is a modified K-W-L, a K-W-L-A (What do you Know? Want to learn? What have you learned? What additions would you make?) The K-W-L strategy is a learner-driven strategy because it asks the learner to generate questions for which they are interested in finding the answers. Use the template below for your note taking needs.

K   What do you already know about helping students become strategic readers in your content area? What challenges do you see students facing when reading to learn in _____?

W   What questions are you seeking answers to regarding strategic reading in your content area?

L   What did you learn or what new insights did you gain from this reading? From your dialogue with team members?

A   What additions would you make to the information that you read?

KWLA

K – What do I already know about teaching reading in my content area?	W- What questions do I have about teaching reading in my content area?	L – What did I learn from the reading and/or my colleagues?	A – What additions would I make to the information provided?

Strategic Reading and the Young Child
Authors, Ellen Billmeyer and Molly House

Rationale

When schools include activities such as storytelling, reading aloud, poetry parties, book fairs, meeting the author events, puppet shows, writing stories, acting out stories, and other wonderful engaging book related activities, children learn that reading is fun.

- Pamela Nevills and Patricia Wolfe

Young children love books; they possess a natural curiosity about books and they like to touch them, look through them, and ask inspiring questions, such as "How come?" or "What does that mean?" Many children eagerly enter school thinking they will learn to read and to write. The secret for granting this wish is easy – exposure to lots of books and plenty of time spent reading them. Reading opportunities such as an extensive classroom library, an inviting school library, special school events such as Books and Bedtime, and those mentioned by Nevills and Wolfe (2009) help develop young children into flourishing readers.

Developing knowledge and providing links to knowledge children already possess are foundations for literacy. As stated earlier in this book, **reading is thinking cued by text**; through watching and listening to teacher modeling, children learn specific strategies and identify the thinking necessary to comprehend text. For example, modeling how to access prior knowledge is essential when reading with young children; conversations about the title, the topic, the cover of the book, and key vocabulary jumpstarts thinking before reading and helps students make connections throughout the story. The sooner the teacher reveals these strategies and thinking, the sooner children will imitate the processes.

Although young children may not be independently reading narrative and informative texts, the teacher's use of strategies to reveal and reflect upon what is being read will show students that reading is more than being able to recognize and pronounce words. Research stresses that phonics instruction cannot stand alone as a reading program. Children need simultaneous instruction to build comprehension and develop vocabulary. The focus during the primary years must be on both **learning to read** and **reading to learn**! A delicate balance between phonics instruction and modeling before, during, and after reading strategies, as well as making connections between reading and writing promotes the development of strategic readers.

Issues and Nuances When Reading with the Young Child

Research indicates that a phonemic awareness program should take no more than 20 hours of *instruction throughout the entire year* (Armbuster, B., Lehr, Fl., & Osborn, J. 2001). While phonics is critical for helping students learn to read, it cannot become the major focus when teaching reading. As stated in chapter three, the goal is for children to become **strategic** readers, children who work actively to construct meaning, not merely to decode words. Research reminds us that children who do not learn to read for meaning in the early grades hit a comprehension wall in fourth grade (Snow, 2002). Children must become familiar with print, how print flows on the page, that combinations of sounds and letters generates words, and how words create meaningful stories. One engaging way to teach phonemic awareness is through the use of old favorites like Dr. Suess's *Cat in the Hat* or *Green Eggs and Ham*. Rhyming books such as these teach children to read while absorbing the structure and phonetic rules of the English language.

It is easy to presume that students will automatically possess the thinking and processes necessary to use reading skills. While reading to a first grade class, a teacher asked students to close their eyes and visualize what it would look like to be a bird in the air. As the story progressed, the teacher noticed one girl "squinching" her face into a "thinking pose." When the class stopped to check for comprehension and alter the predictions made, the teacher asked the children what they were seeing in their minds. The girl's hand went up. "I just see black." What a clear, literal answer to hear! It was time to stop to discuss what it means to visualize in our minds. The little girl's face brightened. "No one ever told me to picture what you are reading." What an "aha" moment for a veteran teacher. Modeling strategies **numerous times** is imperative; students must understand how strategies help them make meaning when reading. Guided instruction not only leads to independent use of strategies but also helps young readers learn to monitor for understanding. Each child is different; learning to decode words, achieving reading fluency, and reading for meaning is not a uniform process. All readers exhibit a wide range of reading potential; it is the individual teacher who must be prepared to meet the needs of all children (Nevills & Wolfe, 2009).

Learner Considerations

The greatest predictor of reading achievement is the actual amounts of time children spend reading real books (not basal selections or worksheets). There is a correlation between the amount of recreational reading time and scores on standardized reading tests; studies indicate that students need to spend 65 minutes a day in recreational reading to make an achievement difference (Allington, 2001). It is imperative children handle real life text early on; while they may not be able to read the words, they can read the pictures or retell the story to a friend.

To ensure that children become avid readers, teachers must concentrate on creating conditions for it to occur. We need to start the students' day energized with reading. Have a book on each student's desk; walk around with an interview notebook and ask questions. "I notice you have read two books on fish. What are you learning about fish?" Informal interviews increase student interest, set purposes for reading, and enhance comprehension. When struggling readers see the teacher writing down what they reported, they know their thoughts, opinions, and questions are valued, and they tend to read more complex texts. Reading a favorite selection aloud is another positive way to start the day; children are exposed to a variety of genres, learn how fluent reading sounds, and that reading is a valued way to spend time.

Young readers must learn skills of independence; extensive recreational reading of self-selected books facilitates independence. Children must have ample opportunities to browse through lots of books in order to find the right one. This means classrooms must include a library containing a span of text, fiction and nonfiction, at a variety of levels. Teaching students how to determine what makes a book a "good fit book" is essential. After modeling the process, a teacher can provide students with a bookmark suggesting ideas such as:

A Good Fit Book
- Look at the cover of the book read the title and the author
- Set a purpose for reading
- Open to a page in the beginning of the book
- Read the page using the 5 Finger Rule (Raise a finger for each unknown word)
    - 0-1 Fingers – too easy
    - 2-3 Fingers – just right
    - 4-5 Fingers – too hard
- Open to a page in the middle of the book and read using the 5 Finger Rule
- Enjoy reading the book or select a new one if too easy or hard

---

Book buddies or mixed ability partner reading allows students to talk about what they read, helping them construct meaning as well as working independently. This approach allows all students to read a variety of texts, even some that might be deemed too hard if they were to read alone. For example, two second grade girls (one an avid and successful reader and the other reading below grade level) make a fabulous duo during partner reading. The struggling reader is capable of reading and discussing a wider variety of books and develops confidence as a reader while the successful reader expands her leadership skills.

Text Considerations

Students need to learn at an early age how to think and process informative text. Nell K. Duke (2004) stresses the importance of informative/nonfiction text in the primary grades. Informative text:

- Creates future success in school (By 6th grade, 80% of school reading is informative text.)
- Appeals to readers' preferences, especially boys
- Addresses children's interests and questions
- Builds vocabulary and knowledge in all content areas
- Prepares students to handle real-life reading

Duke suggests that teachers carefully examine student reading; half of a student's daily interaction with text should be with informative material. In highly effective classrooms, teachers motivate readers with quality nonfiction text, model how to read informative text, and create classroom libraries with a 50-50 balance of narrative and informative text, including those that go beyond the specified curriculum. Research suggests that informative text provides a way to draw in uninterested male readers, those who sometimes turn into reluctant readers. The same young boys who spurn fiction may be eager to read about prehistoric animals, sports, historical figures, or cars.

A **Nonfiction Read-Aloud** provides students opportunities to learn science, social studies, mathematics, and other curriculum concepts (Calhoun, 2001). Because many primary age children cannot read the selection, teachers read the selection aloud. Read-Alouds can be very brief, sharing as little as a sentence or paragraph, or can be longer, reading a chapter over several days. When using the Nonfiction Read-Aloud explain how it is unlike reading a narrative "cover to cover." A great way to model the difference between the two is to show students an example of a narrative book and an informative book and together compare and contrast the similarities and differences.

Introduce readers to informative text containing different formats, such as:

- Concept books like *A Swim through the Sea* by Kristin Pratt
- Picture books like *Red-eyed Tree Frog* by Joy Crowley
- Mature identification books like *Ladybugs* by Mia Posada
- Life cycle books like *Suitcase for Seeds* by Jean Richards
- Experiment books like *The Magic School Bus* series by Joanna Cole
- Magazines such as *Ranger Rick*, *KIDS Discover*, *Boys Life*, *American Girl*, *Sports Illustrated for Kids*, and *Time for Kids*

Informative texts create interest in reading, deepen thinking when reading, and motivate learners to read more challenging text. When primary classroom teachers make sure that plenty of informative text is accessible to their students and model how to make meaning from text, students become strategic readers.

Teacher Considerations/Instructional Practices

Learning how to learn is just as important as what we learn. As teachers model fix-it strategies such as rereading, they show students how to become strategic readers. They see that the most important part of reading is making meaning of print and that strategic readers pay very close attention to their own thinking and comprehension.

Young readers need models to emulate; teachers' motivation and attitudes toward reading affect students' reading behaviors. An important part of a teacher's day is discussing with students what she likes or doesn't like to read, what she is currently reading, and/or when she finds time to read. Encouraging students to share what they read is also important. A classroom bulletin board titled "Take a Bite Out of a Book" encourages students (teacher too) to read and recommend books to others. The title, author, genre, personal opinions, and classmates who might enjoy the read are recorded on a "bite from a book" and displayed.

Ongoing vocabulary development must be an explicit part of reading instruction. Vocabulary is a critical ingredient when learning to read and oral language is the primary source for vocabulary development. Most of the books that primary students read themselves include relatively few words that are not already in their listening vocabularies. Research emphasizes the importance of engaging primary aged children in conversations to increase their exposure to words and to read aloud text that is above their independent reading level but at the cutting edge of their listening comprehension level.

Students should not only hear a wide variety of words but must learn to use a vast array of words when speaking. Incorporating group work in which students teach each other a new skill or play vocabulary games increases their use of rich oral language. Another powerful word learning approach is for the teacher to create word conscious learners by asking open-ended questions about the meaning of unfamiliar words spoken or written, such as "What does the author mean when she said he felt faint?" For more ideas on creating word conscious learners see chapter 5, p. 102.

Comprehension increases when teachers model fix-it strategies, focus on vocabulary development, and explicitly teach strategies for reading both informative and narrative text. The next section outlines specific strategies that help primary students read to learn.

Strategies to Extend Strategic Reading with the Young Child

Strategies are taught before, during, and after teaching, depending on the established purpose. Some strategies focus on vocabulary development and accessing prior knowledge, some are used to engage the mind throughout reading, and others assess understanding after reading a selection. Strategies need to be presented in an organized, planned manner one at a time. Effective instruction occurs when strategies are explicitly taught in meaningful ways, modeled, and reviewed again and again; students are then able to apply them appropriately and independently.

The **SAW Model (Student Action Words)** strategy (Billmeyer, 2006b) assists in teaching critical words for concepts found in informative text. The strategy encourages whole brain learning because students interact with selected words in visual, aural, symbolic, and experiential ways. The SAW Model when used in a Vocabulary Journal format works well as a formative assessment.

1. quote: *in front of the boxcar a pretty little brook*	
page: *31* reference: *Boxcar Children*	
2. word: *brook*	3. definition:
predicted definition: *fountain or a car that has a waterfall*	*a small natural stream*
4. antonym/s: *ocean*	5. association or symbol:
6. one good sentence: *I like brooks because you can splash in them.*	

Example of the SAW model used to enhance vocabulary development.

The **Concept Definition Mapping** (Schwartz and Raphael, 1985) vocabulary strategy is excellent for learning critical terms in science, social studies, and math. Concept Maps cause students to internalize the word rather than merely copy the textbook definition, and it encourages them to make personal connections. Create the Concept Map on chart paper or on a transparency, as well as printing student copies with the concept in the middle. Once students understand the process for completing a Concept Map they can work with a partner or independently.

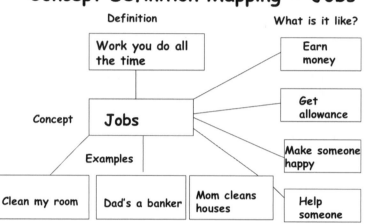

Concept Definition Mapping - Jobs

Example of a Concept Map to reinforce critical vocabulary terms in social studies.

A powerful strategy to reinforce that reading is thinking cued by text is the **L.E.T.S. CONNECT** strategy (Billmeyer, 2006b). This strategy engages the mind of the learner through a read aloud, but the reading is continuous. Periodically the reading is stopped so paired learners share with each other what they are thinking about the topic at that moment. (3-5 stopping points can be marked ahead of time.) For example, if the strategy was used during social studies when studying citizenship the teacher could begin by writing L.E.T.S. Connect horizontally on chart paper and explaining the meaning of each letter.

L: Listen to the selection
E: Engage with ideas in the story
T: Think about important ideas and interesting vocabulary
S: Share your thinking with your partner

Next, read aloud *My Teacher for President* by May Winters, stopping for paired sharing at predetermined places. At the first stopping point model the process with a student, then ask all students to share with their partners. Conclude by discussing what students learned from the selection and how the strategy helped them focus on what was read.

Teachers can use questions to help primary students understand an informative selection. The **Question-Answer Relationship (QAR)** (Raphael, 1986) strategy helps students make connections between ideas in the selection and their prior knowledge, process information at deeper levels of understanding, modify ideas, and elaborate on ideas presented in the story. The QAR strategy incorporates four types of questions organized into two categories:

- In the Book - *right there* and *think and search* questions
- In My Head - *author and me* and *on my own* questions

Explain that answering questions about a selection read requires the reader to use information from the book and information from their own background of experiences. Model the process using an easy fairy tale. Display *right there* and *think and search* questions along with the pages from the book containing the answers on the Smartboard, Promethean Board, or using an Elmo projector. Next, display *author and me* and *on my own* questions but no pages from the book. Questions for the four areas of the QAR strategy have been created on candy wrappers because such questions unwrap meaning and make learning enjoyable (Billmeyer, 2006b). Students use the questions during guided, independent, and paired reading activities. Four different colors of paper are used to differentiate each type of question. Four sample questions are included below:

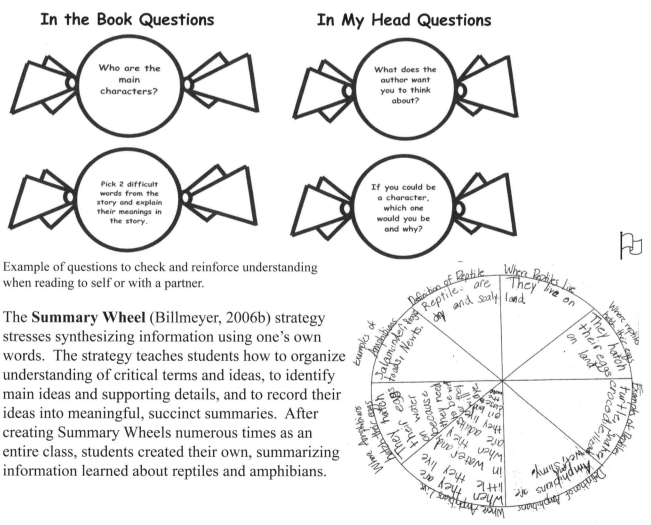

In the Book Questions

Who are the main characters?

Pick 2 difficult words from the story and explain their meanings in the story.

In My Head Questions

What does the author want you to think about?

If you could be a character, which one would you be and why?

Example of questions to check and reinforce understanding when reading to self or with a partner.

The **Summary Wheel** (Billmeyer, 2006b) strategy stresses synthesizing information using one's own words. The strategy teaches students how to organize understanding of critical terms and ideas, to identify main ideas and supporting details, and to record their ideas into meaningful, succinct summaries. After creating Summary Wheels numerous times as an entire class, students created their own, summarizing information learned about reptiles and amphibians.

Example of a Summary Wheel used to check for understanding when studying reptiles and amphibians.

Give 1 to Get 1 (Billmeyer, 2006b) is an interactive strategy that provides students with an opportunity to exchange ideas about a topic before, during, or after learning. This barter system activity encourages oral communication and engages all students in the learning process. Primary students who are learning the different elements of a fictional story are introduced to the elements one at a time during story read alouds. The Give 1 to Get 1 is used as a formative assessment once all elements have been presented. The teacher models the strategy with one student, the teacher giving "Setting of the Story" and getting from the student a "Favorite Character." Students select what they want to share. Students are later placed in small groups to give and get one idea from each group member, writing or sketching the ideas in the right boxes.

Favorite Character	Setting of the Story	Problem in the Story	Your Favorite Part

Conclusions: Implementing an Integrated Approach

A good start in learning to read and reading to learn has long-term advantages for children's overall education. Because students' attitudes toward reading develop early it is imperative they have numerous opportunities to enjoy and learn from informative and narrative text. Informative text represents real-life reading, and students find it engaging and interesting; narrative text allows a chance for fantasy. Strategic reading in the content areas in the primary grades provides excellent opportunities for all students to be members of a reading and learning community.

The ideas and strategies cited in this section support comprehension development with the young child; they not only help children learn to read but also, read to learn. Emphasizing reading in the content areas with primary age students builds a strong foundation for ongoing success as a strategic reader in the content areas. We must remember -- *In every task the most important thing is the beginning... especially when you deal with anything young and tender.* - Plato, *The Republic*

Strategic Reading and the English Language Learner

Author, Peggy Braitsch

Rationale

The number of English Language Learners (ELLs) is continuing to grow at a rapid pace, and their academic achievement is receiving increasing attention as schools are challenged to provide quality education for all students. Enrollment figures of the National Clearinghouse for English Language Acquisition show that of the 49.5 million students enrolled in school during the 2005-2006 school year more than 10% were ELLs, up 57% in ten years (NCELA, 2007).

As educators, we know that teaching English through the academic curriculum is the most successful approach for ELLs since students gain content knowledge as they perfect reading, writing, listening, and speaking in English. Through learner-centered teaching strategies, a methodical focus on academic vocabulary development, and explicit instruction for critical skills, classroom and content area teachers can effectively help their ELL students develop language *and* understanding of new concepts needed for achievement in school.

Literacy Issues for the English Language Learner

There are various factors that affect second language development and academic achievement. These include literacy level in the native language, prior education, language development programs available, and culture. Not surprisingly, one of the most significant influences is the student's literacy level in the native language since these skills transfer to English as the student acquires it. Those who have acquired phonemic awareness, who can recognize a main idea and details, and can analyze an emotional tone in their native language, will transfer those skills as they learn English. As reading skills transfer, so will previously learned content area skills (Cummins, 1980).

Learner Considerations

When considering the needs of language learners, it is important to have a basic understanding of second language acquisition theory (Krashen, 1981). Understanding the two principal aspects of language is essential in order to analyze and prepare appropriate lessons for ELLs. One aspect, Basic Interpersonal Communication Skills (BICS), is the simple social language required to carry on conversations, complete forms, or read menus and directions. The other is referred to as Cognitive Academic Language Proficiency (CALP). CALP is needed to complete more complex tasks such as reading and comprehending a text or writing a report; it includes such skills as literacy, comprehension, and analysis (Cummins, 1980). Well-developed oral communication skills are very important to academic success but do not themselves prepare the students to succeed in academics. Although BICS are usually acquired in one to two years, research by Cummins (1980) shows that it may take students seven years or longer to acquire the CALP skills necessary for academic success.

Students With Interrupted Formal Education (SIFE)

In the past 15 years, an increasing number of immigrant students have entered schools in the US having little or no formal education and/or with very low literacy skills. These students are faced with learning English, developing academic language skills, mastering grade level content, and developing study skills all simultaneously. Research shows that they are among the *most at risk students* in US schools. Current research on SIFE programs by Walsh (1999) indicates that the approaches listed below begin to provide effective support when working with SIFE students:

- Integrating literacy and content instruction thematically
- Instructing in the native language when possible
- Incorporating the ELLs previous cultural and literacy experiences
- Identifying and using cognates, words in English similar to the native language
- Coordinating English language and content instruction in a structured way
- Sheltering instruction to modify content (see below)
- Keeping class sizes small

Teacher Considerations/Instructional Practices

In helping ELLs to become strategic readers in the content areas, classroom teachers need to modify both their instructional strategies and the expectations of the ELLs. Referring to sections in chapter 6 addressing strategic reading in specific content areas will provide additional strategies when designing instruction for ELLs.

Sheltered instructional approaches help immeasurably as ELLs acquire language proficiency support while learning concepts and vocabulary in the content areas. Sheltered approaches include the use of audio aids, visuals (graphic novels, maps, pictures, graphs, and videos), high-interest-low readability books, clear and simplified language (free of colloquial or idiomatic expressions) as well as gestures and demonstrations. Guiding students in *narrow* reading using children's literature is advantageous for ELLs: *narrow* reading refers to reading based on one theme, one subject, or by one author (Hadaway, 2009). Children's literature typically presents more concrete concepts using simpler language than textbooks.

Teachers need many tools and techniques at their fingertips to provide scaffolding for ELL learning. Prior to reading teachers must help ELLs preview materials, access background knowledge with the use of pictures, maps, graphs, or objects, and pre-teach critical vocabulary. Audio recordings of the readings provides ELLs with multiple opportunities to both read and hear the text, helping to develop listening skills, vocabulary, and connections to pertinent concepts. Activities requiring ELL students to brainstorm, sort, and/or analyze vocabulary pertaining to new concepts helps them gain understanding and retain new information. Coupling these tools and techniques with a cooperative learning approach greatly enhances learning.

Let's look at how these approaches have been integrated into a learning experience about "Migration and Why People Move." After an introduction to the concept of migration through pictures, a story about migration, such as *Tomas and the Library Lady*, and discussion (including why their families have moved), students are divided into multi-English level groupings. One student in each group is asked to be the recorder. Groups are provided a question, "Why do people move from one place to another?" to discuss for 5-7 minutes with recorder writing all ideas. Next, the entire class resumes to share ideas recorded in small groups. The teacher records all ideas, creating a **Web Organizer** that incorporates critical terms pertinent to migration. This student-generated web containing key vocabulary can be added to the classroom word wall or used in word-sorts to support ongoing use of the words.

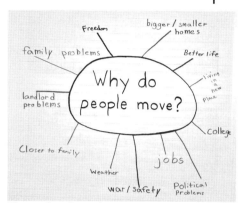
Example of a web organizer for migration.

Next, using texts and visuals, the concept of the "push-pull" factors involved with human migration is introduced. Students are divided into pairs and using the organizer and word banks to model correct spelling or syntax, they create a T-Chart or Venn diagram indicating human migration "push-pull" factors.

Why People Move		
Push Factors	Both	Pull Factors
Family problems	Bigger home	Better life
War	Jobs	Safety
Landlord problems	Closer to family	Live in new place
Political problems		Freedom

Example of a "push-pull" chart created from ideas listed on the web organizer for migration.

Strategies to Extend Reading with the English Language Learner

A *thorough book introduction* can be magical in preparing an ELL to read unfamiliar material. It encourages students to access background knowledge and to build interest. A rich introduction requires that the teacher be aware of the student's language level as well as being very familiar with the text; it can be as simple as bringing in an object that will trigger ideas about the story or as elaborate as ideas listed below.

The **SQ4R** (Survey, Question, Read, Recite, Review, Reflect) strategy (Robinson, 1961) can be used independently or in groups to help ELLs organize information at every stage of reading. This strategy is especially useful because it helps the student self-monitor; the following self-assessment guide (Billmeyer, 2006b) serves as a self-monitoring device for students.

SQ4R Self-Assessment Guide

Reading Assignment:

Please put a check mark on the line after you have completed the following steps.

Survey   **Check**
- Read the title, subheadings, and introduction
- Study new vocabulary, illustrations, graphic aids
- Establish purpose for reading

Question
- Formulate questions about the title, headings, pictures and charts that will guide your reading

Read
- Read to answer your questions
- Reread any sections that were confusing
- Write questions or ideas on sticky notes and attach it to the page

Recite
- Answer the questions
- Study the new vocabulary words

Review
- Review your purpose for reading the information
- Test your understanding of the new vocabulary
- Write a summary of what was learned

Reflect
- Record how the strategy helped you comprehend the selection

In an English/LA class where ELL and native language students together were reading a book about Roberto Clemente, the famous Puerto Rican baseball player, several days were required to prepare the students for the reading. The book introduction consisted of each student selecting one theme from the book and preparing a five-minute oral presentation to the group. The teacher had prepared readings, pictures, and a selection of graphic organizers at different levels, matching activities with student abilities and interests. The topics included Puerto Rican history or geography, baseball rules and history, the current organization on the Major and Minor Leagues, and a look at recent racism in America. By preparing and sharing their work students gained background knowledge, learned key words, and developed ownership of one of the important themes to be explored. To introduce *To Kill a Mockingbird*, an ESL teacher created a map of Maycomb, Alabama complete with the streets, the courthouse, and "Scout" and Boo Radley's houses. As the students read the selection they added ideas to the map to reinforce their new knowledge and understanding.

Vocabulary Development

Developing a rich vocabulary is essential to the academic success of ELLs. Learning English vocabulary is one of the most crucial tasks for ELLs; vocabulary contributes to word recognition, is a significant predictor of reading comprehension, and is an indicator of academic success (Folse, 2004). ELLs face several challenges as they develop vocabulary, such as the lack of basic speaking and reading vocabulary; the need to learn frequently used idioms; and the need to learn new concepts through a foreign language. A multi-faceted approach for vocabulary development is essential for ELLs (Graves, 2006).

The fact that ELLs in the class may not understand words that seem obvious to native language speakers must be in the forefront of all teachers' minds as they prepare lessons; being aware of the ELLs' language levels and being deliberate in the identification and instruction of the vocabulary is essential. Teaching *within a context* helps ELLs build prior knowledge and attach word meanings to content information.

For example, during the Olympics, an ELL teacher teamed up with a classroom teacher to teach vocabulary words and concepts pertaining to the Olympics. Words were investigated as part of the "Words of the Week" classroom routine. Students were encouraged to listen for each word as it was used in other contexts; they also read information about the Olympics to reinforce the new words.

Words of the Week	
Mystery Monday:	Introduce and discuss the words arriving upon a written definition.
Telling Tuesday:	Students talk about the words, multiple meanings, what they know about them.
Wordy Wednesday:	Students write their own definitions sketch what the word means.
Thoughtful Thursday:	Word study focuses on synonyms, antonym, prefixes, and suffixes.
Fun Friday:	Games such as "Who has/I have" are played using targeted vocabulary.

A **Word Sort** using all of the Olympic terms posted on the word wall was created. Students were asked to categorize the words and explain how they organized them to a partner. Students created sentences on sentence strips using the vocabulary and organized the strips into proper order. This approach is an excellent way for students to show their level of understanding of vocabulary and it can be easily differentiated using an open sort (student controlled) or a closed sort (the teacher provides the sorting categories).

Olympics	Sportsmanship	Equipment	Location	Medals
hockey	National Anthem	puck	ice rink	gold
basketball	friendship	ball	court	silver
track & field	handshake	skis	stadium	bronze

Example of a closed word sort using the Olympic terms.

To reinforce the meaning of the words and concepts, students played the "Who has?"/"I have" game. Each student in the group was given a teacher prepared 3x5 card with a word and a question using the targeted vocabulary written on it. The teacher began play with a question and students read their cards to figure out if they had the response. The responder then asked the question on her card. Play continued until all students had an opportunity to participate. This activity can be modified for any content or grade level. A colleague uses this technique to teach 11th grade vocabulary and etymology. An example follows:

Teacher Card	Who has a word that means a person who does sports?
Student 1 Card	I have the word "athlete."
	Who has a compound word?
Student 2 Card	I have the word "sportsmanship."
	Who has the definition of "anthem?"
Student 3 Card	I have "A song to show love for a country."

The **Concept Definition Mapping** strategy (Schwartz & Raphael, 1985) focuses on vocabulary development of critical concept within a content area. Concept Definition Maps cause students to internalize the meaning of words by interacting with the word in different ways. Students are asked to define the meaning of the word using their own words, to provide real-life examples, and to draw what the word means; when ELLs are asked to construct a nonlinguistic representation of the new words their understanding and retention increase. Asking students to explain all facets of a concept map to a partner increases the learning process. There are different types of concepts maps; the map provided is a version developed by middle school teachers.

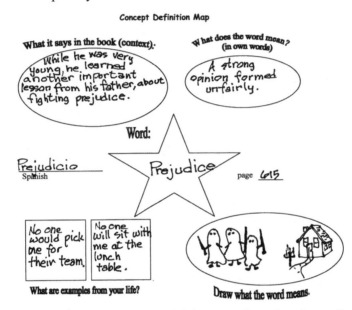

A Concept Definition Map explaining *prejudice* taken from a literature selection.

Conclusions

To provide equal access to the curriculum and to narrow the achievement gap between ELLs and their English-speaking peers, ELLs need to participate in the mainstream academic program, but with appropriate supports to supplement the linguistic input. English language learners benefit from the strategy instruction in all content areas, but require well-planned supports and modifications. Leveled texts, both fiction and nonfiction, provide an excellent supplement to engage ELLs in content exposure. Due to the complexity of vocabulary acquisition, all students, especially ELLs, will benefit from content areas teachers becoming experts in effective vocabulary instruction and the teaching of content area reading strategies.

Strategic Reading and the Special Education Learner

Author, Sue Witter

Rationale

To be literate in the 21st century requires not only the basic skills of reading and writing, but also rapid changes in technology demand that students must be able to view, present, analyze, and evaluate information that comes in a variety of forms—through print and various digital modes. Now, more than ever, all students need to become strategic readers. For some students, this task is accomplished in a seemingly intuitive way. However, for those students who have learning difficulties, the task of making sense of print is an arduous task. The Literacy Bill of Rights (Yoder, Erickson & Koppenhaven, 1996) states that all people, regardless of their disabilities, have a basic right to use print. Special education students deserve to have access and opportunity to the best literacy instruction that we can provide. Doing so will have profound positive implications for their chances to succeed in the fast-paced, information-rich 21st century.

Issues & Nuances When Reading with the Special Education Learner

Two developments in education have had a direct impact on literacy instruction for the special education student—changes in legislation that require school districts to develop a Response to Intervention (RtI) plan, and the growing number of students who are labeled with dyslexia or autism spectrum disorder. These developments not only have resulted in changes in the way we place students and provide services for them, but also directly in the classroom in the way that we deliver instruction.

Response to Intervention

The reauthorized Individuals with Disabilities Education Improvement Act (IDEA, 2004) includes provisions that have led to changes in the way students with learning disabilities are identified. Although the legislation does not explicitly use the term Response to Intervention, it implies that school districts need to develop clear plans as to how they will devise, deliver, and document scientifically based interventions. The onus falls upon both general education and special education teachers to carefully and systematically plan focused instruction and to monitor progress. Now more than ever, teachers need specific and proven strategies to implement learning and ways to monitor students' progress.

Students with Dyslexia and Autism Spectrum Disorder

Another challenge facing both general education and special education teachers is the growing number of students diagnosed with dyslexia and Autism Spectrum Disorder, or ASD. Although it is unclear why the numbers of diagnosed students are increasing, it is clear that this has profound instructional implications for both special and general education teachers.

Dyslexia, an often misunderstood term to describe a student with reading difficulties, actually refers to a very specific type of reading difficulty. Dylexia is a language-based learning disorder that is biological in origin and primarily interferes with the acquisition of print literacy (reading, writing, and spelling). It is characterized by poor decoding and spelling abilities as well as deficits in phonological awareness and/or manipulation (Sawyer, 1993). Though dyslexia is a complex reading disability, it is important for students with dyslexia and teachers to understand that they can still grow as readers and writers; they can benefit from strategy instruction that will help them read rich and engaging texts.

Students with Autism Spectrum Disorder (ASD) represent another fast-growing population of students with disabilities. ASD, is the overarching term used to describe various categories of the disorder ranging from autistic disorder, pervasive development disorder not otherwise specified (PDD-NOS), to a much milder form, Asperger syndrome (NIMH, 2004). Students with ASD have "delayed or abnormal functioning" in at least one of the following areas: 1) social interaction; 2) communication; and/or 3) restrictive repetitive and stereotyped patterns of behavior, interests, and activities (American Psychiatric Association, 2000). Authors Kluth and Chandler-Olcott (2008) argue that the medical model of autism described above represents a deficit model, and they prefer to think about students with autism as having differences, rather than deficits. These differences, which may include movement, sensory, communication, social, and learning differences, will clearly affect literacy development. Teachers who recognize the differences, however, can address them through various strategies and accommodations. Kluth and Chandler-Olcott emphasize that when planning literacy instruction for students with ASD, teachers need to recognize both student's strengths and needs and focus on learning about the individual students with autism rather than upon autism itself.

The increasing number of students diagnosed with dyslexia and ASD provide unique challenges in the classroom and now more than ever teachers need to continue to add strategies to their "toolbox." Searching for a "silver bullet" is futile; students with disabilities need the same high expectations and good teaching that benefit all students. The only real difference is that special education students needs can be characterized by the word "more"—more time, explicitness, and modifications. Otherwise, special education students will benefit from the same effective strategies that work for general education students.

Text/Learner Considerations

Because special education students often have experienced failure, it is imperative that they receive instruction with text that is respectful, engaging, and accessible. Many special education students lag grade levels behind their peers in terms of reading ability, yet they have the same interests as their peers. It is important to seek out text that is age-appropriate but is at a comfortable level of difficulty. Although there are many commercially published books designed to accommodate this need, called "high/lows," (high interest/low vocabulary), it may be necessary to seek out alternate sources of text. Short articles from children's magazines, internet articles, poetry, song lyrics, and teacher-made books provide special education students with respectful and engaging texts.

Another important factor to consider when planning reading instruction for special education students is that many of these students have experienced years of struggle and failure, and have often developed avoidance behaviors. It is important that teachers address this in a direct and respectful way, perhaps by acknowledging the behavior, while reassuring the student that together we can find what is difficult and work to build the necessary skills to be successful. It is important to let special education students know that their failure to learn to read is not their fault; we just need to find strategies that will work. Perhaps one of my most memorable students said it best, "Mrs. Witter, teachers tell me to try harder, but I don't know what to try!" This student needed strategies, or even more importantly, needed assistance in becoming a strategic reader.

Teacher Considerations/Instructional Practices

In planning instruction for special education students, there are several general considerations to guide a teacher's selection of text and strategies. Because special education students have very distinctive learning needs and specific areas of interests, special education teachers should invest extra time in finding out what these needs and interests are. Although there are many commercially produced interest inventories and reading surveys available, teachers can easily find or create their own informal inventories. Questions to possibly include:

- What do you like to read about?
- How do you spend your free time?
- What do good readers do?
- What do you do when you come to a word you don't know?
- What do you do when you don't understand?
- What do you do well as a reader?
- What is difficult for you as a reader?

Teachers not only need to know students well but also be able to bridge the students' prior knowledge to new learning. This is true for all students with special needs but especially so for learners with autism. Using strategies like word webs and KWL charts (Ogle, 1989) will focus students' current knowledge and provide a solid foundation for successful new learning.

Lastly, a final consideration is to select strategies that have simple procedures and are easily transferable to other settings. Getting students to be "metagcognitive" about their strategies—to talk about what strategy works for them, why and when they might use the strategy is especially important for special education students. This will ensure that the students will move closer to becoming strategic readers.

Strategies to Extend Reading with the Special Education Learner

Special education students benefit from ongoing strategy instruction. Strategies outlined in chapter 6 are beneficial for all students. The strategies explained in this section are considered essential for struggling readers.

Word Sorts (Billmeyer, 2006b) help students activate and share prior knowledge. Special education students benefit from this pre-reading strategy because a lack of vocabulary knowledge often impedes the students' ability to make meaning of the text. Additionally, word sorts are especially helpful to special education students because sorting mimics the basic cognitive process of comparing and contrasting information (Ganske, 2000).

The two most common kinds of word sorts are open and closed sorts. In open sorts, the teacher presents words or phrases and asks the students to categorize them into meaningful groups; students must then label the categories. Open sorts encourage divergent thinking, and also provide useful insight about the students' thinking. In closed sorts, the teacher predetermines the categories, and asks students to place the words in the proper category. Closed sorts reinforce students' ability to classify words and ideas. Both kinds of sorts, however, give special education students the opportunity to deepen their knowledge of vocabulary and concepts, see relationships among words, and build interest before they read. For both open and closed sorts, it is imperative that the teacher and students discuss the sorting when finished. Not only will this allow students to articulate their thinking, but it also will allow the teacher to address misconceptions.

Using word sorts as a post-reading strategy is an excellent way to provide more repetition with the vocabulary and concepts of the text as well as a good way to assess the students' understanding. For students who need extra support, using pictures or icons paired with the words helps facilitate understanding. Finally, using word sorts for the purpose of having students categorize sound and letter patterns will strengthen their decoding and spelling abilities (Ganske, 2000). Word sorting for sound and letter patterns is a particularly effective way for students with dyslexia to strengthen their phonological abilities.

Reciprocal Teaching (Palinscar, A. & Brown, A., 1984) is an effective strategy because it incorporates four critical comprehension skills as well as active engagement through discussion. The four reading skills emphasized are:

- *Predicting* provides a purpose for reading. Readers use background information to forecast what the selection will be about and then read to prove or disprove their prediction.
- *Clarifying* promotes understanding of difficult text. Readers seek clarity about difficult concepts, new vocabulary, or unfamiliar reference words.

- *Questioning* causes purposeful reading and deeper understanding of the selection. Readers think about what they do not know, need to know, or would like to know.
- *Summarizing* increases understanding of the passage and encourages reflection. The information read is synthesized into the reader's own words.

Reciprocal Teaching is a labor-intensive strategy requiring the teacher to first teach each comprehension skill individually. Once students understand the thinking each reading attribute demands, the four comprehension skills are combined and the Reciprocal Teaching strategy is modeled. The teacher, serving as discussion leader, begins by discussing the selected passage, either predicting what will happen or summarizing what is known about the topic. Next, the first section of the passage is read aloud with the teacher stopping to clarify new vocabulary words or to ask questions. After reading the section the teacher generates a summary statement.

Once the strategy is modeled, the role of discussion leader is given to a student. Special education students need intensive modeling and guided practice with feedback; many require additional coaching and guidance as they lead discussions. Students can be organized into groups of four with each student responsible for a reading skill, rotating the responsibility to predict, clarify, question, and summarize throughout the reading of the selection. The Reciprocal Teaching strategy ensures understanding and clarity when reading; readers see first hand that reading is thinking cued by text.

The **T+B=I Inference** strategy (Zwiers, 2005) helps students understand the "formula" for making an inference, instead of just thinking that it's something that magically just happens (or doesn't!). The teacher begins by modeling for students using a simple 3-column chart:

Text +	Background Knowledge =	Inference

The teacher reads a portion of the text aloud and does a "think aloud" to show students that she arrived at her inference by looking at the text for clues that the author left, as well as combining her background knowledge with the clues. Next, the teacher asks students to try. It is not necessary for the student to fill out the columns from left to right; often they will read the text, make an inference, and then go back and consider their background knowledge. Using short mysteries and/or picture books works particularly well for special education students when first introducing this strategy. For reluctant and struggling writers, the teacher can have students discuss their inferences orally by pointing out where the clues were in the text and what background knowledge was utilized.

Text Tagging (Billmeyer, 2006b) is another powerful strategy for special education students. Often, special education students expend so much cognitive attention on decoding the text that they often finish a piece of text and wonder, "What did I just read?" Text tagging is a "during reading" strategy that requires students to interact and think about the text as they read. This strategy is particularly beneficial to special education students because it helps them remain focused during the entire text, allows for kinesthetic learners to use manipulatives, and encourages deeper follow-up discussions.

After selecting a text, building background and setting purposes for reading, instruct students to use coded sticky notes/arrows to mark specific parts of the text as follows: *This is new information, information was surprising or shocking, and an idea is confusing.* Students can be encouraged to jot brief notes on the coded sticky notes, but extensive writing while reading might interfere with the flow. Additionally, many special education students find writing to be an arduous task and might avoid placing a sticky note to avoid any extra writing. A follow-up discussion of the sticky notes is necessary, it allows students to co-construct the meaning of the text and will deepen and extend their reading experience.

The **FQR** strategy (Harvey and Goudvis, 2000) requires students to record facts, questions, and responses during reading. Students synthesize information and come to new and deeper understandings.

Facts What are the important ideas?	Questions What does this make you think about or wonder?	Responses So what? Why is this important?
Toads are actually frogs	Why do we call them toads then? What's the difference?	Toads have short hind legs made for walking. Frogs have long hind legs for swimming. I only see toads in my back yard.

Teacher modeling is essential to the success of the FQR strategy, as students may not feel comfortable questioning the facts or responding to the text. For students who are reluctant to write, the teacher could place sticky notes in the text that have an "F," "Q," or "R" written on them. When students come to a sticky note, they must orally respond with a fact, question, or response. This causes the reader to interact with the text more deeply and more frequently.

Conclusions: Implementing an Integrated Approach

To be literate in the 21st century is a daunting task for any student, but it is particularly challenging for students who encounter learning difficulties. The good news is that research strongly indicates that most students can grow as readers and writers when careful attention is focused on diagnosing their difficulties and selecting effective strategies to help them make sense of the dizzying amount of information surrounding them. Reading is not easy undertakings for special education students, but as Yoder, Erikson and Koppenhaven (1996) remind us, access to literacy for all students is not a privilege, but a right. Special education students have the same literacy needs as all students—the need for effective strategies, rich, engaging text, and excellent instruction.

Strategic Reading and the Reluctant Reader

Author, Cheryl Becker Dobbertin

Rationale

Reluctant readers aren't born, they're made. They are most often students who come to school behind their peers in terms of language development. They watch, in many cases bewildered, as their classmates quickly, and invisibly, master something that they themselves cannot do. As their peers take off into a whole new world of vocabulary, information, and imagined places and people, they are left behind. Understanding challenging text requires deep background knowledge, and these readers have not yet acquired that background knowledge. They're frustrated, and frustrated people often avoid the tasks that cause that feeling. It's a downward spiral of avoidance, self-defeat, and lack of learning. Teachers of reluctant readers must address these students' emotional *and* academic needs.

Most teachers recognize and understand the connection between students' reading skill and their capacity for learning, especially as students begin to move up through the grades to more rigorously study the "contents" of the world – science, math, social studies, family and consumer science, for example. But the importance of reaching our reluctant readers is more fully illustrated when we consider life *beyond* school for those not reading proficiently by the time they graduate. According to the 2004 report by the Alliance for Excellent Education:

"In 1950, when opportunities to achieve economic stability and a middle-class standard of living were open to those without a high school diploma, students unable to convert their third-grade reading skills into literacy levels useful for comprehending and learning from complex, content-rich materials could drop out of high school and still hope to achieve a reasonably comfortable and successful lifestyle. In 2004, however, there are few opportunities for the high school dropout to achieve a comparable way of life; jobs, welfare, and social safety nets will no longer be available as they once were." (http://www.all4ed. org/files/ReadingNext.pdf)

I live in Rochester, New York and have seen this phenomenon first hand as a steady stream of friends and neighbors have been released from high-paying manufacturing jobs at the Eastman Kodak Company. Our community's beloved "Big Yellow Box" once employed 60,000 people locally, now only about 7,400 still work locally for the company that was once the foundation of our local economy. And it's not simply that these jobs are going overseas -- Kodak's worldwide employment has also dropped more than half, from 136,500 to 20,300. Our worldwide economy is changing and our expectation, no, our *insistence*, upon our students' need to read, and read well, must change with it.

Learner Considerations

In Chapter 3, a Strategic Reader is defined as one who comprehends text by: making connections to self, to other texts, and to the world, asking questions, determining importance, visualizing, making inferences, and synthesizing information (Keene & Zimmerman, 1997). Most schools and teachers, especially middle and high schools who often (unfairly) lack the preparation to deal with the challenge of struggling and less motivated readers, may believe that what they need is simply a dose of "more phonics." Readers are encouraged to do things like "sound it out," "use the dictionary," or "highlight" without any support as to how to *think* about text. Thinking about text, Keene and others have taught us, is actually the key to comprehension, and it's more often than not the missing link.

Reluctant readers in the content areas often don't know that reading is *thinking*. They don't know that learning to read or making reading interesting involves making connections, actively questioning the author, inferencing, and sorting out the important ideas from the text. They rarely understand that the text is a means to an end – that reading well gives them access to ideas and information that they will need and like. Supporting reluctant readers means helping them as they use metacognitive processes such as making connections or determining importance that they *aren't yet* using, or that they *aren't yet* using in academic settings.

My experience is that it benefits readers to be direct, to be supportively honest about the fact that they do not read well enough to be successful. Put it out there, and let the students know that you have every intention of doing something about it. Then create opportunities for students to *be* successful when reading.

When working with reluctant readers, it is important to use strategies that build on what they know or are already able to do so that they gain confidence and motivation. **Learning Logs** (Billmeyer, 2006b) asks readers to share their thinking while reading, often in a two-column format. Students choose selections from the text to comment on or question. For example, students in health class are reading an article about teen smoking. The teacher asks them to keep a double entry journal that looks like this:

Selections from the Text	My Response

Quinn, who is a very good reader, submits her work, and the teacher is pleased with it, partially replicated below:

Selections from the Text	My Response
"The American Lung Association estimates that every minute four thousand eight hundred teens will take their first drag off a cigarette."	That seems unrealistic to me. Most of my friends don't smoke.
"Research shows that teens between 13 and 17 years of age who smoke daily are more likely to use other drug substances."	I have heard this before. That's one of the reasons why I will never even smoke one cigarette.

But the teacher is also happy to receive the following from Brent, who often fails to complete reading assignments:

Selections from the Text	My Response
"Why is tobacco so addicting? It is because nicotine acts as a stimulant, which is stimulating the mind, body, and spirit."	I am not sure what "stimulant" is exactly, but I know people get addicted to smoking because it makes them feel good or better.
"The amount of teens smoking cigarettes dropped about 28% in 2001. One reason why is because the retail price of cigarettes has gone up 70%"	This is totally true! A few people I know quit smoking because they had to work extra hours to pay for cigarettes!

Learning Logs are the type of flexible strategy that, when combined with text that's interesting and relevant, can engage readers, no matter their skill level. To encourage students to read grade them for participation in active reading and thinking versus skimming text to find the right answers.

A Special Note about Boys and Reading

It's no secret to teachers who work closely with reluctant readers that many, if not most, of the students they work with are boys. Boys are challenged by our existing school systems, as the following data shows (King & Gurian, 2006).

- Boys lag behind girls 1.5 years in reading and writing.
- Boys earn 70% of D's and F's and fewer than half of the A's.
- Boys account for two-thirds of students diagnosed with learning disabilities.
- Boys represent 90% of discipline referrals.
- Boys dominate such brain-related disorders as ADD/ADHD, with millions now medicated.
- Males represent 80% of high school dropouts.
- Males make up fewer than 40% of college students.

It sure appears that most schools are working better for girls than for boys. Check your school's data to see if these trends hold true in your system.

One question that is easy to ask specifically about boys and reading is "what are we *asking* our students to read?" It is true that female teachers make many decisions about the reading materials students are offered in class, and often this decision is made on the basis of what particular teachers themselves find appealing rather than what the students, especially the male students, might like to read. It is one thing to have a variety of reading materials available in your library, it's quite another to offer a variety of materials to students as part of their class work. Over time, boys come to believe that the things they like to read "don't count," and fed on a steady diet of material they find "boring," boys lose interest and become unmotivated.

If we're serious about tackling the problem of reluctant readers, we have to be deliberate and thoughtful about whether we're meeting our students in the middle. Survey boys about their reading interests and then offer a rich variety of easy to read choices, including comic books, graphic novels, newspapers, and magazines.

Text Considerations

Our classrooms present the dual challenge of increasing heterogeneity and the expectation that all students will succeed; we must accept and act on the knowledge that it is impossible to help students become strategic readers if they are working with text that is too hard for them. Reluctant readers *can't learn to read better by reading what they can't read.* When students are offered only one text to learn from, here is what happens:

- Readers for whom the text is too easy don't develop any strategies for reading harder text.
- Readers for whom the text is "just right" understand the text with some support from the teacher, and in the process they may become more able to make meaning independently.
- Readers for whom the text is too hard are either spoon fed the content, circumventing the need to read, or they shut down entirely.

Teachers can no longer support the "one text for all readers" paradigm, developed in an era when only a select few were expected to attend, not to mention graduate, from high school. They must, instead, balance the use of challenging text with authentic strategy instruction using less complex text such as articles from magazines, newspapers, Internet resources, and essays. Consider using excerpts from sample textbooks sent to the district, perhaps those written for a grade level or two below the class being taught.

In addition to ensuring that students are working with text they *can* read well, at least some of the time, it's also important to give students the opportunity to read text they *want* to read. Since readers are people with different interests and backgrounds, it's unlikely that any single text will engage all of the readers in a class. If you're trying to motivate reluctant readers, offering students choices should be a regular part of your practice.

There is no doubt that having different students reading different texts adds another layer of complexity to your planning, delivery, and management. Engaging strategies can be the "glue" that holds everything together. One strategy that helps teachers give students access to multiple texts is the use of **Literature Circles**. Literature Circles make it possible for students to have more choice, more control, and more interest in what they are reading in class. As students practice reading more often with "just right" text or text that they are interested in, they become more confident and motivated.

Literature Circles, when thoughtfully and intentionally designed and implemented, can engage students as text users and critics. A Literature Circle is essentially a discussion group, a meeting in which people who have chosen a book or selection to read come together to discuss it. A popular model of Literature Circles has students prepare for discussion by taking on specific roles. These roles can be "flexed" to meet the needs of readers working in most content areas. For example, small groups of students reading primary source documents in history could select from the following roles to examine and discuss their work.

Historian	**Authenticator**
Your task is to determine the historical context for the document/artifact. In order to accomplish this task, develop answers to the following questions: • What is the artifact's date of origin? • What do you already know about that time period? • What do you know about the concerns and issues of someone from that time period? • What do you see in the artifact that confirms or denies what you expected?	Your task is to determine whether or not the document/artifact is genuine. In order to accomplish this task, develop answers to the following questions: • Who is the author/creator? • Is it likely that the author/creator had first hand knowledge of the events/issues depicted? • Is the creator's point of view credible? Why or why not?
Impact Analyzer	**Content Master**
Your task is to determine whether or not the document served its intended purpose. To accomplish this task, examine the document and read it through at least once. Then develop answers to the following questions: • What type of document is it? How was it developed? • Who is the intended audience? Did they receive the document? • Why was it developed in the form that it was? • Imagine that you are the person who first received this item. How does it make you feel? Why?	Your task is to determine the "gist," main topic(s), or themes of the document/artifact. In order to accomplish this task, read the document twice, once quickly and once slowly. After reading it quickly, write a list of 10 key words and phrases from the document. Then complete the following statement: "This says that _____." Read it again to test your statement. Are you right? What would you change/add?

In his newest book *Mini-Lessons for Literature Circles* (2004), Harvey Daniels encourages teachers to use the discussion roles such as the ones above as a temporary scaffold *only* and to remove them as soon as possible in order to make Literature Circle discussions more authentic. Teachers can also increase the depth of students' Literature Circle discussions, and shift students' reading stance to the "text critic," by purposefully grouping text choices around genre or author studies and focusing students' reading on features of the genre or an author's style. For example, students might choose a book that interests them from a short list of quality historical fiction, read and study the features of the text with their group, then produce a piece of historical fiction of their own. Or they might all be working with historical letters in history, or research studies in science. While engaged in Literature Circles this way, students read not to fulfill a specific discussion role, but more broadly and with the intention of analyzing and critiquing the work they are reading.

Teaching/Instructional Considerations

One of the challenges both teachers and students are facing is "objective overload" – lots of pressure from state tests and huge curriculum guides to cover lots of material in a hurry. This makes it hard to decide what students should learn from any assigned reading and even more challenging for the students when (or if) they do the reading. Recently I worked with a beginning teacher who intended to have her students memorize a list of 51 types of poetry, and read all 51 types, as part of her poetry unit. Yikes! Defining more reasonably and concretely what students should read for will help students follow through with what they should *learn* while reading.

Rick Stiggins and his colleagues (2004), emphasize assessment for learning strategies that research shows close the learning gaps between low performing and high performing students. Struggling students learn more when teachers offer a clear and understandable vision of the learning that is supposed to happen (what Stiggins calls the "learning target"), when teachers provide models, and when teachers focus lessons and offer feedback on one learning target at a time. For example, in an eighth grade classroom, a science teacher decided that she wanted to challenge her students' misconception that the Earth moves closer to the sun in the spring. She collected several short pieces of text that described how seasons are caused by the tilt of the Earth on its axis throughout the year. She asked students to preview the articles and pick the one they felt they could read best. Then she provided them with a **Directed Reading/Thinking Activity** (DR/TA) (Moore, Readence, & Rickelman, 1982) with the learning target for the lesson included at the top.

Directed Reading/Thinking Activity – *The Cause of Seasons* Learning Target: I can analyze the interrelationship of the revolution of the Earth, the tilt of the Earth on its axis, and the sun in the cause of seasons.
Before you begin reading this section, take some time to reflect. What do you already know about how seasons are caused?
What questions do you have about the cause of seasons?
What do you think you will learn while reading your selection?
After reading this section, what have you learned about the interrelationship of the revolution of the Earth, the title of the Earth on its axis, and the sun in the cause of seasons?

Example of DRTA strategy used in 8th grade science.

The first three sections of the DR/TA are completed before the students read, perhaps even after small group discussions or Think-Pair-Shares, and help the students prepare for their new learning. The last section is completed by the students following the reading and helps students make connections, inferences, and synthesize new ideas. All sections are more open-ended than a series of questions and therefore engage students in critical thinking. In addition, the learning target at the top and embedded in the prompts focuses students and helps them know what they are supposed to learn from the reading.

You can develop learning targets for your students' reading assignments by thinking carefully about what it is you ***most*** want your students to know, understand or be able to do as a result of their reading. If you are intending for students to remember the causes of World War I from their reading, then develop a learning target such as "I can read to determine the causes of World War I." If the reading is to expose students to new scientific terms, then the target would be something along the lines of "I can read to identify, define, and make connections between new science vocabulary terms."

Once you have developed your learning targets, share them with students, add them to assignments, and ask students to reflect on whether or not they have met the learning targets prior to turning their assignments to be assessed. In this way, you can help your students become more informed and strategic about their reading and learning.

Conclusions/Toward an Integrated Approach

Engaging reluctant readers in the reading practice they so desperately need takes understanding, patience, and flexibility. It is worth the extra effort, however, because all students deserves to leave school prepared to support themselves and their families – a goal that rests firmly on a literate foundation. Dealing with older struggling readers is a bit like a dance – you have to know your partner and practice, practice, practice.

Early in the year – get to know your readers. Find text they can and want to read. Use strategies such as Learning Logs that enable all students to be successful. Be honest and encouraging, but set very high expectations for student engagement with text. They have to read to get better at reading.

As the year progresses – Build your collection of different levels and choices of text so that all readers are able to work with text that's just right for them. Be clear with your readers about what it is that they need to focus on while reading. Help them understand the purpose for reading so that they can be successful and use strategies such as the Directed Reading/Thinking Activity to help readers stay on track before, during, and after a reading assignment.

Next - Use strategies such as Literature Circles to help your students gain confidence and independence. Working in a focused fashion in small groups will bring new perspectives and depth to their understanding.

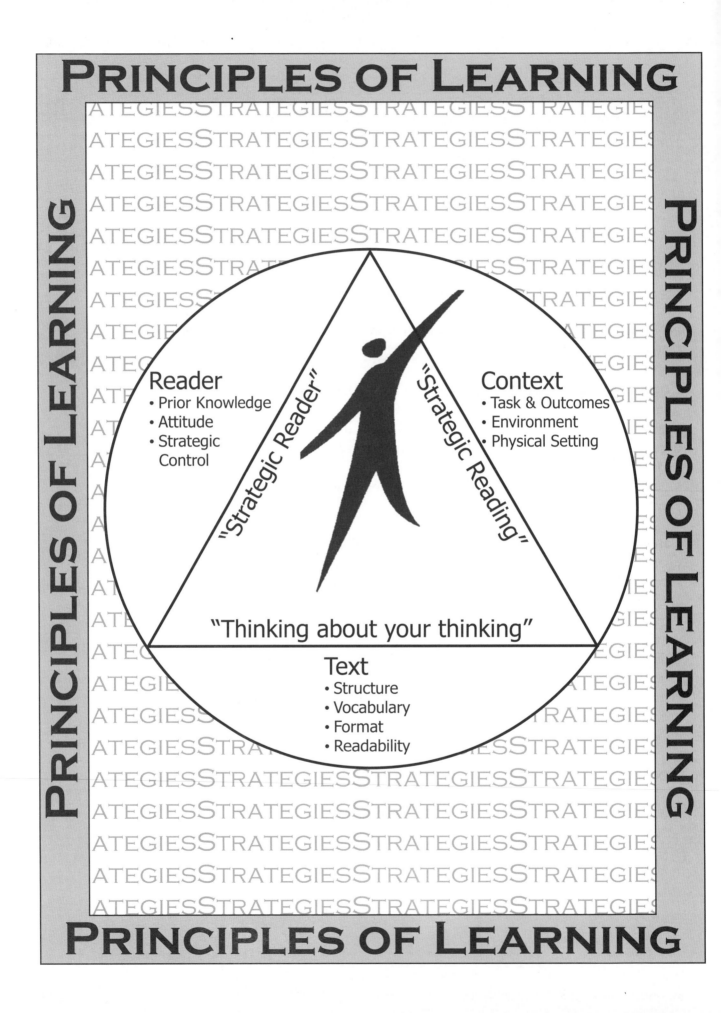

Reader
• Prior Knowledge
• Attitude
• Strategic Control

"Strategic Reader"

Context
• Task & Outcomes
• Environment
• Physical Setting

"Strategic Reading"

"Thinking about your thinking"

Text
• Structure
• Vocabulary
• Format
• Readability

Chapter 8

Essential Reading Components

"Learning Teams"

As a result of working through this chapter you will:
- Know the what, why, and how of reading aloud to students
- Understand the benefits of sustained silent reading
- Examine ways to involve families in developing readers

Questions to ponder before, during, and after reading

Before reading – How often do you read aloud to your students? What are your thoughts/feelings about the benefits of sustained silent reading? In what ways does your school currently involve families to create strategic readers?

During reading – How is the information presented congruent with your experiences and/or beliefs?

After Reading – What new insights have you gained as a result of reading this chapter? How might you support your school's efforts to incorporate essential reading components?

Process Activity

The process activity for this chapter is a vocabulary strategy called Mind-Sketching (Billmeyer, 2006b). This strategy stresses the nonlinguistic representation of critical vocabulary words; when readers sketch word meanings they think analytically and use ideas from their experiences. The Mind-Sketching strategy helps the reader develop accurate and meaningful definitions, increasing retention of words and concepts.

Directions:
1) Preview the chapter to see how it is organized. With learning team members discuss your experiences regarding the three essential reading ingredients: read aloud, sustained silent reading, and family literacy.
2) Fold a piece of plain paper into thirds, label each section with one of the three components, sketch, and descriptive phrase.
3) Read the chapter, sketch what each essential ingredient means, and write a descriptive phrase to define the concept.
4) Share the sketch and descriptive phrase for each concept with other team members.
5) Brainstorm ways you can support our school's efforts in incorporate these three essential reading components.
6) Discuss the benefits of the Mind Sketching strategy and how you might use it with your students.

Read Aloud: Sketch   **Descriptive phrase**
Sustained Silent Reading   **Descriptive phrase**
Family Literacy: Sketch   **Descriptive phrase**

Chapter 8

Essential Reading Components

You may have tangible wealth untold: Caskets of jewels and coffers of gold.
Richer than I you can never be - I had a mother who read to me.
                                                    - Strickland Gillilan, The Reading Mother

"I love it when teachers read aloud. When I am reading, I have to focus on getting the words right, and I miss out on the meaning," explains a high school student. An elementary school teacher states, "I am so thankful we have invested time in Sustained Silent Reading because I get a chance to catch up on some of my reading, and when students see me reading they are intrigued. They want to know what I am reading and why I chose it." A middle school principal exclaims, "We are reaping the benefits of our efforts to involve parents in our school-wide literacy plan. We've gained knowledge about the students' family literacy practices which helps us tap into students prior knowledge, interests, strengths, and reading needs."

To create a literate environment for adults and students, develop a building plan in which the entire staff invests time and effort in the essential reading components: reading aloud, sustained silent reading, and family literacy. The investment will pay big dividends. This chapter will examine the data and research, implementation ideas, and examples of successful results when implementing three reading staples.

Read Aloud
Data and Research
Jim Trelease (2001, p. xiii) states, "Extensive research has proven that reading aloud to a child is the single most important factor in raising a reader. If reading to children were common instead of a rarity, we'd be facing fewer academic and social problems in this nation." Students of all ages enjoy being read to; when teachers read aloud to students on a regular basis it inspires them to read on their own and increases the chances of their becoming life-long readers.

Reading aloud should be an instructional routine in all classrooms at all grade levels. Unfortunately, many teachers associate reading aloud with preschool and elementary aged students. Yet, research emphatically states that reading aloud to students increases vocabularies and boosts comprehension (see p. 102). When teachers read aloud they give a voice and meaning to text that students often cannot give to the reading themselves (Ivey, 2002). For example, Shakespeare is difficult for many students to understand, but once the characters are introduced through a read-aloud they have a real voice and the action of the play unfolds more vividly and meaningfully.

Students benefit the most when they are read to on a daily basis. Reading aloud:
- Increases the love for reading
- Builds a rich vocabulary
- Increases understanding of the target language
- Builds background knowledge
- Creates an understanding of story structure, organization, and language
- Develops sentence sense, patterning, and an ear for the rhythm of language
- Models appropriate phrasing, inflection, and fluency
- Introduces different writing styles and genres
- Introduces a variety of authors and their voices
- Develops better listening skills and longer attention spans
- Develops positive relationships among readers

Implementation Ideas

Any selection can be read aloud. K-12 teachers read novels, short stories, poems, articles from the newspaper, quotes from famous people, passages from textbooks, and letters just to name a few. A read-aloud can serve as a springboard to discussion of an upcoming event, a lurking problem, or a content topic. High school teacher, Cheryl Dobbertin, reminds us that a read-aloud is not intended to replace independent reading; reading aloud to help the struggling reader should be balanced with opportunities for students to work independently with text they can read. Important considerations when reading aloud:

- Read selections you have read and care about to model thoughtful reading.
- Set expectations for how to listen; some students need to doodle.
- Create a relaxing environment by lowering the lights, facing students away from distractions, or allowing students to sit in a comfortable spot.
- Set the stage by showing the cover, sharing the title, and predicting outcomes.
- Personalize the selection by providing information about the author.
- Read slowly and expressively so students can create mental pictures.
- Start small with a quote, poem, or short story (if students have not been read to) and build up to longer selections and/or time frames for reading aloud.

Examples of Successful Results

Secondary literacy experts, Ivey and Fisher (2006), emphasize that the purpose for reading aloud is to build background knowledge, develop vocabulary, and foster a love of reading. A high school art teacher read aloud the picture book *My Name is Georgia* (Winter, 1998) before introducing Georgia O'Keefe's work. As a health teacher read *The House that Crack Built* (Taylor, 1992), she asked students to record interesting and unfamiliar vocabulary words for discussion; student selected words were recorded on the word wall as well as in their word journals for future writing experiences. A favorite success story is about a skeptical high school science teacher who decided to try reading aloud a few minutes at the beginning of each class. He liked the Gary Paulsen selections so he began reading *Hatchet*. He quickly realized numerous benefits: students

∿
∿

were not late for class as they did not want to miss the next reading installment (especially when he ended the reading at a spine-tingling point), connections from the book were made with the science content, and one student who refused to read anything fell in love with Paulsen's books and started poring through anything he wrote. Thanks to reading aloud this student is now an avid reader!

Sustained Silent Reading

Data and Research

Sustained silent reading (SSR) creates students who develop the reading habit! If we want students to become readers we need to give them frequent opportunities to behave as readers. SSR is time set aside for students to read what they choose; the purpose is to build habit, background knowledge, and vocabulary (Marzano, 2004). As emphasized in chapter 5 (see p. 101) independent reading is the largest source of vocabulary growth, especially for older and more able readers.

We have taught students how to read but have forgotten to teach them to **want** to read. A study of 155 capable fifth grade students revealed that 90 percent of them devoted only one percent of their free time to reading but spent 30 percent of their free time watching television (Trelease, 2001). Fewer than 40 percent of teachers surveyed in the United States participated in any form of a SSR program (Trelease, 2001). Students who do not read unfortunately will become adults who do not read. Being aliterate, a person who knows how to read but chooses not to read, is no better than being illiterate, a person who cannot read at all. Students become confident, successful readers by reading **a lot**.

Reading is the cornerstone to learning; it is no surprise that students who read more score significantly higher on standardized tests. Stephen Krashen's (1993) comprehensive study examining the benefits of independent reading reveals that no single literacy activity has a stronger positive effect on comprehension, vocabulary development, and writing than a SSR approach. Janice Pilgreen's (2000) research comparing SSR to traditional skill-building exercises in language arts reveals that students who participate in SSR out-performed students using a skill-based approach on standardized tests of reading comprehension. Working with secondary students engaged in SSR she found that interest and motivation toward reading increased significantly.

In 2000, the National Reading Panel's report claimed they were unable to find a positive correlation between programs promoting independent silent reading and increased reading achievement. These results led to much controversy about the value of SSR. Ten years later, research has confirmed that SSR does increase student achievement, motivation, and engagement (Krashen, 2004; Miller, 2009). Marzano's (2004) meta-analysis of the impact of independent reading on comprehension ability reveals that students involved in SSR show significant reading gains. Students engaged in SSR **one year or longer** scored at the 81st percentile while students participating for less time scored only at the 50th percentile.

Implementation Ideas

Based on these findings, it seems logical that all schools should design and implement SSR programs. Pilgreen's work (2000) highlights eight factors for successful implementation of SSR:

- **Access** suggests classrooms have an extensive variety of reading materials such as, books (fiction and nonfiction), magazines, comics, and newspapers.
- **Appeal** means students can self-select material that they find interesting as well as at their reading level.
- **Conducive environment** refers to a comfortable and quiet climate with uninterrupted time for reading.
- **Encouragement** means teachers model enthusiasm for reading, discuss selections with students, and ask students to share what they read.
- **Staff training** provides information to staff about the goals and procedures for successful implementation.
- **Non-accountability** means students are not required to complete book reports, take tests, or endure forms of accountability.
- **Follow-up activities** encourage students to interact with the information read by discussing ideas with peers or through **informal** writing.
- **Distributed time to read** means that the allotted amount of time for SSR must be provided on a regular basis. To build habit the research recommends that SSR time be provided at least two to three times per week.

For best results introduce SSR early in the school year, beginning with a short amount of time (young children or struggling readers may begin with five minutes and secondary students ten minutes). As the year progresses slowly extend the SSR time, working toward 20 to 30 minutes. Build reading stamina by charting how many minutes students stay focused during SSR. When one student is off task, reading time ends, students share what they read with a partner. The goal is to increase minutes reading in a positive way!

A chart graphing the number of minutes (left side) students were able to read each day (across the bottom).

Three final thoughts regarding implementation of SSR – first, the teacher is critical to the success of the program. Teacher enthusiasm and modeling pay huge dividends in motivating students to read. Second, having a large amount and variety of reading materials in the classroom from which students can select is essential. Books can be checked out from the school and/or the public library, grant money can be used to buy classroom sets of high-interest books and magazines, and books can be purchased at garage sales. Lastly, obeying the non-accountability rule is vital; how many adults write a response to every book they read?

∿∿∿
∿∿∿

Examples of Successful Results

SSR can be implemented by an individual teacher or as a school-wide initiative. A high school English teacher found that ten minutes of independent reading offered significant opportunities for students' language and literacy development (Gardiner, 2001). As he tracked the number of books read, he discovered that students were reading anywhere from ten to 52 books per semester; quite an accomplishment from the typical zero to five books read. He also learned that it is imperative students know why they are expected to participate in SSR time; after all, independent reading time during the school day is not the norm. A middle school initiated a school wide SSR approach incorporating Pilgreen's eight factors; all adults (including cooks and custodians) and students participated. To promote sharing of selections read, teachers invited students or adults to voluntarily complete a "Read and Share" form listing: Title, Author, Why did you like the book/article?, Name, and Date. A highly visible hallway bulletin board displayed "Read and Share" forms; periodically students were asked to share a selection during the morning news.

Family Literacy

Data and Research

Parents are instrumental in developing children as readers; we all know the literacy environment at home has a profound effect on school literacy. Parent involvement and cooperation ranked first, while voluntary reading at home ranked second when discriminating between more and less-effective schools in literacy learning (Postlethwaite & Ross, 1992). The 1998 National Assessment of Educational Progress (NAEP) reported that when students talked about what they were reading with family and friends, reading scores were higher. Researchers Kamil and Walberg (2005) emphasize the benefits of a literate home to enhance vocabulary, comprehension, and knowledge of the world.

The 2008 *Kids and Family Reading Report* found that the time children spend reading at home declines after age eight and continues to drop off through the teen years. Children who have parents who read daily are more likely to read than those who come from homes where parents read only a few times each month. The report revealed also that parents are a key source of book suggestions for their children, but parents (especially parents of teens) say they have a hard time finding information about books their reader might enjoy. More unfortunate, the *Reading Across the Nation* survey (2007) found that the daily ritual of parents reading to their children has dropped below 50 percent. Strengthening parents' involvement in their children's education may be the vital link for increasing achievement. Strong partnerships between schools and parents are needed; parents must be taught how to be strong advocates for their students as well as given the tools to do so (Allen, 2005). Family literacy means parents or guardians, children, and teachers learning together and growing as readers.

Implementation Ideas

Getting families involved in creating a literate home environment may initially be met with some resistance. Finding time to read can be a challenge; some adults work long hours, tempting them to use video or television to entertain rather than reading with children. Children have increased involvement in non-academic activities (such as sports) leaving less time for reading. Families also come from various backgrounds and cultures; they have varying degrees of reading abilities, interests, and understandings of the importance of reading. With this in mind educators must be sensitive to the needs of parents or guardians; family literacy programs must be tailored to the needs of the families they serve (Morrow, 2004).

• **Begin the school year with a literacy plan** in which parents/guardians, children, and teachers learn together and grow as readers. Before the school year begins determine the backgrounds or cultures of students attending the school and interview parents about their reading habits. At a Back to School Night introduce a family literacy plan; educate parents or guardians about the importance of their role in creating life-long readers. Begin the Back to School night with a fun read aloud; teach adults how to read aloud and identify the many benefits associated with reading aloud. A favorite read aloud of mine is the Dedication from *My Life in Dog Years* by Gary Paulsen (1997). Following my reading this aloud at a training, men have contacted me to say that they are reading the book with their sons and have found it to be a positive "guy bonding" experience.

Frequently parents struggle to get their sons to read, some are not interested in reading books, but some lose interest in reading all together as they approach their teen years. Guys Read is a web-based literacy program for boys; the mission is to help boys become self-motivated, lifelong readers. Instead of books only make sure there are newspapers and magazines available. Whatever your teens' interests – from skateboarding to stamp collecting- provide pertinent information to entice them to read. For more ideas and to learn more about boys as readers, visit www.guysread.com.

• **School librarians** are instrumental in opening doors to increased family literacy. Begin the school year by inviting parents and children to a library open house and tour. Read aloud from a popular selection, teach parents how to select reading materials or how to help a child select a book, and encourage families to browse and check out books. Some schools initiate a library card system for adults similar to the public library.

• **School newsletters** sent to parents can devote a section to Family Literacy. A middle school titled their section *Reading Rocks – Let's Create Readers*; the newsletter included titles of popular books to read aloud, books to purchase for an upcoming birthday, suggestions for motivating male readers, snippets of research about family literacy, upcoming reading events at school, ways to increase home reading, descriptions of new books added to the school library, and testimonials from parents and teachers about reading successes.

• **Increase home reading** by providing parents with reading material, such as used books, newspapers, and magazines recycled from garage sales, hotels, and business offices. Suggest that reading material is placed in different parts of the home (nightstand, bathroom, or in the playroom) or that they carry reading material in the car. A fun and interesting way to increase home reading is by creating family literacy stories. Parents and students work together to study family artifacts or events such as immigration, genealogy, careers, or travel. A fifth grader and his parents who were immigrants explored past literacy practices and experiences. The school librarian read aloud, *Miss Bridie Chose a Shovel* (Connor, 2004), a lyrical tribute to the millions of immigrants who left their homes to begin anew in America. This selection paved the way to wide reading and discussion about immigration and the impact on families.

• Don't forget to include **summer reading** as part of the family literacy plan. Research about summer reading loss indicates:
  • Students regress three months in achievement, and these losses are cumulative creating a wider gap each year. By the time a student reaches middle school years, the reading loss can add up to two or more years of lost reading achievement (McGill-Franzen & Allington, 2003).
  • On-going summer reading loss is cumulative and eventually affects high school graduation rates and attendance in college (Alexander et al., 2007).
  • Summer reading loss is greater for low-socioeconomic students; the lack of access to books is the major cause of regression for students living in poverty.

Schools can develop a meaningful and engaging summer reading program for all ages.
  • Start student book clubs and encourage meetings at the school library throughout the summer. Invite parents; they might enjoy participating in their own book club.
  • Allow students to check out school or classroom library books during the summer. Schools might staff the library one evening a week throughout the summer so children can return their books and check out new ones. Schools with summer lunch programs can provide daytime access to the library.
  • Invite students and parents to the school library for "Book and Movie" nights; they read the featured book (or start it) during the first gathering and then return another night to watch the movie. Over a bowl of popcorn they discuss questions such as: Did you think the characters would look like that? Why do you think the filmmakers made the movie different? How did they decide what to include and what to leave out?

Examples of Successful Results
A Partnership With Parents (McNicol & Dalton, 2002) was implemented for parents of primary students. The major goal of the family literacy plan was teaching parents how children are taught to read and write at school, as well as ways to support their development at home. Parents were encouraged to interact with narrative and informative text, including magazines and children's literature.

The project included an introduction to library services inviting parents to join and use the library. Parents participated in book clubs and enjoyed the opportunity to read and respond with other adults.

A high school in Leadville, Colorado created a Parent University that offered Spanish and English speaking parents or guardians meaningful ways of reading and learning with their children. Parents attended with their children to learn reading strategies, check out books from the library, and spend time reading together. Teaching parents reading strategies outlined in this book not only promoted their children's literacy but also increased their own literacy. Modeling how to preview the text before reading, make predictions, pose questions while reading, and summarize the story are powerful comprehension tools for all learners.

Teachers can encourage partner reading by incorporating assignments that require students to share literature selections with their parents. Teachers at a high school in Mountain Brook, AL invited parents to select and read novels with their children. A letter was sent to parents introducing the project.

> *Wouldn't it be great if teenagers wanted to read books instead of watching television? Wouldn't it be great if you and your child could have a conversation about a really terrific book? I believe both are possible. If a child can select a book he/she likes and can have meaningful conversations at home about them, both are possible. I invite you to take part in a different kind of assignment; you and your child choose a book and read it together. The actual report will be a joint venture; each of you will contribute equally to the presentation. Join us for a "show and tell" of books.*

Parents enjoyed coming to school to participate in the "show and tell" of books. The project was an overwhelming success. **Read to Them** (Anderson, 2007) is another form of collaborative reading. Read to Them engages an entire school (including students, parents, teachers, and other staff) in reading the same children's novel simultaneously. To learn more about the program visit www. readtothem.org. Family literacy projects not only increase home reading but also build relationships between parents and their children. Families that read together grow together!

Conclusion

Reading is the platform from which we do most of our learning. Investing time and energy in the essential components – reading aloud, sustained silent reading, and family literacy - pays enormous academic dividends for all students. Our goal is to build the reading habit; each component has the potential to positively affect a wider sphere of influence. Individual teachers can do reading aloud, sustained silent reading can occur as a school-wide initiative, and family literacy reaches beyond the school to involve the community. Parents can make a difference, but teachers must lead the way in involving them. It is worth the time and effort of every educator to actively involve parents in creating students who are avid, capable, and thoughtful readers. **It does take a village to raise a child!**

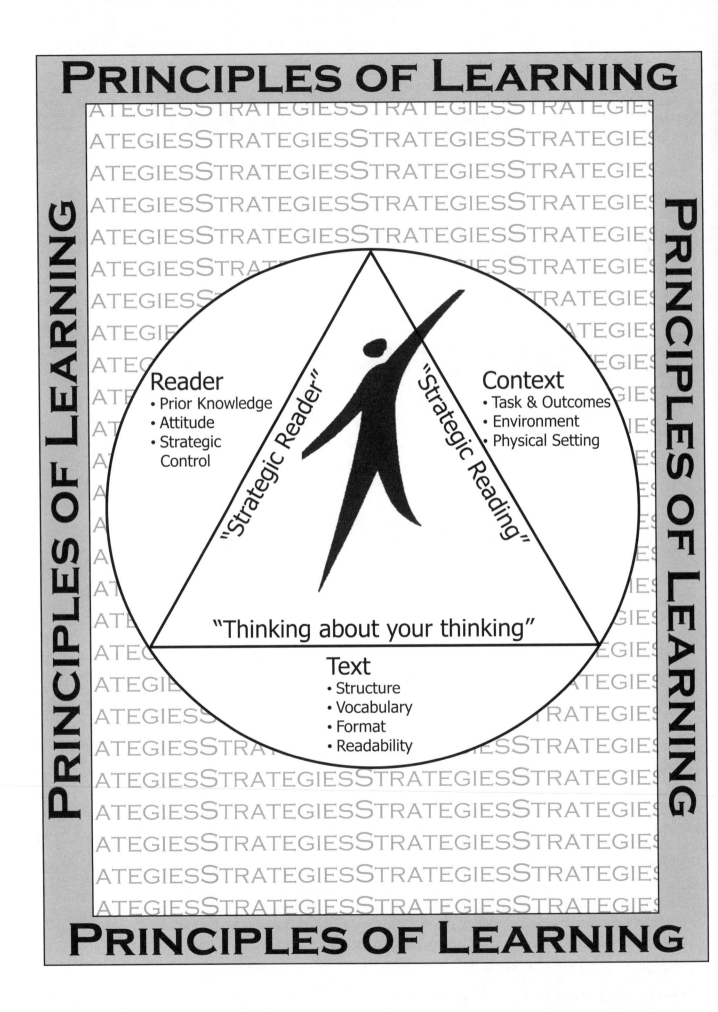

Reader
• Prior Knowledge
• Attitude
• Strategic Control

"Strategic Reader"

Context
• Task & Outcomes
• Environment
• Physical Setting

"Strategic Reading"

"Thinking about your thinking"

Text
• Structure
• Vocabulary
• Format
• Readability

Chapter 9

Creating a Literate Environment Through Children's Literature

There is more treasure in books than in all the pirate's loot on Treasure Island.
- Walt Disney

We all love a good story; literature can be used at all grade levels to motivate students. While picture books have been a staple in the primary classroom for many years, there is growing evidence that using them with older students is also beneficial. Frequently, teachers find students lack motivation when it comes to reading from textbooks. Young adult and children's literature provide a motivating way to approach textbook concepts. Students find picture books to be more interesting than textbooks because they are more "real-life" and focus on a single topic. Once students have an interest in and an understanding of the topic, they can read about it from their textbooks or other resources.

Older students enjoy and benefit from pictures books just as the primary child does. Just because a book is considered to be a picture book does not mean it is accessible at the primary level. Often concepts are inappropriate because the accompanying text is at a high level of sophistication which young children are unable to understand. Children's books can be high-quality fiction as well as informative in nature. They contain universal themes and motivating illustrations as well as bringing events and people to life.

Illustrated books are beneficial for English Language Learners, as well as for anyone who has difficulty reading. English Language Learners and special needs students tend to be visual, verbal learners who greatly benefit from the use of picture books. Just as young children need to associate the words with pictures, so do English Language Learners and special needs students. Through the use of children's literature, these learners strengthen their reading skills and develop an interest for reading.

Reluctant readers tend to enjoy illustrated books, particularly graphic novels, which are fiction and nonfiction text with pictures resembling comics. Graphic novels offer an alternative route to reading a novel; teachers find they motivate the reluctant reader.

Teachers are always asking for good read-aloud books. Many of the selections in this chapter have been recommended by teachers as powerful read-alouds. Some choices are quick, easy reads, while other selections require more time. Pre K-12 teachers have recommended the books listed in this chapter; they comment that their attitude toward the use of picture books greatly influences students' reaction and acceptance for using them. Because picture books have often been viewed as "baby books," students must see that teachers value children's literature for truth, depth, complex ideas, and representations of real life. We want teachers to use this literature for the same reasons we use adult literature. **It's not a tool; it's an experience in thinking.** Even though the books listed in this chapter are recommended for specific levels (P = K-3, I = 3-6, and Sec = 6-12), book selection is based on teaching goals and content objectives. The books are organized into the following categories: Art; Character Education; Graphic Novels; Language Arts; Mathematics; Music; Physical Education and Health; Science; and Social Studies.

ART
Abuela's Weave (1993) Omar Castaneda: Lee and Low Books
A young girl and her grandmother work together to weave a tapestry telling a story with symbols of Guatemala's history. (P-Sec)

Action Jackson (2002) Jan Greenberg: Millbrook Pr Trade
The book is an account of Jackson Pollock creating his painting Number 1, 1950 (Lavender Mist) during the months of May and June1950. (Sec)

Alphabet City (1995) Stephen T. Johnson: Viking
The author draws your eyes to tiny details within everyday objects to find the letters of the alphabet. This is a wordless alphabet book that should appeal to all ages. (P-Sec)

Andy Warhol : Pop Art Painter (2006) Susan Goldman Rubin: Abrams Books
An illustrated biography of Andy Warhol, discussing his early life, family, school, work as an illustrator, and fame as a pop artist. Includes a time line and glossary. (I-Sec)

Anna's Art Adventure (1999), Bjorn Sortland: Carolrhoda
On her search for the art museum's bathroom, Anna meets famous artists, becomes part of some of their paintings, and makes her own art. (P-I)

The Art of Reading (2005) Dutton Books
Presents a collection of essays by popular children's authors celebrating the fortieth anniversary of the Reading Is Fundamental literacy program. (P-Sec)

Art (2006) Patrick McDonnell: Little, Brown
Using play on words throughout the story, Art, a young boy, tries his hand at all kinds of art. (P)

Art From Her Heart (2008) Kathy Whitehead: G.P. Putnam's Sons
Clementine Hunter, a popular African-American folk painter from Louisiana, paints scenes from her life and relates how she was not allowed in the galleries to view her own exhibits. (P-Sec)

A Bird or Two: A Story about Henri Matisse (1999) Bijou Le Tord: Eerdmans Books for Young Readers
Describes the work of French painter, Henri Matisse, particularly his joyful use of color. (P-I)

Calling the Doves (1995) Juan Felipe Herrera: Children's Book Press
This is a poetically told story of a family that emigrated from Mexico to California. The father tells of his parents' lives and his hopes for his children's future. (P-Sec)

Camille and the Sunflowers : A Story about Vincent van Gogh (1994) Laurence Anholt: Barron's Educational Series
A young French boy and his family befriend the lonely painter who comes to their town and begin to admire his unusual paintings. (P-Sec)

Cassie's Word Quilt (2002) Faith Ringgold: Alfred Knopf
A young African American girl takes the reader on a tour of her neighborhood, home, and school. The author's paintings enrich and illustrate a page-by-page study of common words. (P-Sec)

Degas and the Little Dancer: A Story about Edgar Degas (1996) Laurence Anholt: Barron's
Marie helps her poor parents by modeling for an ill-tempered artist; she becomes a famous ballerina but not in the way she had dreamed. (P-Sec)

The Dot (2003) Peter H. Reynolds: Candlewick Press
"I can't draw," says Vashti. "Just make a dot," says her teacher. The dot is just the beginning. A powerful story that focuses on positive acts. (P-Sec)

Emily's Art (2006) Peter Catalanotto: Aladdin
Emily, who loves drawing, loses the first-grade art contest. (P)

The First Starry Night (1997) Joan Shaddox Isom: Charlesbridge Publishing
A fanciful story of Vincent van Gogh's encounter with the beauties of the night sky. It provides an introduction to the artist as a person and to one of his most famous works. (P-Sec)

Georgia O'Keeffe : The Poetry of Things (1999) Elizabeth Hutton Turner: Phillips Collection
Provides an in-depth exploration of the still-life paintings of Georgia O'Keeffe. (Sec)

The Incredible Painting of Felix Clousseau (1990) Jon Agee: Farrar, Straus & Giroux
An unknown painter becomes an overnight sensation when his paintings become alive. (P-Sec)

Ish (2004) Peter Reynolds: Candlewick Press
Ramon loses confidence in his ability to draw, but his sister gives him a new perspective on things. (P-Sec)

Katie Meets the Impressionists (2007) James Mayhew: Scholastic
Visiting a museum, Katie climbs into five Impressionist paintings and has amazing adventures. (P-I)

Klimt and his Cat (2005) Berenice Capatti: Eerdmans Books for Young Readers
The life and work of Viennese painter Gustav Klimt is explored by his favorite cat. (I-Sec)

Leonardo's Horse (2001) Jean Fritz: Putnam Publishing Group Juvenile
A picture book about Leonardo da Vinci and his dream of creating a bronze horse and about Charles Dent, who wanted to make Leonardo's horse a reality. (Sec)

Leonardo and the Flying Boy (2000) Laurence Anholt: Barron's
Introduces Leonardo's life and accomplishments through imagined anecdotes about his apprentices. (P-Sec)

Linnea in Monet's Garden (1985) Christina Bjork: Raben & Sjogren Bokforlag
Linnea visits Claude Monet's garden. The book contains photographs of many of Monet's famous paintings and old family snapshots previously unpublished. (I-Sec)

Listen to the Rain (1988) Bill Martin Jr, and John Archambault: Henry Holt & Co., Inc.
The rhyming text and captivating art describe the rain from a slow, soft sprinkle to heavy drip, drops and back to the silence after a rain. (P-Sec)

The Mad, Mad, Mad World of Salvador Dali (2003) Angela Wenzel: Prestel
Introduces children to the art of Salvador Dali, providing a discussion of his life, and an overview of his dream-like paintings. (I-Sec)

Magic Dogs of the Volcanoes (1990) Manlio Arguenta: Children's Book Press
A colorfully illustrated, bilingual tale from El Salvador telling of campesinos who live at the foot of a volcano and are protected by magical creatures until this tradition is threatened by the landowners who wants to destroy the relationship. (P-Sec)

The Magical Garden of Claude Monet (2003) Laurence Anholt: Barron's
Based on a true story about a little girl who visits Claude Monet in his magical garden. (P-Sec)

Matisse : The King of Color (2007) Laurence Anholt: Barrons
Matisse develops a strong friendship with Monique, a nun who nursed him back to health. He creates stained glass windows to adorn the chapel at the nunnery where Monique lives. (P-Sec)

My Painted House, My Friendly Chicken and Me (1994) Maya Angelou & Margaret Courtney Clark: Clarkson Potter, Inc
Beautiful, never-before-seen, photographs of the Ndebele people in South Africa, taken by Clark, anthropologist/photographer, along with text by Angelou in the voice of a young girl. (P-Sec)

Norman Rockwell: Storyteller with a Brush (2000) Beverly Gherman: Atheneum Books
Describes the life and work of the popular American artist who depicted both traditional and contemporary subjects. (I-Sec)

Now You See It-- Now You Don't, Rene **Magritte** (1998) Angela Wenzel: Prestel-Verlag
This book explores the mysteries of the paintings of twentieth-century Belgian artist Rene Magritte. (I-Sec)

Picasso and the Girl with a Ponytail (1998) Laurence Anholt: Barron's
Sylvette gradually begins to gain self-confidence during the summer she models for the renowned artist Pablo Picasso in the French village of Vallauris. (P-Sec)

The Round Trip (1990) Ann Jonas: Harper Trophy
Every black and white photograph in this book tells two stories. A great book to entice artists to create pictures that use negative space. (P-Sec)

Tar Beach (1991) Faith Ringgold: Crown Publishers, Inc.
Ringgold's painting tells a story written around the edges of an eight-year old African American girl in Harlem in 1939 who can go anywhere she wishes in her imagination. (P-Sec)

Voices of the Heart (1997) Ed Young: Scholastic Press
The author explores twenty-six Chinese characters, each describing an emotion or feeling. Stunning collage art interprets the visual elements within each character. (I-Sec)

Where Are You Going? To See My Friend (2001) Eric Carle & Kazuo Iwamura: Orchard Books
A collage and watercolors tell a story of two friends, one in Japan and one in America. (P-Sec)

The Year with Grandma Moses (2000) W. Lisa-Nicola: Holt and Company
Reproductions of Anna Mary Moses's paintings take children through the seasons. (P-Sec)

CHARACTER EDUCATION
The 7 Habits of Highly Effective Teens (2003) Sean Covey: Simon & Schuster
Describes seven habits for teenagers to help them improve their self-images, resist peer pressure, achieve goals, get along with parents, and make positive changes in their lives. (I-Sec)

The 7 Habits of Happy Kids (2008) Sean Covey: Simon & Schuster Books for Young Readers
A collection of seven stories featuring the Seven Oaks friends who find out how they and the entire community can be happy and productive. (P-I)

A Day's Work (1997) Eve Bunting: Houghton Mifflin
A young Mexican-American lies to help his grandfather get work-stresses honesty and work ethic. (I-Sec)

The Afterlife (2003) Gary Soto: Harcourt Children's Book
The main character is killed by a stranger and is soon floating above his bleeding body. As the story evolves he achieves many things he did not when alive. (Sec)

Alt Ed (2004) Catherine Atkins: Speak
Susan, an overweight tenth grader, develops a better sense of herself through participation in a special after-school counseling class with other troubled students. (Sec)

Americans Who Tell the Truth (2008) Robert Shetterly: Puffin Books
A collection of stories about fifty historical and contemporary writers, labor leaders, artists, environmentalists, reporters, and politicians who spoke out about what they believed. (I-Sec)

Burger Wuss (2008) M.T. Anderson: Candlewick
Hoping to lose his loser image, Anthony plans revenge on a bully which results in a war between two competing fast food restaurants, Burger Queen and O'Dermott's. (Sec)

Buried Onions (1997) Gary Soto: Harcourt Brace
A nineteen-year-old Mexican man drops out of college and joins a gang. He then decides to do something with his life and joins the Navy to get away from "buried onions." (Sec)

Call Me Hope (2008) Gretchen Olson: Little, Brown and Co. Books for Young Readers
Eleven-year-old Hope begins coping with her mother's verbal abuse by devising survival strategies for herself – based on a history unit about the Holocaust. (I-Sec)

Children of Christmas: Stories for the Season (1987) Cynthia Rylant: Orchard Books
Short stories occurring in ordinary places by ordinary people who have extraordinary experiences. (I-Sec)

Cookies: Bite-Size Life Lessons (2006) Amy Krouse Rosenthal: HarperCollins
Defines words such as cooperate, patient, proud, modest, respect, compassionate, and others with sentences about cookies. (P-I)

Every Living Thing (1985) Cynthia Rylant: Aladdin Paperbacks
Twelve short stories whose themes are about how an animal cause a human being to see things in a different way or in some ways changes a person's life. (I-Sec)

The Giving Tree (1964) Shel Silverstein: Harpercollins Juvenile Books
The story tells about the generosity of an apple tree that continues to give to a young boy as he grows older, but the boy continues to ask for more from the tree. (P-Sec)

Going Home (1996) Eve Bunting: Harper Collins
A story of a family currently living in Los Angeles returns to their home in Mexico. When they arrive on Christmas Eve the entire town celebrates their return. (I-Sec)

Harris and Me (1993) Gary Paulsen: Bantam Doubleday Dell Books for Young Readers
Young city boy stays on a farm with relatives. He and his cousin find trouble & fun. (I-Sec)

The Honest-to-Goodness Truth (2000) Patricia C. McKissack: Atheneum Books
Libby learns that telling the truth is not always as simple as it seems, especially when it hurts. (P-Sec)

The House on Mango Street (1991) Sandra Ciseneros: Vintage
A young girl growing up in the Hispanic quarter of Chicago uses poems and stories to tell about the harsh realities and beauty of her environment. (Sec)

The Kissing Hand (2006) Audrey Penn: Tanglewood Press
A raccoon and his mother share their love to reassure each other that all will be well as he goes off to school for the first time. (P-I)

Life is So Good (2000) George Dawson and Richard Glaubman: A Penquin Book
A 102-year old George Dawson, a slave's grandson, learned to read at 98. He reflects on his life offering valuable lessons and his views of the events and happenings in the 20th century. (Sec)

A Long Way from Chicago (1998) Richard Peck: Scholastic
Joe and his sister spend a week every August in Chicago with their grandma. The story is about the relationship with their grandma and how perceptions change as Joe grows older. (I-Sec)

Maniac Magee (1990) Jerry Spinelli: Little. Brown & Company
Jeffrey Magee, whose parents were killed when he was three, lives with his aunt and uncle but runs away in search of a new home-focuses on prejudice, fear, love, and understanding. (I-Sec)

My Life in Dog Years (1998) Gary Paulsen: Bantam Doubleday Dell Books for Young Readers
Each chapter is a special story about a dog that made an impression on the author. (I-Sec)

Niagara Falls, or Does It? (2003) Henry Winkler & Lin Oliver: Grosset & Dunlap
The mostly true confessions of the world's best underachiever. (I-Sec)

People (1980) Peter Spier: Doubleday Book for Young Readers
A global view of all people and showing how we are different but that we can happily live together by understanding and accepting one another. (P-Sec)

Petey (1998) Ben Mikaelsen: Hyperion Press
A relationship between a teenager and an old man, Petey. Petey was placed in an insane asylum by his parents who thought that he was mentally retarded, but he had cerebral palsy. (I-Sec)

Seedfolks (1998) Paul Fleischman: Harper Collins
A neighborhood of Hispanics, Haitians, Koreans work together to make a community garden after a young girl plants a few lima beans in a rat infested vacant lot. (Sec)

She Taught Me to Eat Artichokes (1993) Mary Kay Shanley: Sta-Kris, Inc.
A beautiful story about how friendship can grow – like the artichoke – you peel away the petals and find the gift of the plant - friendship. (I-Sec)

The Skin I'm In (1998) Sharon G. Flake: Hyperion Paperbacks for Children
Maleeka is teased because of the color of her skin and her teacher, who is teased because of a face blemish, helps Maleeka out. (I-Sec)

The 6th Grade Nickname Game (1998) Gordon Korman: Hyperion
Eleven year old friends give nicknames to everyone, but some of the nicknames backfire. (I-Sec)

Shredderman series **(2004)** Wendelin Van Draanen: Knopf
Fifth-grader Nolan, tired of being called names by the class bully, does something about it. (I)

Small Steps (2006) Louis Sachar: Farrar, Straus, & Giroux
The sequel to *Holes* takes place three years after the boys are released from the detention center. (I-Sec)

Smoky Nights (1994) Eve Bunting: Harcourt Brace & Co.
A story about cats and people who could not get along until an evening of riots brought them together. (P-I)

What if the Zebra's Lost Their Stripes (1998) John Reitano: Paulist Press
Helps young minds think about and appreciate how we are all different. (P-I)

What's Wrong with Timmy? (2001) Maria Shriver: Little Brown & Company
A little girl sees Timmy, a child with Down's Syndrome, who looks different and acts differently than the other kids. Her mother introduces her to Timmy and a friendship develops. (P-I)

Wilfrid Gordon McDonald Partridge (1984) Mem Fox: Kane/Miller
A touching story about a young boy who helps an old lady find her memory. (P-Sec)

Woman Hollering Creek: and other stories (1991) Sandra Cisneros: Vintage Contemporaries
Six stories about life on both sides of the Mexican border, tales of discovery and wisdom. (Sec)

GRAPHIC NOVELS
9-11: The World's Finest Comic Cook Writers and Artists Tell Stories to Remember (2002) DC Comics
A collection of comic book stories based on the events of September 11, 2001, when the United States was attacked by terrorists. (Sec)

The Adventures of Tintin: Tintin in America (1979) Herge: Little, Brown & Co.
The story takes place in 1931 when gangster bosses ruled the city. Tintin, a reporter, arrives to clean up the city; but one of the gangsters escapes and the adventures begin. (I-Sec)

Barefoot Gen. Volume one, A cartoon story of Hiroshima (2004) Keiji Nakazawa: Last Gasp of San Francisco
A graphic novel account of the dropping of the atomic bomb on the Japanese city of Hiroshima, based on the experiences of the author who was six-years-old at the time of the attack. (Sec)

The Cartoon Guide to Statistics (1994) Larry Gonick: Harper Resource
The cartoons will introduce the reader to statistics. (Sec)

The Cartoon History of the Universe II (1994) Larry Gonick: Main Street Books
Approaches the fall of the Roman Empire and the history of China and India with humor. (Sec)

Ray Bradbury's Fahrenheit 451 (2009) Tim Hamilton: Hill and Wang
An adaptation of Ray Bradbury's "Fahrenheit 451" about Guy Montag, a career fireman, who realizes the evils of government-controlled thoughts and sets about to change society. (Sec)

Graphic Library: Graphic Science-Max Axiom series (2007-2009) Capstone Press
Max Axiom is a super-cool scientist who uses powers he acquired in a freak accident to demonstrate and explain science in ways never before seen in the classroom. (P-I)

Maus a Survivor's Tale: My Father Bleeds History (1986) Art Spiegelman: Panthem Books
The book is a memoir of Vladek Spiegelman, a Jewish survivor, and his son who is trying to come to terms with his father's terrifying story. (Sec)

Rapunzel's Revenge (2008) Shannon and Dean Hale: Bloomsbury
This graphic novel retelling of the fairy-tale classic is set in the Wild West. (I-Sec)

Robert Louis Stevenson's Strange case of Dr. Jekyll and Mr. Hyde (2008) adapted by Alan Grant: Tundra Books of Northern New York
A graphic novel adaptation of Robert Louis Stevenson's classic story in which John Utterson, a lawyer and friend of the scientist Dr. Jekyll, uncovers the hidden life of Mr. Hyde. (I-Sec)

Stinky (2008) Eleanor Davis: Toon Books
Stinky the Swamp Monster is scared of kids in this Theodor Seuss Geisel Honor Book about friendship and sharing. (P)

The United States Constitution: a graphic adaptation (2008) Jonathan Hennessey: Hill & Wang
An introduction to the United States Constitution detailing important people and events. (Sec)

LANGUAGE ARTS

A Family Apart (1987) Joan Lowery Nixon: Bantam Doubleday Dell Books for Young Readers
The story takes place in 1856 when a young widow makes the ultimate sacrifice and sends her six children on the orphan train to find better lives with western families. (I-Sec)

Baloney (Henry P.) (2005) Jon Scieszka: Puffin
Henry P. is from outer space and has the same problems we do when learning to read. (P-Sec)

Baaa (1985) David Macauley: Houghton Mifflin/Walter Lorraine Books
People disappear and sheep wander into town and begin to pattern their lives like people. A food shortage hits, a new product is invented called "Baaa." Pair with *Animal Farm*. (Sec)

The Bee Tree (1993) Patricia Polacco: Philomel Books
A fun adventure teaching a young girl the importance of reading. (P-Sec)

Cinderella Skeleton (2000) Robert D. San Souci: Silver Whistle, Harcourt, Inc.
This part familiar, part new, story written in verse is described with creative illustrations. (P-Sec)

Dear Deer: A Book of Homophones (2007) Gene Barretta: Henry Holt
Aunt Ant moved to the zoo and speaks in homophones to describe the animals' behaviors. (P-Sec)

Dogku (2007) Andrew Clements: Atheneum
A story of a homeless dog told completely in haiku. (P)

Eats, Shoots & Leaves: Why, Commas Really Do Make a Difference! (2006) Lynne Truss: Putnam's
Humorous comparative illustrations show that the meaning of a sentence can depend upon the placement of a comma. (I-Sec)

Esperanza Rising (2000) Pam Muñoz Ryan: New York Scholastic
Due to family tragedy, Esperanza and her mother leave their ranch in Mexico and immigrate to the United States. The book compares her life in Mexico with her life in California. (P-Sec)

First Day Jitters (2000) ***First Year Letters*** (2003) ***Last Day Blues*** (2006) Julie Danneberg: Charlesbridge
This series is the journey through the school year with Mrs. Hartwell and her class, from first day to the last day of school. (P-Sec)

Kids Pick the Funniest Poems (1991) Bruce Lansky: Meadowbrook Press
The first collection of funny poems selected by children and compiled by Lansky. (P-I)

Love That Dog (2001) Sharon Creech: Harper Collins
A boy finds out he can enjoy and write poetry with the help of his teacher and his dog. (P-I)

Nothing Ever Happens on 90th Street (2004) Roni Schotter: Orchard Books
When Eva sits on her stoop trying to complete a school assignment by writing about what happens in her neighborhood, she gets a great deal of advice and action. (P-Sec)

Miss Alaineus (2000) Debra Frasier: Harcourt, Inc.
The young girl in the story misunderstood one of her weekly vocabulary words. Her mistake in front of her classmates is a humiliating experience but leads to a victorious ending. (I-Sec)

My Dog is As Smelly As Dirty Socks (2007) Hanoch Piven: Schwartz & Wade
Filled with similes and play on words encourages students' creativity. (P-I)

The Mysteries of Harris Burdick (1984) Chris Van Allsburg: Houghton Mifflin
Fourteen intriguing pictures, captions, and story titles make this book a natural for creative writing. (I-Sec)

Once Upon a Time: Writing Your Own Fairy Tale (2009) Nancy Loewen: Picture Window Books
A guide to writing fairy tales, retelling the tale of "Little Red Riding Hood," and including an analysis of different elements of the story with thirteen tools for writing fairy tales. (P)

Petite Rouge: a Cajun Red Riding Hood (2001) Mike Artell: Dial Books for Young People
An original retelling of a classic folktale using rhyme and art where the big, bad gator is no match for a smart young girl and her quick-thinking cat. (P-I)

Punished! (2006) David Lubar: Darby Creek Publishing
Logan and his friend Benedict are playing tag in the library when a mysterious man punishes him for his disrespect by making him speak only in puns. (P-Sec)

Read All About It! (2008) Laura Bush and Jenna Bush: Harper Collins Publishers
Tyrone likes everything about school except reading, until he and his classmates are swept into a mysterious adventure during the class story hour. (P-Sec)

Thank You, Mr. Falker (1998) Patricia Polacco: Philomel Books
A little girl looks forward to school, but has trouble reading. A seventh grade math teacher discovers she can't read and helps her. A personal thank you to all teachers. (P-Sec)

The True Story of the 3 Little Pigs (1989) Jon Scieszka: Viking
The real story as told to the author by A. Wolf. (P-Sec)

The Weighty Word Book (2000) ***Weighty Words, Too (2009)*** Paul M. Levitt, Douglas A. Burger, and Elissa S. Guralnick: Roberts, Rinehart Publishers
Letters of the alphabet are featured with a word and a fanciful story but leads to the correct meaning. (I-Sec)

Words are CATagorical series (2000-2010) Brian P. Cleary: Millbrook Press
This series gives a lighthearted look at language, each book shows, rather than explains, the concept of nouns, verbs, or adjectives. (P-Sec)

MATHEMATICS

Anno's Mysterious Multiplying Jar (1983) Mitsumasa Anno: Philomel Books
About a jar and what is in the jar. Factorials are represented through story and graphically represented with dots. (Sec)

A Remainder of One (1995) Elinor Pinczes: Houghton Mifflin
When the queen of bugs demands that her army marches in even lines, Private Joe divides the marchers into more and more lines so he will not be left out of the parade. (P-I)

Bats on Parade (1999) Kathi Appelt: Morrow Junior Books
Each year the Bat Jamboree, starring 55 adorable bats, draws a standing room only audience for a numbering performance. (P)

The Best of Times: Math Strategies That Multiply (2002) Greg Tang: Scholastic Press
Simple rhymes offer hints on how to multiply any number by zero through ten without memorizing the multiplication tables. (P-I)

The Cat in Numberland (2006) Ivar Ekeland: Cricket Books
Chaos threatens among the numbers and letters in Mr. and Mrs. Hilbert's Hotel Infinity, when the fractions arrive demanding rooms. (I-Sec)

Do You Wanna Bet? (2007) Jean Cushman: Clarion Books
The book has short passages about two boys and most ordinary situations that depend on chance and probability. (P-I)

The Doorbell Rang (1986) Pat Hutchins: Mulberry Books
Ma has made a dozen cookies for her two children. Will they be able to share when the doorbell rings, and rings, and rings? A good introduction to division. (P- I)

The Dot and the Line: A Romance in Lower Mathematics (2001) Norton Juster: SeaStar Book
It is the story of incompatible love and an exploration of the possibilities for geometrical relationships. (I-Sec)

Each Orange Had 8 Slices (1992) Paul Giganti Jr.: Greenwillow Books
A counting book with an introduction to repeated addition or multiplication. (P)

The Everything Kids' Money Book: Earn it, Save it, and Watch it Grow! (2008) Brette McWhorter Sember: Adams Media
A guide to personal finances for children that explains the history of money, currency, banking, earnings, investing, saving, spending, and other related topics. (P-Sec)

Feast for 10 (1993) Cathryn Falewell: Clarion Books
Numbers from one to ten explain how a family shops and works together to prepare a meal. (P)

Fermat's Enigma: ***The Epic Quest to Solve the World's Greatest Mathematical Problem*** (1998) Simon Singh: Walker and Company
The book tells the story of the search to solve Pierre de Fermat's Last Theorem. (Sec)

Grandfather Tang's Story (1990) A. Tompert: Crown Publishers
A good book to introduce Tangrams, an ancient Chinese puzzle. A tale of two fox fairies who change their shapes into different animals and find themselves in a predicament. (P)

G is for Googol: A Math Alphabet Book (1998) David M. Schwartz: Tricycle Press
Explanations and illustrations of math terms from abacus, binary, probability to zillion. (I-Sec)

The Grapes of Math (2001) Greg Tang: Scholastic
Introduces the art of problem solving through a series of math riddles. The riddles challenge children and adults to think creatively as they learn tricks to help solve problems. (I-Sec)

The Great Graph Contest (2005) Loreen Leedy: Holiday House
Two amphibian friends hold a contest to see who can make better graphs. (I)

The History of Counting (1999) Denise Schmandt-Besseral: Harper Collins
A renowned archaeologist traces the evolution of counting. It is a fascinating book that introduces children to one of our most important inventions. (I)

How Much is a Million? (1985) Schwartz: Lothrop, Lee & Shepard Books
The book helps children and adults to understand the concept of how much is a million. (P-I)

How Do You Count a Dozen Ducklings? (2006) In Seon Chae: Whitman
Faced with keeping track of twelve ducklings, Mama Duck finds different ways to group them so that they are easier to count. (P-I)

How Long or How Wide?: A Measuring Guide (2007) Brian P. Cleary: Millbrook Press
A humorous introduction to measurement, including a definition of length, and discussing inches, feet, yards, millimeters, centimeters, decimeters, meters, and rulers. (P-Sec)

Is the Blue Whale the Biggest Thing There Is? (1993) Robert E. Wells: Albert Whitman
As students think about sizes of things in nature they are helped to realize the importance of scientific notation for large numbers. (I-Sec)

If You Hopped Like a Frog (1999) David Schwartz: Scholastic Press
Hilarious mathematical explanations of what people could do if they had the amazing abilities of animals. (P-Sec)

If You Made A Million (1989) David M. Schwartz: Harper Trophy
The book is follow-up to *What is a Million* and tells how to earn and save money. (P I)

It's Probably Penny (2007) Loreen Leedy: Holt
After learning about probability at school, Lisa has to complete an assignment and find things that fit into the categories of what will, might, and cannot happen. (P)

The King's Chessboard (1988) David Burch: Dial Books for Young Readers
A wise man asks the king to place rice on his chessboard and double the amount each day for 84 days and deliver that amount to him. A look at exponents and exponential notation. (I-Sec)

The Librarian Who Measured the Earth (1994) Kathryn Lasky: Little Brown
About the life of a geographer whose notable achievement was an ingenious method of using geometry to measure the circumference of the earth. History and science in picture format. (P-I)

The Man Who Counted: A Collection of Mathematical Adventures (1993) Malba Tahan: Norton
Tahan, a Brazilian mathematician, shares through stories, math puzzles and numerical intrigue in human situations. (Sec)

Math Curse (1995) Jon Sciezka and Lane Smith: Penguin Books USA
A funny story in which everything becomes a problem and math anxiety becomes a curse. Children think mathematically about many of life's issues. (I-Sec)

Math Fables (2004) Greg Tang: Scholastic Press
A series of rhymes about animals introduces counting and grouping numbers. (P-Sec)

Math Fables Too: Making Science Count (2007) Greg Tang: Scholastic Press
Fables about ocean, jungle, desert, and lake animals focus on number groupings and counting. (P-Sec)

Measuring Penny (1997) Loreen Leedy: H. Holt
Lisa measures her dog Penny with units, including pounds, inches, dog biscuits, and cotton swabs. (P)

More M & M's (1998) Barbara Barbieri McGrath: Charlesbridge
M&M's are used to teach estimation, simple graphing, factoring, multiplication, problem solving, and division. (P-I)

The Number Devil (2000) Hans Magnus Enzensberger: Henry Holt
A cleverly written mathematical adventure in narrative text about math history and theory. (I-Sec)

One Grain of Rice: A Mathematical Folktale (1997) Demi: Scholastic
Written in folk tale format with traditional miniature illustrations, the author demonstrates how numbers doubled grow from one to one billion in 30 days. (I-Sec*)*

One Hundred Hungry Ants (1993) Elinor Pinczes: Scholastic
Regrouping is taught as one hundred hungry ants are marching to a picnic. (P-I)

Pizza Counting (2003) Christina Dobson: Charlesbridge
Decorated pizzas are used to introduce counting and fractions. (P-I)

Sir Cumference series *(1997-2009)* Cindy Neuschwander: Charlesbridge
Through these stories, Sir Cumference and his friends teach diameter, radius, pi, and many other geometry terms. (I-Sec)

2x2=BOO (1995) Loreen Leedy: Holiday House
A Halloween book filled with spooky multiplication stories. (P-I)

Ten Black Dots (1986) Donald Crews: Greenwillow Books
The book is a good introduction to counting and conservation of numbers. (P)

Two Ways to Count to Ten (1988) Ruby Dee: Henry Holt and Co.This Liberian folktale includes creative thinking and skip counting as the king of the jungle uses a mathematical problem to choose his successor. (P)

MUSIC
Bravo! Brava! A Night at the Opera (2001) Anne Siberell: Oxford University Press
Discusses the history of opera, profiles of famous composers, brief descriptions of some well-known operas, and a detailed discussion of what is involved in the staging of an opera. (I-Sec)

The Bat Boy & His **Violin** (1998) Gavin Curtis: Aladdin Picture Books
The manager of the Dukes, a Negro National League team, needs his son to be a batboy not a "fiddler." This is a story of family ties and team spirit with beautiful watercolor paintings. (P-I)

Chicka Chicka Boom Boom (1989) John Archambault: Simon & Schuster
Repeating rhythmic patterns are presented as the alphabet letters race to the top of the coconut tree. Students can create ostinato to accompany the book. (P-I)

Do Re Mi: If You Can Read Music, Thank Guido d'Arezzo (2006) Susan L. Roth: Houghton Mifflin
A fictionalized account of the childhood and early life of Benedictine monk Guido d'Arezzo, the "Father of Music" and inventor of the musical staff. (P-I)

Jake the Philharmonic Dog (2006) Karen LeFrak: Walker & Co.
Jake the dog, who comes along to work with New York Philharmonic stagehand Richie Norton and becomes a hit with the musicians and the audience-teaches several orchestral terms. (P-I)

Jazz on a Saturday Night (2007) Leo & Diane Dillon: Blue Sky Press
A crowd gathers to groove to an evening of jazz played by Miles Davis on trumpet, Max Roach on drums, Charlie Parker on alto saxophone, John Coltrain on his sax, plus others. (P-Sec)

John was a Jazz Giant (2008) Carole Boston Weatherford: Henry Holt
A biography of John Coltrane that focuses on his childhood and adolescent years and discusses his inspirations, influences, family, the development of his musical talent, and more. (P)

Love to Langston (2002) Tony Medina: Lee & Low Books
Life of poet Langston Hughes who used rhythms of black music in his poetry. (Sec)

Meet the Orchestra (1991) Ann Hayes: Harcourt Brace
Describes the features, sounds, and role of each musical instrument in the orchestra. (P-I)

Music Through Children's Literature: Themes and Variations (Revised Edition) Donna B. Levene: Teacher Ideas Press
A book of lesson plans based on children's books and divided into sections related to rhythm, melody, form and style, instruments, dances, and history. (P-I)

Pet of the Met (2008) Lydia and Don Freeman: Viking
Maestro Petrini, a musical mouse at the Metropolitan Opera House, gets so carried away by the music that he is nearly apprehended by the music-hating cat who lives in the basement. (P-I)

Satchmo's Blues (1999) Alan Schroeder: Bt Bound
Set in New Orleans, Louis Armstrong earns the money to buy his first horn. (Sec)

***The Story of the Incredible* Orchestra** (2000) Bruce Koscielniak: Houghton Mifflin
Traces the development and trends of music and instruments over the last 400 years. (I)

***This Land is Your Land* (2008)** Woody Guthrie: Little, Brown
Illustrations of classic American landscapes accompany the lyrics of Woody Guthrie's classic folk song. Includes the sheet music for the song's chorus and a brief overview of Guthrie's life. (P-Sec)

Tiger Woman (1995) Laurence Yep: Bridgewater Books
The story is based on a Shantung folk song about a greedy old woman and what happens to her after she does not share her white bean curd with a raggedy old man. (P-I)

PHYSICAL EDUCATION and HEALTH
The Babe and I (1999) David Adler: Harcourt Brace
A boy selling newspapers during the Depression sells a paper to Babe Ruth. (I-Sec)

The Bare Naked Book (2006) Kathy Stinson: Annick Press
Includes the various parts of the body such as toes, noses, teeth, and belly buttons. (P)

Baseball Saved Us (1993) Ken Mochizuki: Scholastic, Inc.
A true account of how the author and his family were moved to an internment camp in Idaho during World War II. (I-Sec)

Bump! Set! Spike! : You Can Play Volleyball (2006) Nick Fauchald: Picture Window Books
Teaches how to play volleyball through a story about a school game- how to serve, set, bump pass, and dig pass. (P-I)

The Edible Pyramid: Good Eating Every Day (2007) Loreen Leedy: Holiday House
Uses the U.S. Department of Agriculture's food pyramid to show the healthy way to eat. (P-Sec)

Food Fight (2002) Carol Diggory Shields: Handprint Books
Just after midnight the food in the refrigerator starts to party and make quite a mess; if you want the whole story ask the cat about what happened last night. (P-Sec)

For the Love of the Game: Michael Jordan and Me (1999) Eloise Greenfield: Harpercollins Juvenile Books
- The author's poem with accompanying paintings will inspire children to find the strength to follow their dreams. (P-Sec)

From Head to Toe (1997) Eric Carle: HarperCollins
Encourages the reader to exercise by following the movements of various animals. (P)

Get up and go! (2006) Nancy Carlson: Viking
Encourages readers to turn off the television and exercise. (P)

Good For Me and You (2004) Mercer Mayer: HarperFestival
Little Critter helps his family and friends have fun while getting fit after he learns about the food pyramid and exercise in school. (P)

The Gym Teacher from the Black Lagoon (1994) Mike Thaler: Scholastic, Inc.
School is getting a new gym teacher and he is coming from the Junior High. The kids say he is really mean. The story tells what they have heard that makes him so mean! (P-I)

Hoops (2001) Robert Burleigh: Voyager Books
The author presents a poetic description of the game of basketball. (P-Sec)

J is for Jump Shot: A Basketball Alphabet (2005) Mike Ulmer: Sleeping Bear Press
An A to Z alphabet book that describes the history, major players, and basic basketball moves using simple rhyming text. (P-Sec)

Let Them Play (2005) Margot Theis Raven: Sleeping Bear Press
In 1955, the dreams of South Carolina's only all-black Little League team are dashed as prejudice prevents the state champions from competing in the Little League World Series. (I-Sec)

My Daddy is a Pretzel: Yoga for Parents and Kids (2004) Baron Baptiste: Barefoot Books
This picture book revolves around children participating in a yoga class and discussing their parents' occupations. (P)

Riding the Tiger (2001) Eve Bunting: Clarion
An allegory. The tiger could symbolize drugs, gangs or any form of temptation faced by inner city youth. Illustrated with beautiful woodcuts, a very powerful book to use with teenagers. (Sec)

Salt in His Shoes (2000) Deloris Jordan and Roslyn M Jordan: Simon & Schuster
Michael Jordan's story of how he learns from his father and mother that in order to be a champion you need to have patience, determination, and hard work. (I)

The Skin You're In: Staying Healthy Inside and Out (2008) Diane Webber: Franklin Watts
A guide to good health for teens, discussing issues of self-esteem, nutrition, exercise, weight management, preventive maintenance, and the dangers of teen life. (Sec)

Swish: The Quest for Basketball's Perfect Shot (2009) Mark Stewart and Mike Kennedy: Millbrook Press
This book has an engaging history of the sport, followed by profiles of some of the most impressive shots of all time and the players who made them. (I-Sec)

Touchdown: The Power and Precision of Football's Perfect Play (2010) Mark Stewart and Mike Kennedy: Millbrook Press
Examines the history of football, focusing on touchdowns, and discusses players, memorable plays, and NFL records. (I-Sec)

Wilma Unlimited: How Wilma Rudolph Became the World's Fastest Woman (2000) Kathleen Krull:
Voyager Books - A book about how Wilma became the world's fastest woman. (I-Sec)

You are Healthy (2008) Todd Snow: Maren Green Pub.
Encourages young children to stay healthy by playing, eating fruits and vegetables, drinking water, sleeping well, washing their hands, and enjoying time with loved ones. (P)

Your Tongue Can Tell (2000) Vicki Cobb; Brookfield, CT: Millbrook Press, Inc.
An entertaining story with suggested activities that explores the sense of taste, how it works, and how it can help children detect which foods are sweet, sour, salty, or spicy. (P-Sec)

SCIENCE

11 Planets: A New View of the Solar System (2008) David Aguilar: National Geographic
Profiles the eight planets from Mercury to Neptune, the dwarf planets and discusses meteorites, comets, the Kuiper and asteroid belts, the Oort cloud, and other solar systems. (I-Sec)

Almost Astronauts: ***13 Women Who Dared to Dream*** (2009) Tanya Lee Stone: Candlewick
Nearly 20 years before the U.S. officially admitted women into the astronaut program, 13 women, known as the Mercury 13, fought for the right to soar into space. (I-Sec)

A Sand County Almanac (1972) Aldo Leopolud: Ballentine Books
Essays on conservation from Round River. (Sec)

Antarctic Antics (1998) Judy Sierra: Harcourt Brace & Co
The book uses poetry to teach about the life of the penguin. (P-I)

Being Caribou: Five Months on Foot with a Caribou Herd (2007) Karsten Heuer: Walker
Wildlife biologists follow the five-month migration of 123,000 caribou over mountain ranges and icy rivers to their calving grounds in Alaska's Arctic National Wildlife Refuge. (I-Sec)

Bigfoot Cinderrrrrella (1998) Tony Johnston & James Warhola: G.P. Putnam's Sons
The book is a new version of Cinderella with the theme of saving the forest. (P-Sec)

Bringing the Rain to Kapiti Plain: A Nandi Tale (1981) Verna Aardema: Dial Press
A cumulative rhyme relating how Ki-pat brought rain to the drought-stricken Kapiti Plain. Multicultural, science, storytelling. (P-Sec)

Brother Sister, Eagle Sky: A Message from Chief Seattle (1991) Susan Jeffers: Dial/Delacorte
A Suquamish Indian chief describes his people's respect and love for the earth, and concern for its destruction. (I-Sec)

Cell Division and Genetics (2008) Robert Snedden: Heinemann Library
The book explains how cells divide, the relationships between chromosomes and genes, and how DNA determines whether an organism will be an oak tree or a human being. (I-Sec)

Cloud Dance (2000) Thomas Locker: Silver Whistle/Harcourt
Clouds of many shapes and sizes drift across the sky. The book has factual information on the formation of different kinds of clouds. (P-Sec)

Dear Mr. Blueberry (1991) Simon James: Aladdin Paperbacks
A young girl exchanges letters with her teacher about finding a whale in her pond. The book is a great way to learn about whales and letter writing. (P)

Dinosaur Food: Unearth the Secrets Behind Dinosaur Fossils (2008) Rupert Matthews: QEB
Explores the hunting and feeding habits of dinosaurs and how paleontologists determine the habits and behaviors of these prehistoric creatures. (P-Sec)

Earth Then and Now: Amazing Images of our Changing World (2007) Fred Pearce: Firefly
Presents three hundred before-and-after photos of places throughout the world, taken between five and one hundred years apart, exploring environmental change, industrialization, urbanization, natural disasters, war, travel, and tourism. (I-Sec)

Extreme Animals: The Toughest Creatures on Earth (2009) Nicola Davies: Candlewick Press
Describes the physical characteristics and biological processes that enable particular animals to survive in extremely hot and cold climates. (I-Sec)

Face To Face With Animals Series (2007-2010) National Geographic
A behind-the-scenes look with the people who research and photograph wild animals--the reader is put right into the action! (P-Sec)

Flashy, Fantastic Rain Forest Frogs (1997) Dorothy Hinshaw Patent: Walker and Co.
The author describes the physical characteristics, behavior, reproduction, and habitat of frogs that live in the rain forest. (I-Sec)

The Great Kapok Tree (1993) Lynn Cherry: Harcourt Brace & Co
 A man planning on cutting down a great Kapok tree learns from the animals how important every tree is in the Amazon Rain Forest. (P-Sec)

How to Hide a Crocodile (1994) Ruth Heller: Grosset & Dunlap
This book is from the author's "How to Hide" series. Learn about camouflage in nature. (P)

How Monkeys Make Chocolate: Unlocking the Mysteries of the Rainforest (2006) Adrian Forsyth: Maple Tree Press
Describes mysteries of tropical rainforests and the connections between plants and animals. (P-I)

The Human Body (2008) Seymour Simon: Smithsonian/Collins
An investigation of the human body, looking at what technological developments have revealed about the twelve major body systems and how they work together. (I-Sec)

Insectlopedia (1998) Douglas Florian: Harcourt Brace
A book of poems that gives interesting facts about certain insects. (P-I)

Inside Ralphie: A Book About Germs (1995) (Science Concepts Series) Joanna Cole: Scholastic, Inc.
Ms. Frizzle and her class learn what happens when germs enter our body and make us sick. (P-Sec)

It's Disgusting and We Ate It*! (1988) James Solheim: Simon & Schuster Books, Young Readers
Shares food facts from around the world and throughout history. (I-Sec)

Joyful Noise (1992) Paul Fleischman: Harpercollins Juvenile Books
A choral poetry book about insects. (I-Sec)

Ladybugs: Red, Fiery, and Bright (2002) Mia Posada: Learner Publishing Group
The book is written in rhyming text that describes the life cycle of the ladybug. (P-I)

Letting Swift River Go (1992) Jane Yolen: Little, Brown
Tells of the flooding of towns in western Massachusetts to form the Quabbin Reservoir. (I-Sec)

The Lorax (1971) Dr. Seuss: Random House
The Lorax speaks for the trees that are being chopped down. What happens when the trees are gone? The book delivers an ecology message for all of us. (I-Sec)

Michael Recycle (2008) Ellie Bethel: IDW & Jonas Pub
Michael Recycle teaches a town where trash is piled high, about recycling their garbage. (P)

Mountain Dance (2001) Thomas Locker: Silver Whistle/Harcourt
Provides a poetic description of various kinds of mountains and how they are formed. (P-Sec)

My Season with Penguins: An Antarctic Journal (2000) Sophie Webb: Houghton Mifflin
Describes the author's two-month stay in Antarctica to study and draw penguins. (P-Sec)

Open Wide, Tooth School Inside (2000) Laurie Keller: Doubleday
A book filled with students who are teeth and will keep the children's interest with the illustrations and jokes. The information is accurate and oral hygiene is stressed. (P)

One Small Square: Woods (1997) Donald M. Silver: McGraw-Hill/Contemporary Books
A trip to the woods where you are asked to explore and investigate one small square of space, provides students an opportunity to appreciate nature. (P-I)

Over the Mountains: An Aerial View of Geology (2007) Michael Collier: Mikaya Press
A collection of aerial photographs that profile the remote regions of the world that reveal some of the geological phenomena that have shaped the planet. (I-Sec)

Parts (1997) ***More Parts*** (2001) ***Even More Parts*** (2007) Tedd Arnold: Puffin Books
Humorous books about a young boy's fear of losing his body parts. (P)

The Periodic Table: Elements with Style (2007) Adrian Dingle: Kingfisher
Combines science and art to create a simple way for students to learn the periodic table. (I-Sec)

Red-eyed Tree Frog (1999) Joy Cowley: Scholastic Press
Learn about a frog in the Central America rain forest that hunts for food while trying not to be dinner for other animals. (P)

Salmon Creek (2002) Annette LeBox: Douglas & McIntyre
This beautiful, poetic text tells the life cycle of the Coho salmon. (I-Sec)

Smack (1998) Melvin Burgess: Holt
The story is about the hazards of drugs. (I-Sec)

Snowflake Bentley (1998) Jacqueline Martin: Houghton Mifflin
This is a story of Wilson Bentley, the photographer-scientist who discovered that no two snowflakes are alike. His persistence may be an inspiration to young scientists. (I-Sec)

The Spider and the Fly (2002) Mary Howitt: Simon & Schuster
An adaptation of an old story, this book has stunning artwork and a letter from the spider at the end of the story. Could use as an anticipatory set for an insect unit. (I-Sec)

Starry Messenger: Galileo Galilei (1996) Peter Sis: Farrar, Straus & Giroux
Beautiful illustrations and quotes from his own writings tell the story of the life of Galileo, scientist, mathematician, astronomer and philosopher. (I-Sec)

Suitcase for Seeds (2002) Jean Richards: Millbrook Press
The book is an excellent introduction to seeds, their purpose, growth, and how they travel. (P)

Swim Through the Sea (1994) Kristen Joy Pratt: Dawn Publications
Take an illustrated tour of the undersea environment of Seamore the seahorse. (P)

Swimmy (1963) Leo Lionni: Pantheon
Swimmy is a little fish in a big ocean trying to find a way to protect himself and his friends. (P)

Tracking Trash: Flotsam, Jetsam, and the Science of Ocean Motion (2007) Loree Griffin Burns: Houghton Mifflin
Describes how a scientist tracks trash traveling great distances by way of ocean currents. (I-Sec)

Tree in the Ancient Forest (1995) Carol Reed-Jones: Dawn Publishing
Step deep into a northern forest and see the beauty of one hundred foot trees and the interdependence of the plants and animals that live in that ecosystem. (I-Sec)

The Tree That Time Built: A Celebration of Nature, Science, and Imagination (2009) Mary Ann Hoberman and Linda Winston: Sourcebooks Jabberwocky
Collects over one hundred poems from various authors that explore the worlds of nature, science, and the imagination. (P-Sec)

Verdi (1997) Janell Cannon: Harcourt Brace
A young python learns the ways of the tropical jungle. (P-Sec)

A Walk in the Rain Forest (1992) Kristin Joy Pratt: Dawn Publications
"XYZ, the ant, went for a walk in the rain forest, and what do you think he saw?" Follow him on his journey and explore the vegetation and see the unusual animals. (P-I)

Water Dance (1997) Thomas Locker: Harcourt Brace & Company
Water speaks of its existence in such forms as storm clouds, rivers, mist, and rainbows. Factual information is given on the water cycle. (P-Sec)

The Way We Work: Getting to Know the Amazing Human Body (2008) David Macaulay: Houghton Mifflin
A visual exploration of the inner workings of the human body that uses close-ups, cross-sections, and perspectives to look at the different body systems and how they function. (I-Sec)

The Wump World (1970) Bill Peet: Houghton-Mifflin
The Wump World is an unspoiled place where huge monsters bring hordes of tiny creatures from the planet Pollutus. This is an environmental story about the need to protect the Earth. (I-Sec)

SOCIAL STUDIES

A. Lincoln and Me (2001) Louise Borden: Scholastic
A young boy compares himself to Abraham Lincoln. (I-Sec)

America, A Patriotic Primer (2002) Lynne Cheney: Simon & Schuster
This is an alphabet book celebrating our nation, its history, and the American people. (P-Sec)

The Bracelet (1993) Yoshiko Uchida: Philomel Books
A young girl is being sent to a Japanese American internment camp during World War II. She discovers she lost a bracelet, a parting keepsake, given to her by a friend. (P-Sec)

Bull Run (1995) Paul Fleishman: Harper Trophy
A Civil War story as told through 16 individuals' viewpoints. (I-Sec)

The Butterfly (2000) Patricia Polacco: Philomel Books
Takes place during the French Resistance and is based on the lives of the author's aunt Monique and her aunt's mother. A Jewish girl and her family are hiding from the Nazis in Monique's basement. (I-Sec)

Chains (2008) Laurie Halse Anderson: Simon & Schuster Books for Young Readers
After being sold to a cruel couple in New York City, a slave named Isabel spies for the rebels during the Revolutionary War. (I-Sec)

Children of the Dust Bowl (1993) Jerry Stanley: Crown Books for Young Readers
A true story of a school at Weedpatch, one of several farm-labor camps run by the federal government. The book is a researched portrait of the "Okies" driven to California during the Dust Bowl days. (I-Sec)

Colonial Voices: hear them speak (2008) Kay Winters: Dutton Children's Books
Ethan must deliver an important message to the Patriots, and as he makes his way through the streets of his city, he witnesses the daily events and practices of diverse groups of people. (P-I)

Dakota Dugout (1989) Ann Turner: Aladdin Paperbacks
The book tells of life in a sod house on the Dakota prairie during the 1800s. (I-Sec)

Family Pictures (1990) Carmen Lomas Garza: Children's Book Press
Written in Spanish and English, about the author's family and daily happenings in the village. (P)

The Gettysburg Address (1995) Foreword by Gary Wills: Houghton Mifflin
The most famous American History speech with illustrations reflecting Lincoln's words. (I-Sec)

Ghosts of the White House (1998) Cheryl Harness: Simon & Schuster
A picture book presenting American presidents. (P-Sec)

Grandfather's Journey (1993) Allen Say: Houghton Mifflin
The Japanese American author tells how his grandfather loved two different countries. (P-I)

Home to Medicine Mountain (1998) Chiori Santiago: Children's Book Press
Based on a true story, this tells of two young Native Americans who were taken to live at a government-run boarding school in the1930s. (I-Sec)

House Mouse, Senate Mouse (1996) Peter and Cheryl Barnes: VSP Books
The Squeaker of the House and Senate Mouse-jority Leader has a big task, creating a law to declare a National Cheese. The book takes the reader through the legislative process. (I-Sec)

I Have a Dream (1997) Foreword by Coretta Scott King: Scholastic
An illustrated edition of the famous speeches by Dr. Martin Luther King, Jr. (I-Sec)

I Pledge Allegiance (2004) Bill Martin Jr. and Michael Sampson: Candlewick Press
The pledge is explained and illustrated. Historical anecdotes are also included. (P-Sec)

If you're not from the prairie... (1995) David Bouchard: Aladdin Paperbacks
Experience the beauty and vastness of the prairie through the book's verses and images. (I-Sec)

If the World Were a Village (2002) ***If America Were a Village*** (2009) David Smith: Kids Can Press
To make the idea of a world of 6.2 billion people more understandable, Smith suggests that children imagine the population of the world as a village of just 100 people. (P-Sec)

John, Paul, George & Ben (2006) Lane Smith: Hyperion Books
A humorous look at the early lives of five founding fathers of the United States, including George Washington, John Hancock, Paul Revere, Ben Franklin, and Thomas Jefferson. (P-Sec)

The Keeping Quilt (1988) Patricia Polacco: Aladdin Picture Books
Family triumphs and disappointments as a beautiful quilt is passed from generation to generation. The quilt idea originated when great gramma left Russia leaving her belongings behind. (I)

The Last Brother: a Civil War Tale (2006) Trinka Hakes Noble: Sleeping Bear Press
Eleven-year-old Gabe enlists in the Union Army in Pennsylvania along with his older brother Davy and as bugler, does his best to protect Davy during the Battle of Gettysburg. (P-Sec)

Listen to the Wind (2009) Greg Mortenson: New York: Scholastic
Learn about Dr. Greg's work to educate the children of Pakistan by building schools, the children's version of *Three Cups of Tea* written by Greg Mortenson. (P-Sec)

More than Anything Else (1995) Marie Bradby: Orchard Books
Nine-year-old Booker T. Washington wants to learn to read. Pair this with *Richard Wright and the Library Card* for units on black Americans. (I)

N. C. Wyeth's Pilgrims (1991) Robert San Souci: Chronicle Books
Tells of the pilgrims' lives in the New World up to the first Thanksgiving. Illustrated by N. C. Wyeth. (Sec)

Nim and the War Effort (2002) Milly Lee: Farrar, Straus and Giroux
A story that talks about life on the home front during World War II. (Sec)

Number the Stars (1989) Lois Lowry: Bantam Doubleday Dell Books
It is 1943 and 10 year-old best friends are living in Copenhagen, Denmark when the Nazis invade. (I-Sec)

The Other Side (2001) Jacqueline Woodson: Putnam
Two girls, one white and one African-American, gradually get to know each other as they sit on the fence that ⋯des their town. (P-Sec)

Our White House: Looking In, Looking Out (2008) introduction by David McCullough: Candlewick Press
A collection of essays, personal accounts, historical fiction, and poetry that traces the history of the White House through the eyes of the children who have lived and visited there. (P-Sec)

Pearl Harbor Child (1998) Dorinda Makanaonalani Nicholson: Arizona Memorial Museum Association
Describes the aftermath of the attack at Pearl Harbor. Photographs of burning battleships, bomb shelters, and people standing in line for food explain what life was like then. (I-Sec)

Pink and Say (1994) Patricia Polacco: Scholastic Inc.
A black soldier saves the life of a young white soldier during the Civil War. (I-Sec)

Richard Wright and the Library Card (1997) William Miller: Lee & Low Books
Based on a scene from Wright's autobiography, *Black Boy*. Wright borrowed a library card from a white co-worker because black people were not allowed to use the public library. (I)

Rose Blanche (1996) Roberto Innocenti: Creative Editions/Harcourt Brace
During World War II a German girl discovers a concentration camp and carries food to the prisoners. (I-Sec)

Rudy Rides the Rails: A Depression Era Story (2007) Dandi Daley Mackall: Sleeping Bear Press
In 1932, during the Depression in Ohio, thirteen-year-old Rudy, determined to help his family during the hard times, hops a train going west to California and experiences the hobo life. (I-Sec)

The Scarlet Stockings Spy (2004) Trinka Hakes Noble: Sleeping Bear Press
In 1777 Philadelphia, young Maddy Rose spies for General Washington's army by using an unusual code to communicate with her soldier brother. (P-Sec)

Star of Fear, Star of Hope (1995) Jo Hoestlandt: Walker
Nine-year-old Helen, who lives in France during the Nazi Occupation, can't understand why her Jewish friend, Lydia, must leave her birthday party in such a hurry. (I)

T4: A Novel in Verse (2008) Ann Clare LeZotte: Houghton Mifflin
After the Nazi party takes control of Germany, thirteen-year-old Paula, who is deaf, is forced to go into hiding because of Adolf Hitler's Tiegartenstrasse 4--T4--which was put in place to kill any mentally ill or disabled people. (I-Sec)

Through My Eyes (1999) Ruby Bridges: Scholastic Press
A true story told by one of the first five African Americans to enroll in an all white school. The book includes quotes and pictures of that era. (P-Sec)

The Wall (1990) Eve Bunting: Clarion
In the picture book a father takes his young son to the Vietnam War Memorial to find the name of the grandfather he never knew. (I-Sec)

The Watsons Go to Birmingham—1963 (1995) Christopher Paul Curtis: Scholastic, Inc.
This novel is about a family that goes to Birmingham, Alabama, during one of the darkest moments in American history. (I)

White Socks Only (1996) Evelyn Coleman: A. Whitman
The story focuses on segregation in Mississippi. A little black girl drinks from a "whites only" drinking fountain and is beaten by a white man. (I)

William's House (2001) Ginger Howard: Millbrook Press
In 1637 a family from England builds a house in the New World. (Sec)

The Yellow Star: The Legend of King Christian X of Denmark (2000) Carmen Deedy: Peachtree
All Jews had to wear a yellow star when the Nazis occupied Denmark. King Christian proclaimed that all Danes would wear the star so the Nazis would not be able to tell the Jews from Christians. (Sec)

Chapter 10
References

ACTFL. (1998). *ACTFL performance guidelines for K-12 Learners.* Available at www.actfl.org.

Allen, J. (2007). *Inside words.* Portland, ME: Stenhouse Publishers.

Allen, J. (2000). *Yellow brick road: Shared and guided paths to independent reading.* Portland, ME: Stenhouse, 4-12.

Allen, R. (2005). New paradigms for parent involvement. *Education Update*, 47(30), 3-5.

Alexander, K., Entwisle, D., & Olson, S. (2007). Lasting consequences of the summer learning gap. *American Sociological Review*, 72, 167-180.

Allington, R. (2002). You can't learn much from books you can't read. *Educational Leadership*, 60(3), 16-19.

Allington, R. (2001). *What really matters for struggling readers.* New York: Addison Wesley Longman.

American Psychiatric Association. (2000). *Diagnostic and statistical manual of mental disorders* (4th ed., text revision). Washington, DC: Author.

Anderson, G. (2007, 2010). One school, one book. *Reading Today*, Newark, DE: International Reading Association.

Anderson, N.J. (1991). Individual differences in strategy use in second language reading and testing. *The Modern Language Journal.* 75(4) 460-472.

Anderson R. C. and Freebody, P. (1981). Vocabulary knowledge. In J. T. Guthrie (Ed.), *Comprehension and teaching: Research reviews* (pp. 77-117). Newark, DE: International Reading Association.

Armbuster, B., Lehr, Fl., & Osborn, J. (2001). *Put reading first: The research building blocks for teaching children to read.* Center for the Improvement of Early Reading Achievement.

Armbruster, B. & Nagy, W. (1992). Vocabulary in content area lessons. *The Reading Teacher*, 45(7), 550-551.

Au, K. (2010). NAEP data show little change. Reading Today, 27(5), 1-6.

Baker, L. & Brown, A.L. (1984). Cognitive monitoring in reading. In J. Flood (Ed.), *Understanding Reading Comprehension* (21-44). Newark, DE: International Reading Association.

Barnett, M. (1988). Teaching reading in a foreign language. On-line ESL Articles, ERIC Digest.

Beck, I. & McKeown, M. (1985). Teaching vocabulary: Making the instruction fit the goal. *Educationl Perspectives*, 23(1), 11-15.

Beck, I. & McKeown, M. (1991). Conditions of vocabulary acquisition. In R. Barr, M.L.Kamil, Pl Mosenthal, & P.D. Pearson (eds.), *Handbook of Reading Research, Vol. II.* NY: Longman, 789-814.

Beck, I. L., McKeown, M. G., Hamilton, R. L., & Kucan, L. (1997). *Questioning the author: An approach for enhancing student engagement with text.* Newark, DE: International Reading Association.

Beck, I., McKeown, M., & Kucan, L. (2002). *Bring words to life: Robust vocabulary instruction.* New York: Guilford Press.

Biancarosa, G. & Snow, C. (2004). *Reading next: A vision for action and research in middle and high school literacy.* (A report to Carnegie Corporation of New York.) Washington, DC: Alliance for Excellent Education.

Biemiller, A. (2001). Teaching vocabulary: Early, direct, and sequential. *American Educator*, 25(1), 24-28, 47.

Biemiller, A. (2003). *Teaching vocabulary to kindergarten through grade two children.* Paper presented at the annual meeting of the American Educational Research Association, Chicago, IL.

Billmeyer, R. (2006a). *Capturing all of the reader through the reading assessment system* (2nd ed.). Rachel & Associates: Omaha, NE.

Billmeyer, R. (2006b). *Strategies to engage the mind of the learner* (2nd ed.). Rachel & Associates: Omaha, NE.

Billmeyer, R. (1996). *Teaching reading in the content areas: If not me then who?* (1st ed.). Alexandria: Virginia, Association for Supervision and Curriculum Development.

Billmeyer, R. & Barton, M. L. (1998). *Teaching reading in the content areas: If not me then who?* (2nd ed.). Alexandria: Virginia, Association for Supervision and Curriculum Development.

Blachowicz, C. & Fisher, P. (2004). Vocabulary lessons. *Educational Leadership*, 61(6), 66-69.

Bransford, J. D., et. al. Editors. (2001). *How people learn: Brain, mind, experience, and school.* Washington, D.C.: National Academy Press.

Buehl, D. (2001). *Strategies for interactive learning.* Newark, DE: International Reading.

Bybee, R. W. (2002). Scientific Inquiry, Student Learning, and the Science Curriculum. In Rodger Bybee (Ed.), *Learning science and the science of learning* (25-36). Arlington, VA: National Science Teacher's Association Press.

Buehl, M. & Fives, H. (2009). Exploring teachers' beliefs about teaching knowledge: Where does it come from? Does it change?. *Journal of Experimental Education,* 77(4), 367-408.

Calhoun, E. F. (2001). *Every child reads.* Iowa Department of Education, DesMoines, IA.

Calkins, L. (1994). *The art of teaching writing.* Portsmouth, NH: Heinemann.

Cambourne, B. (1995). Toward an educationally relevant theory of literacy learning: Twenty years of inquire. *Reading Teacher*, 49(3), 182-190.

Campbell, J.R. & Ashworth, K.P. (Eds.). (1995). *Report in brief: A synthesis of data.* National Association of Educational Progress' Integrated Reading Performance Record at Grade 4 (4). Washington, DC: National Center for Educational Statistics.

Carter, J. (2009). Going graphic. *Educational Leadership*, 66(6), 68-72.

Ciardiello, A. (1998). Did you ask a good question today? Alternative cognitive and metacognitive strategies. *Journal of Adolescent & Adult Literacy.* 42(3), 210-218.

Clarke, M. A. (1979). Reading in Spanish and English: Evidence from adult ESL students. *Language Learning.* 29, 121-150.

Coiro, J. (2003). Rethinking comprehension strategies to better prepare students for critically evaluating content on the Internet. *The NERA Journal*, 39, 29-34.

Cook, D. (1989). *Strategic learning in the content areas.* Madison, WI: Wisconsin Department of Public Instruction.

Costa, A., & Kallick, B. (2000). *Discovering & exploring habits of mind.* Alexandria, VA: Association for Supervision and Curriculum Development.

Covey, S.R. (1989). *The 7 habits of highly effective people.* New York, NY: Fireside.

Covington, M. (1992). *Making the grade: A self-worth perspective on motivation and school reform.* New York: Cambridge University Press.

Cummins, J. (1980). The construct of language proficiency in bilingual education. In J.E. Alatis, *Georgetown University Roundtable of Language and Linguistics,* Washington, DC: Georgetown University Press.

Cunningham, A. & Stanovich, K. (1998, Spring/Summer). What reading does for the mind. *American Educator*, 8-17.

Daggett, W. R. (2004). "Achieving Reading Proficiency for All." International Center for Leadership in Education. Available: http://www.icle.net.

Daniels, H. (2004). *Mini-lessons for literature circles.* Portsmouth, NH: Heinemann.

Davey, B. (1983). Think aloud: Modeling the cognitive processes of reading comprehension. *Journal of Reading*, 27 (1), 44-47.

Davis, F. (1944). Fundamental factors in reading comprehension. *Psychometrika*, 9, 185-197.

Demski, J. (2009). Learning to speak math. *The Journal*, *36*(8), 18-22.

Dickinson, D., Cote, L., & Smith, M. (1993). Learning vocabulary in preschool. In C. Daiute (Ed.), *The development of literacy through social interaction: No. 61. New directions for child development: The Jossey-Bass Ed Series* (pp. 67-78). San Francisco: Jossey-Bass.

Dillon, A. (1992). Reading from paper versus screens: A critical review of the empirical literature. *Ergonomics* 10.35, 1297-326.

Driver, R., Squires, A., Rushworth, P., & Wood-Robinson, V. (1994). *Making sense of secondary science.* London: RoutledgeFalmer.

Duke, C. (1984). Integrating reading, writing, and thinking skills into the music class. ERIC Document Reproduction Services (ED278029).

Duke, N. (2004). The case for informational text. *Educational Leadership*, 61(6), 40-44.

Duke, N. (2000). 3.6 minutes per day: The scarcity of informational texts in first grade. *Reading Research Quarterly*, 35, 202-224.

Elmore, R. (2002). Hard questions about practice. *Educational Leadership*, 59(8), 22-25.

Fisch, K., McLeod, S., & Bestler. L. (2010, Feb. 10). *Did You Know 4.0*. XPLANE, Available: http://www.xplane.com/company/news/2009/09/16/did-you-know-4-0.

Fisher, D. & Frey, N. (2003). Writing instruction for struggling adolescent readers: A gradual release model. *Journal of Adolescent & Adult Literacy*, 46(5), 396-407.

Fisher, D. & Frey, N. (2004). Improving adolescent literacy: Strategies at work. Upper Saddle River, NJ: Merrill/Prentice Hall.

Fisher, D. & Ivey, G. (2007). Farewell to a farewell to arms: Deemphasizing the whole-class novel. *Phi Delta Kappan*, 88(7). 494-497.

Folse, K.S. (2004). *Vocabulary myths: Applying second language research to classroom teaching.* Ann Arbor: University of Michigan Press.

Fountas, I. & Pinnell, G. (2001). *Guiding readers and writers (Grades 3-6): Teaching comprehension, genre, and content literacy*. Portsmouth, NH: Heinemann.

Frayer, D.A., Frederick, W.C., & Klausmeier, H.J. (1969). *A schema for testing the level of concept mastery* (Technical Report No. 16). Madison, WI: University of Wisconsin Research and Development Center for Cognitive Learning.

Ganske, K. (2000). *Word journeys: Assessment guided phonics, spelling and vocabulary instruction.* New York, NY: Guilford Press.

Gardner, H. (1982). *Art, mind, and brain.* New York: Basic Books.

Gardiner, S. (2001). Ten minutes a day for silent reading. *Educational Leadership*, 58(2), 32-35.

Geer, P. & Geer, S. (2008). *Picture these SAT words*. Hauppauge NY: Barron's Educational Series, Incorporated.

Gerber, T. & Gerrity, K. (2007). Attitudes toward the teaching of language reading skill in the music classroom. *Bulletin of the Council for Research in Music Education*, 173, 71-87.

Gerrity, K. (2009). No Child Left Behind: Determining the impact of policy on music education in Ohio. *Bulletin of the Council for Research in Music Education*, 179, 79-93.

Gillespie, C. & Rasinski, T. (1988). Making the case for coursework for content-area teachers. *The High School Jounal*, 71, 206-209.

Goodlad J. (1984). *A place called school: Prospects for the future.* New York: McGraw-Hill, 107.

Graff, G. (2003). Clueless in academe. New Haven and London: Yale University Press.

Graves, M. (2006). *The vocabulary book: Learning and instruction.* Newark, DE: International Reading Association.

Graves, M. & Slater, W. (1987). *The development of reading vocabularies in rural disadvantaged students, inner city disadvantaged students, and middle-class suburban students.* Paper presented at the meeting of the American Educational Research Association, Washington, DC.

Hadaway, N. (2009). A narrow bridge to academic reading. *Educational Leadership*, 66(7), 38-41.

Harp, B. (1996). *The handbook of literacy assessment and evaluation.* Norwood, MA: Christopher-Gordon Publishers, Inc.

Harvey, S. & Goudvis, A. (2000). *Strategies that work. Teaching comprehension to enhance understanding.* Portland, ME: Stenhouse.

Hashey, J.M. & Connors, D.J. (2003). Learning from our journey: Reciprocal teaching action research. *The Reading Teacher*, 57:3, 224-232.

Heller, R. & Greenleaf, C. (2007). *Literacy instruction in the content areas: Getting to the core of middle and high school improvement.* (A report to Carnegie Corporation of New York.) Washington, DC: Alliance for Excellent Education.

Henriksson, Anders. (2001). *Non campus mentis: World history according to college students.* New York, NY: Workman Publishing.

Henry, L.A. (2006). SEARCHing for an answer: The critical role of new literacies while reading on the Internet. *The Reading Teacher*, 59, 614-627.

Herber, H. (1978). *Teaching reading in content areas*. (2nd ed.). Englewood Cliffs, NJ: Prentice-Hall.

Hirsch, E. (1993). *What your 6th grader needs to know*. New York, NY: Dell Publishing.

Hirsch, E. (2004). Many Americans can read but can't comprehend, *USA Today*. 2(25).

Holt world history: The human journey, (2003). Austin, TX: Holt, Rinehart and Winston.

Individuals with Disabilities Education Act of 2004, Pub. L. No. 108-446, (2004).

Ivey, G. (2002). Getting started: Manageable literacy practices. *Educational Leadership*, 60(3), 20-23.

Ivey, G. (2010). Texts that matter. *Educational Leadership*, 67(6), 18-23.

Ivey, G. & Fisher, D. (2006). *Creating literacy-rich schools for adolescents*. Alexandria, VA: Association for Supervision and Curriculum Development.

Jenkins, J., Stein, M., and Wysocki, K. (1984). Learning vocabulary through reading. *American Educational Research Journal*, 21(4), 767-787.

Johnson, K. (1998). *Readability*. [On-Line]. http://www.timetabler.com/readable.pdf.

Johnston, P. & Pearson, D. (1982). *Prior knowledge, connectivity and the assessment of reading comprehension*. (Technical Report No. 245). Champaign: University of Illinois, Center for the Study of Reading.

Jones, B., Palinscar, A., Ogle, D., & Carr, E. (1987). *Strategic teaching and learning: Cognitive instruction in the content areas*. Alexandria, VA and Elmhurst, IL: Association for Supervision and Curriculum Development and North Central Regional Educational Laboratory.

Jukes, I. & McCain, T. (2008, May). *Closing the digital divide: 7 things education and educators need to do*. The Info Savvy Group, Web. Available: http://www.committedsardine.com.

Kamil, M. & Walberg, H. (2005, January). The scientific teaching of reading. *Education Week*.

Keene, E. & Zimmermann, S. (1997). *Mosaic of thought*. Portsmouth, NH: Heinemann.

Kids and Family Reading Report. (2008). New York: Scholastic. http://www.scholastic.com/aboutscholastic/news/readingreport.htm

King, K. & Gurian, M. (2006). Teaching to the minds of boys. *Educational Leadership*, 64(1), 56-61.

Kluth, P. (2006). *Hanging in there: Keeping students with autism comfortable, relaxed, and focused*. Available: http://www.paulakluth.com.

Kluth, P. (2005). Supporting literacy development of students with autism. Available: http://www.paulakluth.com.

Kluth, P. & Chandler-Olcott, K. (2008). *A land we can share: Teaching literacy to students with autism*. Baltimore, MA: Paul H. Brookes Publishing.

Krashen, S. (1981). *Principles and Practice in Second Language Acquisition*. English Language Teaching series. London: Prentice-Hall International (UK) Ltd. 202.

Krashen, S. (1993). *The power of reading*. Englewood, CO: Libraries Unlimited.

Krashen, S. (2004). False claims about literacy development. *Educational Leadership*, 61, 18-21.

Kuhrt, M. & Farris, P. (1990). Empowering students through reading, writing, and reasoning. *Journal of Reading*, 33(6), 436-441.

Langer, L.A. (1981). From theory to practice: A prereading plan. *Journal of Reading*, 25, 152-156.

Lapp, D., Flood, J., & Farnan, N. (1996). *Content area reading and learning*. Needham Heights, MA: Allyn and Bacon.

Lautzenheiser, T. et. al. (2000). Essential Elements 2000. A Comprehensive Band Method. Volume 2, *Teacher Edition*. Milwaukee, WI: Hal Leonard Corporation, Inc. 36.

Leu, D.J. & Zawilinski, L. (2007). The new literacies of online reading comprehension. *New England Reading Association Journal*, 43(1), 1-7.

Leu, D., et al. (2007). What is new about the new literacies of online reading comprehension? In L. Rush, J. Eakle, & A. Berger, (Eds.). Secondary school literacy: What research reveals for classroom practices. (37-68). Urbana, IL: National Council of Teachers of English.

Luke, A. & Freebody, P. (1999). Further notes on the four resources model. Reading Online. www.readingonline.org/past/past.

Marzano, R. (2004). Building background knowledge for academic success. Alexandria, VA: Association for Supervision and Curriculum Development.

Marzano, R. (2009). Six steps to better vocabulary instruction. *Educational Leadership*, 67(1), 83-84.

Marzano, R., Pickering, D., & Pollock, J. (2001). *Classroom instruction that works: Research-based strategies for increasing student achievement*. Alexandria, VA: ASCD.

Mathison, C. (1989). Activating student interest in content-area reading. *Journal of Reading*, 33(3), 170-176.

Maxim II, H. H. (2002). A study into the feasibility and effects of reading extended authentic discourse in the beginning German language classroom. *The Modern Language Journal, 86* (1), 20-35.

McGill-Franzen A. and Allington, R. (2003). Bridging the summer reading gap. *Scholastic Instructor*.

McKenzie, J. (1998). The new plagiarism: Seven antidotes to prevent highway robbery in an electronic age. *Now On - The Educational Technology Journal,* 7(8), Available: http://fno.org/may98/cov98may.html.

McKeown, M. (1993). Creating effective definitions for young word learners. *Reading Research Quarterly*, 28,16-31.

McNicol, S. & Dalton, P. (2002). The best way is always through the children: The impact of family reading. *Journal of Adolescent & Adult Literacy*, 46(3), 246-253.

McVerry, J., Zawilinski, L., & O'Byrne, W. (2009). Internet reciprocal teaching: Navigating the C's of change. *Educational Leadership*, 67(1), 62-65.

Miller, D. (2009). *The book whisper*. San Francisco, CA: John Wiley & Sons, Inc.

Moats, L. (1998). Reading, spelling, and writing disabilities in the middle grades. In B.Y.L. Wong (Ed.), *Learning About Learning Disabilities* (2nd ed., 367-389). San Diego, CA: Academic Press.

Moeller, A. (2006-2007). Motivating the language learner through reading: From Theory to Practice. *AP German Language Professional Development Workshop Materials, Special Focus: Reading Strategies and Skills.*

Mokhtari, K., Rosemary, C., & Edwards, P. (2007). Making instructional decisions based on data: What, how, and why. *Reading Teacher*, 61(4), 354-359.

Moore, D.W., Readence, J.E., & Rickelmen, R.J. (1982). *Rereading activities for content area reading and learning.* Newark, DE: International Reading Association.

Morrow, L. (2004). Family literacy: Home and school working together. *Reading Today*, 6-7.

Mraz, M., Rickelman, R. & Vacca, R. (2009). Content-area reading. Past, present, and future. In Wood, K. & Blanton, W. (Eds.). *Literacy Instruction for Adolescents. Research-Based Practice.* (pp. 77-91). New York, NY: The Guilford Press.

Nagy, W. (1988/89). *Teaching vocabulary to improve reading comprehension*. Urbana, IL: National Council of Teachers of English. *16*(5), 1-5, Newark, DE: International Reading Association.

National Assessment of Educational Progress. (1998). Results showing heartening gains. *Reading Today*, 16(5), 1-5.

National Clearinghouse for English Language Acquisition. (2007). [On-Line]. Available: http://www.ncela.gwu.edu/askncela@gwu.edu.

National Institute of Mental Health. (2004). *Autism spectrum disorders – pervasive development disorders* (NIH Publication No. 09-5511). Bethesda, MD: National Institute of Mental Health.

National Reading Panel. (2000). *Teaching children to read: An evidence-based assessment of the scientific research literature on reading and its implications for reading instruction*. Washington, DC: National Institute of Child Health and Human Development.

National Research Council (NRC). (1996). *National science education standards*. Washington, DC: National Academy Press.

Newkirk, T. (2006). Media and literacy: What's good? *Educational Leadership*, 64 (1), 62-66.

Nevills, P. and Wolfe, P. (2009). *Building the reading brain*, 2nd edition. Thousand Oaks, CA: Corwin Press.

Nielsen, J. & Pernice, K. (2007). *Eyetracking web usability (Voices that matter)*. New York: New Riders, Available: http://www.useit.com/eyetracking/.

Ogle, D.M. (1989). The know, want to know, learning strategy. In K.D. Muth (Ed.) *Children's Comprehension of Text.* (pp. 205-223). Newark, DE: International Reading Association

O'Neil. (1994). Rewriting the book on literature. *Curriculum Update*, Alexandria, VA: Association for Supervision and Curriculum Development.

Palinscar, A.S., & Brown, A.L. (1986). Interactive teaching to promote independent learning from text. *The Reading Teacher, 39*(8), 771-777.

Palinscar, A.S., & Brown, A.L. (1984). Reciprocal teaching of comprehension-fostering and comprehension-monitoring activities. *Cognition and Instruction*, 1(5), 117-175.

Palincsar, A.S., & Klenk, L.J. (1991). Dialogues promoting reading comprehension. In C. Means, M. Chelemer, & S. Knapp (Eds.), *Teaching Advanced Skills to At-risk Students* (176-203). San Francisco: Jossey-Bass.

Paris, S., Lipson, M., & Wixson, K. (1994). Becoming a strategic reader. In R. Ruddell, M. Rapp, & H. Singer (Eds.), *Theoretical models and processes of reading*, Fourth Edition. Newark, Deleware: International Reading Association, 788-806.

The Partnership for 21st Century Skills. (2010, Feb.). Partnership for 21st Century Skills, Available: http://www.21stcenturyskills.org/index.php.

Pearson, D., Cervetti, G. & Tilson, J. (2008). Reading for understanding. In L. Darling-Hammond. *Powerful learning* (71-111). San Francisco: CA Jossey-Bass.

Pearson, D. & Gallagher, (1983). The instruction of reading comprehension. *Contemporary Educational Psychology*, 8, 317-344.

Penno, J., Wilkinson, I., & Moore, D. (2002). Vocabulary acquisition from teacher explanation and repeated listening to stories: Do they overcome the Matthew effect? *Journal of Educational Psychology*, 94(1), 23-33.

Perkins, D. (1992). *Smart schools: Better thinking and learning for every child.* New York: Free Press.

Perkins-Gough, D. (2006). Do we really have a "boy crisis"? *Educational Leadership*, 64 (1), 93-94.

Pierce, M., & Fontaine, L. (2009). Designing vocabulary instruction in mathematics. *Reading Teacher, 63*(3), 239-243.

Pilgreen, J. (2000). *The SSR handbook.* Portsmouth, NH: Boynton/Cook Publishers.

Postlethwaite, T.N., & Ross, K.N. (1992). *Effective schools in reading.* The Hague: International Association for the Evaluation of Educational Achievement.

Pratt, D. (2008). Lina's letters: A 9-year-old's perspective on what matters most in the classroom. *Phi Delta Kappan*, 89(7), 515-518.

Quinn, S. & Stark-Adam, P. (2008, Oct.). What are the differences in reading news in print and online? *Eye Tracking the News.* Poynter Institute, Available: http://eyetrack.poynter.org.

Raphael, T.E. (1986). Teaching question-answer relationships, revisited. *The Reading Teacher*, 39, 516-522.

Rasinski, T., & Padak, N. (2000). *Effective reading strategies.* (Second Edition). Columbus, OH: Merrill, an imprint of Prentice-Hall.

Readability - An experiment. (2010). *Readability.* ARC90 Labs, 2009. Available: http://lab.arc90.com/experiments/readability.

Reading Next. (2004). Available online: http://www.all4ed.org/files/ReadingNext.pdf.

Resnick, L.B. (1987). *Education and learning to think.* Washington, DC: National Academy Press.

Resnick, L. B. (1983). Toward a cognitive theory of instruction. In S. Paris, G. Olson, & H. Stevenson (Eds.), *Learning and motivation in the classroom*, Hillsdale, NJ: Erlbaum.

Rhodes, N.C., & Pufahl, I. (2009). *Foreign language teaching in U.S. schools: Results of a national survey.* Center for Applied Linguistics. Available: www.cal.org.

Rigby, J.W. (1978). Learning strategies: A theoretical perspective. In H.F. O'Neil (Ed). *Learning strategies* (165-205). New York: Academic Press.

Robinson, F. (1961). *Effective study.* New York: Harper and Row.

Rooney, J. (2009). Teaching two literacies. *Educational Leadership*, 66(6), 92-93.

Rosenblatt, L. (1978). *The reader, the text, the poem.* Carbondale, IL: Southern Illinois University Press.

Rosenshine, B., Meister, C., & Chapman, S. (1996). Teaching students to generate questions: A review of the intervention studies. *Review of Educational Research*, 66, 181-221.

Russ S, Perez V, Garro N, Klass P, Kuo AA, Gershun M, Halfon N, Zuckerman B. (2007). *Reading Across the Nation*. Available: http://www.reachoutandread.org.

Sadoski, M. & Paivio, A. (2004). A dual coding theoretical model of reading. In R.B. Ruddell & N.J. Unrau (Eds.), *Theoretical models and processes of reading* (pp. 1329-1362). Newark, DE: International Reading Association.

Santa, C. (1988). *Content reading including study systems*. Dubuque, IA: Kendall Hunt.

Santa, C.M. & Alvermann, D.E. (Eds.). (1991). *Science learning: Processes and applications*. Newark, DE: International Reading Association.

Sawyer, D. (1993, August). *What is dyslexia?*. Available: http://dyslexia.mtsu.edu/about/whatisdyslexia.html.

Schoenback, R., Braunger, J., Greenleaf, C., & Litman, C. (2003). Apprenticing adolescents to reading in subject-area classrooms. *Phi Delta Kappan*, 85(2), 133-138.

Schomoker, M. (2007). Radically redefining literacy instruction: An immense opportunity. *Phi Delta Kappan*, 88(7), 488-492.

Schomoker, M. (2006). *Results now*. Alexandria, VA: Association for Supervision and Curriculum Development.

Schwartz, R. & Raphael, T. (1985). Concept definition: A key to improving students' vocabulary. *The Reading Teacher*, 39(2), 676-682.

Scott, J. & Nagy, W. (2004). Developing word consciousness. In J.F.Baumann & E.J. Kame'enui (Eds.), *Vocabulary instruction: Research to practice* (pp. 201-217). New York: Guilford Press.

Sheppard, N. (2006). The trouble with Newsweek's cover story about boys. *American Thinker*, http://www.americanthinker.com.

Schoenback, R., Braunger, J., Greenleaf, C., & Litman, C. (2003). Apprenticing adolescents to reading in subject-area classrooms. *Phi Delta Kappan*, 85(2), 133-138.

Snow, C. (2002). *Reading for understanding: Toward an R&D program in reading comprehension*. Santa Monica, CA: RAND.

Stephens, Elaine C., Brown Jean E. (2005), A Handbook of Content Literacy Strategies: 125 Practical Reading and Writing Ideas Second Edition. Norwood, MA: Christopher Gordon Publishers, Inc.

Stevenson, V. H. (2008). *Statistical abstract of the United States*. New York, NY: Communications Industry Forecast & Report.

Stewart, O. & Tei, E. (1983). Some implications of metacognition for reading instruction. *Journal of Reading*, 27, 36-43.

Stiggins, R.J. (1991). *Assessing reading proficiency*. Portland, OR: Northwest Regional Educational Laboratory.

Stiggins, R., Arter, J., Chappuis, J. & Chappuis, S. (2004). *Classroom assessment for student learning – Doing it right, using it well*. Portland, OR: Assessment Training Institute.

Strong, R., Silver, H., Perini, M., & Tuculescu, G. (2002). *Reading for academic success*. Thousand Oaks, CA: Corwin Press, Inc.

Sullivan, E.P. (1979). Using music to teach reading: State of the art review. ERIC Document Reproduction Services (ED184109).

Swiggum, R. (1993). Strategies for critical reading in the arts. In Chapman, A. (Ed.). *Making Sense: Teaching Critical Reading Across the Curriculum*. New York, NY: The College Entrance Examination Board, 109-124.

Taillefer, G. F. (1996). L2 reading ability: Further insight into the short-circuit hypothesis. *The Modern Language Journal, 80*(4), 461-477.

Taylor, G. C. (1981). ERIC/RCS Report: Music in language arts instruction. *Language Arts*, 58(3), 363-367.

Terban, M. (2002). *Building your vocabulary*. New York, NY: Scholastic Inc.

Tucker, A. (1981). Music and the teaching of reading. A review of literature. *Reading Improvement*, 18(1), 14-19.

Tovani, C. (2004). *Do I really have to teach reading? Content comprehension grades 6-12*. Portland, ME: Stenhouse Publishers.

Tovani, C. (2000). *I read it, but I don't get it: Comprehension strategies for adolescent readers.* York, Maine: Stenhouse Publishers.

Tyre, P. (2008). Boy trouble. *Instructor*, September/October, 35-41.

Vacca, R. (2002). From efficient decoders to strategic readers. *Educational Leadership*, 60(3), 6-11.

Vacca, R. & Vacca, J. (2001). *Content area reading: Literacy and learning across the curriculum* (7th ed.). Boston: Pearson Allyn & Bacon.

Vaughn, J. & Estes, T. (1986). *Reading and reasoning beyond the primary grades*. Boston, MA: Allyn and Bacon.

Venezky, R., Kaestle, F., & Sum, A. (1987). *The subtle danger*. Princeton, NJ: Educational Testing Service.

Vygotsky, L. (1986). *Thought and language*. Cambridge, MA: MIT Press.

Walsh, C. E. (1999). *Enabling academic success for secondary students with limited formal schooling.* Providence: Northeast and Islands Regional Education Laboratory.

Weigel, M. & Gardner, H. (2009). The best of both literacies. *Educational Leadership*, 66(6), 38-41.

Weiner, B. (1980). *Human motivation*. New York: Holt, Rinehart & Winston.

Wientjes, G. (2010). *WordSift - Visualize text*. Stanford University, Web. 10 Feb. 2010. http://www.wordsift.com.

Wiggins, G. & McTighe, J. (1998). *Understanding by design.* Alexandria: Virginia Association for Supervision and Curriculum Development.

Wilson, P. (1995). Does a content area reading course change preservice teachers' attitudes? ERIC Document Reproduction Services (ED384021).

Wolf, M. & Barzillai, M. (2009). *The importance of deep reading*. Educational Leadership, 66(6), 33-37.

Yang, K., & Lin, F. (2008). A Model of Reading Comprehension of Geometry Proof. *Educational Studies in Mathematics*, 67(1), 59-76.

Yoder, D., Erickson, K., & Koppenhaver, D. (1996). *A literacy bill of rights.* Durham, NC: Duke University, Center for Literacy and Disabilities Studies.

Yore, L. D., Bisanz, G. L., & Hand, B. (2003). Examining the literacy component of science literacy: 25 years of language arts and science research. *International Journal of Science Education*, 25(6), 689-725.

Zwiers, J. (2005). *Building reading comprehension habits in grades 6-12: A toolkit of classroom activities.* Newark, DE: International Reading Association.

Children's and Adolescent Literature Cited

Albom, M. (1997). *Tuesdays with Morrie*. New York: Bantom Doubleday.

Anderson, L. H. (1999). *Speak*. (2007). *Twisted*. New York, NY: Penguin Group.

Arnold, T. (2007). *Fly guy*. New York, NY: Scholastic.

Babbitt, N. (1975). *Tuck everlasting*. New York, NY: Farrar, Strauss and Giroux.

Briggs, R. (1998). *Ethel and Ernest: A true story*. New York, NY: Pantheon Books.

Canfield, J., Hansen, M., & Kirberger, K. (1997). *Chicken Soup Series*. Health Communications.

Climo, S. (1989). *The Egyptian cinderella*. Harper Collins.

Colon, R. (1997). *Tomas and the library lady*. New York: Dragonfly Books.

Connor, L. (2004). *Miss Bridie chose a shovel*. New York: Houghton Mifflin.

Cutting, J. (1996). *Fall*. Bothell, WA: The Wright Group.

Demi. (1990). *The empty pot*. New York, NY: Henry Holt & Company.

Dickens, C. (2009). *A tale of two cities*. New York, NY: Puffin.

Dr. Seuss. (1957). *Cat in the hat*. (1988). *Green eggs and ham*. New York: Random House.

Feelings, T. (1995). *The middle passage: White ships/black cargo*. NY: Dial Books.

Frank, A. (1993). *The diary of Anne Frank*. New York: Bantam.

Golding, W. (1954). *The Lord of the flies*. New York, NY: Libri.

Gwynne, F. (1976). *Chocolate moose for dinner*. New York: Simon & Schuster.

Gwynne, F. (1970). *The king who rained*. New York: Simon & Schuster.

Haislip, P. (2002). *Lottie's courage*. Shippensburg, PA: White Mane Kids.

Hesse, (2005). *Out of the dust*. New York: Scholastic.

Hickam. H. (1998). *Rocket boys*. New York, NY: Delta.

Hunt, I. (1964). *Across five Aprils*. New York: Follett.

Lederer, R. (2006). *Get thee to a punnery*. Layton, UT: Gibbs Smith.

Lee, H. (1995, 1960). *To kill a mockingbird*. New York: Harper Collins.

Miller, A. (1952). *The crucible*. New York, NY: Penguin Books.

Morrison, T. (2003). *Love*. New York: Knopf a Division of Random House.

Munsch, R. (1992). *Paper bag princess*. Toronto, Canada: Annick Press.

Nixon, J. L. (1996) *A family apart*. New York: Bantam Doubleday Dell Books.

O'Connor, J. (2008). *Fancy Nancy's favorite fancy words*. New York: Harper Collins.

Palatini, M. (1995). *Piggie pie*. New York: Clarion Books.

Parish, P. (1963). *Amelia Bedelia*. New York: Harper Collins.

Paulsen, G. (1987). *Hatchet*. New York: Bradbury.

Paulsen, G. (2000). *Soldier's heart*. New York: Dell Laurel-Leaf.

Paulsen, G. (1998). *My life in dog years*. New York: Bantam.

Pinkwater, D. (1977). *The big orange splot*. New York: Scholastic.

Reeder, C. (1999). *Shades of gray*. New York: Aladdin Paperbacks.

Rylant, C. (1985). *Pappa's parrot*. *Every Living Thing*. New York: Aladdin Paperpacks.

Sachar, L. (1998). *Holes*. New York: Yearling Books.

Spier, P. (1980) *People*. New York: Bantam Doubleday Dell Books.

Spinelli, J. (2002). *Loser*. (2002). *Star girl*. New York, NY: Scholastic.

Taylor, C. (1992). *The House that crack built*. San Francisco, CA: Chronicle Books.

Tompert, A. (1997). *Grandfather tang's story*. New York, NY: Dragonfly Books.

Tsuchiya, Y. (1951). *Faithful elephants*. New York: Houghton Mifflin.

Winter, J. (1988). *Follow the drinking gourd*. New York: The Trumpet Club.

Winter, J. (1998). *My name is Georgia*. San Diego, CA: Harcourt Brace.

Winters, M. (2004). *My teacher for president*. New York, NY: Scholastic.

Yep, L. (1996). *Tiger woman*. Mahwah, New Jersey: Bridgewater Books.

Young, E. (1996). *Lon Po Po*. New York, NY: Puffin Books.

Appendix

Learning Teams

Purpose

The purpose of a learning team is to create a community of learners interested in processing information on the same topic. Learning teams meet to study the latest research, monitor the impact of students learning, collect, analyze and interpret student data. *Strategic Reading in the Content Areas* is formatted so that 4 or 5 interested individuals can read the information and learn together how to develop strategic readers. Each chapter begins with questions to ponder before, during, and after reading, and a process activity to focus the readers' minds.

Learning Teams

- Are homogeneous or heterogeneous groupings
- Meet on a regular basis
- Establish a set of norms
- Rotate leadership responsibilities
- Monitor progress with an agenda distributed to group members in advance
- Use agreed upon effective communication tools

Roles

Three major roles foster productive learning teams:

Engaged Participant

- Monitors own and other's adherence to the learning team agenda and norms
- Seeks and provides data
- Clarifies processes when needed
- Opens the door for others to speak
- Listens to other team members
- Is conscious of own assumptions and knowledge and how these interfere with listening

Facilitator

- Focuses group energy
- Keeps group on task
- Directs processes
- Encourages everyone to participate
- Elicits clarity regarding meeting follow-up

Recorder

- Keeps record of learning team meeting
- Supports the facilitator
- Records basic ideas
- Uses participant's language
- Asks group members for corrections
- Asks group members what not to record
- Writes legibly

Adapted from: The Adaptive School: Developing Collaborative Groups, Robert Garmston and Bruce Wellman

Learning Team Format

Productive learning teams allow 45 minutes to one hour time for learning together. The following format works well:

Focus Activity or Opener	5 minutes
Share the purpose of the learning team time (Examples: read and learn, study student work, reflect on strategy use).	3 minutes
Review process activity used to study the concept	5 minutes
Complete process/product as a group Team members process the activity independently. They share recorded activities and reflect on learning.	25-35 minutes
Decide on next steps/next meeting	5 minutes
Reflect on effectiveness of group functioning	3-5 minutes

Communication Tools

Productive learning teams use the following communication tools to make their learning time most effective.

Pausing. Waiting to respond or ask a question allows time for team members to think, and enhances the dialogue, discussion, and decision-making of the learning team.

Paraphrasing. Using paraphrases that restate what learning team members have said assists the group to hear and understand each other as they formulate new learning and decisions. Paraphrasing sends three messages: I am listening, I understand you (or I'm trying to), and I care about what you are saying.

Probing. Using open-ended probes increases the clarity and precision of the learning team's thinking and learning. Members of a learning team might probe/inquire in the following ways:

- To invite introspection on the part of the speaker
- To ask for an example of what was said
- To ask for specific sources
- To ask about values and beliefs held by the speaker
- To ask about certain conditions
- To elicit significance/importance of what was said

Learning Team Log

Date _____   Time _____

Location _____

Facilitator_____   Recorder_____

Engaged Participants _____
_____
_____

This learning team session focused on:
____ Studying an article, book, etc.   ____ Looking at student work

____ Reflecting on previous learnings   ____ Sharing strategies and benefits
       and student applications   for student learning

Process used:

We are learning:

Questions we still have:

Next we will:

Learning to be communicated to others:

Date/time/location of next learning team session:

Assignments for next learning team session:

Contributing Authors

Ellen Billmeyer, a teacher for Papillion-La Vista Public Schools in Papillion, Nebraska, completed her masters of education through Doane College. Ellen works to create strategic readers by incorporating numerous strategies and differentiating instruction to meet individual needs. Ellen can be reached at ebillmeyer@paplv.esu3.org.

Jody Bintz is currently a science educator with Biological Sciences Curriculum Study in Colorado Springs, Colorado. She previously taught high school science and served as a science education and school improvement consultant with Loess Hills Area Education Agency 13 in Council Bluffs, Iowa. Jody can be contacted at jbintz@bscs.org.

Peggy Braitsch is an ESL teacher for Monroe 2 Orleans BOCES in Spencerport, New York. Peggy has taught children and adults in the U.S and abroad; she has also worked in the field of international education at the college level and has consulted for universities and corporations in the area of cross-cultural communications. Peggy can be reached at pbraitsc@monroe2boces.org.

Pat Branson teaches German, serves as high school department chairperson and coordinates the 7-12 world language department for Bellevue, Nebraska Schools. She received the Certificate of Merit from American Association of Teachers of German (AATG)/Goethe Institute and the Nebraska Outstanding Foreign Language Teacher. Pat can be reached at bransonp@hotmail.com.

Cindy Cronn has taught art at all grade levels for 40 years. She is currently head of the Fine Arts Department at Papillion-La Vista South High School and teaches. In addition to her teaching experience, she has been a CADRE Associate at the University of Nebraska at Omaha, mentoring first year teachers. Cindy can be reached at cronn.cynthia4@gmail.com.

Abdelhafid Djemil has a Masterís Degree in Mechanical Engineering and recently received his PhD in Education, Curriculum, and Instruction from Capella University. He has worked as an engineer and a college instructor. Currently he is teaching math at W.E.B. Dubois High School in Brooklyn, New York. Abdelhafid can be reached at ADjemil1@gmail.com.

Cheryl Becker Dobbertin is a secondary English/Language Arts teacher and former school administrator with a deep passion for adolescent literacy and differentiated instruction. Cheryl has also been published in ASCD's *Differentiation in Practice: 9-12*. She is a school designer with Expeditionary Learning, a national school reform organization. Cheryl can be reached at books4teachers@gmail.com.

Tim Dobbertin is a secondary social studies teacher and high school assistant principal in Hilton, New York; he developed the school's Instructional Support Team program based on Response To Intervention principles. Tim was a founding member of a regular education alternative high school. Tim can be reached at TDOBBERTIN@hilton.k12.ny.us.

Shawna Gareau-Kurtz, an Instructional Specialist, works with teachers at WE-MO-CO Career and Technical Education Center in Spencerport, NY to integrate research-proven strategies into instruction to improve student learning. Shawna can be reached at sgareau@monroe2boces.org.

Kevin W. Gerrity, an Assistant Professor of Music Education at Ball State University in Muncie, Indiana, holds a Doctor of Philosophy degree from The Ohio State University. In addition to serving as Ball State's secondary music specialist, Kevin teaches a course regarding the integration of music teaching and content reading. Kevin can be reached at kgerrity2@aol.com.

Wendy Grojean is a library media specialist with the Bellevue, Nebraska Public Schools. She has taught high school English and holds a Masters degree in Educational Administration and an endorsement in library science. She provides training on ways to incorporate reading strategies when working with students in the media center. Wendy can be reached at grojean@hotmail.com.

Molly House is currently a reading/writing consultant working in Des Moines, Iowa. She has years of experience working with K-12 children in the areas of reading and writing. Molly can be reached at molly@netins.net.

Pam Krambeck is an instructional technology support specialist at Educational Service Unit #3 in Omaha, Nebraska. Pam previously taught middle school and served as a curriculum and technology support specialist for 20 years in the Papillion-La Vista School district. Pam can be reached at pkrambeck@gmail.com.

Lindsey Post is an ELA teacher and literacy consultant for Monroe 2-Orelans BOCES in Spencerport, NY. She has taught grades 7-12 with a focus on career and technical education; her graduate studies at the University of Rochester led to research on students' perception of the Internet and online reading strategies. Lindsey can be reached at lpost@monroe2boces.org.

C.J. Potter is an Enrichment Specialist (Gifted & Talented) in the Webster Central School District in upstate New York; he is also an adjunct professor at Nazareth College of Rochester. He presents nationally on differentiated instruction, gifted education, and learning through the arts. C.J. can be reached at differentiated.instruction@gmail.com.

Elizabeth Scheppers teaches third grade for Papillion-La Vista Schools in Papillion, Nebraska. She serves as a district Math Toolbox member helping to create and write math curriculum and assessments for the elementary grades. She works with teachers in using the student inquiry method for learning mathematics. Elizabeth can be reached at escheppers@paplv.esu3.org.

Debbie Schwartz, an English teacher and literacy consultant, works with students and teachers at WE-MO-CO Career and Technical Education Center in Spencerport, NY to integrate literacy strategies. She has years of experience working as a teacher, clinical instructor, and diagnostician with teachers and adult learners. Debbie can be reached at dschwart@monroe2boces.org.

Elizabeth Smallwood has taught all areas of science for the past 18 years. She is currently teaching at Tapestry Charter High School, an expeditionary learning school in Buffalo, New York and serves as an adjunct professor for STEM education at Niagara University. Elizabeth can be reached at smallwoode@tapestryschool.org.

Janine Theiler taught Spanish for Omaha and Lincoln, Nebraska Public Schools. She is currently pursuing a Doctor of Philosophy degree in Education while assisting with research on foreign language teacher quality, student goal setting and achievement, and elementary foreign language learning. Janine can be reached at jtheiler@lps.org.

Sue Witter is a reading specialist and professional developer at Monroe 2-Orleans BOCES. Sue has worked as a special education teacher, reading teacher, and literacy coach. She currently provides professional development and literacy coaching for teachers in many districts, helping teachers meet the needs of struggling readers. Sue can be reached at switter@monroe2boces.org.

About the Author

Internationally known educational consultant Rachel Ann Billmeyer has extensive experience putting educational theory into practice. She has taught elementary, secondary, and university level classes, and is known for her work with reading in the content areas and reading assessment practices. Rachel is author of the ASCD publication, *Teaching Reading in the Content Areas: If Not Me Then Who?* Her recent publications include *Strategies to Engage the Mind of the Learner* and *Capturing ALL of the Reader Through the Reading Assessment System*. Rachel has served in leadership positions, including Director of Professional Development and Instruction, Grant Director for the Nebraska Literacy Program, and Program Chair for the Midwest Association for Supervision and Curriculum Development (ASCD) Conference. In 1993 Rachel received the Nebraska Literacy Award.

For a complete overview of the Literacy and Learning Trilogy see www.rachelbillmeyer.com

Rachel is a dynamic presenter. She conducts workshops, seminars, and training sessions in the following areas:

- Strategic Reading in the Content Areas
- Strategies to Engage the Mind of the Learner
- The Reading Assessment System

To learn more about her workshops, seminars, and training sessions, contact Dr. Billmeyer at—

Dr. Rachel Billmeyer
17445 Riviera Drive
Omaha, NE 68136
phone: (402)932-1417
e-mail: rachelb2@cox.net
website: www.rachelbillmeyer.com

Literacy and Learning: A Trilogy By Rachel Billmeyer

ITEM	ITEM DESCRIPTION	PRICE
Literacy and Learning: A Trilogy 3 Book Set		
TRG	Contains all three volumes of the Literacy and Learning Set: **Vol. I -** *Strategic Reading in the Content Areas* **Vol. II -** *Strategies to Engage the Mind of the Learner, Building Strategic Learners* **Vol. III -** *Capturing All of the Reader Through the Reading Assessment System* **⁺⁺(VOLUME DISCOUNTS DO NOT APPLY TO THE TRILOGY SET)**	**$85.00⁺⁺** **($94.85 Value)**
Vol. I - *Strategic Reading in the Content Areas* *Practical Applications for Creating A Thinking Environment* *Second Edition*		
1BK	**Vol. I -** *Strategic Reading in the Content Areas* *Practical Applications for Creating A Thinking Environment - Second Edition* Volume 1 Foreword by Arthur L. Costa, 259 pages examining the current information about the role of metacognition; the interactive reading ingredients (context, reader, text) and current research on vocabulary development. Book features guidelines and strategies for teaching reading in all content areas, children's bibliography for all content areas and grade levels, and resources for special education, English Language Learners, and the young child.	$29.95
1WP	**Text Structure Wall Chart** Chart is 20" x 24" and contains the Narrative Text Story Elements and Informative Text Organizational Patterns. Poster is ready to be laminated.	$5.00
1SR	**Summarizing Rules Wall Chart** Chart is 20" x 24" and is ready to be laminated.	$5.00
1BCD	**Strategic Reading Blackline Masters CD** 30 Blackline Masters to make overheads or student copies.	$15.00
1RP	**Strategic Reader Wall Chart** Single wall chart with definition of a strategic reader.	$5.00
1FH	**Facilitator Handbook for Strategic Reading Learning Team Study**	$8.00
Vol. II - *Strategies to Engage the Mind of the Learner* *Building Strategic Learners* *Second Edition*		
2BK	**Vol. II -** *Strategies to Engage the Mind of the Learner* *Building Strategic Learners - Second Edition* Volume 2 Foreword by Robert J. Garmston, 258 pages containing 92 strategies for all grade levels and all content areas. Strategies focus on vocabulary development, narrative and informative text, questioning, graphic organizers, discussion, energizing and grouping activities, information building, and reflection.	$29.95

2QCD	**Questioning Activities From *Strategies to Engage The Mind of the Learner* - CD***
	    CD contains all premade questions for the three questioning activities explained in Section 4: Chat & Go, Enlighten Your Thinking & Unwrap Your Thinking
	    • **Chat and Go - (Questions that Promote Conversation)**
	    31 Questions for narrative and informative each in a text box
	    • **Enlighten Your Thinking - (Habits of Mind strategy)**
	    50 Questions on lightbulbs
	    • **Unwrap Your Thinking (SAR Strategy)**
	    40 Questions on candy wrappers
		$15.00

2QP	**Print each set of questions and then copy on colored paper, laminate, and cut.* **Questioning Activities From *Strategies to Engage The Mind of the Learner* - Complete Set** 3 sets of premade questions assembled on rings for each questioning activity explained in Section 4:	$15.00
2CG	• **Chat and Go - (Questions that Promote Conversation)** *31 Questions for narrative and informative each in a text box (Approx. 8" x 1")*	$3.00
2ET	• **Enlighten Your Thinking - (Habits of Mind strategy)** *50 Questions on lightbulbs (Approx. 4.25" x 5.5")*	$7.00
2UT	• **Unwrap Your Thinking (QAR Strategy)** *40 Questions on candy wrappers (Approx. 8.5" x 3.5")*	$5.00
2BM	**Focused Reading Bookmarks** Each bookmark has icons to focus the reader's thinking when reading	$1 for 10
2BCD	**Strategies Blackline Masters CD** 72 Blackline Masters to make overheads or student copies.	$15
2RT	**Reciprocal Teaching Tents** 8 Sets of Reciprocal Teaching Tents (4 Tents Per Set - 32 Tents Total)	$15
2RBM	**Reciprocal Teaching Bookmarks - Two-Sided Bookmarks** Each bookmark contains key verbs and questions to stimulate thinking when reading.	$3 for 20
2RTP	**Reciprocal Teaching Wall Chart** Contains key verbs and questions to stimulate thinking when reading. (5 wall charts in set)	$20
2QAP	**Question-Answer Relationships Wall Chart** Contains cue words and question starters. (2 wall charts in set)	$10
2T&RBM	**Think and Read Bookmark** Bookmarks contain icons and ideas to assist comprehension	$3 for 20
2MBM	**Reading to Solve Story Problems - Two-Sided Bookmark** Bookmarks contains icons, ideas, and key questions to support problem solving	$4 for 20
2RRBM	**Reading Rocks Bookmark - Two-Sided Bookmark** (Elementary Students) Folded bookmark containing questions to support comprehension Before-During-After Reading and a reading "Place Marker"	$5 for 20
2SRBM	**Be a Strategic Reader Bookmark - Two-Sided Bookmark** (Secondary Students) Folded bookmark containing ideas to support comprehension Before-During-After Reading and a reading "Place Marker"	$5 for 20

ITEM #	ITEM DESCRIPTION	PRICE
3BK	**Vol. III - *Capturing All of the Reader Through the Reading Assessment System*** *Practical Applications for Guiding Strategic Readers - Second Edition* Volume 3 Foreword by Richard J. Stiggins, 255 pages explaining the 4 traits and attributes of a strategic reader, scoring guides for each trait in narrative and informative text, strategies, graphic organizers, checklist, and 17 assessment tasks.	$34.95
3MM	**Strategic Reader Memory Mats** Laminated memory mats serve as a "desk mat" for quick reference to the 4 traits and attributes of a strategic reader or the scoring guides to accompany the traits and attributes.	**4 Sets $30** 8 mats, 16 sides tota
3MM1	Set 1 - Outlines the 4 traits of a Strategic Reader and the narrative and informative attributes associated with each trait. (Red)	**1 Set $8** 2 mat, 4 sides tota
3MM2	Set 2 - Outlines the 4 traits with 4 Reading Continuums of attributes for grades K-3 (Yellow)	
3MM3	Set 3 - Outlines the 4 traits with 4 Narrative Scoring Guides of attributes for grades 3 - 12 (Orange)	
3MM4	Set 4 - Outlines the 4 traits with 4 Informative Scoring Guides of attributes for grades 3 - 12 (Blue)	
3MRY	**Sets 1 & 2**, Traits and Attributes (Red) & K-3 Continuums (Yellow)	**2 Sets $15** 4 mats, 8 sides tota
3MRO	**Sets 1 & 3**, Traits and Attributes (Red) & 3-12 Narrative Scoring Guides (Orange)	
3MRB	**Sets 1 & 4**, Traits and Attributes (Red) & 3-12 Informative Scoring Guides (Blue)	
3MOB	**Sets 3 & 4**, 3-12 Narrative Scoring Guides (Orange) & 3-12 Informative Scoring Guides (Blue)	
3MOY	**Sets 2 & 3**, K-3 Continuums (Yellow) & 3-12 Narrative Scoring Guides (Orange)	
3MBY	**Sets 2 & 4**, K-3 Continuums (Yellow) & 3-12 Informative Scoring Guides (Blue)	
	* PLEASE INDICATE SET NUMBERS WHEN ORDERING MEMORY MATS	
3WC	**4 Traits of a Strategic Reader Wall Charts** Sets contain 5 charts total: • 1 chart is 10" x 24" titled Traits of a Strategic Reader • 4 charts are 20" x 24" each containing one trait with complete description Each set contains 5 posters ready to be laminated and hung in the classroom.	$20.00
3BCD	**Capturing Reading Blackline Masters CD** 79 Blackline Masters to make overheads or student copies.	$15.00

Vol. III - *Capturing All of the Reader Through the Reading Assessment System*

Practical Applications for Guiding Strategic Readers

Second Edition

BILL TO:

Name _____

Institution _____

Address _____

City _____ State _____ Zip _____

Daytime Phone _____

SHIP TO: (if different from bill to)

Name _____

Institution _____

Address _____

City _____ State _____ Zip _____

Daytime Phone _____

METHOD OF PAYMENT:

<u>Individuals</u>: Check ❑ Money Order ❑ VISA ❑ MASTERCARD ❑ DISCOVER ❑ **Make Checks & Money Orders Payable to: Rachel & Associates**

<u>Schools and Institutions</u>: Check ❑ Money Order ❑ VISA ❑ MASTERCARD ❑ DISCOVER ❑ Signed P.O. ❑

Card # _____ Expiration Date _____ Please bill. (Attach signed P.O.) P.O. # _____

ITEM #	QTY	PRICE	TOTAL	ITEM #	QTY	PRICE	TOTAL
							—
							—
							—
							—
							—
							—

* SALES TAX (except for not-for-profit institutions) • Nebraska residents pay 7% sales tax

**SHIPPING AND HANDLING COSTS:
Continental United States Orders: <u>Standard Shipping</u> - 10% of purchase price before discount, $5 minimum. (Shipping is 5-10 business day delivery) <u>Priority Shipping</u> - 20% of purchase price before discount, $15 minimum. (Shipping is 2-3 business day delivery). Shipping and handling for the Trilogy Set is $9.50 per set.

Alaska, Hawaii, U.S. Territories & International Orders: Orders will ship via UPS and will incur additional shipping charges which will be added to your order. To request a quote, please contact the distributor at 402-593-1080 prior to ordering.

***PLEASE ORDER CAREFULLY. We do not accept returns of books or merchandise. If your order is incorrect or damaged, please contact Kelly at Printco Graphics 402-593-1080.

25-49 Books/Products	10% Discount	
50+ Books/Products	15% Discount	

Quantity discounts on single title volume purchases only

Subtotal	
* Sales Tax	
** Shipping	

Total Due

Mail or fax your order to the distributor:
14112 Industrial Road Omaha, NE 68144
Phone: 402-593-1080 or 1-888-593-1080
Fax: 402-593-1077

Order form 7/08

Prices subject to change.